# ANTI-NAZI MODERNISM

*Cultural Expressions of
World War II: Interwar Preludes,
Responses, Memory*

*Phyllis Lassner, Series Editor*

# Anti-Nazi Modernism

## The Challenges of Resistance in 1930s Fiction

## Mia Spiro

NORTHWESTERN UNIVERSITY PRESS | EVANSTON, ILLINOIS

Northwestern University Press
www.nupress.northwestern.edu

Copyright © 2013 by Northwestern University Press. Published 2013. All rights reserved.

Printed in the United States of America

10  9  8  7  6  5  4  3  2  1

**Library of Congress Cataloging-in-Publication Data**

Spiro, Mia.
   Anti-Nazi modernism : the challenges of resistance in 1930s fiction / Mia Spiro.
       p. cm.
   Includes bibliographical references and index.
   ISBN 978-0-8101-2863-7 (pbk. : alk. paper)
   1. Woolf, Virginia, 1882–1941—Criticism and interpretation. 2. Barnes,
Djuna—Criticism and interpretation. 3. Isherwood, Christopher, 1904–1986—
Criticism and interpretation. 4. American fiction—20th century—History and
criticism. 5. English fiction—20th century—History and criticism. 6. Modernism
(Literature)—History and criticism. 7. Anti-Nazi movement in literature.
I. Title.
   PR888.M63S65 2013
   823.9120935843086—dc23

                                                                    2012022483

*For David*

# CONTENTS

## ACKNOWLEDGMENTS

In the Talmud there is a wise Jewish saying: "Provide yourself with a teacher and get yourself a friend; and judge every person towards merit." I have been so fortunate in receiving unsurpassed guidance, mentorship, and encouragement from teachers and friends as I embarked on this scholarly journey. I would like to express my sincerest gratitude to Phyllis Lassner for inspiring me with her enthusiasm, critical inquiry, and exciting intellectual conversation; and for her time, energy, and incisive readings as she encouraged my scholarship and helped this book take shape. As a dissertation adviser and teacher, Lesley Higgins taught me to be thorough, inquisitive, and critical, but most importantly, she infected me with her love of modernist literature and poetry. Her wit, kind patience, and years of dedication in mentoring me as a scholar, and her continued encouragement and advice, have been a rare and wonderful gift. And I am so grateful to have benefited and to continue to learn from Sara Horowitz's mentorship and teaching. Her learned wisdom, gracious critique, and nuanced approach to literature, ethics, and Jewish culture — and her compassion and generosity as a scholar — are a guiding example. This book would not be possible without the assistance, guidance, and care of these three remarkable and illustrious scholars.

I would also like to thank Henry Carrigan, assistant director at Northwestern University Press, Sara Dreyfuss, and the helpful staff at the press. My sincerest gratitude also goes out to the faculty, colleagues, and friends at York University's Department of English, and especially Art Redding, who helped me to probe further in my research as a conscientious reader, teacher, dissertation committee member, and adviser. Marie-Christine Leps has also guided me as a scholar with her passionate scholarly enthusiasm and encouragement. In addition, I am grateful to Harold Troper for his wise counsel and to Doris Bergen for sharing with me her extensive knowledge and guidance. My appreciation goes out to Andrea Knight for her support as well as Naomi Azrieli and my colleagues at the Azrieli Foundation for assisting me in building my career as a Holocaust scholar.

My research and writing was greatly assisted with the help of generous scholarships and fellowships. Research for my dissertation was funded by the Social Sciences and Research Council of Canada, York University's President Susan Mann Dissertation Scholarship, an Ontario Government Scholarship, a Fleischer Award for Jewish Studies, and a Henry and Barbara Bank Fellowship for Jewish Studies. I am so grateful to the Israel and Golda Koschitsky Centre for Jewish Studies at York University for supporting my research and providing me with travel funds, space, and resources as I revised my manuscript, and the Crown Center for Jewish Studies at Northwestern University for hosting me as I put the finishing touches on my book. This book was made possible in part by funds granted to me through a Charles H. Revson Fellowship at the Center for Advanced Holocaust Studies, United States Holocaust Memorial Museum. I am also grateful to Steve Feldman and the Emerging Scholars Publication Program at the Center for Advanced Holocaust Studies for its support in the preparation of the manuscript. Discussions with colleagues at the museum helped me develop and refine my argument for this book, including the generous advice of senior fellow Susan Suleiman, and helpful feedback from Brett Kaplan, Clifton Spargo, Anika Walke, Alexandra Budabin, and Daniel Brewing.

Last but not least, I want to thank my family and friends for having faith in me and for their dedication and love. My parents, Rabbi Solomon and Syma Spiro, and Elliott Spiro, Chani Sacharen, Zippy Livneh, Robert and Sandra Birnbaum, Elisa Birnbaum, and my near and dear family of friends who supported me and facilitated with food and laughter. I reserve the most important and crucial thank-you, however, for David Birnbaum. For believing in me, for making me laugh, for making me tea, and for being the best partner in life I could ever hope for. I dedicate this book to him.

## ABBREVIATIONS

**Djuna Barnes**

| | |
|---|---|
| NW | *Nightwood* |
| NWOV | *Nightwood: The Original Version and Related Drafts.* Ed. Cheryl Plumb |

**Christopher Isherwood**

| | |
|---|---|
| CHK | *Christopher and His Kind* |
| GTB | *Goodbye to Berlin* |

**Virginia Woolf**

| | |
|---|---|
| A | "Anon" |
| AROO | *A Room of One's Own* |
| BTA | *Between the Acts* |
| D | *The Diaries of Virginia Woolf* |
| DM | *Death of the Moth and Other Essays* |
| E | *Collected Essays of Virginia Woolf.* Ed. Andrew McNeillie |
| L | *The Letters of Virginia Woolf.* Ed. Nigel Nicolson and Joanne Trautmann |
| M | *The Moment and Other Essays* |
| PH | *Pointz Hall: The Earlier and Later Transcripts of "Between the Acts."* Ed. Mitchell A. Leaska |
| TG | *Three Guineas* |

# ANTI-NAZI MODERNISM

Who live under the shadow of war,
What can I do that matters?
—STEPHEN SPENDER, *POEMS* 31 (1933)

In *Three Guineas*, Virginia Woolf suggests that writers need to "find out new ways of approaching 'the public'; single it into separate people instead of massing it into one monster, gross in body, feeble in mind" (117). The burden for many politically engaged writers in the 1930s was how to warn the "public" to resist the harmful and alienating effects of Nazism as it began to overtake Europe. Many writers asked themselves these questions: What cultural role could their novels play in a time of political crisis? What kind of narrative voice and style was appropriate to reach the larger public? Moreover, could fiction and reading constitute a mode of resistance and effect political change? As in Stephen Spender's poem, many writers of the era wrestled with the same dilemma: "What can I do that matters?"

*Anti-Nazi Modernism* grapples with the question of how modern art and literature can "matter"—an issue that has been debated since the 1930s and is still important for politically conscious writers and critics today. More precisely, this book offers a historically based approach to the study of antifascist, and particularly anti-Nazi, literature by examining the narrative methods used by three writers of the late modernist period whose novels warn readers of the approaching political shadow of their time: Christopher Isherwood, Djuna Barnes, and Virginia Woolf. Although they are often considered champions of subversion by literary scholars of the modernist period, oddly enough these three writers are seldom read within the historical and political context of Nazi resistance. Yet, as this book argues, their works not only resonate with the psychological and social theories of the period but also are key examples in exploring how ideology and political discourse filter into literary works of the period. As I demonstrate, British and American writers and intellectuals were in conversation with European politics, and their works were far more integrated with international concerns than many scholars consider.[1] Deploying what I call an "anti-Nazi aesthetic," Woolf, Barnes, and Isherwood carefully warn against Nazism's suppression of individuality and sexual and racial difference and expose Nazism's murderous discourse of exclusion and its reliance on the culture of the "spectacle" in parades, film, rallies, mass media, and propaganda. Both thematically and through modernist narrative techniques, their texts encourage critique, promote alternate perspectives, and function as interventions into the image of unity, group cohesiveness, and heroic violence that was perceived by many as Nazism's most serious threat to artistic freedom. By highlighting representations of Others that Nazism oppresses — particularly the Modern Woman, the Jew, and the homosexual — these writers also provide important clues to the sexual and racial politics that were endemic to Western Europe in the years leading up to World War II. A close examination of these crucial works can thus reveal how political imagination develops, how literary resistance is produced through discursive and aesthetic strategies, and also the implication and problems of ethics that come to the fore within those literary experiments.

What makes these authors especially fascinating subjects for a study of this kind are the ambiguities and problematic elements that result from their use of a modernist mode of artistic resistance that only indirectly and obliquely uncovers the insidious elements of Nazism. By encrypting their messages within experimental texts to avoid being polemical or "propaganda-like," these writers risked being obscure to the point that their meanings may have been too difficult to decipher. My study thus asks: can experimental fiction function as a meaningful mode of resistance if it risks excluding those readers who do not understand its message? Another key aspect is that the discourses in which Woolf, Isherwood, and Barnes participate are not all (or at least not all to the same degree) as resistant to misogyny, antisemitism, or homophobia as so many critics have claimed. Each author, in recurring instances and to various degrees, uses stereotypes or condones the prejudices they aim to reveal. In analytical response to this phenomenon, my book addresses the following crucial questions: When do novelists, in uncovering oppressive ideologies, become complicit in the prejudice they are targeting? Can literary figures and their work be effective in political resistance? On whom does resistance writing rely: the writer or the reader? By raising these critical questions, this study aims to probe both the ethical potential and limits of anti-Nazi strategies in literature and thus to add an alternative dimension to inquiries into the late modernist period and its relation to fascism and Nazism.

In the last decade, there has been a renewed interest among scholars of the modernist period to examine the interwar years — often known as an "age of catastrophe" or, as Claud Cockburn coins it, the "Devil's Decade" — in the context of art, politics, and resistance. Works that focus on "Recharting the Thirties" (Quinn), "Rewriting the Thirties" (Williams and Matthews), "Revision" of 1930s writing (Shuttleworth), and reexaminations of women writers between the two world wars (Gill Plain, Maroula Joannou, Phyllis Lassner, Maren Linett, and Judy Suh, among others) all suggest that our time is germane for analyses of "crisis" literature.[2] A number of studies have usefully demonstrated how feminist, socialist, antifascist, and leftist writers of the 1930s oppose the oppressive ideology of fascism in poetry, essays, and realist prose. Other film, literary, and cultural critics (along the lines of Siegfried Kracauer, Saul Friedländer, and Susan Sontag) have defined what could be called a "fascist aesthetic" — that is, overt expressions of fascist ideology in art and literature. Among the many elements they include are extreme nationalism, nostalgia for a glorified past, kitsch, order, veneration of the family, aestheticization of war and violence, worship of masculine virility, and the embrace of Absolutes while simultaneously conflating contradictions. This book situates itself in conversation with these various discussions, but most importantly it extends and complicates them by employing a theoretical approach that produces close readings of the literature within its specific political, ideological, and historical contexts.

There has not yet been a cogent, sustained analysis of a method or approach that specifically links fiction writing and modernist aesthetics with resistance to Nazism, as opposed to a more general "Ur-Fascism," to use Umberto Eco's term, and other fascist movements such as the British Union of Fascists (BUF), Action Française, or Spanish and Italian fascism. Nor has there been a study that reveals how closely Woolf's,

Isherwood's, and Barnes's works resonate with contemporaneous conversations, theories, and discourses regarding the psychology and ideology of Nazism, its reliance on mass culture spectacles, and its effect on the "masses." Of course, the seemingly contradictory ideologies within fascism itself have resulted in scholars agreeing upon only one thing — that defining fascism is contested. It has been variously defined as an economic movement; a political anti-Communist ideology (Nolte); a fanatically violent nationalist, racist movement (Paxton); a reaction to modernity (Herf); an outcome of social Darwinism (Payne); a development of European moral and sexual conservatism (Mosse); and an extension of sexism, misogyny, and patriarchy (Theweleit, Bock). For the purposes of this book, however, I choose to focus on National Socialism as theorized and practiced by the Nazi Party. Although various movements in Europe were gaining in popularity in the 1930s and were of a concern for many antifascist English and American writers living in European centers, generally other fascist movements — including Action Française, Italian fascism, Spanish fascism, or even the BUF — did not attain the level of significance that National Socialism did in England and the United States in the late 1930s. The BUF, headed by Oswald Mosley (established in 1932), at its most popular boasted an estimated membership of 40,000 to 50,000 and had considerable support among London's East End working class (Thurlow, *Fascism in Britain*, 140). Yet, controversy surrounding Mosley's increasingly antisemitic stance, violent exchanges at BUF rallies, and the rise of National Socialism in Germany and threat of war caused many to withdraw their support. Following the 1934 Olympia rally, where antifascists were beaten badly by Mosley's Blackshirts, and the infamous "Cable Street battle" in the East End of London in 1936, membership dropped to fewer than 8,000.[3] Nazism, on the other hand, with its clear agenda of biological determinism, sexism, homophobia, and antisemitism, presented a more menacing and direct threat to writers such as Barnes, Isherwood, and Woolf than did any other movement. Ultimately, it was only in Nazi Germany that the horrific and murderous potential of fascism was fully realized.

In *Anti-Nazi Modernism*, I identify an "anti-Nazi aesthetic" as a form of literary resistance to Nazism that punctuates the connection between Nazism and the notion of the "spectacle"—the aesthetics that Hitler's National Socialist Party used to appeal to the public and draw them toward its ideology. In effect, I am interpreting these works as "antispectacle" narratives, an aspect that adds a crucial, critical component to more general studies of antifascist writing in literary modernism. Focusing on aspects of "seeing" reformulates the link between how writers of the late modernist period witnessed and were thus implicated as spectators of the racial laws against Jews and the oppression of Roma, Sinti, Jehovah's Witnesses, homosexuals, and political activists who became victims of Nazi policies. It also refocuses attention to how scholars of the modernist period often situate works written and published in the late 1930s in England and the United States as external to, or remote from, the looming crisis in Europe and the genocide of the Jewish population that lived there. By 1938, news regarding Hitler's vision for Germany was clearly filtering into the public sphere through newspapers and radio broadcasts. The 1933 English translation of Hitler's *Mein Kampf* was in print and widely available (it had sold 100,000 copies by that time), and Jewish refugees who had experienced persecution were streaming into London. It thus becomes more apparent that those who didn't "see" the spectacle of Nazism and fascism perhaps chose not to. Theories of the Nazi spectacle also provide one way to understand or explain *why* Hitler's party was seductive and *how* it managed to garner support from both intellectual elites and the masses in Europe. As Alice Yaeger Kaplan suggests, "Participation in fascism was not as selflessly masochistic as its most outraged, disbelieving critics would have it appear." Instead, it "gave the masses the impression of intimacy, not just with the leader, but with the myriad representations of themselves supplied by the state" (*Reproductions of Banality*, 35). It provided individuals with the illusion that they were a part of a unified, harmonious whole that was beautiful and noble in its pursuit of supremacy.

German social critics, psychologists, and philosophers living in Europe during this period were among the first to recognize that the mass rallies, pageantry, and images of harmonious crowds were key elements to the draw and allure of Nazism and that it was these factors that posed the greatest threat to individuality and critical thinking. As anyone could read clearly in *Mein Kampf*, the image of the self as part of the crowd was at the foreground of the movement. As Hitler advocated, *"The mass meeting is also necessary for the reason that in it the individual . . . for the first time gets the picture of a larger community, which in most people has a strengthening, encouraging effect*" (435). The perception that the appeal of this form of mass gathering was dangerous because of the way it erased individual freedom and turned spectators into a mesmerized, passive group was being discussed by those theorists who had experienced the direct threat of Nazism as Jews in Germany, such as Walter Benjamin and members of the Frankfurt School, as well as psychologists Sigmund Freud and Wilhelm Reich, among others. Many wrote and published their works from exile in America, England, or prewar France after fleeing persecution by the Nazis. But even British and American writers, political thinkers, and intellectuals who wrote from safety in England and the United States echoed similar views of Nazism in antifascist books and essays. What is key to observe, then, is that no discursive field is solitary. These writers and theorists were all fundamentally analysts of the social plots that came into play during the rise of Nazism, and correspondingly registered their fear that any ordinary person from *any* country could be lured into believing the Nazi myth if he or she became enthralled enough by the promise of harmony to blindly follow an ideology.

Although more recent studies have problematized this "mesmerized mass" conception of German society's support of Nazism, as these theories are central to my understanding of aesthetic resistance to the Nazi spectacle in the 1930s, I cite them here as a framework for discussing Woolf's, Isherwood's, and Barnes's works.[4] Most notably, Walter Benjamin, in his 1935–36 essay "The Work of Art in the Age of Mechanical Reproduction," argues that fascism works to provide an image of unity through aesthetic means, especially in mass spectacles such as political rallies and parades. The appeal of Nazism, Benjamin suggests in his oft-cited passage, is due in no small part to humanity's "self-alienation"—a condition of modernity that by the 1930s had "reached such a degree" that society could "experience its own destruction as an aesthetic pleasure of the first order" (*Illuminations*, 241–42). Members of the Institute for Social Research, founded in 1923 in Frankfurt, Germany, were also at the forefront in advancing theories of contemporary society that focused on the alienating aspects of the modern condition. Theodor Adorno and Max Horkheimer's 1940 analysis of mass culture, for example—which they termed "culture industry" to differentiate it from positive cultural expression arising from the masses—posited that forms of mass entertainment could distract individuals from their own oppression and transform perceptions of their reality. This had far-reaching implications for those who speculated on how Nazism, in its employment of mass cultural productions for propaganda, captivated the German masses. Unlike the writers in this study, Adorno and Horkheimer's objective was to extend Marxist theories of revolution to answer to the emergence of totalitarianism; nevertheless, the notion that mass spectatorship could inhibit individual critique and thinking resonates with the fear that compelled such writers as Woolf, Barnes, and Isherwood to register parallel observations in their novels.

Contemporary theorists have continued to offer analyses of Nazism that link the popular appeal and even seductiveness of the party with concepts of spectacle, image, and illusion. Susan Sontag, in her 1975 essay "Fascinating Fascism," for example, describes the essentials of Nazi culture as the "rendering of the movement in grandiose and rigid patterns . . . for such choreography rehearses the very unity of the polity" (91–92). Included among Sontag's description of fascist aesthetics are the following:

> the massing of groups of people; the turning of people into things; the multiplication or replication of things; and the groupings of people/things around an all-powerful, hypnotic leader-figure or force. The fascist dramaturgy centers on the orgiastic transaction between mighty forces and their puppets, uniformly garbed and shown in ever swelling numbers. Its choreography alternates between ceaseless motion and a congealed, static, "virile" posing. Fascist art glorifies surrender, it exalts mindlessness, and it glamorizes death. (Sontag, "Fascinating Fascism," 91)

Nazism's ability to reinforce an image or "drama" of collectivity, unity, and an illusion of harmony is a similar thread running through numerous descriptions of fascist aesthetics and theories of how Germany became mesmerized by the allure of Nazism. Alice Yaeger Kaplan's argument that fascism functions on the basis of "splitting and binding" also contributes to contemporary perceptions of how the Nazi Party was able to inhabit contradictory or seemingly opposite ideologies at one and the same time, making compatible pairs of what seemed incompatible. "Splitting and binding in fascism empty its language of the kind of content or consistency that usually helps explain political doctrines" (*Reproductions of Banality*, 24). The hypnotic magnetism of Nazism is thus couched in the positive rather than negative workings of power—as a unifying counterpoint to alienation and fragmentation. This is the essence and the effect of the Nazi spectacle.

Reading Woolf, Isherwood, and Barnes in the context of the Nazi spectacle extends the discussion of literary resistance among British and American writers to an important international context and places them as witnesses to the rise of Hitler's tyrannical regime. Using historical documents, media, and social and political theories of the era, my book focuses on their late modernist works: Barnes's *Nightwood* (set in Paris and Europe in 1930; published in 1937), Isherwood's semiautobiographical *Goodbye to Berlin* (a portrait of Berlin between 1930 and 1933; published in 1939), and Woolf's *Between the Acts* (set in rural England in 1939; published in 1941). While these three novels are often acknowledged as crucial texts of the era, and appear regularly on college course lists, comparing these texts for a study of Nazi resistance is rarely considered. Woolf is a key figure in British modernism, and although she reacted to fascism in politically inflected literary writing, she remains firmly grounded in British political and cultural discourses through personal and political identity. Isherwood and Barnes occupy more liminal positions in literary modernism. Isherwood's most notable writing derives from his experiences in Berlin, and he had already immigrated to California when his novel was published. Barnes was an American living in Paris, yet she herself identified with a British and cosmopolitan modernist cultural coterie, wrote her novel while living in England, and is often read alongside British modernists. Yet, as I argue, these three novels deploy an anti-Nazi aesthetic and warn their readers against its allure in strikingly complementary ways. Rather than cautioning against the perils of fascism and National Socialism using polemical style and voice in service of propaganda goals, Woolf, Isherwood, and Barnes use experimental narrative strategies such as nonlinear plots, time shifts, unreliable narrators, and parodic modes to challenge the illusion of harmony and unity in Nazi ideology.[5] They therefore not only promote a transformation in viewpoint but also expand how people can think and respond ethically to oppressive political policies. They also use similar character choices and themes to emphasize how Nazism appeals to the masses but also oppresses those who do not belong to the ideal image of a unified community.

As I emphasize throughout, and as the selection of these writers and following chapters demonstrate, it is the novelization — and particularly, the experimental novelization — that is key to these writers' anti-Nazi strategies. I use the term *novelization* to highlight how the particular narrative forms and strategies of these experimental texts convey their critical ambiguities through construction of character, scene, and plot or plotlessness associated with the modernist novel. I also employ Mikhail Bakhtin's notions of "dialogism" and "heteroglossia" (multivoiced discourse) in my analysis to describe how these novels rely on the reader to make sense of the various political, historical, and cultural discourses that circulate outside the margins of these novels. Comparing Barnes's, Woolf's, and Isherwood's novels suggests that if the Nazi spectacle relies on unifying forces of propaganda and the visual image of harmony, then resistance is more likely to occur when the visual is mediated through experimental fiction, a space in which contrasting voices can exist in a dialogic relationship to expose tensions and contradictions. Their works thus focus on tropes of individual acts of reading and performing as an alternative to consensus-driven spectatorship promoted by mass culture spectacles.

There are, however, elements that are highly problematic with a mode of artistic resistance that uncovers the dangerous elements of Nazism in this manner. For one, by showing *how* Nazi ideology works, by laying bare what is obscured by fascist ideologies in their fictions, these novelists also run the risk of unwittingly supporting the very belief system they intend to undermine. In highlighting how gender, sexuality, and national identity are interrelated along the political spectrum, for example, these writers also rely on accepted modes of stereotyping that draw attention to, or even justify, the essentializing way women, gay men and lesbians, and especially Jews were encoded in early twentieth-century Western European society. At the same time as focusing on "queer" representations of women who are not mothers, men who are not fathers, and Jews who are not "true" citizens or members of society, they often reiterate discriminatory discourses in disturbing ways. Thus, while their texts all work to defamiliarize totalitarianism and oppression, and refuse to allow spectators to consume passively, with fascination, it is also important to read Barnes's, Isherwood's, and Woolf's works carefully and skeptically. *Anti-Nazi Modernism* reveals how public intellectuals perceived the threat of Nazism. Yet, it also interrogates how modern anti-Nazi writers did not foresee the ultimate peril of their own ideologies of exclusion — in particular antisemitism and the destruction of the Jews of Europe.

Clearly, even the notion that modernist or avant-garde art can "enlighten" the masses to make them think differently is decidedly problematic. Andreas Huyssen notably insists that a polarizing discourse based on "the Great Divide" between "high" modernist art and mass culture simply affirms a false hierarchy based primarily on a self/Other binary. The so-called transformative potential of modernist art pitted against the destructive capabilities of "consuming and engulfing" mass culture ignores important considerations in the production and reception of art and culture (*After the Great Divide*, vii). First and foremost, one cannot assume that the "masses" of the interwar period were a homogeneous, gullible group without variances or complexities. The public played a large role in choosing what it wanted to consume. Adorno, "theorist par excellence" of the Great Divide, had an especially influential role in proposing avant-garde and experimental art as resistant to the alienating aspects of mass media and mass culture (ibid., 24). Considering the historical context of his writing, one can understand why Adorno had valid reasons for wanting to draw a divide between modern art and mass culture. In the 1930s, Adorno had seen how art produced for mass consumption could distract an entire population from the reality of their suppression and how propaganda could sway a whole nation to accept and embrace Nazi ideology. Art, for Adorno, was meant to be subjective, oriented against existing power structures, and with a potential to dismantle, "solely through artistic form, the course of the world, which continues to hold a pistol to the heads of human beings" (Adorno, *Notes*, 80).[6] American art critic Clement Greenberg, in the same period, argued similarly that modernist art could provide an alternative to the manipulation of capitalist consumer culture. In his groundbreaking 1939 essay "Avant-Garde and Kitsch," Greenberg used the now-common German/Yiddish word *kitsch* to describe that which is passively consumed by mass culture, juxtaposing it with avant-garde art, which could "save" culture by more accurately describing individual experience.

Avant-garde art is nevertheless often construed as sharing a common goal with fascist aesthetics, posing an additional challenge to its deployment as a strategy of resistance. As Peter Bürger proposes, the aim of numerous interwar political avant-garde movements (especially Dadaism, Surrealism, and Futurism) was "to reintegrate art into the praxis of life" (*Theory of the Avant-Garde*, 22) or "to organize a new life praxis from a basis in art" (49). As Bürger maintains, the politicized avant-garde's goal was to merge art and life so that art could become politically productive and transform societies. In the context of Nazism, rendering life into an aesthetic practice poses considerable ethical problems. Even Huyssen, who considers it our "task" to "retain the image of the now lost unity of the political and artistic avantgarde," admits that "false sublation of reality in fascism and reality status for fiction in socialist realism made breaking down the art/life divide a project with moral and ethical problems" (*After the Great Divide*, 6, 8). Fascist (and especially Nazi) culture, after all, was based on the aestheticization of life and politics, which, as Kaplan argues, explained the draw to fascism on the part of many interwar intellectuals: "Fascism seems to be about making life into art—a transformation that promises to give artists an enormous role" (*Reproductions of Banality*, 32). Closing the gap between art and life—between representation and reality—became horrifyingly real in the context of the Third Reich.

In considering relations among experimental artistic movements, and the political left and right, even placing Barnes, Isherwood, and Woolf among those affiliated with modernist "high art" or the avant-garde is problematic, especially because the issue of how to define these various movements is still a topic of intense debate. Radical modernist experimentation, or "high modernism," typically identified with poets and writers such as James Joyce, T. S. Eliot, and Ezra Pound, was considered by many 1930s critics on the Left to be elitist and classist, catering to a select group of highly educated readers that often excluded women or those belonging to social groupings that would not have access to, or opportunities to acquire, formal education.[7] Although Isherwood has never been considered a "high modernist," Barnes and Woolf were often criticized for being "aesthetes." Barnes was severely criticized by social ist critic Philip Rahv, whose 1937 review of *Nightwood* scorned her intellectual snobbery and "decadence," which he deemed destructive to "genuine values."[8] Similarly, many critics of her time accused Woolf of failing to act politically. Most notably, E. M. Forster in a 1941 Rede lecture assessed that Woolf "has all the aesthete's qualities . . . [with] no great cause at heart" (*Two Cheers*, 240). Even Christopher Isherwood, in his autobiography *Christopher and His Kind*, ruefully admits that he and other young 1930s writers "used Virginia Woolf as an enemy-image of the ivory-tower intellectual" (90).[9]

I would argue that there are distinctions to be made, nonetheless, among "avant-garde" and "modernist" movements and those independent artists who use experimental art as a strategy to interrogate accepted notions of meaning or to revolutionize society for ethical purposes. Although the works examined in this book contain elements of avant-garde, modernist experimentation, realism, and even kitsch or "camp" parody, any attempt to situate Barnes, Isherwood, or Woolf within a single one of these modes would be artificial, at best. As members of what Virginia Woolf in *Three Guineas* would call the "Outsiders' Society" (122)—either because of gender or sexual orientation (or both)—their writings trouble if not negate the existing paradigms constructed around the discourse of modernism/avant-garde, high/low, Left/Right, realism/experimentalism. The allusiveness of an experimental approach to writing, no matter how one would define it, nonetheless allowed for a more democratic, individualist mode of interpretation that defied a totalitarian unity of meaning and could provoke a critical response to the cultural moment of the interwar period. The textual disruptions, parataxis, shifts in viewpoint, irony, and intertextuality that characterize their modes of writing had revolutionary potential for writers like Barnes, Isherwood, and Woolf, and show how they are preoccupied by similar questions about identity, subjectivity, art, and political crisis. To quote Adorno, "Modern art is as abstract as the real relations among men" (*Aesthetic Theory*, 45). In this regard these writers reflect, perhaps in a more "truthful" manner, and in contrast to the Nazi illusion of harmony and unity, the unintelligibility of the political climate and incipient threat of totalitarianism.

Of the three writers, Woolf (1882–1941)—whose essays, short stories, and novels won her critical acclaim in the 1930s and earned her the reputation of being one of the greatest innovators of English literature in the twentieth century — is widely acknowledged by recent critics for her antifascist stance, and especially for linking gender politics with war and fascism.[10] In her often-quoted political treatise *Three Guineas* (1938), Woolf argues that gender politics is at the core of militaristic tyranny and imperialism, and draws vivid parallels between English patriarchy and fascist dictatorships. In *Three Guineas* Woolf insists that the most active form of resisting war is through complete "indifference": "not to incite . . . brothers to fight, or to dissuade them, but to maintain an attitude of complete indifference" (123). Nevertheless, Woolf herself by no means maintains an attitude of indifference — neither in *Three Guineas* nor in any of her other works. Moreover, as I will argue, *Between the Acts* performs resistance *in difference* — that is, the act of positioning difference as a strategy to counter not only fascist ideology in general but also the Nazi dictatorship in particular.

Diaries and letters from the late 1930s suggest that as the war began and the threat of a Nazi invasion in England became a distinct possibility, Woolf became more troubled and began to wonder if writing could be politically effective (Schneider, *Loving Arms*, 111). In a letter to Ben Nicolson on August 24, 1940, Woolf makes these remarks:

> What puzzles me is that people who had infinitely greater gifts than any of us had — I mean, Keats, Shelley, Wordsworth, Coleridge and so on — were unable to influence society. They didn't have anything like the influence they should have had upon 19th century politics. And so we drifted into imperialism and all the other horrors that led to 1914. Would they have had more influence if they had taken an active part in politics? Or would they only have written worse poetry? (*L*, 6: 421)

Perhaps what Woolf means by "worse poetry" is verse that, as the speaker in *Three Guineas* claims, "prostitutes culture" and "encourage[s] intellectual slavery" (*TG*, 113, 114). For this reason Woolf was especially concerned that her political writing avoid any similarity to propaganda.[11] Besides listening to Hitler's speeches on the radio, which greatly disturbed her, Woolf also critiqued the BBC and Churchill for fabricating "BBC-generated emotion," which she felt parodied "real feelings" (*D*, 5: 292, 302).

Woolf's concern regarding the effectiveness of political writing and her fear of "intellectual slavery" is why I argue that *Between the Acts*, particularly as an antispectacle novel, is a more explicit critique of Nazism than her other 1930s work. Unlike her more general comment on fascism in polemical texts such as *Three Guineas*—which elides differences among various types of oppressions—*Between the Acts* identifies the more specific threat of a Nazi dictatorship. Set in June 1939 (published in 1941), the novel has a constant undercurrent of war, with planes droning overhead and fragments of newspaper headlines interrupting whimsical conversations. The history pageant at the center of the novel not only interrogates ideas of nationalistic pageantry but also becomes a site that exposes the constructed nature of social hierarchies, the workings of discrimination, the collusion between public and dictator in relations of power, and the potential of art to create critique. Yet, her anti-Nazi sentiments are nevertheless complicated by her stereotypical and prejudiced portrayal of Jewish characters. One therefore wonders the following: Does Woolf becomes complicit in the discourse of exclusion that she is targeting? How does the discrimination against Jews in her texts affect her resistant strategies?

Similar to Woolf, Christopher Isherwood (1904–1986) was also concerned with depicting social attitudes toward "difference" as a way of political protest. By virtue of his close friendship with W. H. Auden and "his gang," the group of young, left-wing British writers of the 1930s (which included, among others, Stephen Spender, Louis MacNeice, John Lehmann, and C. Day Lewis), Isherwood is recognized as an important literary figure of the interwar period. Although many tend to read *Goodbye to Berlin* as a portrayal of Isherwood himself—an uncomplicated autobiographical text—Isherwood more precisely experiments with what he calls a novel of "example," a literary mode that could reflect more faithfully the complex and threatening political climate of Berlin. In an unpublished lecture entitled "What Is a Novel," Isherwood contends that a novel "is not journalism, is not a political pamphlet, is not a religious sermon, is not a historical essay, is not a sociological treatise. . . . [T]he novel is made up of examples" (quoted in Carr, *Queer Times*, 22). That is, it can contain different types of discourse, but it should allow the reader to elicit meaning from it rather than presenting a definite point of view. Isherwood's "examples" in *Goodbye to Berlin* become politicized specifically because they challenge how sexual and racial identities are defined in interwar Europe. Furthermore, a close analysis of the way in which image, performance, and theatricality operate in *Goodbye to Berlin* reveals not only how identities are constructed but also how a nation loses its sense of reality when the illusion of unity and harmony has completely replaced reason.

A clear condemnation of Nazism is more difficult to detect in American writer Djuna Barnes's *Nightwood* than in any of the other texts. Already a successful New York journalist and playwright, Barnes (1892–1982) went to Paris in 1921 to spend most of the twenties living among the circle of expatriate artists and literary figures in the Left Bank, including Natalie Barney, Colette, Nancy Cunard, Sylvia Beach, and James Joyce. *Nightwood*, written while she was living in England in the 1930s (she returned to New York after suffering a breakdown in 1939), was based on her experiences there. Stylistically, *Nightwood* is more experimental, parodic, whimsical, and ultimately cynical, and its anti-Nazi message is therefore difficult to educe. Moreover, critics tend to disregard *Nightwood*'s engagement with international politics by focusing on Barnes's life in Paris, her lesbianism, and her love affair with Thelma Wood. In fact, it is only in the past fifteen years or so that studies have begun to situate the novel within its political and historical contexts.[12] Barnes's biographer Andrew Field reports that in later years Barnes vehemently denied that the novel was in any way connected with "the spirit of Nazism" (quoted in Field, *Djuna*, 15). Yet, I would agree with Field, who comments, "If one understands the spirit of the Thirties at all, it is quite clear that . . . *Nightwood* does not speak only to the question of lesbianism or the private life of Djuna Barnes but also to its time" (214). The carnivalesque cast of outcast characters undermines the determination of normative gender and sexual roles by completely overturning the ideas of social order that Nazi ideology promoted. The absurd conflations of high literary expressions, folk idioms, sentimental kitsch, and obscenities also challenge the way her novel is consumed as a cultural product. Thus, by multiplying the possibilities of perspective, the novel confounds the homogeneous "truths" encouraged by Nazi culture, propaganda, and totalitarian thinking.

Dissimilar as they are, the common characteristic that all three texts share is the manner in which they function as modes of resistance by upsetting the complacency of interwar European society and by im-

pressing upon the reader an awareness of how Nazism suppresses difference and subjugates Others. Only now do readers possess the hindsight
to perceive how Nazi ideology could lead to genocide. Yet each of the
three writers, in eerily prescient segments of their novels, foresees the
perils of Hitler's National Socialist Party and attempts to respond to
the crisis by warning readers to see, and to witness, rather than simply
to stand by and watch. As Woolf in *Three Guineas* describes the distinct
viewpoint of Outsiders, "though we look at the same things, we see them
differently" (7). *Anti-Nazi Modernism*'s analysis of the ethical potential
of modernist innovation as a strategy that "sees differently" to uncover,
expose, and resist Nazi culture adds historical complexity and significance to current studies of antifascist literature. Moreover, through the
wider historical and cultural analysis that this study provides, and the
close examination of the interrelated aspects of spectacle, bodies, and
identities (national, racial, gender, and sexual), I offer an alternative perspective on interweaves between politics and cultural production of the
late modernist period.

By integrating historical, political, and cultural contexts with close
readings of the texts in each chapter, I demonstrate how Barnes, Isherwood, and Woolf challenge the Nazi spectacle's image of unity, harmony, and racial superiority and at the same time warn of the fundamental danger inherent in Nazism's anti-Jewish, sexist, and homophobic
agenda. This is not to suggest that racism, sexism, and homophobia are
analogous or were treated similarly under National Socialism. As Judith Butler proposes, we need to "resist the model of power that would
set up racism, homophobia and misogyny as parallel or analogical relations" lest we risk ignoring their specific histories and the ways each are
interrelated (*Bodies That Matter*, 18). Mindful of these considerations,
and because I am interested in showing the many continuities and simi-
larities among these three diverse writers, I have organized *Anti-Nazi
Modernism* according to a problematics model. In this way, the texts
are reexamined from different perspectives, and parallels can be drawn
according to each thematic consideration. The first chapter lays out the
theoretical foundations of the Nazi spectacle to discover how these texts
counter the spectacle and what tropes and methods constitute their anti-
Nazi aesthetic. The subsequent three chapters consider the different aspects of their literary resistance by isolating themes pertaining to the

representation of bodies that the Nazi spectacle suppresses: sexism and the representation of Modern Woman; antisemitism and the image of "the Jew"; and homophobia and "queer" resistance. Finally, the conclusion briefly explores the link between cultural production and politics by considering the impact of resistance writing and the cultural bearing it has on politically engaged readers today.

Chapter 1, "Spectacular Nazism and Subversive Performances," establishes the theoretical basis for a discussion of the Nazi spectacle, its reliance on illusion and visual media, and the various aesthetic and thematic methods writers use to subvert it. This chapter outlines various theories of the Nazi spectacle and how it relates to fascism and National Socialism in particular. Especially important are the effects of the spectacle on its audience, and its connection to technology, mass media, and crowd mentality. Drawing attention to how Barnes, Isherwood, and Woolf engage with tropes of visual media, performance, and reading in their works, the chapter then explores the manner in which they highlight the tensions between the illusion of harmony in mass culture performances and the heterogeneity of private acts of interpretation. The "snapshots" and cabaret performances in Isherwood's *Goodbye to Berlin*; the circus performers in Barnes's *Nightwood*; and the pageant in Woolf's *Between the Acts* all require viewers and readers to participate in acts of individual interpretation and critique. In many ways these performances act as *mises-en-abyme* of the novels that frame them — the onlookers in the audience, as well as the reader, are simultaneously implicated as participants in the dynamic of the spectacle and as witnesses to the Nazi threat. Chapter 1 thus investigates the inconclusiveness and ambiguities of modernist writings as they attempt to dismantle the totalitarian paradigm from within, undermining the lure of crowd mentality and engendering a new way of reading, listening, and understanding.

To expose how gender and national identity are interrelated all along the political spectrum, the second chapter, "Vamps, Tramps, and Nazis: Representations of Spectacular Female Characters," examines how women are represented in popular European culture, in fascist and Nazi propaganda, and in antifascist fiction. Woman, and especially the Modern Woman, becomes a metaphor that both Nazi and anti-Nazi discourses use in a parallel manner — as threat or beacon of a new, more liberal age; as victims or accomplices in the allure of mass culture; and as champions or collaborators of fascist ideology. Barnes, Isherwood, and Woolf overturn the typical ways women are constructed, especially in the Nazi scenario, by portraying compelling, individualistic, emancipated female characters. The novels critique Nazism in its oppression of women not only by anticipating current gender theory (by focusing on the performative aspects of gender) but also by drawing attention to the ways in which sexism and "the female spectacle" function in oppressive regimes. Sally Bowles in *Goodbye to Berlin*, Robin Vote in *Nightwood*, and Mrs. Manresa in *Between the Acts* all challenge patriarchy by revealing that ideas of "womanhood" are constructs, or images that need to be rethought. Nevertheless, women in these works also become vehicles for an exploration into the ethical responsibility of the private individual toward a larger public. As my analysis suggests, these works show that if subversive performance loses its self-consciousness and slips into fantasy — a way of evading responsibility toward others — then it ultimately supports fascism, Nazism, and their oppression of others.

Chapter 3, "Seeing Jewish or Seeing 'the Jew'? The Spectral Jewish Other," analyzes the construction and portrayal of "the Jew" in the three works and in the larger European imagination. Specifically, this chapter extends extant approaches to this issue by considering whether these authors' critiques of Nazism are compromised by the evident prejudice they convey in their stereotyping of Jews. Jewish characters feature prominently in all three novels, often with sympathy and recognition of their status as the "ultimate Others" and victims of the cruel and unjust racial policies of Nazi Germany. Yet, although Barnes, Isherwood, and Woolf express some of their most unambiguously anti-Nazi sentiments in their representation of Jewish characters, troubling these portrayals is the fact that they reiterate a discourse that imagines "the Jew" as always and inescapably Other.[13] *Nightwood*, *Between the Acts*, and *Goodbye to Berlin* reinforce exclusivist racist thinking by depicting Jewish characters with stereotypical physical markers and moral traits — frequently portraying them as morally corrupt, as overly urban, or as social climbers. As this chapter demonstrates, these writers might confront aspects of antisemitism, but despite their personae as critical "Outsiders," they are also entrenched in a cultural moment, thus revealing the conditions in everyday European life that allowed for antisemitism to go unchecked.

The final chapter, "Eventually We're All Queer: Fascism, Nazism, and Homosexuality," considers how homosexual characters are portrayed in the texts in a manner that confronts the era's sexual anxieties. Especially in their portrayal of gay and lesbian characters, Barnes, Isherwood, and Woolf highlight the way gender, sexual politics, and textual politics are decisively linked in oppressive political ideologies. This chapter explores how the authors "queer" their texts as a strategy to manipulate the textual potential of the "unrepresentable." By laying out the discourse of homosexuality in England, France, and Germany, and the historical and cultural context that is the background of these texts, I clarify the risks involved in exposing homosexuality, even in fiction — censorship, career sabotage, and, for Isherwood, possible arrest. Nevertheless, by featuring characters that challenge the idea of a "natural" gender, *Nightwood, Goodbye to Berlin*, and *Between the Acts* become sites of struggle, dismantling ideas of belonging and absolute truth, and exposing that identity itself — national, racial, and sexual — is perpetually unstable. This chapter will contextualize these discourses within the historical context of the notorious Paragraph 175 that criminalized homosexuality and that the Nazis expanded to justify the murder of homosexuals.

Final considerations about the impact and effect of literary resistance are offered in the conclusion, "Can Fiction Make a Difference? Writing and Reading Resistance." This study begins with the assumption that support for Nazism did not stem from a momentary lapse of sanity in the history of Europe or a freak accident.[14] With this idea in mind, what opportunity is there for current readers and writers to learn from literary resistance in the 1930s? In *The Society of the Spectacle* (1967), Guy Debord states that "A critical theory of the spectacle cannot be true unless it joins forces with the practical movement of negation within society" (143). This chapter accordingly probes and evaluates responses to the deployment of an "anti-Nazi aesthetic" as a mode of resistance during the interwar period and discusses the role of the current reader and critic within that resistant process. It is my contention that in studying the past, today's critics, readers, and teachers have the opportunity to take another look at modern culture and its link to fascism and Nazism, and to reject the outcome of the Holocaust as "a temporary illness" of modern society. More importantly, as I propose, the canon of modern English fiction implicitly demonstrates that it is not invested enough with these types of political and ethical questions.

## CHAPTER 1

# Spectacular Nazism and Subversive Performances

The entire educational system, the theatre, the cinema,
literature, the Press, and the wireless — all these will be used
as a means to this end and valued accordingly. They must all
serve for the maintenance of the eternal values present in the
essential character of our people.

—ADOLF HITLER, SPEECH GIVEN ON MARCH 23, 1933

The masses have never thirsted after truth. . . . Whoever can
supply them with illusions is easily their master; whoever
attempts to destroy their illusions is always their victim.

—GUSTAVE LE BON, *THE CROWD* (1903); REFERRED TO BY SIGMUND

FREUD, *GROUP PSYCHOLOGY AND THE ANALYSIS OF THE EGO* (1921)

In Eric Rentschler's 1996 collection of essays on German cinema, film-maker Wim Wenders comments, "Never before and in no other country have images and language been abused so unscrupulously as here, never before and nowhere else have they been debased so deeply as vehicles to transmit lies" (*Ministry of Illusion*, 128).[1] In the past two decades, considerable scholarly attention has been focused on the way Nazi Germany exploited images and visual culture to captivate the public and rally people to the National Socialist cause. It is well understood that Nazism could not have garnered as much support from the public as it did by political arguments alone or by fear and policing.[2] In 1933 social critic Frederick Schuman observed that it was the "meetings, parades, flags, music" that lent Nazism its allure and made it so appealing: "There was a hypnotic oratory, great drama, tremendous excitement and exaltation" (*The Nazi Dictatorship*, 77). As Schuman comments on his impressions of the 1927 Nuremberg convention, Hitler was "the symbol artist *par excellence*. . . . He was an actor and stage director, as well as scene-painter, costumer, and property man. The pageantry of the great parades and mass meetings was his" (82). Aside from the colorful rallies and family events, the Nazi Party used the newest forms of technology — radio, cinema, newsreels, photography — to transform ideology into enthralling and mesmerizing modes of entertainment. To quote Rentschler, "The Third Reich [was] a grand production, the world war a continuing movie of the week" (222).

For many modernist writers, Hitler and the Nazi Party's reliance on image, illusion, spectacle, and propaganda threatened to eclipse their own roles as artists and fiction-makers. In "The Artist and Politics" Woolf remarks that the artist must become involved in politics because "two causes of supreme importance to him are in peril. The first is his own survival; the other is the survival of his art" (M, 182). But how can the artist's work become a site of political struggle against the perilous effects of the Nazi spectacle? What does this struggle look like? Is it possible to convince a public to resist Nazism and its ideology without resorting to the very same rhetorical strategies used in its propaganda? This chapter attempts to probe some of these questions by examining both the ethics and aesthetics of these writers' resistance to the Nazi spectacle in fiction. Later, I examine how Woolf's *Between the Acts*, Isherwood's *Goodbye to Berlin*, and Barnes's *Nightwood* challenge aspects of Nazi culture through metaphors taken from photography, film, theater, and cultural performances. Before I launch into an analysis of the texts, however, I will outline some of the ideological and political aspects of the "spectacle" to explain how it functioned in the 1930s and how it is then reproduced and challenged in anti-Nazi fiction.

## The Politics of the Spectacle

The exploitation of mass spectacle for political purposes, unsurprisingly, has historical precedents to its use by the Nazi Party. The lavish, dramatic, and public nature of a spectacle and its particular impact on a community of viewers had potential to lend significance to the notion of "spectacle" in social and political thought. Among the first to politicize the word *spectacle* is, notably, Friedrich Nietzsche. In *The Birth of Tragedy in the Spirit of Music*, Nietzsche discusses spectacle and spectatorship in relation to politics and antiquity when describing ancient Greek theater. He uses the term "spectacle" in a discussion of whether life can be represented in art, basing his main conceit on an analysis of the role of the Chorus in ancient Greece. Nietzsche contends that although commentators generally view the Chorus as an "ideal spectator," mirroring the mood or will of the people in contrast to the "passionate excesses and extravagances" of the aristocrats, such a role would be impossible in a community that has no concept of equality, democracy, or unity. According to Nietzsche, the members of the audience "knew of no constitutional representation of the people in *praxi*, and it is to be hoped that they did not even 'have intimations' of it in tragedy." From this point he derives his notion that the Chorus and the "chorus of ideal spectators" could not possibly coincide: "The spectator without the spectacle is an absurd notion" (*Birth of Tragedy*, 56–57). Instead Nietzsche posits that the pleasure and rapture derived from tragedy by the Dionysian audience stems from the Chorus acting as a wall between art and reality. It erases the need for an "ideal spectator" to differentiate art from reality by "nullifying" the role of the spectator, thus giving comfort in the illusion that life is larger, grander, and more powerful than it actually is (ibid., 58–59). Once Euripides introduces a consciousness of art and its separation from reality in an aesthetics that is "Socratic" rather than Dionysian (in that "to be good everything must be conscious"), a "second spectator" arises—an individual who is no longer passive or incapable of action (ibid., 85–86). This, as explained by Andrew Hussey, is "the theoretical man"—a person, like the artist, who can disconnect from the past and the present and imagine a different future (*Game of War*, 190).[3]

The "pleasure and rapture" that Nietzsche perceived as the sentiment Dionysian audiences experienced when art and reality melded into an ideal illusion were also crucial components in the dynamics of the Nazi mass rally. In a single mass, individuals could be released from the burden of consciousness and disenfranchisement that was part and parcel of the modern condition. The role of the Nazi rallies, meetings, and cultural displays in creating this sense of bliss and combating modern alienation through the image and illusion of a unified whole cannot be overemphasized. In *Mein Kampf*, Hitler describes how the spectacle is at the foreground of the movement when he advocates the necessity of the "mass meeting":

> The community of the great demonstration not only strength-ens the individual, it also unites and helps to create an *esprit de corps*. The man who is exposed to grave tribulations, as the first advocate of a new doctrine in his factory or workshop absolutely needs that strengthening which lies in the conviction of being a member and fighter in a great comprehensive body. And he obtains an impression of this body for the first time in the mass demonstration. When from his little workshop or big factory, in which he feels very small, he steps for the first time into a mass meeting and has thousands and thousands of people of the same opinions around him, when, as a seeker, he is swept away by three or four thousand others into the mighty effect of sugges-tive intoxication and enthusiasm, when the visible success and agreement of thousands confirm to him the rightness of the new doctrine and for the first time arouse doubt in the truth of his pre-vious conviction — then he himself has succumbed to the magic influence of what we designate as "mass suggestion." (435)

The passage indicates how the mass rally contributes to a feeling of be-longing that is lost as a result of modern industrialization; the spectacle of the rally promotes instead a feeling of "intoxication and enthusiasm" that comes with harmony and consensus. Hitler's perception that mass suggestion could become a vehicle to imagining a grander reality was unanticipated in its shrewdness and political efficacy, but also worrisome.

The individual's vulnerability toward becoming "swept away" into a unified, passive group of spectators to avoid the discomfort of modern "tribulations" was simultaneously registered by those "second spec-tators" of the 1930s. Aside from modernist writers such as Woolf, Ish-erwood, and Barnes, at the time many American and British writers, intellectuals, psychologists, sociologists, and political scientists tried to warn their readers about the menace of Nazism.[4] Their strategies included not only exposing Hitler's oppressive policies but also trying to comprehend how and why the German masses were drawn to Hitler and Nazi culture. Echoing earlier studies on crowd mentality such as Gustave Le Bon's *The Crowd: A Study of the Popular Mind* (1903) and Freud's *Group Psychology and the Analysis of the Ego* (1921),[5] for instance, Frederick Schuman in *The Nazi Dictatorship* (1936) points out the "spellbinding" effect of the Nazi rallies on the crowds: "the voice from the platform, assisted perhaps by songs, images, banners and other appropriate paraphernalia, reaches out to its multitudes of auditors" and "evokes a spiritual orgasm leading to whatever type of violent mass behaviour the orator is seeking to produce" (79). Emil Lengyel, author of *Millions of Dictators* (1936), contends, "The mass soul . . . is different from the individual soul. The kindly Dr. Jekyll may turn into a horrid Mr. Hyde in a crowd, and the ruffian may rise to heights of selfless exaltation" (259). Similarly, John Strachey's widely published *The Menace of Fascism* (1933) warns that German fascism's purpose is to drive the masses "back to the unquestioning acceptance of lives of unrelieved drudgery" (41).

German-Jewish social critics of the 1930s who witnessed the emerging threat of totalitarianism from a more direct vantage point were also developing strategic responses to the ever-expanding political and social turmoil in Europe between the two world wars. Siegfried Kracauer's "Masse und Propaganda" (commissioned by Theodor Adorno in 1936 for the Institute for Social Research in New York), for example, explains how in German mass culture the masses are "forced to see themselves everywhere; thus, they are always aware of themselves, often in the aesthetically seductive form of an ornament or an effective image" (translated by Witte in "Introduction," 62). In other words, the danger of the Nazi spectacle was that it was enticing because of the pleasure that spectacle produced: it satisfied a desire to be seen and observed by fellow citizens and by Hitler and the state; to sacrifice and submit to the rules; and to relinquish responsibility for the self. Adorno and Max Horkheimer expand on this notion of manipulation in their critique that "culture industries" were contributing to the manipulation of the masses by concealing social structures and dulling the individual's desire to struggle against those same structures. As they claim in *Dialectic of Enlightenment* (written in the early 1940s, published in 1947), mass forms of media and entertainment are vehicles of "mass distraction" that inhibit subjective thinking and imagination. Individuals, diverted from the reality of their oppression, thus unquestioningly accept the existing order of society. The culture industry becomes the linchpin of oppression under fascism and Nazism because it imposes ideology from the top down, eroding more "authentic" forms of culture, and at the same time shutting down opportunities for individual thought and revolutionary struggle.[6] For this reason Adorno and Horkheimer direct their strongest critique of the culture industry's power of manipulation toward film: "Far more strongly than the theatre of illusion, film denies its audience any dimension in which they might roam freely in imagination . . . it trains those exposed to it to identify film directly with reality" (*Dialectic of Enlightenment*, 100). Even so, as discussed in the introduction, the idea that the masses are unified in their desires, or utterly passive and vulnerable to manipulation (or even that mass culture is always negative), is decidedly problematic, a point that I will address in more detail later.

From a slightly different perspective, but still writing from the critical viewpoint of a witness to current German policies, Walter Benjamin supported the types of mass culture, like film, that could break down the institutions of bourgeois hierarchies that dictated culture, and in this way provide critical consciousness to the masses. Even Benjamin, however, concludes in his renowned essay "The Work of Art in the Age of Mechanical Reproduction" (1935–36) that there are circumstances in which the use of technology for mass culture spectacles, as it is used in Nazism, could lead to the "aestheticization of politics." Benjamin observes this in a frequently quoted passage:

> Mankind, which in Homer's time was an object of contemplation for the Olympian gods, now is one for itself. Its self-alienation has reached such a degree that it can experience its own destruction as an aesthetic pleasure of the first order. This is the situation of politics which Fascism is rendering aesthetic. (*Illuminations*, 242)

How Benjamin comes to this conclusion from his support of film and technology as a means for promoting individual expression and revolution is often deliberated in critical assessments of his work. His theory is important to how we read experimental works such as Woolf, Isherwood, and Barnes, however, in that it brings into focus and enables a clearer articulation of both the possibilities and challenges that come into play when particular types of art are used to reveal hidden "truths" by shocking the viewer. Breaking the routine of everyday thought, as Benjamin posits, a work of art can "innervate" a person into awareness and revolutionary action (avant-garde art and film being crucial examples), but the by-product of this "shock" also has negative effects. As Miriam Hansen aptly points out, although Benjamin welcomes the decay of the "aura"—which he defines as a "unique phenomenon of a distance" that represents "the cult value of the work of art" (*Illuminations*, 243)—he also modifies this position as World War II draws near.[7] Based on Freud's theory of shock and the defensive numbing toward stimuli that happens in the body, Benjamin argues that shock is necessary to promote change by disrupting routine and habit-forming sensory perceptions; yet, the numbing caused by too much stimulation from media and modern industry results in the "decay of experience." Concomitantly, the individual experiences a loss of memory and perception of the past and thus surrenders the future (Hansen, "Benjamin and Cinema," 44–45). Fascism, according to Benjamin, combines the most damaging aspects of both the decay of the aura and the numbing experience of modernity. Man himself becomes the contemplated image, and combined with the overstimulation, distancing, and self-alienation caused by the "shock" of the Nazi spectacle, he becomes a spectator of his demolition. That is how he experiences war as an "aesthetic pleasure."

Taking Benjamin's concept of the aestheticization of politics one step further, Russell Berman in his introduction to Alice Yaeger Kaplan's *Reproductions of Banality* (1986) explains how in Nazi aesthetics the decay of the aura, and the consequential rise of the image, transforms into the basis for murder. "Mechanical reproduction permits an aesthetic practice emancipated from the auratic image," Berman asserts, "but the compulsive fixation on the image and the associated fear of language . . . turn into a search for origins and an extermination of the different as nonoriginal, as outside the sacred image" ("Wandering Z," xx). In other words, by making the image itself sacred, the Nazis promote the fantasy of an auratic original. The impossible search for origins leads to the identification and obliteration of that which interferes with the illusion of originality — the Other. The terrible result is "mass murder as the an-swer to mass media" (ibid.). The Nazi rallies, holidays, flags, and uni-forms, as well as the methodical use of technology such as cinema and radio, were thus central to the party's racial policies. The Nazi spectacle, by creating an enthrallment with the illusion of a cohesive, undivided community, simultaneously persuaded a nation to support a policy of exclusion that annihilated all those individuals who did not belong in the image of a sacred, unified nation.

Being so invested in maintaining the illusion of harmony, Nazism was not surprisingly adamantly opposed to modernist and avant-garde art and literature, while making optimum use of the dramatic potential of mass cultural productions and especially film. Even before the Second World War was launched, many scholars suggest, audiences were primed for war by the images presented to them on film.[8] Kaplan references me-dia critics Robert Brasillach and Maurice Bardèche's 1943 statement in Histoire de cinéma as a prime example of the significance of cinema in the public's support of the Third Reich: World War II, as they perceived, "was staged in our collective imagination, in our moviegoing imagina-tion, before the war actually began" (quoted in Kaplan, Reproductions of Banality, 29). As Kaplan argues, in particular the newsreel, shown to audiences at the cinemas between the two world wars, promoted a situation whereby "destruction in the real [was] justified beforehand by an aesthetic device." For the moviegoing public, the newsreel "distances and controls war, rendering it a safe fantasy, and ultimately, a real pos-sibility" (ibid., 29). The audience, therefore — not only in Germany but also in other Western countries — could accept the negative aspects of war as an aesthetic experience rather than a lived one.[9] For those spec-tators in France, England, and the United States, Hitler's expansionist motives and impassioned speeches displayed on screen kept them up-dated on international politics but could also reinforce a remoteness that facilitated the choice for audiences to remain "in the dark" — as passive spectators to an alienated reality. For this reason as well, critical works that highlighted the fragmentary nature of reality could potentially threaten the fantasy of harmonious accord and rouse the individual into awareness. As I demonstrate later, it is specifically this choice to remain remote and passive, relieving individuals from feeling a moral or ethical obligation to respond to the political climate, that Woolf, Isherwood, and Barnes expose in their novels.

As these writers perceived, the danger to the wider public was not only that Nazism oppressed the rights of Jews, women, and homosexuals and used spectacle as a vehicle to encourage the German public to "un-see" those who did not belong to the ideal image of a unified community. Nazism was more than a political movement—it was a way of living and perceiving reality that was illusory. As Linda Schulte-Sasse asserts in her assessment of the Third Reich's use of cinema, Nazism not only exploited leisure activities and modes of entertainment to distract the masses—it was "virtually *synonymous with* illusion, theatre, or spectacle" (*Entertaining the Third Reich,* 3). Monies invested in the film industry by the Third Reich's Ministry of Propaganda are further evidence of the importance of promoting that illusion on the big screen. As Hitler maintains in *Mein Kampf,* "The picture in all its forms up to the film has greater possibilities. Here a man needs to use his brains even less; it suffices to look, or at most to read extremely brief texts, and thus many will more readily accept a *pictorial representation* than *read* an *article* of any *length*" (427; italics in original). Ironically yet aptly, the Nazi era is often considered the "Golden Age" of German film history. Eric Rentschler indicates that more than 1,000 feature films were produced during the period. These figures demonstrate the growth and popularity of film at the time: in 1933, approximately 5,071 cinemas nationwide witnessed 245 million admissions; by 1940, more than 7,018 cinemas had 834 million admissions. Even at the height of the war, in 1944, there were 6,484 cinemas and 1.1 million tickets sold (Rentschler, *Ministry of Illusion,* 13). The early establishment of the Reich Ministry for Popular Enlightenment and Propaganda and The National Chamber of Culture also suggests the crucial positioning of mass public forms of entertainment within Nazi ideological formation (especially cinema, theater, radio, staged rallies, and revues). On March 11, 1933, only three months after Hitler was appointed chancellor, Paul Joseph Goebbels was made propaganda minister responsible for the entire nation's cultural production.[10]

Goebbels recognized the crucial role mass culture and "art" played in promoting "invisible propaganda" (*unsichtbare Propaganda*). In a speech given on March 5, 1937, at the Berlin Kroll-Oper, Goebbels makes the following shrewd remarks:

> At the moment that propaganda is recognized as such it becomes ineffective. However, the moment that propaganda, mes-

sage, bent or attitude as such stay in the background and appear to people only as storyline, action, or side-effect, then they will become effective in every respect. . . . All art has a message. Art has an aim, a goal, a direction. . . . Thus I don't want art for the sake of a message but to insert that message into the greater overall design. (quoted and translated by Schulte-Sasse in *Entertaining the Third Reich*, 33)

The assertion that "all art has a message" would imply that fascism not only aestheticized politics in rallies and mass spectacles, as Benjamin and Kracauer claim, but also politicized art. "Works of art" promoted by the National Socialist Party, especially those that fell into the category of mass culture entertainment, such as film, could thereby transform spectators from "culture consumers" into "political beings" or at the least recipients of political indoctrination (Hake, *Popular Cinema*, 79). The 1935 Nuremberg Laws, which restricted Jews from going to public events, worked to politicize further the act of mass cultural consumption. Simply by going to the cinema, spectators were affirming membership in a privileged majority; moviegoing thus became "an experience with political implications" (ibid., 72). Furthermore, while entertainment — especially moviegoing — is inextricably linked to propaganda and indoctrination, it is also principally linked to profit. This is supported by the Third Reich's other motive for promoting film — economics. To quote Schulte-Sasse, "Moneymaking and ideological dissemination were perceived as one and the same"; at the same time that Nazi filmmaking was heavily regulated, it was also "privileged with huge budgets to ensure they became monumental, star-studded spectaculars" (*Entertaining the Third Reich*, 4). Metaphorically, profit was concurrently gained on the part of the spectator, who consented to be manipulated in order to be rewarded with the power and privilege of being a part of the ideal community.

This so-called profit secured by the audience constitutes the main problem with basing theories of Nazi control on the idea of mass manipulation, which assumes that the German public was utterly passive and unaware of the violence, oppression, and hideous truths that lay behind Nazi ideology. Although there is no doubt that fear of the repercussions of opposing the Nazis played a part in public support, and it is certainly true that mass culture swayed public opinion and provided fantasies, I would concur with Kaplan that it is giving Goebbels and the Nazis too much credit to assume that all members of German society were entirely submissive to their indoctrination. Can one truly believe that fascism worked as well as it did by secretly imposing propaganda in a one-way relationship inflicted upon a nation of childlike automatons? Certainly there were those intellectuals and members of society who could differentiate between reality and illusion. As Kaplan astutely reasons, "We can no more reduce fascist media to maniacal manipulation than we can reduce the rest of fascism to pied piperism: too many people's desires and too many hard working imaginations stand in the way" (*Reproductions of Banality*, 34). It is thus crucial to look at a more complex set of desires on the part of the public to understand how mass media and mass spectacle worked.[11] Any careful assessment of the Nazi spectacle must bear in mind the willingness on the part of the spectators to endorse an image of social harmony due to the pleasure it supplied — even if this pleasure entailed ignoring the social freedom of others. Only then can one examine modes of resistance to that spectacle.

## Writing Resistance: Art, Mass Media, and Political Consciousness

The problem with all of the preceding theories regarding the public's susceptibility to the Nazi spectacle is that one wonders if there is any way "out" of the conception of social harmony as reliant on fantasy. Are we inescapably trapped in our dependency on an inauthentic illusion of social reality? How then can anyone imagine a society that is more liberal, tolerant, or less violent and oppressive? Clearly, even social and political theorists of the period such as Benjamin, Adorno, and Horkheimer had their doubts as to whether human beings would allow themselves to be manipulated or controlled beyond hope. Resistance through critical awareness or disruption, they concede, has the possibility of creating new viewpoints and subject positions. In their view, one way to "free" members of society from the effects of the culture industry and the mass spectacle was through aesthetic means. It is specifically for this reason that theorists of the period often promoted modernist art as a way of resisting oppression and transforming life. Benjamin, as mentioned previously, argues that the avant-garde can have a role in political revolution by destroying the aura — the institution by which art is consumed — and thereby dismantle perceptions to facilitate active revolution. Adorno and Horkheimer were perhaps more skeptical of the potential of art to revitalize freedom of the subject, yet they too in *Dialectic of Enlightenment* claim, "The promise of the work of art to create truth by impressing its unique contours on the socially transmitted forms is as necessary as it is hypocritical. . . . [I]t is only in its struggle with tradition, a struggle precipitated by style, that art can find expression for suffering" (103). The ambiguous implication here is that experimental art can perhaps be a vehicle to oppose mass culture and express the misery of oppression, with the important disclaimer that representing "truth" in art is nevertheless unfeasible since both art and the individual are productions of a socially transmitted culture.

Reflecting the view that modernist experimentation could provide a valid response to the spectacle of fascism and Nazism, many artists and writers of the 1930s, such as Woolf, Isherwood, and Barnes, did employ experimental strategies based on nonunified narrative structures as a "truer" if not truthful reflection of the political climate. We must nevertheless keep in mind the pitfalls of assuming that modernist or avant-garde art can "open our eyes" but mass culture in the form of Nazi art and the spectacle is "blinding." Critics of the "Great Divide" such as Andreas Huyssen rightly point out that a polarizing discourse based on the transformative potential of "high" modernist art and the destructive capabilities of "consuming and engulfing" mass culture works primarily to affirm a false hierarchy based on a self/Other binary (*After the Great Divide*, vii). The appeal to consumers of modernist art, in other words, is that they now belong to an "in" group of intellectual elites who can appreciate the nuance and profound message of the experimental aesthetics. Yet, to assume that all "highbrow" writers imagined the wider public as a homogeneous, uncritical, mass group without variances and complexities is also injudicious, to say the least. "Mass" culture, as Melba Cuddy-Keane determinedly insists in her study of Woolf's public audience, is not necessarily synonymous with "popular" culture. The public of 1930s Britain, for example, played a large role in choosing what it wanted to read, listen to, and watch — and while modernist highbrow art may not have been "widely favoured," a complex, heterogeneous group of "ordinary" readers could enjoy popular intellectually challenging material (Cuddy-Keane, *Virginia Woolf, the Intellectual*, 14–15).[12]

Writers of the 1930s such as Woolf, Isherwood, and Barnes were well aware that they depended on the public to support their art; if their writing was too obscure, or relied on a specialized class-based knowledge, they risked losing their audience. Unlike their German contemporaries, British and American writers were allowed to publish their critiques not only of Germany but also of their own political systems with relative freedom—but they still relied on their messages reaching a market of consumers.[13] As Woolf remarks when describing the leaning-tower writers of that era, a critique of society might be necessary, but, "How can you altogether abuse a society that is giving you, after all, a very fine view and some sort of security?" (M, 115). George Orwell questioned this same thing when he observed in his essay "Poetry and the Microphone" (1943) that a breach between popular media and experimental art (or more specifically poetry) "tends to widen simply because of its existence, the common man becoming more and more anti-poetry, the poet more and more arrogant and unintelligible" (Collected Essays, 378). Even so, as Aldous Huxley concedes in "Writers and Readers" (1936), in a time of political upheaval it is perhaps more important to reach a few individuals who can effect change instead of expecting a message to spread to a mass audience. "It is possible to argue that the really influential book is not that which converts ten millions of casual readers," he remarks, "but rather that which converts the very few who, at any given moment, succeed in seizing power" (ibid., 14). Taking these various viewpoints into consideration, one wonders if experimental art, poetry, and writing can be effective if they only reach the culturally privileged elites who have the educational and cultural means to access the work; or, as Orwell implies, perhaps isolating the "common man" (or woman) empties the artistic project of its relevance by widening the divide between artist and public.

Another predicament that politically conscious writers of the thirties encountered was that they relied on mass media outlets such as radio, newspapers, film newsreels, and photography for their source of political information but at the same time were understandably suspicious of the media. As Keith Williams observes, tensions between mediated and direct experiences placed many antifascist writers of the thirties in a position of conflict, especially in England. Even when British writers of the 1930s tried to gesture to events happening in the larger political sphere, their own knowledge of politics was mediated through newspapers that were often owned by members of the political Right who hesitated to criticize government policies, resulting in a "problematic transaction between real and vicarious experience" (Williams, *British Writers*, 18).[14] The Astor family, who owned *The Times* and *The Observer*, were staunch supporters of the political Right, as was Lord Rothermere, who ran the *Daily Mail*. These newspapers reinforced Britain's position of appeasement and remained uncritical of Prime Minister Neville Chamberlain's 1938 Munich agreement with Hitler. Rothermere even provided a media platform for Mosley and the British Union of Fascists (BUF) until Mosley's openly antisemitic statements at the 1934 Olympia rally caused substantial public controversy and Rothermere withdrew his support.[15]

Even violent episodes perpetrated against Jews in Germany—which were reported in British and American newspapers—were for the most part portrayed as incidental rather than a key part of National Socialism's racial policy. In his antifascist polemic *The Menace of Fascism*, for instance, John Strachey recorded twenty-six reports of attacks on Jews in *The Times* and *The Manchester Guardian* in 1933 but still claimed that the terror against Jews was an outcome of the passionate hatred of the masses, egged on by propaganda, rather than fundamental to the Nazi agenda (ibid., 72–73). In Brigitte Granzow's 1964 review of the newspaper coverage of the rise of Nazism, she concludes that many of the main papers in Britain reflected the phenomenon of "non-recognition" of Nazi violence—an almost "conscious flinching away by eye-witnesses from registering the sinister events they saw." In Granzow's words, "The idea that a fanatical petty-bourgeois [like Hitler] could . . . direct a mass movement and that he might be victorious . . . was sociologically too novel and politically too unwanted to be readily comprehended." As late as 1933, newspapers such as the London *Times* projected a picture of Hitler as a relatively moderate and decent leader (*Mirror of Nazism*, 186–88).

Mass media not only influenced 1930s writers' perceptions of what was occurring in the larger political sphere but also forced them to reconsider their role in society. C. Day Lewis, for one, acknowledged a somewhat positive side to the rise of film, radio, and mass-produced print since it would "enable us to distinguish more easily between serious writing and entertainment" and "compel literature to decide what its real job is" (Lewis, "Revolution in Writing," 70). Virginia Woolf also recognized the role of media in thirties writing when she compared contemporary writers to those of the previous century.[16] As Woolf notes, "In 1815 England was at war, as England is now," but "wars were then remote." The difference in 1940 is that "we hear the gunfire in the Channel. We turn on the wireless; we hear an airman telling us how this very afternoon he shot down a raider; his machine caught fire; he plunged into the sea. . . ." (M, 107). Walter Scott and Jane Austen, on the other hand, never "heard Napoleon's voice as we hear Hitler's voice as we sit at home of an evening" (M, 107). Woolf's comments undoubtedly indicate how radio influenced her own household and writing. According to Victoria Glendinning, the Woolfs had a new radio installed in March 1938, just in time to hear the news of Germany's invasion of Austria, and Leonard Woolf "took a furious interest in the medium," as both a broadcaster and critic of the British Broadcasting Corporation (*Leonard Woolf*, 331). Certainly when radio entered the home of the private citizen, it became all the more difficult for the artist to remain oblivious to the political environment. The result, as Woolf professed, was that books of the thirties "were written under the influence of change, under the threat of war" (M, 114).

Aside from radio, the effect of other forms of media, such as film, was not lost on writers of the thirties, especially Woolf. Perceiving that cinema could fulfill a critical role in society in ways that novels or other forms of art and culture could not, in her 1926 essay "The Cinema," Woolf lauds the new medium as having the capability to allow the public to "see life as it is when we have no part in it" (E, 4: 349). She imagines the potential for cinema to contain "within its grasp innumerable symbols for emotions that have so far failed to find expression" (E, 4: 350).[17] Woolf observes that cinema has the capability to "make images run side by side with itself, to create a likeness of the thing thought about," thus promising to be a medium that can change the perception of time. "The most fantastic contrasts could be flashed before us with a speed which the writer can only toil after in vain," Woolf notes. "The past could be unrolled, distances could be annihilated" (E, 4: 351).[18] In his 1938 essay "Are Films Worth While?" critic Charles Davy also claims cinema has the capability to "unite time and space," much like a poem. Cinema, Davy asserts, "will find its nearest models in the poetic novel," which he defines as a "novel which conveys an experience of values and does not merely report events." As Davy maintains, "the cinema and the novel alike are free to move to and fro in time and space and to mould both to their own needs" (288).[19] Cinema of the thirties, from this viewpoint, rather than being a vehicle of propaganda and mass manipulation, incorporates groundbreaking creative potential; it promises to transmit new experiences, alter perceptions of time and space, and create new critical roles for the viewer.

The preceding comments by Woolf and Davy highlight some of the contextual differences in the uses and attitudes toward new media in Germany as opposed to England or America. Whereas in Nazi Germany new media nurtured under the auspices of the Third Reich appeared to be yoked to a fantasy of the collective, in Britain and America media also embraced the promise of critique. This is not to say that British and American governments did not use film as propaganda during the war or exploit it to promote consensus.[20] Jo Fox, for instance, outlines many parallels between British and German propaganda in World War II cinema. Even in the context of war propaganda, however, Germany's mission of altering its own population's vision of itself (and values) was vastly distinct from British and American purposes. In prewar Britain and the United States in the 1930s, the critical or political potential of overtly anti-Nazi film was nevertheless difficult to realize. Although there were some Hollywood films that dealt indirectly but recognizably with European antisemitism and promoted antifascist messages, similar to the twenty-first century, the problem for nonpopulist, overly political, or experimental film was largely economic.[21] In 1938, Sidney Bernstein commented that catering to a discerning minority "whose demands were not met by the ordinary run of pictures" was unquestionably complicated. Even at that time, the "initial outlay of capital on the production of a film is great, and it can only be recovered if the finished product reaches a wide market." Novels thereby had a practical advantage over film — they cost less and could therefore risk reaching a potentially small market. To quote Bernstein, "The film producer is not in the fortunate position of the producer of a play or the publisher of a book, whose expenses are lighter and whose costing factors of production can be more easily adjusted to suit the probable demand of the markets" ("Walk Up!" 228).

An additional benefit for novels, especially political fiction, was that they were subject to less censorship than film.[22] Author and film critic Forsyth Hardy remarked in 1938 that the "platform and the pulpit, books and plays, can be used with comparative freedom by anyone with something new and vital to say about religion, politics or the relations between men and women: but censorship would deny this right to the screen" ("Censorship," 265). Especially in Britain, since the official government position was one of appeasement, a section of the prohibited categories for film was "themes likely to wound the just susceptibilities of Friendly Nations"—which included anti-Nazi films. Fox notes that the British Board of Film Censors (BBFC) in 1938–39 prevented a number of high-profile anti-Nazi films from being shown, including the *March of Time, Inside Nazi Germany* (Jack Glenn, 1938), censored in February 1938; *Swastika* (1939), censored since its theme was "mainly concerned with relating the horrors of Jewish persecution in Germany today" and was therefore "classed . . . as unsuitable for exhibition"; and *Professor Mamlock* (Adolf Minkin/Herbert Rappaport, 1938), a story of a Jewish professor persecuted by the Nazis (Fox, *Film Propaganda*, 140).[23] Even when presented, audiences found representations of the enemy "a bore" and persecution a "horror" that should be avoided. They wanted messages of hope, resulting in "the virtual exclusion of the suffering of the Jews from British cinema during World War II" (ibid., 141, 143).[24]

The complex relationship between writers and the redemptive or destructive aspects of technology, mass media, mass culture, and political expression is clearly apparent when examining *Between the Acts, Goodbye to Berlin,* and *Nightwood.* These works draw explicit attention to various forms of new media and audience reactions to mass culture to simultaneously highlight and critique the effects of the Nazi spectacle. At the same time, however, Woolf, Isherwood, and Barnes refuse to succumb to modernist nostalgia for a past that is no longer relevant or that does not include them. Woolf, unusually echoing Mathew Arnold, describes the era's prose and poetry as a "curious bastard language" that is "not the rich speech of the aristocrat: it is not the racy speech of the peasant. It is betwixt and between. The poet is a dweller in two worlds, one dying, the other struggling to be born" (*M*, 119).[25] In distinctly self-conscious, experimental, and modernist modes of writing, Woolf, Isherwood, and Barnes attempt to bridge the two worlds—a present on the brink of destruction and an uncertain future—by pointing toward an alternative future, one in which members of society are aware, conscious, and accepting of contradictions and multiple viewpoints. Their texts, both thematically and aesthetically, explore the psychology behind the consumption of mass media and Nazi ideology, probe the limits of writing and reading and their influence on political consciousness in the public sphere, and investigate the correlations among art, culture, and critical thinking.

An intriguing question to ask of these novels, nevertheless, is if the texts consistently reference and interrogate mass media and modes of mass culture (especially visual culture such as photography, film, circuses, and pageants)—and if they wish to reach as wide a spectrum of society as possible—why do these writers choose fiction rather than another, perhaps more public, artistic medium as a vehicle for resistance? As Michael Tratner provocatively asks in his essay's title and argument: "Why Isn't *Between the Acts* a Film?" Similarly, one can ask why *Goodbye to Berlin* is not a book of photographs, or *Nightwood* a circus. Obviously, the question is somewhat absurd, yet it raises the query of whether the act of reading itself can make a difference in the way that resistance can be performed or effected. After all, Woolf, as discussed previously, was profoundly interested in new media and used photographs to a great effect in *Three Guineas*; Isherwood was a screenwriter and playwright as well as a novelist; and Barnes was a graphic artist and playwright in addition to being a successful journalist. Yet, for their most pointed critiques of fascist ideology and Nazism they chose fiction.

Using Mikhail Bakhtin's theory of the novel is one way I approach my interpretation of why specifically novelization and fiction-writing, as opposed to other media, is a key aspect to analyzing these works as examples of social resistance. In "Discourse in the Novel," Bakhtin privileges the novel as a mode that permits "a multiplicity of social voices and a wide variety of their links and interrelationships" (263). His concept of "heteroglossia" (*raznorecie*, or "multi-speeched") can lend nuance to the way we as readers perceive how literary texts register internal social and historical forces in societies. From a Bakhtinian perspective, *Between the Acts*, *Goodbye to Berlin*, and *Nightwood* are heteroglot novels since their purpose is to register the various voices, opinions, and points of view of the period. The way in which the novels work against propaganda and Nazi ideology is that they resist what Bakhtin perceives as the "unifying, centralizing, centripetal forces of verbal ideological life" ("Discourse," 273). Experimental novel writing could be an especially appropriate mode to register the intensity of the political atmosphere in the 1930s since languages, nationalities, and identities are "dialogized" in the novel and "can fully unfold, achieve full complexity, depth, and at the same time artistic closure" (ibid., 278).[26]

Considering that the three novels examined in this study are works that represent visual culture and public performances in novelistic writing, the questions regarding the limits of representation are manifold. In some ways, taking the pageants, circuses, and photographs out of their visual context is itself a gesture that demands that the reader probe the distinction between reality and its representation. For readers in interwar Europe, there were distinct differences between witnessing the political spectacle and reading fictionalized representations of spectacles and their audiences. Arguably, the individual reader picking up a new Woolf novel at the library would differ from the mass spectator. Since written representations of visual spectacles create more distance, and often more room for contemplation, if anything, questions regarding the borders between perception and reality are reinflected and intensified by appearing in novelistic form.

In many ways, all artistic representation, to quote Vivian Patraka, "is always a site of struggle between history and its representations, between desire and loss, and between the unmanageable and the manageable" (*Spectacular Suffering*, 8). Yet, unlike visual representations such as theater, film, circuses, or pageants, novelization does not attempt to make certain events and practices visible to the eye, fixed in time and place. If there is a struggle between the experience, the image, the moment, and its reiteration in the novel, then perhaps that struggle is even more profound when the image is mediated through writing and can be reiterated and reimagined each time the book is put down, picked up, reread, and reinterpreted. Thus, both writing and reading resistance occurs not as a community of spectators, but at the level of the subject—whom Hitler, in *Mein Kampf*, describes as "the seeker" or "the man who is exposed to grave tribulations" (435). For it is within that loneliness and doubt that the individual can probe the epistemological questions that are necessary at a time of political chaos. Where Woolf's, Isherwood's, and Barnes's works differ, however, is to what degree they indicate what happens then. In *Between the Acts* awareness, critique, and discourse hold the promise of change in a wider community, but it is not clear whom Woolf envisions as included in that community; for Isherwood and Barnes, the broader potential of resistance is not as clear—it appears that the Europe of *Goodbye to Berlin* and *Nightwood* may already be lost to the spectacle's allure.

## "Dispersed are we": The Reading "I/Eye" and Communal "We" in *Between the Acts*

In *Three Guineas*, Woolf suggests that writers, especially women, need to "find out new ways of approaching 'the public'; single it into separate people instead of massing it into one monster, gross in body, feeble in mind" (*TG*, 113). It is toward a public of "separate people" with multiple subjectivities and voices that Woolf's *Between the Acts* is specifically geared. Perhaps that is why Woolf, subsequent to the essay format of *Three Guineas*, chooses the novel, a medium better suited for multivoicedness, to express her protest against the totalizing Nazi pageant of war and to generate critique toward fascist ideologies and propaganda. Despite only oblique references to war and fascism in the work, the range of interpretations inspired by the novel spans the entire scope of the political spectrum. *Between the Acts* has been hailed as an elegy for a lost culture; a suicide note; an expression of extreme despair; a reaffirmation of Woolf's protest and fight against patriarchy; a reiteration of pacifist views expressed in earlier essays and diaries; or even a change in political outlook from pacifism to an acceptance of the necessary evil of military protest.[27] In line with many of these critical analyses, I explore *Between the Acts* as an expression of Woolf's antiwar views, perhaps her strongest to date, but also as a manifestation of her deep ambiguity as to how antiwar protest can be achieved. At a time when Nazism presented a genuine and imminent threat to her (and her Jewish husband's) existence, the attitude of "indifference" that Woolf proposes in *Three Guineas* to resist an overarching pan-fascism and patriarchy is clearly insufficient. I examine how the pageant, as opposed to books, newspapers, and reading, highlights Woolf's uncertainty as to how, strategically, to reach individual members of the larger British public in order to encourage opposition to Nazi ideology. Is it the private "I," who interprets, reads, and witnesses the coming of war, that is crucial to fighting Hitler? Or, is it the communal "we"—the same group that can most easily be manipulated by nationalist propaganda and pageantry—that is necessary (if reluctantly so) to support a significant struggle against the risk of a Nazi invasion? By drawing attention to both the perils and the necessity of cohesion within a community of spectators, Woolf presents a vision of a group of dispersed, heterogeneous, and isolated individuals who begin the experience of watching the pageant desiring unity, only to emerge with a third option—a different kind of critical "we" that is ostensibly capable of imagining change.

Woolf's choice of a historical pageant on which to base her critique of Nazi ideology is also no coincidence. The historical pageant experienced a particular resurgence in popularity and acclaim at the beginning of the twentieth century. Among those in Woolf's circle who produced pageants at the time were E. M. Forster, whose village pageant, *England's Pleasant Land*, was performed at Milton Court in July 1938 (Beer, *Common Ground*, 145), and Edith Craig, whose productions of suffragist pageants and Shakespearean matinees Woolf had attended (Snaith, *Public and Private*, 150–51).[28] The first distinctly "modern" British pageant, however, was said to have taken place in 1905 in Sherborne, Dorset, directed by Louis Napoleon Parker (1852–1944). *Macmillan's Magazine* attests to the status of Louis Napoleon's decidedly "modern pageant" when comparing it to the pageants that were at one time performed in small towns throughout England. To quote the *Macmillan's* reviewer (1905), "other pageants may have had as fair and beautiful a setting, notably those of Warwick or Kenilworth, but they do not seem to have had a Mr. Louis Parker to direct them" (452). The purpose of the Parker pageant, as many recognized, was to stimulate patriotism and pride in British history and heritage at a time when industrialization, immigration, and the possibility of a Great War threatened to jeopardize traditional ways of living. Thus the pageant had a political function of which Woolf was only too aware. Ayako Yoshino, who interprets *Between the Acts* as a response to the Parker pageants, notes that in the years leading up to World War I, "the pageant was often used for raising money for war charities and even for war propaganda in both England and in America." Although the popularity of pageants waned after 1918, friends of Woolf, such as Forster and Craig, were still involved with writing and producing them (Yoshino, "*Between the Acts*," 52, 51).

The significance of communal pageants in the early twentieth century, especially their role in politics and nationalism, is reflected in the popularity of the *Guide to Community Drama and Pageantry*, written by Mary Porter Beegle and Jack Randall Crawford in 1916 and published in both England and the United States. "The story of a pageant," as they define it, is "the life of a community" told "chiefly through appeal to the eye, rather than to the ear. The spectacle is of vastly more importance than the dialogue." Pageantry, they proudly insist, is "a conscious attempt to restore to the people a share in the creation and development of dramatic art." Although drama was once a populist form of entertainment performed by community members for each other, when it became a "professional art" it lost its ability to compete with other forms of entertainment. Yet the modern pageant, as they envisioned it, has the potential to be "the art work of the future." Aside from generating cohesion and feelings of community, Beegle and Crawford ascribe a moral and psychological purpose to the pageant: "a rational and joyous form of recreation, a sane outlet for the unconquerable play-spirit, which, when lacking outlets, may become a source of danger instead of a benefit" (*Community Drama*, 13, 7, 10, 16). In retrospect, and in the context of National Socialism's rise to power, it is difficult not to notice the echoes of Hitler's designs for the mass rally in this statement. The anxiety associated with the lonely and bored modern individual who, left to his or her own devices, might rebel, revolt, or fail to be a good citizen, is quite clear. The pageant as festival — drama revived in the hands of the folk — would be used to the advantage of the Nazi Party only twenty years later in giving the public an "outlet" in the ceremonies, holidays, and party rallies.[29]

Yoshino draws numerous parallels between the pageant in *Between the Acts* and those directed by Louis N. Parker, even comparing Parker to Woolf's domineering pageant-master, Miss La Trobe. Taking into consideration historical contexts, however, and Woolf's attitudes toward nationalism and propaganda, the pageant appears to be all that the Parker pageant is *not*.

The Parker pageant's celebration of nationalism, imperialism, and patriotism surely resonated with Woolf's views on propaganda as a "parody," an idea plainly stated in her diary: "feelings that war breeds: patriotism; communal &c, all sentimental & emotional parodies of our real feelings" (D, 5: 302). Yet, while the pageant in *Between the Acts* is often read as a parody of the "sentimental & emotional" performances of nationalism and communal unity, it also gestures toward aspects that have more to do with the relationship between audience and pageant, and by extension reader and writer, than with actual performance of the pageant itself.

Woolf's preoccupation with the role of the writer or artist and audience is discussed in the notes to her uncompleted work "Anon" (1940), an essay in which she traces a history of literature to a time in Britain when the artist was anonymous. The connection between the folk pageant and the role of Anon is noted by Brenda Silver, whose edition of the unfinished text provides a glimpse at Woolf's concerns regarding the individual artist within the community as World War II begins. According to Silver, Woolf's notes indicate that she planned to begin the work "as she had begun the pageant in her novel — with the early forms of English literature and society, and with the anonymous men and women who created them." Silver also observes that when writing both "Anon" and *Between the Acts*, "the importance of the audience to the writer became poignantly clear to her as her own sense of isolation increased" ("'Anon' and 'The Reader,'" 357, 360). Anon is described as "sometimes man; sometimes woman. He is the common voice singing out of doors" (A, 382). As an outsider, the figure is "tolerated" because he or she "say[s] out loud what we feel, but are too proud to admit" (A, 383). Yet, Anon's voice is neither the originator nor owner of the song, "lifting a song or a story from other peoples [sic] lips, and letting the audience join in the chorus" (A, 382). Rather than a controlling master of text (the "Parker" of the pageant), Anon cannot be differentiated from the audience — he or she is a communal part of the folk.

Woolf traces the demise of Anon through the invention of the printing press, the advent of royal patronage, and the birth of the individual artist. Parallels between the pageant in *Between the Acts* and "Anon" are unmistakable. The relationship among the audience, the actors from the village, the domineering pageant-master, the voice of the dictator, and the individual author all reiterate Woolf's concern with the transformation from public communal voice to individual artistic expression. As

Woolf observes in the essay, the "death of Anon" occurs when "the play has outgrown the uncovered theatre where the sun beats and the rain pours. That theatre must be replaced by the theatre of the brain. The playwright is replaced by the man who writes a book. The audience is replaced by the reader. Anon is dead" (A, 398). So, too, the main characters of *Between the Acts* occupy themselves with reading and writing, and the reader experiences the pageant as a book to be read in the "theatre of the brain," in isolation, rather than as a participant in a play or a communal song. As I argue later, however, in *Between the Acts*, Woolf remains ambiguous about whether the communal experience of early literature and theater, such as the pageant, is necessarily superior to the isolation of reading and writing. After all, "common belief" can also imply narrow-mindedness or discrimination, and "herd" mentality is also a feature of communal unity; yet, to effectually oppose tyranny, some form of unanimity and agreement is necessary in a realm that extends beyond the mind's eye.

A fundamental aspect of the pageant in *Between the Acts*, however, is that it neither falls into the category of the Parker pageant nor that of other types of folk performances. In actuality, it is not even a parody of a pageant — it is a novelized version of one. Critics who treat *Between the Acts* only in terms of a performance perhaps miss this important detail. *Between the Acts* works to undermine the pageant because the novelized elements that occur "between the acts" of the play — on the lawn of Pointz Hall — become sites where public and private, and aesthetics and ethics, are linked through critique. The audience's reactions, the interruptions, the narrator's comments, the intrusion of the wind, the animals, the birds — these are all a part of the novelized heteroglossia that allows parody, and thus a critique, to occur. *Between the Acts* anticipates Linda Hutcheon's model of postmodern parody in that it uses parody to distance the reader so that he or she is freed to participate in both a historical and a political critique. The audience of the pageant, therefore, is not the only one poised to form an opinion of what is occurring on that day in June 1939. The dialogic relationship that develops between the reader, the text, and the discourse surrounding the pageant signals to the reader that *all* nationalist performances that reaffirm a dominant view of British history ought to be critiqued. It thereby demands of readers "to be active not passive viewers" (Hutcheon, *Politics of Postmodernism*, 32).[30]

The role of History (with a capital "H") parodied in the pageant is also fundamental to Woolf's understanding of Hitler's ideological and racial platform. The evocation of ancient history and the link to Aryan ancestry played a key role in Nazi culture and was a consistent theme in speeches, books, plays, films, and public cultural events. Ancient ceremonial festivals such as those reflected in Leni Riefenstahl's depiction of the Greek Olympics in *Olympia*, for example, were common. This type of historical narrative reinforces a fictional fantasy of a unified community because it allows an illusion of a coherent past to disguise contradictions. It imposes "an organization on disorganized happenings, pulls together fragmentary sentiments and ideas, and structures disperse events in a narrato*logical* context" (Schulte-Sasse, *Entertaining the Third Reich*, 30). *Between the Acts*, as a heteroglossic novel, provides the social discourse that subverts standardized versions of History. It highlights the contrast between the unifying force of "we" thinking and the "I/eye" that sees, reads, evaluates, and creates. The fragmented, fictionalized version of the pageant in *Between the Acts*, replete with interruptions and intrusions, is arguably the more "accurate" representation of history since it exposes the contradictions and conflicts inherent in the social life of a community. Granted, Woolf's vision of an English community still does not envision certain ethnic and social groups as belonging to that group of individuals. Nevertheless, as an anti-Nazi strategy that avoids a more polemical approach, Woolf's ersatz pageant can underscore the illusionary nature of historical representation and point to the "reality" of spectacle as an abstraction and fabrication.

Woolf's strategy to connect English nationalism and patriarchal versions of History in the pageant to dictatorship and Nazi ideology is compelling since both are based in subjugating Others. The audience (and reader) can thus extend the familiar English context to the larger, more remote threat overseas. On the other hand, correlating English patriarchal oppression with despotic and murderous dictatorships is especially obtuse, not least because this oversimplification results in obscuring the particular histories and conditions of the groups who are victims of Nazi violence and brutality. Small wonder that England, played by the little girl Phyllis Jones, forgets her lines (*BTA*, 70–71), or that the words of the villagers singing patriotic songs of "armed and valiant" warriors are "blown away" by the wind (*BTA*, 72). In the political context of a German invasion, patriotic maxims are insufficient to register the gravity of the circumstances. Nevertheless, British partisanship is still poles apart from Nazi propaganda and its racialist policies — which Woolf recounted as "the ravings, the strangled hysterical sobbing swearing ranting of Hitler" (D, 5: 245). What remains ambiguous in the novel, moreover, is whether in a time of crisis the individual writer or reader can expedite political transformation only through reading and writing fiction, and whether any type of effective political change can be negotiated without a larger community consensus to support it. Can one mandate change without appealing to the public to become a "we"? And who does this "we" include?

The role of the individual writer and reader as opposed to the "we" of audience, community, and country is probed in an April 1938 diary entry, as Woolf is thinking of her new book: "'I' rejected: 'We' substituted: to whom at the end there shall be an invocation? 'We' . . . composed of many different things . . . we all life, all art, all waifs & strays" (D, 5: 135). This type of wavering between the private "I" and the public "we" is an aspect of Woolf's work that critics such as Anna Snaith claim dominates her world of the 1930s.[31] It is a "we" that obviously includes different social classes and genders. Woolf's diary entry on April 15, 1939, as the war begins, reflects her feelings of uncertainty regarding the role of the individual in the community: "the community feeling: all England thinking the same thing — this horror of war — at the same moment. Never felt it so strong before. Then the lull & one lapses again into private separation —" (D, 5: 215). Instead of an expression of powerlessness, Woolf's oscillation between community and individuality can be interpreted as a gesture that resists the type of ideology, such as Nazism, that destroys divisions between the private and the public. Even so, the "we" of "all art, all waifs & strays" also oversimplifies a vision of English society. For instance, it notably does not include ethnic minorities like Ralph Manresa, "the Jew" who is absent on the day of the pageant. What, then, is the social and political nature of this communal "we"?

In Between the Acts, spectators waver between feelings of unity and disparity, echoed by the gramophone's refrain, "Dispersed are we" (BTA, 86). Thus the pageant mirrors the workings of spectacle in the false sense of harmony and unity that it engenders only for these same effects to be undermined by the narrator's comments on the events and points of view revolving around the pageant. This is one way Woolf highlights the overlap between the characters' individual lives and their collective identities and roles in the public sphere. Individual voices and interruptions disturb the pageant so that it can include the "waifs & strays." While propaganda, and especially Nazi propaganda, seeks to unify a multiplicity of voices, the novel attempts to register a variety of voices and mentalities that constitute a community. As Christine Froula aptly observes, "before the play has progressed six lines, we hear at least seven voices: Mrs. Carter, the narrator, the gramophone . . . little Phyllis, whispering spectators, the kind old man, and the director in three vocal modes, cursing sotto voce, calling in vain for music, then promoting from the script, a sort of eighth voice" (Froula, *Bloomsbury Avant-Garde*, 304). This does not even include the thoughts, observations, and interruptions of the key characters in the novel—Isa and Giles Oliver, Mrs. Manresa, Lucy Swithin, and William Dodge. The narrator thus widens the lens for readers to see beyond the pageant to include an enlarged perspective of English experience, which includes literature, art, religion, family, world events, and war. On the other hand, if the pageant registers the present moment at Pointz Hall in the summer of 1939— which, as the reader knows, is about to change drastically due to war—it also excludes significant aspects of that historical moment. The "scraps and fragments" that ruminate on the coming war include: "D'you believe what's in the papers?" (*BTA*, 109); "And what about the Jews? The refugees . . . the Jews . . . People like ourselves" (*BTA*, 109). There are no answers to these questions since the news and refugees continue to hover beyond the margins of the text and of the English community as remote, far-off problems. The Jewish refugees are people with problems "like ourselves" but not a *part* of "ourselves."

I am tempted to ask, had La Trobe's pageant gone on as planned, would its antispectacle effect be the same? While the play itself challenges traditional, patriarchal notions of English history, there are times, after all, when spectators are meant to be caught up in the illusion of the spectacle. The narrator clearly indicates that La Trobe knows that in groups people can be influenced. She is fully aware of the malleability of spectators, counting on their willingness to be drawn into illusion: "No one liked to be ordered about singly. But in troops they appealed to her. Someone must lead. Then they could put the blame on her"

(*BTA*, 58). The narrator thus insinuates that individuals are culpable in their desire to submit to leadership. Woolf's notebooks indicate she read Freud's *Group Psychology and the Analysis of the Ego* in 1939, in which Freud claims, "A group is an obedient herd, which could never live without a master. It has such a thirst for obedience that it submits instinctively to anyone who appoints himself its master" (18: 81). Dictators alone do not produce social movements — they cannot exist without a participating "herd." Especially in military-like "troops," *Between the Acts* suggests, people like to be told what to do; thus Bart Oliver aptly remarks, "Our part . . . is to be the audience. And a very important part too" (*BTA*, 54). The narrator observes how easily the audience can be manipulated by expressing an overall statement to describe their condition: "We aren't free, each of them felt separately, to feel or think separately, nor yet to fall asleep. We're too close; but not close enough" (*BTA*, 60). These words are not stated within any enclosing quotation marks. Instead the narrator is describing the overall feeling of entrapment and silence that overwhelms the audience at the beginning of the pageant. Consequently they find the view "stupefying" (*BTA*, 61); the "tick, tick, tick" of the gramophone easily holds them in a "trance" (*BTA*, 75); the dancing of the Elizabethan age becomes "a mellay; a medley, an entrancing spectacle" (84); and the music "intoxicated" both dancers and audience (*BTA*, 85).

The culpability of the audience in accepting propaganda is highlighted in Woolf's text. Aldous Huxley, in his essay "Writers and Readers" (1936), which Woolf likely read, insists that dictatorial propaganda "is acceptable because it encourages men and women to give free rein to their pride, vanity, and other egotistical tendencies, and because it provides them with psychological devices for overcoming their sense of personal inferiority" (26). The crowd that accepts the dictator hears what it wants to believe, Huxley stresses. I would concur with Natania Rosenfeld's observation that Woolf underscores the audience's culpability in supporting the dictator because of its "desire for certainty rather than . . . subtleties" ("Monstrous Conjugations," 127).[32] Nevertheless, as soon as the audience becomes too caught up in the spectacle, the novelized elements surrounding the pageant intervene to give voice to subjective viewpoints. The interval arrives, and the gramophone laments its refrain, moaning, "*Dispersed are we*" (*BTA*, 86). The trance of spectatorship broken, Isa Oliver comments, "All is over. The wave has broken. Left us stranded, high and dry. Single, separate on the shingle. . . ." (*BTA*, 87). Following the disruption of the interval is a series of subjective viewpoints, personal decisions, and individual observations. Isa declares, "Now I follow . . . to have tea" (*BTA*, 87); Dodge wonders, "Shall I . . . go or stay?"; and other members of the audience turn to personal observations and memories to comment on the pageant. La Trobe, who knows the power of illusion, laments, she "hadn't made them see. It was a failure, another damned failure!" (*BTA*, 88). Apparently, La Trobe is the one who does not see — she fails to notice that the audience is beginning to observe elements that lie beyond the scope of the pageant. By the end of the interval, when the audience gathers once more, the members of the audience are no longer a mass: "some sat down; others stood a moment, turned, and looked at the view" (*BTA*, 108). This time the audience can look at the view without being stupefied. Moreover, they muse on matters of psychology, politics, and philosophy: "D'you think people change? . . . I meant ourselves . . . —do we change?" (*BTA*, 109). Once the illusion is broken, critical thinking is set into motion. Time and time again, whenever the audience is lulled back into trancelike behavior, mesmerized by the music or the pageant, this is exactly when the "words died away" and "the illusion had failed" (*BTA*, 126). Finally, La Trobe's dictatorial control over the audience breathes its last breath: "This is death, death, death. . . ." La Trobe murmurs from behind the stage, "when illusion fails" (*BTA*, 161–62).

I will stress again, however, that these disruptions are not part of the plot of the pageant — they are the novelized representation of what occurs around the pageant. The pageant is not heteroglossic, but the novel framing the pageant is. Moreover, it is particularly novelization that holds the potential to offset the effects of the spectacle through its dialogic relationship with the reader, who makes meaning by inserting the historical and politicized discourse outside the text and by taking into account those voices and viewpoints that the narrator does not include. It is no coincidence, then, that books, novels, reading, and the library play just as central a role in *Between the Acts* as does the pageant. As mentioned by a guest and reiterated by Isa, the library is said to be "the nicest room in the house" (*BTA*, 15, 17). "Books are mirrors of the soul" and "'The mirror of the soul' books were" is stated, and then repeated by Isa (*BTA*, 15, 17–18). Nevertheless, both statements are pointedly exposed as clichés, perhaps because the books to which Isa refers — those of English patriarchal cultural heritage and ancestry — are mirroring "a spotted soul" and the "soul bored" (*BTA*, 15).

The kind of book that could be the right one to reflect a multifaceted and changing soul is not only what Isa seeks but also what Woolf provides for the reader. Isa is searching for "a new plot" that can allow her to "forget the rhyme" and embrace contradictions. As she asks, "Did the plot matter?" — especially if it is a plot only there "to beget emotion"? (*BTA*, 82). Woolf seems to imply that if books can truly mirror life, the first thing one needs to do is break with the conventions of historical novel-writing. Yet, given the lack of stability the present moment holds for those at Pointz Hall living under the threat of war, the characters turn to books to dictate cultural conventions. To "remedy" the insecurity faced by their generation, they seek solace in the past. Reflecting on this struggle, Isa asks,

> What remedy was there for her age — the age of the century, thirty-nine — in books? Book-shy she was, like the rest of her generation; and gun-shy too. Yet as a person with a raging tooth runs her eye in a chemist shop over green bottles with gilt scrolls on them lest one of them may contain a cure, she considered: Keats, Shelley; Yeats and Donne. Or perhaps not a poem; a life. The life of Garibaldi. The life of Lord Palmerston. Or perhaps not a person's life; a country's. . . . (*BTA*, 18)

Even Isa, the poet, who hides her compositions in an account book lest her husband see them, looks for rhymes and seeks out platitudes "conveniently provided by fiction" to affirm her place in the world. She repeats, "The father of my children" or "He is my husband" to accept her social positioning as wife and mother (*BTA*, 13, 44). Isa nevertheless also peers into other types of looking glasses, aside from those books that confirm and reflect patriarchal assumptions and clichés, and sees something further. She looks into "the three-folded mirror, so that she could see three separate visions of her rather heavy, yet handsome, face" (*BTA*, 12). There, in the mirror, Isa perceives both "her eyes" and her "I"s, her multiple selves that comprise contradictions and a variety of viewpoints. As

Woolf observes in *A Room of One's Own*, "Women have served all these centuries as looking-glasses possessing the magic and delicious power of reflecting the figure of man at twice its natural size. Without that power probably the world would still be swamp and jungle" (53). Isa's multiple subjectivities and range of desires, however, contradict the clichés and gendered structures provided by patriarchy, by fiction, by the pageant, and by history. She is "in love" with Mr. Haines, the gentleman farmer; she also loves her husband and children; and she is "Sir Richard's daughter" (*BTA*, 13). Isa thus incorporates within her a reflection of the self as a product of emotions, social positioning, history, and politics. Yet, she still desires "a new plot" that can locate her "I" outside a relational positioning to male figures.

In contrast to Isa, who looks to writing to provide a medium that can effectively express ambiguity and contrast, Lucy Swithin draws on books for precisely the opposite reason — to indulge in the illusion of harmony and unity. Here, once again, Woolf indicates her ambiguity regarding the purpose of artistic representation (especially writing) and probes the problematic aspects of "unity" versus "disparity." A clear indication that Woolf is critiquing the manner in which Swithin uses books for escape is demonstrated by the way the narrator associates Swithin with religion and the cross. As Rosenfeld observes, Swithin's character is "ultimately questionable" because she is drawn toward authority and patriarchal structures that are oppressive to others. She "wears a cross around her neck in a novel that invokes yokes, rings, and nooses as images of enslavement by convention" ("Monstrous Conjugations," 128). Swithin's escape into books serves a similar function to her attachment to religion — it solves discord, embraces historical and ancestral origins, and allows her to lose herself in an illusion of wholeness. For example, Swithin often caresses the cross she wears conspicuously in a gesture of "one-making." In one of the pageant's intervals, Isa and William Dodge guess, perhaps correctly, that Mrs. Swithin is "on a circular tour of the imagination — one-making."

> Sheep, cows, grass, trees, ourselves — all are one. If discordant, producing harmony — if not us, to a gigantic ear attached to a gigantic head. And thus — she was smiling benignly — the agony of the particular sheep, cow, or human being is necessary; and

so — she was beaming seraphically at the gilt vane in the distance — we reach the conclusion that *all* is harmony, could we hear it. (*BTA*, 157)

This illusion of harmony, however, can be perilous if it completely ignores the present reality. Especially if that reality is beset by an oncoming war.

Paradoxically, the work Swithin uses to escape into illusion is H. G. Wells's best-selling *The Outline of History* (1920). The book, which presents history as one long evolutionary line from "primitive" man to present times, refutes both nationalism and division between cultures. It made its mark in post–World War I Europe as an appeal for unity and peace between nations. Aldous Huxley comments in "Writers and Readers" (1936) that it was a "well-written and persuasive piece of propaganda" (11). Perhaps not coincidentally, Wells also believed that since they refused to assimilate and abandon exclusivist tradition, Jews were the biggest hindrance to a utopian world state.[33] As Bryan Cheyette maintains, Wells "was able to associate the latter exclusivist tradition of Judaism with a degenerate, contemporary world" ("Wells and the Jews," 29). Not that Huxley considers this type of antinationalist propaganda to be necessarily evil, but he questions its relevance in the context of the 1930s. "In Europe and America many millions of people read . . . the Englishman's plea for internationalism," Huxley notes. "With what results? It is hard indeed to say. All we can be sure of is that nationalistic feeling was never so acutely inflamed as it is to-day."[34] In 1936 Huxley presumed that oppression and despair drive people "to seek consolation and a vicarious triumph in the religion of nationalism" and to succumb to the desire to worship "gods that can be actually seen and heard" — i.e., dictators — rather than utopian universalism or Christian dogma (11).[35]

Lucy Swithin clings to this historical account of a world before English culture not realizing that a utopian narrative view of "history as unifier" is inapt for a population under threat of a nationalist and unifying German invasion. Daydreaming of a land before nations is an insufficient response to the risk of war. Swithin "belonged to the unifiers" (*BTA*, 106), as her brother Bart observes, but she cannot promote change because her unifying dream eclipses individuals and their multifarious sets of desires. Her utopian dream appears everywhere in her mind's eye, but nowhere in the actual world. Swithin's gaze often roams into oblivion, prompting the other characters to interpret what she is seeing. Isa thinks she is gazing at "God on his throne" (*BTA*, 21); Mr. Oliver presumes childish innocence; Giles, an "old fogey" (*BTA*, 49); Dodge assumes compassion and understanding (*BTA*, 67). When Swithin tells Dodge, "We live in others. . . . We live in things" (*BTA*, 64), she thus reveals the ways in which people project harmony and meaning onto empty structures like convention, authority, and religion. Lucy Swithin's fantasy of a harmonious whole might seem trivial, but it is hazardous indeed — not only because it ignores Hitler's "rantings" but also because it stifles the cacophony of voices, views, subjectivities, and tones of a multivoiced dialogue within society.

If a new fictional plot can include multiple voices, subjectivities, and individual interpretations of meaning, then the monologic tendency of the newspaper is surely its opposite. Hours before the pageant, Isa observes, "For her generation the newspaper was a book" (*BTA*, 18). The newspaper, however, is one-way communication, and as a representation of mass media in the novel, it also reflects an "ideological force for building nation-hood and consensus." The role of British papers in "stirring jingoistic frenzy" for the nation against the enemy did not go unnoticed by writers of the 1930s (Williams, *British Writers*, 21–22). At the same time, as mentioned previously, the medium was criticized for obscuring the true nature of Hitler, downplaying the racial policies of Nazi Germany, and blinding the public to the severity of the threat toward England. As Snaith's research indicates, "Out of thousands of articles on Germany in the weeklies" only twenty-five explicitly outlined the Nazi's race doctrine and ideology (*Public and Private*, 134–35). *The Times*, the newspaper read by both Bart and Giles, backed Chamberlain's appeasement agreement with Germany and avoided anti-German commentary.[36] Retaining a picture of Hitler as a "normal politician," other newspapers aside from *The Times* continued to portray Nazism as simply a version of nationalism and downplayed news of conflict from abroad throughout the 1930s (Granzow, *Mirror of Nazism*, 188). Although *The Times* published extracts and multiple reviews of the English abridged version of *Mein Kampf* (entitled *My Struggle*) in 1933, exposing English readers to Hitler's doctrine and his antisemitism for the first time, reviews were not as critical as one would expect (Barnes and Barnes, *Hitler's "Mein Kampf,"* 64, 68). Understandably, then, Woolf—who by 1940 had collected no less than three scrapbook volumes of newspaper clippings of Hitler's speeches and Nazi policies—would be skeptical and fearful of a medium that tried to shore up nationalist fervor while at the same time promoting indifference by masking the menacing nature of Nazi ideology.

The representation of the newspaper in *Between the Acts* is indeed frightening. The "mask" made out of newspaper that Bart Oliver puts on to frighten little George appears as "a terrible peaked eyeless monster" (*BTA*, 11). Moreover, Bart Oliver is not the only one to be associated with the newspaper; Giles, too, reads about sixteen men "shot, others prisoned, just over there, across the gulf" (*BTA*, 42–43) and is filled with wordless rage and visions of violence: "his vision of Europe. Bristling with guns, posed with planes" (*BTA*, 49). The newspaper is blinding in its focus on the military to prepare and buttress support for yet another war against Germany, yet at the same time it overlooks the human suffering of civilians. Giles is moved to violence by the thought of imprisoned soldiers, but the focus on military conflict ignores and dehumanizes the murderous outcome of Hitler's oppression of Jews, women, homosexuals, people with disabilities or mental illness, minority cultures, political opponents, and other "threats" to the nation. As Woolf observes in *Three Guineas*, mass media, the "coarse glare of . . . publicity," is a kind of "limelight" that "paralyses free action of human faculties and inhibits the human power to change and create new wholes" (*TG*, 131). Newspapers encourage men like Bart Oliver and Giles to fight, but they do not address the implications of discrimination or, for that matter, articulate the possibility that cruelty toward Others can be found in England, among people at home.

Much like the other ambiguous gestures in *Between the Acts*, however, the newspaper is not solely an emblem of repression. While the newspaper reflects values of nationalism, heroism, and militarism (associated with Bart and Giles Oliver), it is still the main source of political information and criticism in the public sphere for 1930s readers and writers. Paradoxically, the newspaper thereby also gives voice to human suffering, such as that of the 14-year-old girl raped in the barracks by British troopers, about whom Isa reads. Thus, while the medium has the potential to mask brutality, at the same time it articulates resistance: the girl, after all, does not suffer her rape in silence — she "screamed and hit him about the face with a hammer" and then reports the crime (*BTA*, 20).[37] Her publicized story, moreover, has the potential to move readers toward compassion for victims of violence and to promote intolerance for injustice. Thus, to reference Snaith's argument, one can distinguish once again Woolf's "negotiation" or movement in relation to private and public forms of communication. Narratives that embrace "a new plot" can be read by individuals in private to encourage transformation, but to promote change in society at large it is necessary for readers to become part of an aware, discerning, critical community that can convey resistance to a larger assembly of individuals in the public sphere.

To quote Woolf in "The Leaning Tower," "Literature is no one's private ground; literature is common ground. It is not cut up into nations; there are no wars there" (*M*, 125). For this reason in particular — because literature is "no one's private ground" — by the end of *Between the Acts* there is no consensus as "to whom at the end there shall be an invocation" — "I" or "we" (*D*, 5: 135). The necessity is instead for both: a reading "I" who can observe, interpret, critique, and effect change; and a "we" who can be part of a community that takes responsibility in responding to the Nazi threat. As the pageant reels to its end in a cacophony of "scraps, orts, and fragments," all the spectators have become critics — and to be a critic one needs first to be an independent reader. The spectators are unified in their desire to seek interpretations, but they are no longer part of the kind of unity described in *Three Guineas* "that rubs out divisions" (*TG*, 163). The ending implies that there is a third option — coming together in difference. Thus, when Lucy Swithin asks Isa if she feels "we act different parts but are the same?" Isa answers, "Yes . . . No . . . It was Yes, No" (*BTA*, 193). This same ambivalence is evident when Isa and Giles come together at the end of the book to fight, and then to love and perhaps create a new life. This is the novel's most direct indication that Woolf concedes, differently than she did in *Three Guineas*, that perhaps peace must be fought for. As Leonard Woolf writes in *The War for Peace*, published in 1940, "If you are on the side of civilization, you must be against the use of force. But that unfortunately does not settle the matter. In human affairs the choice is rarely between what is good and what is bad; it is usually between what is bad and what is worse" (216).[38] A skepticism and ambiguity that can ethically encompass and explore conflict is the "new plot" that the book embraces. It does so even if hindsight indicates that something more ethically coherent would soon be needed to protect the "waifs & strays" from destruction by the Nazis.

Woolf claims in *Three Guineas* that society needs both private and public realms to avoid the deterioration of either: "For such will be our ruin if you, in the immensity of your public abstractions forget the private figure, or if we in the intensity of our private emotions forget the public world" (*TG*, 163). Yet, even in this statement, Woolf associates the artist's stance along with the private, with the "we . . . of private emotions" rather than with the "you" or "they" camp of public spectators — the villagers, the Lucy Swithins, and the Bart and Giles Olivers and the Manresas. Similarly, in *Goodbye to Berlin*, Christopher Isherwood places his first-person narrator apart from the public as an observing I/ Eye. Nevertheless, in contrast to Woolf, this positioning is even more problematic — for it is impossible to remain an unfeeling, objective outsider when witnessing the infringement of freedoms as the Nazi spectacle overtakes Berlin. But it is also clearly hopeless to even attempt to change the situation.

### I Am Not a Camera: *Goodbye to Berlin*

Unlike the central *mise-en-abyme* placement of the pageant in *Between the Acts*, Isherwood's *Goodbye to Berlin* presents a more oblique but no less pointed assessment of the link between spectator and spectacle in Nazi dramaturgy. At first glance, the novel appears unambiguously realist — a straightforward documentary or diary account of the young protagonist's life in Berlin in the early thirties. Upon closer examination, however, one realizes that, like *Between the Acts*, Isherwood's Berlin stories incisively critique the Nazi spectacle and its effect on individuals within German society. As Antony Shuttleworth observes of Isherwood's 1930s novels, "rather than voicing uncomprehending alarm at the horrors of the time, [the Berlin stories] delve into the possible causes of totalitarian politics" ("Populous City," 151).

The narrator's observations underscore the insidious nature of the Nazi Party's exploitation of illusion, drama, and pageantry, but the narrative also strongly condemns and implicates the spectators who passively stand by to watch—not support—the rise of the Third Reich. The recurring trope of the photographic image emphasizes how the line between image, illusion, and reality becomes progressively blurred for the population of Berlin. Even more so, the camera image becomes a metaphor for the novel as a whole, a document that purports to capture accurately a single moment in time to be viewed and reflected upon in the future. Forms of German mass entertainment, such as movies and cabarets, are central to the work—a clear indication that for Isherwood questions regarding the role of author as illusion-maker, as opposed to the Nazi mass propaganda machine, become germane.[39]

For many critics the obligatory starting point of any critical discussion of Christopher Isherwood is his most famous sentence: "I am a camera with its shutter open, quite passive, recording, not thinking. . . . Some day, all this will have to be developed, carefully printed, fixed" (*GTB*, 9). As the opening of the second paragraph of *Goodbye to Berlin*, these words place the narrator, Christopher, or "Herr Issyvoo," in the self-conscious position of being outside the space and time of the events depicted, an onlooker or observer of the actions he describes. The camera, however, is no innocent or objective recorder, nor does the novel purport to be an impersonal record of reality—it is an artistic representation of it. As Antony Shuttleworth proposes, the key to understanding the camera image is Isherwood's "concern with the falsely authentic" and his "suspicion towards claims of authenticity" ("Populous City," 157).[40] To expand on this point, it is through the idea of a camera image that Isherwood explores the question of whether an accurate representation of the truth can be recorded. Photographs are always "developed, carefully printed, fixed" (*GTB*, 9). Isherwood thereby insinuates that the creator of such images is always complicit in making meaning and "developing" or "fixing" a story from the scene. He "draws attention to the subjective rather than objective lens of the camera" (Williams, *British Writers*, 124).

Strikingly similar to the way in which Benjamin in "The Work of Art in the Age of Mechanical Reproduction" describes Eugène Atget's photography of deserted Parisian streets in the early 1900s, Isherwood's portraits of Berlin are captured "like scenes of a crime" that are "photographed for the purpose of establishing evidence" that take on historical and political significance (Benjamin, *Illuminations*, 226).[41] Since there are no captions or "signposts" to point the reader in the direction of a specific political analysis, Isherwood's "portraits" of life in Berlin similarly demand that the reader interpret the historical context behind the scenes and approach the documentary-type novel with a political framework in mind. To quote Samuel Hynes's description of Isherwood's camera trope, "If the camera is the instrument of documentary, then one must conclude that in a world that contains fascism documentation is not enough. What the camera eye can document is the apparent city, smiling in the sun; but it cannot record possible death, or terror, or reality of evil." Similar to *Between the Acts*, evidence of the Nazi rallies, Hitler's speeches, and reports of Nazi atrocities remain at the margins of the text. The narrator's description of the characters and their experiences, however, are in a constant dialogic relationship with the political background and cannot be disentangled from the looming sense of peril that surrounds them. As Hynes observes of *Goodbye to Berlin*, "In the stories, the Nazis are never in the foreground for long, but their hovering presence is always felt; fascism is as much a part of the tone of Berlin as the poverty and perversions are" (*The Auden Generation*, 357–58).

In contrast to Woolf's omniscient narrator, the first-person "Christopher Isherwood" of *Goodbye to Berlin* narrows the scope of what can be seen rather than enlarges it. Isherwood thereby injects the narrative with dramatic irony, doubt, and suspicion as to the reliability of the subjective story being told. Often readers mistake the main character of the novel as being synonymous with Christopher Isherwood, the author—a gross oversight considering Isherwood's views on subjectivity. It is clearly apparent that Christopher in the novel is a fictional character meant to highlight the complex relationship between authorship and story. Choosing to call the narrator by the name of the author underscores the idea that memory, diary, and historical witnessing are also forms of narrative with specific points of view that can never encompass the entire picture.[42] Christopher the narrator thereby introduces the concept that the reliability of any first-person representation is suspect—especially when what individuals are witnessing has become indescribably unreal. For this same reason, in Isherwood's overtly autobiographical works and memoirs he mixes third person to refer to his younger, past self and first person for observations in the writing present (see, for example, the subsequent quotation from *Christopher and His Kind*). The different selves observing and interpreting any moment in the work—the "I/Eye" of the observer, the writer, and the reader — constantly change as perceptions are altered in relation to past and present experience. From this perspective, the character portraits and observations in *Goodbye to Berlin* become pieces of a puzzle that gain significance as the story proceeds. Instead of self-contained short stories, each vignette in the novel adds a clue to understanding the bigger "crime scene" of Nazi Germany as more information about the political context is revealed and Hitler becomes more influential.

In his 1977 memoir, *Christopher and His Kind*, Isherwood provides a more unconcealed depiction of what goes on behind the scenes, or "between the acts," of the stories in *Goodbye to Berlin*. Isherwood writes this of himself in 1930:

> Christopher became increasingly aware of the kind of world he was living in. Here was the seething brew of history in the making. . . . The Berlin brew seethed with unemployment, malnutrition, stock market panic, hatred of the Versailles Treaty and other potent ingredients. On September 20, a new one was added; in the Reichstag elections, the Nazis won 107 seats as against their previous 12, and became for the first time a major political party. (*CHK*, 43)

By March 23, 1933, when Hitler is named "master of Germany," Isherwood takes further note of the widespread and ubiquitous spectacle of Nazism:

> The street itself, like all others, was hung with black-white-red swastika flags; it was unwise not to display them. Uniformed Nazis strode along the sidewalks with stern official expressions on their faces; it was advisable to step aside for them. . . . On the loudspeakers blaring forth speeches by Goering and Goebbels. "Germany is awake," they said. People sat in front of the cafes listening to them — cowlike, vaguely curious, complacent, accepting what had happened but not the responsibility for it. (*CHK*, 96)

The complacency described by Isherwood in his memoir turns into passive acquiescence as Jewish businesses are boycotted and "boy bars" are raided. Before leaving Berlin and sitting down to write his recollections, Isherwood notes that he has "hallucinations" that Nazism is invading every corner of his life: "He fancied that he heard heavy wagons drawing up before the house, in the middle of the night. He suddenly detected swastika patterns in the wallpaper. He convinced himself that everything in his room, whatever its superficial colour, was basically brown; Nazi-brown" (*CHK*, 100).

If one interprets *Goodbye to Berlin* as colored Nazi-brown, then the images portrayed therein all take on a more pronounced political nuance. Moreover, in contradiction to the opening lines of the novel, the depictions of Berlin life provide anything but a "passive" or "not thinking" viewpoint (*GTB*, 9). The novel becomes a form of resistance writing that is clearly political. Like the disruptions to the pageant in *Between the Acts*, the observations of Germany that surround the character portraits are meant to dispel any British or American media impressions that Germany is politically benign or Hitler a moderate. The smiling sunny photograph of Berlin is repeatedly undermined by the narrator, who, rather than being stuck in isolation or helplessness (as is often claimed by critics), is very much involved in what is going on.[43] Even Stephen Spender, a close companion of Isherwood's at the time the novel was written, comments in his autobiography, "Christopher, so far from being the self-effacing spectator he depicts in his novels, was really the centre of his characters, and neither could they exist without him, nor he without them" (*World Within World*, 124). It is clear, as Lisa Schwerdt argues at length, that "except for that one line ['I am a camera'], there is nothing in the novel to support the narrator's statement of passivity" (*Isherwood's Fiction*, 80). From the very first page the claim that the narrator is "unthinking" is disrupted by descriptions of the external atmosphere that are infused with feeling.

The camera image is pointedly meant to be a metaphor, not a literal technique, especially considering that the narrator continually, and transparently, tries to influence not only the characters with whom he interacts but also the reader. Christopher expresses clear opinions on life, love, and politics; becomes involved with people; moves in with families; and introduces characters to one another. Nevertheless, analogous to the narrator's interruptions in *Between the Acts*, Christopher's astute observations of the public atmosphere surrounding the characters — in the streets and city — distance the reader and deflect any desire to become too caught up in the lives of any particular character. I would even argue that Isherwood explicitly refuses to structure the episodes of the novel in logical sequence so that rather than being drawn into a conventional character- or plot-based story, the reader is encouraged to focus on the political context that causes characters to react to their environment in the way that they do. Instead of individuals, the characters become examples of personality types that make up German society during the rise of Nazism. Furthermore, by disrupting the normative linear sequence of events and shifting time and place without logical progression, Isherwood insists that the only accurate representation of Berlin in the 1930s is the one that leaves a blank space for all those "unseen" portraits that become occluded by the irrationality of the Nazi regime.

The opening section of the novel, in which Christopher describes his room in Frl. Schroeder's boardinghouse, provides one of the primary hints that a more threatening political undercurrent underlies the supposedly innocent, camera-like image of Berlin. Christopher describes the room as "gorgeously coloured, like an altar" but at the same time a hat stand, by all accounts innocuous, is depicted as menacing and foreboding. It is formed out of "three sham medieval halberds," which Frl. Shroeder "unscrews the heads of . . . and polishes. . . . They are heavy and sharp enough to kill" (*GTB*, 10). If the image of the halberd hat stand is not ominous enough, Christopher goes on to describe the rest of the room as being "unnecessarily solid, abnormally heavy and dangerously sharp" and filled with metal objects in shapes of fierce animals or weapons: "candlesticks shaped like entwined serpents, an ashtray from which emerges the head of a crocodile, a paperknife copied from a Florentine dagger. . . ." (*GTB*, 10). All are objects that allude to poison, danger, and death. Musing on the fate of the room and its objects, Christopher sets the context for a world on the verge of destruction. Eerily foreshadowing the imminent war, Christopher wonders, "What becomes of such things? How could they ever be destroyed? They will probably remain intact for thousands of years: people will treasure them in museums. Or perhaps they will merely be melted down for munitions in a war" (*GTB*, 10). Thus the narrator insinuates right from the start of the novel that an image, if one looks closely enough, can reveal much about the violent and ominous political context.

Even more overtly, the chapter "On Reugen Island" supplies a not-so-subtle message that the political backdrop of an image can change its meaning. The beach at the Baltic Sea resort, like Frl. Shroeder's boardinghouse, is depicted in terms of a snapshot:

> Each family has its own enormous hooded wicker beach-chair, and each chair flies a little flag. There are German city-flags — Hamburg, Hanover, Dresden, Rostock and Berlin, as well as the National, Republican and Nazi colours. Each chair is encircled by a low sand bulwark upon which the occupants have set inscriptions in fir-cones: *Waldesruh. Familie Walter. Stahlhelm. Heil Hitler!* Many of the forts are also decorated with the Nazi swastika. (*GTB*, 110)

The seemingly static snapshot of the beach nevertheless introduces a certain amount of irony into the section since what is *not* depicted is more important than what is — Jews, for one (in this way, it is not so different from the lawn of Pointz Hall in *Between the Acts*), and rationality for another. As the passage portentously reveals, even before the legal segregation of Jews and Aryans was formally put into place in 1933, it was reflected in places with significant Nazi support and a fundamental aspect of the Nazi Party's ideology (published in their Party Program in 1920). Not coincidentally, in 1936 part of the island—which before World War II was a popular holiday destination for both German Jews and non-Jews—was slated as a Nazi resort spot for its "Strength Through Joy Program" (*Kraft durch Freude*, or KdF) to provide a "healthy" Aryan vacation spot for working-class party members.[44] Immediately following the description of the beach in *Goodbye to Berlin*, now connected with a national, racial, and political expression by the presence of the flags, Christopher remarks, "The other morning I saw a child of about five years old, stark naked, marching along all by himself with a swastika flag over his shoulder and singing 'Deutschland uber ales'" (*GTB*, 110). The juxtaposition between the depiction of the beach and the recollection of seeing the child makes the political implications quite obvious: the families are just as obtuse as the little boy — the flags and the city "teams" give the impression that Nazism is a game. It is also a fundamental example of how the Nazi spectacle worked to exploit an image of national grandeur and thus play into a nostalgic desire for unity on the part of the German public.

Aside from the static photographic images, references to moving images — cinema — are also crucially placed in *Goodbye to Berlin* to emphasize the empty promise of Nazi public culture. Woolf is one of the first to note how due to "the influence of films," leaning-tower writers such as Isherwood "lack . . . transitions in their work and [feature] violently opposed contrasts" (*M*, 118). More recent critics have also noted that elements of Isherwood's experimental style were due to the impact of cinema. Brian Finney claims that Isherwood's experience as a screenwriter in England helped him "to visualize his scenes to a much greater extent than before, ruthlessly to prune his prose and to treat his dialogue with a dramatist's economy" (*Critical Biography*, 25). Similarly, Keith Williams attributes the "disorienting changes in perspective and location in Isherwood's novel" and "cinematic intertextuality" to Isherwood's attempt to "emulate camera angles and editing to suggest the narrator's subjective state" (*British Writers*, 145). While the relationship between film and Isherwood's writing style is well noted, I will reiterate my contention that the connection between film and novelization, like the correlation between Woolf's pageant and the novel, is not parallel. Visual media such as cinema and theater are not the same as fiction. In a novel language is dialogized; the representation is not fixed in space and time; and, moreover, the reading experience is individualistic. As Alistair Cooke suggests in "The Critic in Film History" (1938), "Whether we like it or not, we are *in* a movie all the time." Unlike reading, "there is no means of getting a context clearer, thinking twice about it, for you can't go back, as you can with literature, or painting, or music, and ponder the thing over" (ibid., 252–53). Even if writers like Isherwood use film and photography as a symbol or metaphor, as Williams fittingly points out, Isherwood, much like W. H. Auden, is well aware of the ways in which writing is neither like still nor motion-picture photography (*British Writers*, 127). Williams cites W. H. Auden's poem "Letter to William Coldstream, Esq." (1937) to illustrate this point. The speaker of the poem starts out by audaciously suggesting, "Let me pretend that I'm the impersonal eye of the camera/Sent out by God to shoot on location." After proving that objective visualization is impossible since the writer always also gives his impressions and associations along with the image, the speaker decides that the novelist and the film director have different ways of "stating experience" and thus leaves "each man to his medium" (ibid., 223, 227).[45]

In the context of *Goodbye to Berlin*, film-watching is directly connected with Nazi propaganda and is juxtaposed with the life of the characters Christopher and Sally Bowles. Sally and Christopher go to see "a film about a girl who sacrifices her stage career for the sake of a Great Love, Home and Children" (*GTB*, 58), shortly before an episode in which Sally gets an abortion. Film scholars such as Linda Schulte-Sasse, Mary-Elizabeth O'Brian, Patrice Petro, and Terri Gordon all describe Nazi films that emphasize themes of sacrifice for the good of the whole, order, and family values. As O'Brian states, in Nazi productions "deviant behaviour is repeatedly played out and then reined in and overcome at the conclusion" to "reaffirm fascist institutions" and reiterate or "validate the prevailing order" (*Nazi Cinema*, 10). The reaction to the film in *Goodbye to Berlin*, however, parodies and thus undermines the effect of the propaganda, much like the satirical elements of the historical pageant in *Between the Acts*. Christopher and Sally, who are so clearly outsiders to the Nazi ideal, both "laughed so much that we had to leave before the end" (*GTB*, 58). Their response implies that ideology can be reversed if its seriousness is destabilized by skepticism. Yet, as the Nazi spectacle becomes progressively more threatening, it also becomes less funny. The observation that parody loses its transgressive effect when the reality of ideology becomes implausibly far-fetched is reiterated in Isherwood's memoir. Christopher cites a letter he wrote to Stephen Spender describing Hitler in comical terms: "we are having a new government, with Charlie Chaplin . . . in the ministry. All words fail" (*CHK*, 94). A few months later, however, when the Reichstag is set on fire and the Nazis accuse the Communists of setting it (events that lead up to the Nazi Party overtaking the parliament), Isherwood bleakly remarks, "Charlie Chaplin had ceased to be funny" (*CHK*, 95).[46]

Films like the one Christopher and Sally watch, which confirm Nazi culture and promote an illusion of a unified, healthy state, are juxtaposed with other forms of mass entertainment in the novel—namely, the cabaret. Although *Goodbye to Berlin* mentions the cabaret only briefly, it subsequently captured the imagination of film and stage adaptors, occupying a central role in John Van Druten's 1951 play, *I Am a Camera*, and Bob Fosse's 1972 film adaptation, *Cabaret* (with Liza Minnelli playing Sally Bowles).[47] One can see how the Berlin cabaret could so easily become a trope that frames the characters and vignettes presented in *Goodbye to Berlin*. The eclectic and decadent liberalism of the popular Weimar cabaret, like the diverse range of individuals whom Christopher meets, would soon be stamped out in favor of more sanctioned, ideologically charged forms of Nazi public life.[48] As opposed to Van Druten's play or Fosse's movie, however, the nightclub associated with Sally Bowles — the Lady Windermere — is not as significant as some of the narrator's descriptions of other local "dives."[49]

The Lady Windermere, the narrator relates, is "an arty 'informal' bar" decorated to resemble Montparnasse (*GTB*, 37). The entire experience of Sally's performance in the bar is described quite briefly: "Sally sang badly, without any expression" except for a "take-it-or-leave-it grin on her face." Applause ensues; the pianist kisses her hand, she sings a couple more songs in French and German (which are not "so well received") and then subsequently tries to make advances toward an elderly gentleman for some "business" (*GTB*, 38). This is what sums up the Sally Bowles-as-cabaret singer section of the novel. Since the episode appears so early in the chapter about Sally, however, her identity as a performer — and a somewhat dodgy one at that — becomes fixedly connected with her character. Of greater consequence is that the Lady Windermere, among the other nightclubs described in the novel, provides a surreptitious look at Weimar night life. Isherwood portrays other cabaret-like bars such as the Troika, where there is "a big dancing-hall" and some "girls did figure-tableaux behind gauze." The sexual energy there is palpable in the depiction of couples "dancing with hands on each other's hips, yelling in each other's faces, streaming with sweat" (*GTB*, 51). Christopher also goes to a "boy bar," the Alexander Casino, where young men with open-necked shirts and tattoos work as pickpockets and pick up elderly "respectable-looking" gentlemen (*GTB*, 150). It is bleakly described as a "dingy room" that is "lit by red chinese lanterns and festooned with dusty paper streamers" (*GTB*, 149).

Accounts of Christopher's visits to "dives" become even more significant in retrospect, since by the end of the book it is clear that all these establishments will be raided or shut down. Portrayals of the cabaret and their patrons, therefore, are added to the collection of objects and "photographs" of a lost Berlin, soon to be committed to memory. Eventually, only this trace of them will remain. The book's reference to the crackdown on Berlin cabarets in 1933 and the "clean up" of Weimar Berlin by National Socialists once again points to the suppression of local performances in exchange for the spectacle of a harmonious, robust, unified Nazi *Volksgemeinschaft*, or "people's community." As Linda Mizejewski notes, until 1933 the cabaret performances were "points of resistance" that "often took on the Nazis as their targets of satire" (*Divine Decadence*, 27–28). Examining at length how the landscape of cabaret changed from the Weimar period to the Nazi era, Peter Jelavich also observes that the cabarets of Weimar Berlin mocked and satirized a host of contemporary issues such as politics, sexuality, gender, and fashion. Under the Nazis, however, most of the Jewish entertainers were forced to flee and satirists came under watch of "cultural watchdogs," leaving "insipid variety-show programs" in their wake (*Berlin Cabaret*, 5). The last cabaret show that Christopher visits is one example of those insipid displays. Christopher goes to a cabaret nightclub called the Salomé "in the nature of a farewell visit for the Police have begun to take a great interest in these places. They are frequently raided, and the names of their clients are written down" (*GTB*, 237). Described as "painted gold and inferno-red" with "crimson plush inches thick, and vast gilded mirrors," the Salomé is a place where "respectable middle-aged tradesmen" watch a cabaret of lesbians and transvestites (*GTB*, 237–38). Christopher inevitably finds the scene "depressing" (*GTB*, 237). This is most probably because the spectators, instead of attending the cabaret as an expression of sexual emancipation, have come to "sightsee" and gawk. "It wasn't even genuine," Christopher's friend Fritz tells him (*GTB*, 237). By 1933, the cabaret has transformed into a shell of empty fakery — and the rest of Berlin society is soon to follow.

The description of the Salomé conspicuously follows a scene in which a Nazi, patrolling a street to watch for "anti-Nordic" activity, tries to stop two young Jewish men in a car from picking up a couple of German women. A little crowd of spectators gathers to watch but does nothing. "Very few of them sided openly with the Nazi," the narrator comments, "several supported the Jews; but the majority confined themselves to shaking their heads dubiously and murmuring: 'Àllerhand! [of all the things]'" (*GTB*, 236). Their reaction, similar to the pageant audience in *Between the Acts*, is to imply that "all sorts of things" are going on, but they do nothing. The passive audience of spectators who allow Jews to be terrorized is the same group that the narrator observes "could be made to believe in anybody or anything" (*GTB*, 235). The collusion in the fantasy on the part of the spectators is what increasingly comes into focus as the novel progresses. Never is this more pointedly emphasized than in the last section of the work. As the narrator is about to leave Berlin, he records static images of the city he is soon to abandon. No specific character is outlined in any detail; instead, short, disjointed paragraphs describe a multitude of different impressions. The last chapter provides a montage of sorts, jumping without transitions from one image to the other in lean, terse, laconic, and paratactic prose. The stylistic divergence from the previous chapters implies that words have become insufficient to describe the decline into irrationality to which Berlin has succumbed. One of the images in this montage is of a Jewish writer dragged out of a café by the Nazis and taken away. The reaction of onlookers is static: "Nobody moved a finger. You could have heard a pin drop, till they were gone" (*GTB*, 251). Another image is of the narrator's student, Herr N., an enemy of the Nazis, who sometimes "will bend forward to the window and regard a building or a square with a mournful fixity, as if to impress its image upon his memory and to bid it goodbye" (*GTB*, 254). Like Herr N., the narrator impresses upon his memory images of Berlin before he says goodbye. The narrator, however, juxtaposes the external, visual image of "the sun is brilliantly shining" to what it obscures: "The sun shines, and Hitler is master of the city. The sun shines, and dozens of my friends — my pupils at the Workers' School, the men and women I met at the I. A. H. — are in prison, possibly dead" (*GTB*, 255).

As the book opens with the camera image, so it closes, framing the entire text and thus intimating that any attempt to represent Berlin accurately must necessarily include the various viewpoints, aspects, experiences, and characters that make up a time and a place. In other words, the novel can only gesture toward "an image" of Berlin during the rise of the Third Reich, but neither a visual nor a textual representation can truly encompass its entirety.[50] *Goodbye to Berlin*, like *Between the Acts*, is a warning to readers of the dangers of becoming indifferent to the precarious political environment in Europe. Woolf, however, implies that there might be a potential for a third option — exposed in the mirrors held up to the audience at the end of the pageant, witnesses of the 1930s are implored to look at themselves, critique the pageantry of war, and change their way of thinking. For the narrator in Berlin, the predicament is much bleaker. The curtain does not rise to introduce a "new plot" at the end of Isherwood's book, as it does in Woolf's. Instead it falls on a show that is a sham. Christopher recognizes that all those individuals whose experiences he has observed and shared during his stay in Berlin "are doomed" (*GTB*, 255). The only logical way for him to disentangle himself from the narrative is to say "goodbye" and leave it behind.

## Circus or Spectacle? Djuna Barnes's *Nightwood*

The foreboding desire for an illusion of wholeness linked with the Nazi spectacle is expressed in an even more oblique manner and thus is more difficult to discern in Djuna Barnes's *Nightwood*. Significant more in its absence than its presence, Nazism lurks in the shadows, lying in wait for the alienated outsiders portrayed in the novel. As Jane Marcus bluntly observes, "What is absent is the Nazi who will burn this book" ("Laughing at Leviticus," 228). Similar to *Between the Acts* and *Goodbye to Berlin*, it is a novel that highlights the dangerous allure of the spectacle's promise — a promise of harmony that leaves the characters grasping for an image of something that does not exist while passively accepting their own destruction. Like Woolf and Isherwood, Barnes demands that the reader look beyond the constructs of sense-making to examine the political context of the novel.

Specifically in its refusal to adhere to a conventional plot or accepted style of prose, *Nightwood* challenges the reader to recognize how novelization can subvert the unifying force of fascism that looms over the streets of Paris. Even so, its parodic, whimsical prose style, confounding language, and criticism of "truth" tales make it difficult to discern a theme as serious as Nazism. A vivid example of novelized heteroglossia, Barnes's work is a mélange of the languages, voices, nationalities, and hierarchies that provide the social framework of interwar European society. I would concur with Jane Marcus that "*Nightwood*'s hysterical heteroglossia is a perverse and almost postmodern folk-text in which language and its possibility for figuration is as potent and explosive as it is in

Shakespeare or Joyce" ("Laughing at Leviticus," 222).[51] In other words, *Nightwood* rejects the type of ideology that imposes order and clear definitions of what does and does not belong by embracing and merging various voices, viewpoints, and ideologies in a cacophony of discourses. Like Woolf and Isherwood, Barnes thus resists totalitarian modes of thinking by affirming that ambiguity is the only accurate way to represent reality. Satiric, ironic, and self-reflexive gestures that question the idea of "truth," "history," and "knowledge" are even more common in *Nightwood* than they are in Woolf's and Isherwood's works. For example, most of the characters' backgrounds are unknown or fabricated; history and origins are all exposed as story; language is often circular and confounding; there is no obvious plot to follow; and the ending presents no resolution. Highly experimental and parodic, as Donna Gerstenberger argues, *Nightwood* "destabilizes the traditional idea of narrative" by subverting the confining categories of official language and historical narrative imposed in fascist dictatorships, yet at the same time it is entrenched in its own positioning as story ("Radical Narrative," 131).

Barnes emphasizes the novel's ironic status as a "story," or work of fiction, rather than a "truthful" depiction of its time, from the start. As soon as the reader first encounters Dr. Matthew O'Connor, the mouthpiece for the novel's most bizarre and paradoxical statements, he states that "legend" is composed of "the stories that do not amount to much," as opposed to "history," which is "the best the high and mighty can do with theirs" (NW, 15). Both legend and history are storytelling, he implies; whether either is significant depends on who is doing the telling and how the story is remembered. O'Connor could also be insinuating that *this* story, *Nightwood*—made up of small stories that "do not amount to much"—can be interpreted as either legend or an "accurate" historical depiction of the atmosphere in Europe between the two world wars. This is especially valid if *Nightwood* is to be read as a novel of resistance. Appropriately, the Tiresias-like Dr. O'Connor, who is neither a doctor nor much of a storyteller (the majority of his pronouncements make little sense), is only identified by the tales he tells. He himself is all story.[52] O'Connor's critical positioning as a self-reflexive gesture in the novel is evident from Barnes's insistence on keeping O'Connor's "loquacious ravings" in the text throughout *Nightwood*'s numerous revisions, defending her position against the advice of editors and friends such as

Emily Coleman and T. S. Eliot.[53] It is also no coincidence that the first time we encounter O'Connor the storyteller, he is in the middle of relating a story at a gathering of circus performers, Jews, transvestites, and other outcasts from various locations in Europe, "Prague, Vienna, Hungary, Germany, France and Italy" (NW, 11). The group is assembled in the house of Count Altamonte, who claims he is related to "every nation" (NW, 11). At a time in history when racial and national origins are of ultimate consequence, it is surely significant that the crowd gathered there is unified only in their mutual Otherness. Everyone at the gathering seems to come from "somewhere else." Barnes in this manner conveys the idea that all nationalities, personalities, sexual identities, social hierarchies, are "stories"—constructions of history that ultimately "do not amount to much" (NW, 15).

O'Connor's confounding way of telling his story, and the mesmerized manner in which his audience is lured into listening to his tale, can be interpreted in a number of ways: as a revolt against the "Absolute" of fascist ideology; as celebration of the nonsensical; and even as a parody of the mystifying language of Nazi propaganda. Within one short storytelling occasion, he spouts numerous pronouncements that upon close examination make no sense at all. They even sound like clever adages: "every nation with a sense of humour is a lost nation, and every woman with a sense of humour is a lost woman"; "Vienna . . . the bed into which the common people climb, docile with toil, and out of which the nobility fling themselves, ferocious with dignity"; or "Youth is cause, effect is age" (NW, 15–16). Saul Friedländer claims that Nazi propaganda worked because it eluded logical or linear thinking. Its circular and repetitive language obscured any contradictions in its content by relying on "a play of images sent back, in turn, from one to the other in echoes without end, creating a kind of hypnosis" (Friedländer, *Reflections*, 50). The difference between Nazi propaganda and O'Connor's repetitive, declarative, and essentializing statements—including those about "The Jew," "The Christian," "The Irishman," "The Woman," and "The Invert"—is that they only *appear* as dicta that represent universal truths. When these declarations are scrutinized carefully, it is quite clear that O'Connor's words parody the type of language that blinds admiring spectators and fools them into thinking they are listening to truth. Especially since the statements are iterated by such a ludicrous character, who so clearly speaks from the perspective of the outsider rather than from a perpetrator's position of power, the ideology of the content is undermined.

There are ways, nonetheless, that Barnes implicates the audience that actually believes the irrational stories and succumbs to the desire to choose illusion over reality, which is why *Nightwood* also highlights the characters' magnetism toward spectacles such as the circus. The circus features prominently and provides the connecting thread between the characters. Like the pageant in *Between the Acts* and the photographs in *Goodbye to Berlin*, the circus becomes a metaphor for the novel as a whole and for the political environment that is its backdrop. The circus in *Nightwood* becomes a locus of resistance to Nazi propaganda and the sanctioned forms of entertainment that will soon impinge on the life of the performers. Yet, it also accounts for the way in which characters can suspend disbelief to be drawn into the allure of the spectacle. Granted, if the audience members of a circus are willing to believe in illusion in order to be entertained, at least they are aware that what they are watching is an act — just as in a work of fiction readers are conscious of the story. As Isherwood depicts in his final portrait of 1933 Berlin, this is not so in life under National Socialism. *Nightwood*'s international cast of fake dukes, duchesses, and barons who move from Berlin, to Vienna, to Italy, to America, and back to Paris would surely be more than aware of the perils of any ideology that believes in its own myth of origins and uses pageantry as a political tactic. At least characters like O'Connor, much like La Trobe in *Between the Acts*, recognize the workings of the spectacle. As O'Connor claims, "I tuck myself in at night, well content because I am my own charlatan'" (NW, 96).

As opposed to the Nazi spectacle of the "real" world, which tyrannizes "deviants" such as Jews, blacks, and other "queer" characters, the circus, as Felix Volkbein observes, is a space in which no one is "alien" because everyone realizes that social positions, race, sexuality are performances — the "reeking falsification" that links everyone to "the pageantry of kings and queens" (NW, 11). The implication in the novel, however, is that the world of circus ribaldry is "decaying." This is why Felix, the "Wandering Jew," moves among the "mysterious and perplexing" circus performers with a feeling that he is walking in a museum (NW, 11). The circus, then, as a parodic form of resistance to real fakery, is represented as a dying practice in the novel, soon to be taken over by political mass spectacles. Laura Winkiel, whose research provides a valuable analysis of Barnes's relationship with the circus, emphasizes the double-function of the circus in Barnes's work: to comment on and critique the effects of mass culture on local forms of entertainment. To understand the role of the circus in *Nightwood*, Winkiel examines Barnes's earlier journalistic work on P. T. Barnum's circus and her assessment of the changing nature of the circus from "heterogeneous sites of entertainment" to modernity's "capitalized, homogenized culture industry." As Winkiel maintains, nineteenth-century traveling circuses such as Barnum's were collective, interactive performances that featured "freaks" and other acts that interrogated and challenged ideas about gender, body, and the self versus the Other. By the 1920s, however, these types of "circus street parades" all but vanished, replaced by more uniformed, ordered, "cleaned up" versions of the circus. Barnes, in her journal articles, specifically critiques these modern spectacles, which gain profits from immense sets, exotic costumes, and large audiences (Winkiel, "Circuses and Spectacles," 8–9).[54]

Winkiel's research is especially helpful in considering how characters such as Felix Volkbein and Nora Flood, intimately connected with the circus as they are, can be interpreted as resisting a homogenized public culture in their Outsidership while concurrently serving as negative examples of what lies in store for spectators who mistake the illusion of the spectacle for reality. After all, the purpose of the circus is to mesmerize spectators and fill them with longing for the magical fantasy to be real. (The number of stories based on "running away with the circus" is a point in fact.) This is similar to the major goal and effect of the Nazi spectacle and mass rallies. At the same time, the spectacle of the circus is positioned in Barnes's novel in juxtaposition to the Nazi spectacle in the way the former embraces marginal characters, ignores national and racial borders, and highlights performances of gender and class. Within the gathering of circus performers described in *Nightwood*, a subversive Bakhtinian type of carnivalesque operates through reversals, the use of mask and grotesquery, and the breakdown of delineation between art and life. Bakhtin attributes the carnivalesque to a disruption of dominant structures of knowledge — a moment of cultural crisis partly due to a contention between "high" and "low" languages (*Rabelais*, 5–7).

Barnes's representation of a world turned upside down is much like Bakhtin's interpretation of the carnival. The performances of the characters therein challenge and deliberately violate the categories of identity fostered by Nazi propaganda. The most heart-wrenching breakdowns, however, occur when the main characters forget that the spectacle is fake. As Winkiel notes, "Unless members of the audience impose resistant readings to counter the alienation of the spectacle, they run the risk of becoming what they see" ("Circuses and Spectacles," 19). Through their desire to overcome alienation, spectators such as Felix and Nora are drawn into believing in the spectacle's image, thereby becoming hollowed-out specters of themselves.

Felix, for example, describes the circus in terms of a desire and yearning that can never be satisfied — in other words, in the same terms with which theorists characterize the dangers of spectacle, pageantry, and illusion. As the narrator of *Nightwood* relates, "The emotional spiral of the circus, taking its flight from the immense disqualification of the public, rebounding from its illimitable hope, produced in Felix longing and disquiet. The circus was a loved thing that he could never touch, therefore never know" (NW, 12). As described by those contemporaneous German theorists such as Adorno, Horkheimer, Kracauer, and Benjamin, who analyze the social plots occurring during the period, Felix's sense of alienation from himself and from the real triggers in him a yearning for an image that has no content. Not knowing himself, and rejected as a part of society due to his racial construction as a Jew, Felix has no capability of feeling accepted anywhere else except by the circus's "disqualification of the public." Even there, however, his belief in the "illimitable hope" of illusion is misguided, leading him to misery. Felix's infatuation with Robin Vote corresponds with this same doomed attraction to the circus. For Felix, Robin is an "image." Despite marrying Robin, or even having a child with her, it is impossible for Felix to succeed in capturing her because Robin, as a spectacular image, is intangible. Felix the spectator, though alienated, submits to her allure without knowing what or who she really is. Likewise, all characters in the novel who succumb to the spectacle participate in "a dark drama of loss and betrayal" instead of a liberating or emancipating carnival (Winkiel, "Circuses and Spectacles," 19).

One of the most intriguing self-reflexive gestures in the book that links the circus, spectatorship, and writing as resistance is the story of "Nikka the Nigger" and his tattoos. It is the first story that O'Connor tells and the first time the reader witnesses Felix's susceptibility to becoming drawn in as spectator. The tattooed narrative on Nikka's body draws attention to the way in which politics are read onto bodies and highlights the metafictional manner in which "writing resistance" turns into a body of work. The fact that Nikka's story is immediately followed by Felix's question about Vienna and its "military superiority" appears to be a clear indication that Nikka's body is meant to be contrasted with politics and the beautiful Aryan-looking "rosy-cheeked, bright-eyed" youth who will soon populate the Nazi army (NW, 17).

Nikka, the African bear wrestler at Cirque de Paris, is decorated in ink from head to toe. The tattoos force his audience to see an alternative visual spectacle that puts into question cultural myths regarding race, religion, economy, history, and sexuality:

> There he was, crouching all over the arena without a stitch on, except an ill-concealed loin-cloth all abulge as if with a deep sea-catch, tattooed from head to heel with all the *ameublement* of depravity! Though he couldn't have done a thing (and I know what I am talking about in spite of all that has been said about black boys) if you had stood him in a gig-mill for a week, though (it's said) at a stretch it spelled Desdemona. Well then, over his belly was an angel from Chartres; on each buttock, half public, half private, a quotation from the book of magic, a confirmation of the Jansenist theory, I'm sorry to say and here to say it. Across his knees, I give you my word, "I" on the one and on the other, "can," put those two together! Across his chest, beneath a beautiful caravel in full sail, two clasped hands, the wrist bones fretted with point lace. (NW, 16)

Details of the tattoo—the "caravel" warship associated with European imperialism, slavery, and exploitation; the French Jansenist quotation linked to seventeenth-century French Catholicism and the Counter-Reformation; the angel from the great medieval cathedral of Chartres—place (or displace) Nikka in Paris within a historical and religious narrative of domination and intolerance. Both Jane Marcus and Laura

Winkiel have examined the tattooed body of Nikka as a text that conveys stereotypes about race and sexuality. Marcus interprets Nikka's body as "an invitation to read the body of the Other as a book" that inscribes the "white man's projection of desire for the white woman onto a black man" and "a text of Western culture's historical projections and myths about race" ("Laughing at Leviticus," 228, 224, 225). Winkiel's analysis is similar in reading Nikka's body as a text that "re-inscribes the easy meanings by which the audience reads him as a black man and circus freak" ("Circuses and Spectacles," 21). Nikka, however, is not only a political or sexual body but also a textual gesture that points to the positioning of narrative in *Nightwood* as a whole. As I maintain, Nikka's body is not only meant to be read as a circus performance or body-as-text. It is also a visual spectacle related to an audience *as story* rather than as performance. Moreover, the reliability of the story is somewhat suspect, given that it is transmitted by O'Connor. Three times removed from its original "truth," it combines the multiple ways a story can be communicated — visually, verbally, and textually. As a performance that is seen by O'Connor, related to an audience, and then in turn read by someone else, Nikka becomes a site for readings that proliferate beyond the body.

Paradoxically, the Nikka story is removed from its original context through narrativization, but tattooing itself is completely tied to its original political and physical context — the body. As Marc Blanchard observes in his study of tattooing in late capitalist societies: "Tattooing, like writing, is a socially significant practice. Unlike writing, however, it is absolutely context-specific" ("Post-Bourgeois Tattoo," 288). Since *Nightwood* refuses to link itself overtly with its political context, Nikka's tattooed body underscores right from the start what the novel purposely obscures — the body politic, its fascist opposite. Blanchard specifically notes the way tattooing blurs the boundaries between image (the tattoo) and reality (the body):

> Not only does tattooing . . . impose a distinction between marked and unmarked subjects, it also forces upon the viewer the perception of a special relation between image and support or frame. . . . There are cases of tattooing so extensive, for instance, that distinguishing the limits between the body and the image becomes impossible. ("Post-Bourgeois Tattoo," 288)

At times, Blanchard observes, a tattoo can even become a *"trompe l'oeil."* If one interprets Nikka's tattooed body as a metaphor for Barnes's experimental novel of resistance, then, like the tattooed body, *Nightwood* demands to be read and interpreted. On the other hand, the tattoos "from head to toe" can also obscure and draw attention away from the frame. The body politic becomes unreadable and opaque, fooling spectators into seeing only what the subject decides to project.[55] Nikka chooses his own form of communication by controlling the gaze of the viewer, much in the same the way as O'Connor lures his audience's attention with his story, and, in turn, Barnes as author draws the reader. By manipulating the viewer and taking ownership of the gaze, Nikka, and by extension O'Connor, subverts the reality of his position — that he is a commodity displayed for mass consumption to a desiring audience who projects a fantasy of primitive and deviant sexuality onto his body. Could this not be said of Barnes's novel as well?

## Conclusion

One wonders if *Nightwood*, like Nikka's tattoos, obscures the flesh and blood of a clear anti-Nazi message. Barnes's gesture of resistance recalls O'Connor's claim to Nora: "I have a narrative, but you will be hard put to find it" (NW, 32). In his 1937 introduction, T. S. Eliot insists one should not read the book as "a psychopathic study"—confirming that there is a tendency to read the book in just that way. Barnes asks readers to recognize themselves in the mesmerized audience who listen to O'Connor's tale, just as Woolf and Isherwood demand that their readers look at themselves in the audience of spectators. As Eliot asserts, readers are not supposed to be watching the group of outcasts from outside, considering themselves to be morally superior. They are asked to take themselves outside the "we" to examine closely the spectacle's effect — and in this way recognize and resist its allure. What remains unclear is whether these novels are successful in conveying a "story" of awareness and tolerance, or even a clear warning of the threat of Nazism and its ideology. Perhaps their position is best indicated by what O'Connor states: "Life is not to be told, call it as loud as you like, it will not tell itself" (NW, 129). These writers "tell" the story, but more important is how the reader participates in creating a life out of these novels by bringing them into conversation with the social, historical, and political contexts that lie outside the novel. Eliot is correct to caution readers to broaden their appraisal to extend it beyond the characters themselves. One could say the same about the readers of *Goodbye to Berlin* and *Between the Acts*. These three novels present examples of the "Other voices" that disrupt the easy categorization of human experience that the spectacle of fascism and Nazism promotes, but the onus is also on the reader to inspect these works as "crime scenes" that give clues to what lies beyond the borders of the page.

If Nikka's tattooed body can be a symbol for *Nightwood*, *Between the Acts*, and *Goodbye to Berlin*, then the message would be "writing resistance hurts." As Blanchard reminds his readers, tattooing "signifies the particular pain of having a message written or painted on and sent by one's own body" ("Post-Bourgeois Tattoo," 288). But it also has no purpose unless that body is seen and read by others. The next three chapters will examine how Woolf's, Isherwood's, and Barnes's texts portray the particular bodies that Nazism dominates and tries to obliterate from its unified utopian community — those of the Modern Woman, the Jew, and the homosexual. By making visible and celebrating those bodies that are exploited by Nazi propaganda to construct defined categories of self and Other and produce a nation of "pure" Aryans, *Between the Acts*, *Nightwood*, and *Goodbye to Berlin* challenge the hierarchies and social constructions upon which the myth of a Nazi *Volksgemeinschaft* relies. Nevertheless, I will demonstrate in the next chapter on the representation of female characters that the strategies Woolf, Isherwood, and Barnes use, and the discourses their texts participate in, are not all (or at least not all to the same degree) as resistant to misogyny, antisemitism, or homophobia as one might hope or expect. By analyzing the intersections of gender, race, and sexuality in these novels, I explore how it may be possible to resist fascist oppression toward women yet still convey misogynist viewpoints; oppose racism yet still be influenced by antisemitic attitudes; and support freedom of sexuality yet still rely on homophobic stereotyping.

CHAPTER 2

# Vamps, Tramps, and Nazis: Representations of Spectacular Female Characters

> The mission of women is to be beautiful and to bring
> children into the world. This is not at all as rude and
> unmodern as it sounds. The female bird pretties herself for
> her mate and hatches the eggs for him. In exchange, the mate
> takes care of gathering the food, and stands guard and wards
> off the enemy.
>
> —JOSEPH GOEBBELS (1929)

In *Between the Acts*, two paintings hang opposite a window: one is an image of a woman, "bought by Oliver because he liked the picture"; the other, a painting of a man, "an ancestor" (*BTA*, 33). The man "had a name." The woman did not. The uncanny silence and emptiness surrounding the image with no history and no story points to the stark reality of woman as image: "empty, empty, empty; silent, silent, silent" (*BTA*, 33). As the narrator observes, "He was a talk producer, that ancestor. But the lady was a picture. In her yellow robe, leaning, with a pillar to support her, a silver arrow in her hand, and a feather in her hair, she led the eye up and down, from the curve to the straight, through the glades of greenery and shades of silver, dun and rose into silence. The room was empty" (*BTA*, 33).

The images of the man and the woman that hang in the English country manor in Woolf's novel expose the significance of context in interpreting ideas of masculinity and womanliness during the 1930s. The man is an ancestor, linked with historical, familial, national, and even regional ties. The lady in the yellow robe, on the other hand, is just "a picture." Empty of its own historic context, the image of the woman is there solely to reflect those meanings that are projected onto her, filling the empty void of the "real" with a fantasy that points to a more beautiful, shimmering world of a mythic past. Indeed, the patriarchal icon of woman as mother, as nation, as savior, as temptress, and as past humanity now in ruins has had a long and durable history in Western literary and artistic imaginations. It is an image that never speaks back, that becomes a shell, "holding the still, distilled essence of emptiness, silence" (BTA, 34). Even today, the symbolic connotations of "woman" and "mother" remain irrevocable in contemporary media and national rhetoric. Essentialized "woman" has long stood as a representation of home, morality, religion, and even geographical location. Especially in modernity, the age of the reproduced image and spectatorship, the female body has functioned in a complex and often paradoxical manner — as a receptacle for fears, hopes, desires, and despair. Even as an icon for modernity itself. As Adrian Bingham observes in his study of the interwar British press, in both positive and negative conceptions, the modern young woman became "one of the most prominent and characteristic figures of post-war culture" (Gender, Modernity, 48). Modern Woman not only became an influential figure because she joined the work force, could vote, and began to participate in public culture; she was also considerably more visible in film, advertising, and magazines.

In the past few decades, numerous feminist and modernist scholars have observed the multiple ways in which the female figure in modernity came to define urban cosmopolitan culture while at the same time embodying a threat to patriarchal order through her new visibility in public culture.[1] In this chapter, I explore how popular media in England, in the United States, and in Weimar and Nazi Germany utilized "Modern Woman" allegorically to represent the allure, enthrallment, and dread of interwar liberalism, as well as the terror of the political, industrial, and social crises taking place in Europe between the two world wars. By setting up the context for female representation in the interwar period, I hope to unravel the historical complexities of how woman becomes a symbol of both adulation and revulsion in popular discourse, which was reflected and mirrored in anti-Nazi modernist fiction. Woolf's, Isherwood's, and Barnes's anti-Nazi strategies are often characterized by ambiguity and complicated by the discourse of their era, resulting in multifaceted but sometimes problematic expressions of resistance. In this chapter, I am specifically interested in interrogating how these writers — all of them marginal due to gender or sexual preference — use women as icons in their works. I thus probe how the concept of "image" and "woman" are joined in a metaphor that both Nazi and anti-Nazi discourses use in a parallel manner — as threat or beacon of a new, more liberal age, as victims or accomplices in the allure of mass culture, and as champions or collaborators of fascist ideology.

## Sexism, National Socialism, and the Female Spectacle

Although examples of antifeminine thought can be found in numerous societies, in every century, and within a variety of texts and cultural productions, it may be arguable that specifically within Western modern culture the image and function of "woman" begins to undergo a crucial transformation. The social, political, and scientific advances of modernity, which extended suffrage and opened more professions to women, undoubtedly increased their opportunities and influence.[2] This transformation did not necessarily indicate, however, that sexism and discriminatory attitudes toward women began to wane. As women's literacy increased and they began to acquire more prominent roles in social and political institutions, often men in positions of power — including clergy, government officials, economists, and members of the intelligentsia — increasingly pushed for more limitations on women's sphere of influence. As Elizabeth Fox-Genovese observes, "The more advanced the economy, the more likely the society was to advance an ideology of separate spheres to justify separate and unequal education for women and the exclusion of women from the emerging professions and political life" ("Culture and Consciousness," 542).[3] Bram Dijkstra, too, illustrates in his renowned analysis of images of women in fin-de-siècle paintings that representations of weak, sickly, morbid, or perverse women in visual cultural productions reveal modern man's preoccupation and anxiety with regard to women's place in the social order. Since modern scientific and economic developments "proved" women's natural inequality based on evolution, Dijkstra argues, what resulted was a "cultural war" over woman's image (*Idols of Perversity*, vii). At the same time, however, the image of woman played an important role as a national symbol. As George Mosse emphasizes in his influential work *Nationalism and Sexuality* (1985), "Always, woman exemplified virtue. . . . She was to be a guardian, protector, and mother" of the nation. Those women who could not live up to the ideal image of nationhood were consequently firmly put in their place, viewed, in Mosse's terms, as a "menace to society and the nation" (16, 90).[4]

These limiting configurations of woman in modernity can best be described as a process that feminist critic Alice Jardine calls "gynesis," whereby woman and the feminine become a discursive space for both the overrepresented "women" and the unrepresentable "woman" or "woman-in-effect" (a signifier rather than a subjective human being).[5] In other words, as a metaphor for modernity, woman becomes intrinsically connected with the crisis of subjectivity, identity, and new, visible conceptualizations of the self. Yet, the various observations of woman's ideological positioning in modern society do not contradict the fact that the Modern Woman had immense appeal and support in public culture. Liz Connor, for instance, argues that as a consumer of goods, as an audience member for cinema and other forms of cultural production, and as a reader and writer, the Modern Woman could now determine and manipulate the circulation of her own image in mass media. Connor aptly coins the term "Modern Appearing Woman" to connote those ways in which women emerged through conditions of modernity and also identified themselves with that image in the urban scene (*Spectacular Modern Woman*, 2). The woman as reproduced media image (rather than as a "real" person), Connor observes, increasingly highlighted modernity's relationship with the visible and thus challenged ideas of identity and subjectivity.[6] Likewise, as I argue later, Woolf's, Barnes's, and Isherwood's female characters indicate that women of the period could simultaneously resist their constructions as objects or fetishized spectacles, while at the same time manipulating those same conditions that make them visible for personal gain. Nevertheless, at the base of those constructions, as these novels imply, there must be an element that is part of a social, political entity with ethical responsibilities toward humanity.

The expectation that the Modern Woman had moral and ethical obligations to uphold, as well as her association with popular and mass cultural spectatorship, not surprisingly also made her the ambiguous target of antifascist intellectuals and left-wing artists. Andreas Huyssen, for example, notes that mass culture is gendered feminine and woman mediated male modernists' fear of it. Commenting on the late nineteenth- and early twentieth-century views of the masses, especially Gustave Le Bon's influential book *The Crowd*,[7] Huyssen observes:

> The fear of the masses in this age of declining liberalism is always also a fear of woman, a fear of nature out of control, a fear of the unconscious, of sexuality, of the loss of identity and stable ego boundaries of the mass. The male fear of woman and the bourgeois fear of the masses become indistinguishable. (*After the Great Divide*, 52)

By extension, in the context of the Great Divide between high art and mass culture, the dichotomy was traditionally gendered male/female as well.[8] The notion that a masculine high modernism could resist the ruinous effects of mass culture was reflected in the hostile attitudes that modern theorists such as Adorno and Horkheimer expressed toward "feminized" forms of entertainment, including film. In *The Dialectic of Enlightenment*, they additionally insist that women are more vulnerable to the allure of totalitarianism because they are easily drawn to the passive acceptance of mass culture.[9] Their attitudes, as Patrice Petro posits, may well have been influenced by the emergence of a new audience of women in cinema theaters, which threatened the illusion of male cultural authority and "distinctions preserving traditionally defined male and female gender roles" (*Joyless Streets*, 8). Yet, while these observations are germane to my study of how women were constructed in discourse of the period, I nevertheless restate my view here that these binary paradigms of modernity and gender division fail to take into consideration the differentiation among that "mass" of culture and the various attitudes toward popular culture at the time. More recent studies on female public intellectuals problematize nuanced terms like "modernism," "popular culture," and "mass culture."[10] Moreover, these types of binary paradigms do not account for the influence and popularity of female intellectuals and producers (and consumers) of interwar

British and American modernist writing such as Woolf, Storm Jameson, Rebecca West, Gertrude Stein, Harriet Monroe, Mina Loy, Dorothy Parker, and Edna St. Vincent Millay, among the many other significant female poets, writers, journalists, and artists whose audiences were both male and female.

The gendered divide of the spectator-subject relationship, too, often assumes a somewhat limiting conception of who is doing the looking and who is being looked at. In most conceptions of modern spectatorship, the spectator is male while the spectacle-object is female. I would like to contest this type of categorization by linking the two types of modern spectatorship that are the basis of my argument—female spectacle and Nazi spectacle. Since Nazi culture transforms or "bends" the relationship between spectacle and spectator, I propose that women's construction of their own image challenges the idea at the base of Nazi spectatorship. Bearing in mind that women were both spectators (and readers) and creators of public art, I investigate how Woolf's and Barnes's novels overturn the paradigm of the female spectacle. Specifically, they position certain female characters as what Connor calls "Modern Appearing Women" to function as metaphors or narrative strategies in their critiques of fascist ideologies. I also examine how Isherwood more problematically represents female characters in his critique of the public's acceptance of Nazism in Germany. As I demonstrate, as allegories, "spectacular" female characters reveal the multiple and contradictory ways that "Modern Woman" is used within a political discourse in a way that both idealizes and castigates her behavior in moral terms.

I base my conception of the female spectacle largely within the theoretical context of what Susan Buck-Morss identifies as a "dialectics of seeing" in modernity most commonly identified with Benjamin's theories of the flâneur. In "The Flaneur, the Sandwichman and the Whore," Buck-Morss explains that even more than a social type, Benjamin's flâneur—based on Baudelaire's gentleman city stroller as detached observer of the modern urban experience—was an emblem of modern subjectivity and a symbol of the changes brought on by the transformation of space (and movement through space) due to capitalism, consumerism, and technology. The flâneur epitomized the "modern" man, moving through the urban scene to observe and be observed as spectacle and spectator. Because modern mass production spilled over into the streets, Benjamin's flâneur "could maintain a rhapsodic view of modern existence only with the aid of illusion" (Buck-Morss, "Flaneur," 101–3). That is to say, the noise, shops, and fast pace of the modern urban scene contributed to the individual's desire for fantasy — an image of an ideal city. As Buck-Morss makes clear, the privilege of the male in the public space is obvious — "all women who loitered risked being seen as whores." What is key to gendered paradigms of viewing based on "flânerie," Buck-Morss explains, is that the flâneur becomes a figure that corresponds to modern ways of seeing and perceiving, while the "whore" symbolizes "the transformation of objects, the world of things" (ibid., 120). Since her sexuality itself acts as a commodity, it not only "takes on [the commodity's] allure" but also frees men to consume without the "elaborately regulated and constrained exchange of women as gifts" in courtship and marriage (ibid., 119–20).[11]

The paradigm of the "male gaze" situating itself on a commodified female object is elaborated upon repeatedly in feminist film theory. Most famously, Laura Mulvey in her 1975 essay "Visual Pleasure and Narrative Cinema" maintains that women have been reduced to objects of the male gaze that "projects its phantasy on to the female figure" in Hollywood movies. She coins the term "female spectacle" to explain how the icon of woman itself connotes "to-be-looked-at-ness" (11). As Mulvey argues, the spectator's fascination with film is based in the patriarchal order that involves an erotic pleasure of looking as well as a fear of castration that "freezes the look, fixates the spectator, and prevents him from achieving distance from the image in front of him" (18). Similar to the way Woolf describes the empty silence surrounding the "picture" of the woman in the yellow robe in *Between the Acts* (33), for Mulvey, to be a female spectacle is to remain always "the silent image of woman still tied to her place as bearer of meaning, not the maker of meaning" (7). This notion of the objectified female figure of male voyeurism on screen has been the foundation for extremely productive discussions of gender and spectatorship for the past three decades. One of the problems with this model, however, as only a few critics have noted, is that it does not include other types of spectatorship that extend beyond the typical gender divide.[12] For example, Mulvey's theory eliminates possibilities such as female fantasy, same-sex desire, and transsexual spectatorship (something she herself addresses in later works). It also relegates female creators of the spectacle to assuming "a masquerade" of male perspective to produce their art. For the female to be spectator, in Mulvey's conception, a female viewer would have to assume a male viewpoint. Moreover, because the female spectator overidentifies with the spectacle, she is unable to separate herself from it. Thus, according to Mulvey, as well as those critics whose analyses are influenced by her, there are only two ways a female spectator can participate in this paradigm: to either identify with the male gaze or be the passive object of desire.[13]

Although Mulvey's view of the female spectacle broke ground for new ways of theorizing gender and spectatorship in feminist film theory, it leaves the female viewer, the female artist, and the same-sex-identified viewer with extraordinarily limited options. Even more so, to take a close look at representations of women in literature, film, and magazines of the interwar era is to observe multifarious, heterogeneous, and often paradoxical representations of gender in both art and mass media. After all, the modern era ushered in a period when women appeared more frequently in public culture and also began playing more vital roles in the public sphere. Female intellectuals, writers, artists, and public figures such as Woolf, Barnes, Rebecca West, and Dorothy Parker spoke out in public, wrote articles for newspapers, and frequently appeared in the media, thus bridging gaps between (feminine) private and (masculine) public spheres. Melba Cuddy-Keane and Anna Snaith, for instance, examine Woolf's involvement in the public sphere and influence among "common readers" as a writer of informal essays and supporter of women's causes.[14] Various other studies on female writers, journalists, and artists of the 1930s (Plain, Joannou, Lassner, Suh) also indicate that female public intellectuals had varying degrees of cultural and political sway on the public.

Rather than imagining woman as a passive object in a long history of female objectification, then, close readings of cultural texts from the period can also reveal how representations of the Modern Woman often illustrate conflicting ideas of gender identity and possibilities for female subjectivity. As Connor asserts, Modern Woman often chose to "appear," placing herself as the center of media and public attention to produce new opportunities for subjectivity. Thus her positioning in the public eye could also be seen as a purposeful, active construction of her own subjectivity (*Spectacular Modern Woman*, 2). At the same time, however, when real women were attempting to break out of preconceived notions of femininity — to be "glamorous spectacles" rather than virtuous and faithful caregivers — they were also perceived with suspicion (ibid., 25). In Britain and the United States, for example, the "flapper" of the twenties often appeared in fashion magazines and film as a figure that was whimsical, but at the same time associated with illusion, guile, and duplicity.[15] Surveys of English media indicate that numerous newspapers and magazines perceived the Modern Woman's or flapper's unisex clothing and short hair as "unnatural" and morally dubious and suspected her of jeopardizing "healthy" conceptions of female and male sexual identities (Petro, *Joyless Streets*, 119). Attitudes toward the Modern Woman arguably became even more conservative in the 1930s, when competition for jobs and lower birthrates gave rise to a morally conservative backlash toward women.[16]

Parallel conflicting attitudes concerning the Modern Woman are reflected in studies on female representation in the German media from 1920 to 1940 with some very significant differences. Whereas most often Weimar Berlin is associated with sexual freedom, broadminded views, and decadence, many scholars have argued that, for women, the sexual liberation movement hid a more normalizing agenda which readily transformed into systematic oppression by the Nazis. Renate Bridenthal, Atina Grossman, and Marion Kaplan, for example, observe that while Weimar culture produced "a certain heady and intoxicating sense of freedom in the big cities," it also recognized that the emergence of the Modern Woman was a threat to the family and postwar attempts to increase population (*When Biology Became Destiny*, 11). Similar to Connor's observations, they contend the Modern Woman in Germany was much more than "images of the flapper or sexy saleslady convey" — these were individuals who had a powerful impact on society. Women were influential consumers of cinema, clothing, and other cultural products. For this reason, rather than only signaling female emancipation in Weimar Germany, to some the Modern Woman "stood at the nexus of the 'morality question,'" illustrating a much larger social and moral crisis. As the close examination of Weimar liberalism in *When Biology Became Destiny* reveals, the images of women "captured the imagination of progressives who celebrated her" and also that of "conservatives who blamed her for everything from the decline of the birth rate and the laxity of morals to the unemployment of male workers" (ibid., 13). At either end, and despite her inspiration for reform, woman remained an instrument for the ideological agenda of both liberals and conservatives alike. Atina Grossman's study of the sex reform movement in Germany in the 1920s emphasizes that even the so-called sexual emancipation of Weimar Germany that sought to legalize abortion and contraception and provide sex education hid a more insidious social engineering agenda. As she asserts, the image of the Modern Woman was conflated with images of the "young stenotypist and working mother" whose "sexual satisfaction [could provide] an antidote to the depressed family or social crisis." Rather than sexual freedom, the focus on expressions of female sexuality was "made functional for the good of society" (Grossman, "New Woman," 158, 166–67). Sexual satisfaction became a woman's duty.

The image of the Modern Woman is transformed into a far more sinister character in Germany after 1933, when representations of modern decadence become far more malicious than in Britain or the United States.[17] Sabine Hake, in particular, notes how the attack on the liberalism of Weimar culture became more prominent after 1933—as did the enlistment of female filmic characters to represent the depravity of an oppressive modernity. Similarly, Petro's observations of Weimar German cinema reveal that by the mid-1930s film began to associate modernity "with difficult domestic settings and inappropriate personal choices" that focused specifically on the "troublesome incarnation in the single career woman and her (ill-advised) quests for individual self-fulfillment" (*Joyless Streets*, 60). The Modern Woman in 1930s Nazi mass media, rather than appearing defiant or morally ambiguous, was now portrayed as sexually aggressive and seditious, blamed for the moral decay of Weimar society. The emancipated woman in Germany soon became the target of an attack on "immorality" and "race defilement" that Nazism promised to squelch. In 1938, for example, *Das Schwarze Korps* (The Black Corps), the popular weekly newspaper of the Schutzstaffel (SS), showcased two full-page photo spreads contrasting the "beautiful and pure" Aryan female body, depicted by wholesome nude women at the beach, with the "shameless, money-making" Weimar woman, portrayed excessively made-up and half-clothed (Herzog, *Sexuality and German Fascism*, 12).[18] Often womanliness was also linked to Jews, who defied clear national or racial categorization and were accused of defective moral qualities and "effeminate" emotional weakness. These concepts were largely based on Otto Weininger's immensely influential 1903 *Geschlecht und Charakter* (Sex and Character), which asserted that Jews were "saturated with femininity" (306). At the same time, female Jews were characterized as "manly," responsible for the promotion of women's emancipation that was eroding the nation.[19]

The intersections of both sexism and racism become clear when examining the role women and the female spectacle played in imagining a unified German *Volksgemeinschaft*, the "people's community." The blame the Nazis tried to place on capitalists, Marxists, and Jews for the misery of social and economic depression extended to women as well. In particular, the German "stab in the back" myth became increasingly popular in right-wing propaganda, blaming women, Jews, and Communists for the army's defeat in World War I due to their subversion "on the home front" (Bridenthal, Grossman, and Kaplan, eds., *When Biology Became Destiny*, 7). Middle-class women, as Gisela Bock indicates, were held responsible for the drop in population, while poor women were blamed for too many children: a phenomenon perceived as "racial degeneration" or "race suicide." Aryan women, on the other hand, were expected to play a crucial role in building a new, wholesome, racially correct society by staying home and raising healthy children, as the propagandist motto *Kinder, Küche, Kirche* (Children, Kitchen, Church) implied. Propaganda had the difficult task, as Bock shows, of persuading racially "superior" women to have more children, while forcing "inferior" women to have fewer or none at all ("Racism and Sexism," 276).

In 1933, soon after Hitler became chancellor, the Nazis removed married women under the age of thirty-five from civil service positions, introduced a 10 percent quota for female students at universities, and closed birth control clinics in urban centers (Bridenthal et al., *When Biology Became Destiny*, 20–21). The most terrifying outcome of reducing women to reproductive objects, however, was the Nazi regime's sterilization policies, which were part of a larger race policy between 1933 and 1939. Even before 1933, the medical establishment lobbied for legislation that would require mandatory sterilization for promiscuous women, prostitutes, schizophrenics, and other "undesirables" (Bock, "Racism and Sexism," 276; Heineman, "Sexuality and Nazism,"

50). By 1933 the Law for the Prevention of Hereditarily Diseased Off-spring firmly established the Nazi agenda for social control by means of repressive measures toward women. The sterilization law, enforced in 1934, applied to a wide range of "just causes" for women's sterilization, including mental health, "feeblemindedness," alcoholism, physical "in-validity," and "defective kin" (Bock, "Racism and Sexism," 280).[20] As Bock records, "During the nearly five and one-half years preceding the outbreak of World War II, about 320,000 persons (nearly 0.5 percent of the population) were sterilized under the terms of this law" (280–81).[21] Race sterilization soon spread to the outright execution of 5,000 "unde-sirable" children under the age of sixteen in 1939–40 (ibid., 282). Thus oppression of women occurred even before the mass murder of Jews and political enemies through legislation regarding who was "fit" to repro-duce and who was not.[22]

For theorists such as Klaus Theweleit, Nazi sexism was not only deadly — it was also the core of National Socialism's relationship to a "life-destroying reality" (*Male Fantasies*, 227). Men who embraced fascist violence, according to Theweleit's well-known 1987 study of the *Freikorps*, did so to battle the "fluid" and "messy" threat of women (linked with the image of Communist revolutionary movements) and to establish an orderly, unified conception of self.[23] To examine Nazism, he thus asserts, one must examine male-female relations as an extension of how these men built a relationship with their reality. This premise, however, still makes it difficult to understand how National Socialism became as popular as it did. After all, the party was widely supported by both men *and* women. Moreover, the danger in conceiving the *Frei-korps* (or other Hitler supporters, for that matter) as monstrous killers created by specific historical and psychological contingencies is that one risks failing to learn the lessons of history and to recognize other elements that could have led to the Nazis' gross abuse of power. It is im-portant to consider the reasons why women, too, voted for the Nazis.[24] Since so many women supported, even championed, Hitler, it would appear that the kind of desires or fantasies National Socialism fulfilled went beyond the material aspects of women's freedoms and rights under the Third Reich.[25] Dagmar Herzog, for example, pertinently insists that rather than working to consolidate power through fear alone, the Nazis "also used sexuality to consolidate their appeal" (*Sexuality and German*

*Fascism*, 3). Premarital sex (and sexual freedom in general) was not necessarily taboo, as Herzog and Elizabeth Heineman have convincingly argued, as long as it was "healthy sex" between genetically favorable partners. Moreover, women who played key roles in the Nazi Party felt that National Socialism protected and secured their power and positions in society as mothers and family caretakers. The fantasy and empowerment that National Socialism provided nevertheless hid a malevolence that both eradicated their rights and created the atmosphere of denial that facilitated genocide — even made it possible. Then again, women who gained influence in the party chose to be ignorant of the racial policies and terror tactics of the state, or "organized motherliness" that covered up the brutality of the Nazis, "so the world would appear normal and virtuous to the average German citizens and to the most murderous SS men" (Koonz, *Mothers*, 228). It is specifically this dangerous aspect of the Nazi spectacle, and women's willing participation in it, that Woolf, Isherwood, and Barnes explore in their works.

With these historical aspects of the female image in mind, I begin my analysis of the female spectacle and its relationship to the Nazi spectacle in *Between the Acts*, *Goodbye to Berlin*, and *Nightwood* with a number of questions. Firstly, while these writers clearly acknowledge sexism as a precursor to more dangerous forms of terror, there is still a paradox in the way women are depicted stereotypically in the novels to mediate the anxieties surrounding Nazi ideology and women's position in a fascist dictatorship. Often the representations of women in these works are ironic, clear parodies of how women are socially and culturally constructed, but it is unquestionably female characters who are the most eager devotees of mass culture, crowd mentality, and even Nazi racism in the novels. To point to the title of this chapter, women in these texts are either "vamps, tramps, or Nazis." To what degree, then, do Woolf's, Barnes's, and Isherwood's narrative strategies resist sexism, and at what point do they inevitably participate in the processes of "gynesis" that reduce women, to use Jardine's term, to "woman-in-effect"? Or would it be just as narrow-minded and irresponsible to portray only "good" female characters rather than figures who reflect popular trends of the time? What possibilities exist for the modern female spectator, or viewer, within a gendered spectacle/spectator binary theoretical framework? Is she the spectacle? The mass audience? Or, is she theorized completely out of consideration except as the object or victim of Nazi oppression?

Mindful that one cannot project contemporary feminist theory onto these writers, I contend that Woolf, Barnes, and Isherwood include representations of women as critiques of fascism in a way that extends beyond the binary logic of the Nazi spectator as passively female, or the female spectacle as passive object of an aggressively male (subject) gaze. Woolf, Barnes, and Isherwood understood that national identity, oppression, and even racism are all related to sexuality and sexual difference as it is perceived visually. Their novels share the common feature of destabilizing sexual identities by overturning perceptions of gender norms. As I will illustrate, in parallel manners the three novels highlight the fact that the "feminine" is a performance — a "story" or visual construct and manifestation, as opposed to a set of biological traits. Women's "fictional" bodies become, like the author's text, a body of work that challenges the illusion-inspiring spectacle with their own brand of illusion-making. Yet, each of these authors also reveals ambivalence toward the notion that an individual's interaction with society can only be based on a self-centered resistant "act." To various degrees, the novels imply that although it is important to resist society's cultural constructions, women must not reject their ethical responsibilities as individuals in society. When the fantasy of the created self facilitates discrimination, or obscures the fate of Others, as these texts warn, that is when fascist ideology has room to maneuver. It would thus seem that these novels, to various degrees, imply that the "ideal woman" not only engages in self-fulfillment and self-creation, but also participates in, and is responsible for, resisting the oppressive ideologies of the larger group. Yet, once again, one wonders what kind of community these writers envision, and how much they are affected by their own cultural assumptions of "ways of being" that are then projected onto and judged using the ubiquitous metaphor of the "Modern Woman."

### Tramps: "How they bored her — her own sex!" In Defense of Mrs. Manresa

Starting with Woolf is an obvious choice when examining the connection between sexism and political oppression. Her reading notes, newspaper clippings, diaries, and essays during the 1930s all point to her perpetual preoccupation with the effects of patriarchy and sexism on women's private lives and on entire political systems. Dictatorship, for Woolf, was not a remote and distant threat — it existed in the everyday relations between the sexes. For many feminist scholars, a common way to read Woolf's work is to be uncritical of her assumptions, projecting the scholars' own beliefs, hopes, and desires onto an "ideal Virginia Woolf." As Brenda Silver points out in *Virginia Woolf Icon*, analyses of Woolf are often filtered by "those who insist on a Virginia Woolf made only in their image, an 'authentic,' legitimate Virginia Woolf to whom, they assert, they have a direct line" (5). She becomes second-wave feminist, historical materialist, avant-garde feminist, postfeminist, and even antifeminist. To quote Christy Burns, Woolf is "the American feminist's favorite cultural icon, the mother to whom we turn in hope of finding a mirror of ourselves." Of course, as Burns aptly notes, the tendency to project one's own desires onto Woolf is, in essence, "another bad cliché of the woman who can mutate to become whatever society demands of her" ("Re-Dressing Feminist Identities," 343). In other words, using Woolf to fit one's image of her would defeat the purpose of reading her critically, skeptically, and closely. Burns's observations certainly ring true when considering the various interpretations of *Between the Acts* that glorify Woolf as icon of pro-feminist pacifism. It is probably more realistic and productive to view Woolf in light of the ambiguities in her work rather than imposing "easy polarizations that make assumptions about male and female character" (Beer, *Common Ground*, 133). Indisputably, Woolf is one of the most astute critics of the sex-gender system of her time, whose thinking clearly anticipates contemporary theories of gender, but she is also a product of her social, class, and cultural context.

In *Three Guineas*, for example, Woolf proposes that sex-based oppression in Britain is directly linked to fascism, but history has shown that this type of analogy distorts the stark distinctions between Nazism and democratic patriarchy. In retrospect, a correlation between British discrimination against women and the violence and murderous outcome of National Socialism is highly problematic — even, I would argue, obscene. I would agree with Laura Frost, who points out that some contemporary feminists are "deeply invested in an analogy between fascism and patriarchy," especially since it buttresses the argument for the very real potential dangers of sexism. The comparison of these two distinct types of oppression nevertheless discounts the specific aggressiveness and racism of fascist violence while also building upon an extremely narrow view of female (and male) desire (Frost, *Sex Drives*, 121). Woolf's idea that the male psyche is somehow inherently attuned toward an impulse for violence is clearly contentious. Moreover, as Phyllis Lassner suggests, there is much to challenge in Woolf's attitude that "women are only passive war victims, war protesters, or complicit with the power of a masculinist war machine" (*British Women Writers*, 4). The complexity of women's attitudes to war in the 1930s, as Lassner shows, is much broader. Absolute adherence to the pacifist doctrine in the context of World War II and the rise of Nazism was increasingly seen by many formerly pacifist male and female intellectuals as unfeasible, and even unjust, in light of the brutal and cruel antisemitic and racist agenda promoted by the Nazi regime.[26]

Despite Woolf's views in *Three Guineas* that the only justifiable war protest is through "indifference," it is possible to read *Between the Acts* as a work that proposes an alternate, wider possibility for resistance to Nazism. In agreement with critics such as Alex Zwerdling, Pamela Caughie, and Anna Snaith, I interpret Woolf's work as a reflection of her ambiguous attitudes toward and mistrust of partisanship and militarism. One is reminded of Zwerdling's insistence that "Hers was a writer's resistance. She used her pen to undermine what she took to be the foundations of war: militarism and nationalism" (*Real World*, 274). In the context of World War II, it is possible to interpret Woolf's fictional resistance as extending beyond her critique of what Lassner refers to as a "metahistorical and pancultural construction of fascism" (*British Women Writers*, 4) to a more specific reaction to Hitler and the threat of a Nazi invasion. Even so, as mentioned previously, Woolf also participates in a social discourse that reflects problematic constructions of gender and sexuality and ignores some of the more serious implications of Nazi oppression. The supposedly confusing opaqueness of *Between the Acts* paradoxically provides a less occluded view of the hesitant nature of Woolf's stance toward gender, sexuality, and fascism than do the more frequently analyzed political essays.

Appropriately, as a reflection of the wide spectrum of human experience in interwar Europe, in *Between the Acts* female characters appear as alternately virtuous, spirited, and unsure, and also sanctimonious, overbearing, insipid, or even downright malevolent. In short—they represent human beings. Undoubtedly, it is nonetheless Miss La Trobe who draws the most attention from critics seeking to discern Woolf's critique of dictatorships, totalitarianism, and patriarchal sexism in *Between the Acts*.[27] For a novel that contains no clear protagonist, Woolf scholars are determinably fascinated by La Trobe, the "bossy" lesbian pageant-master whose lack of personal appeal and charm drives her to the sidelines, or "behind the bushes," of Pointz Hall society. "Oh to write a play without an audience," La Trobe laments (*BTA*, 161). Often La Trobe is interpreted as the key to understanding the novel. Michele Pridmore-Brown, for example, examines La Trobe as "the antithesis of the fuehrer figure" since she "destabilizes not only gender dichotomies but also political ones . . . the very dichotomies that lead to war and systematized oppression" ("Woolf, Gramophones, and Fascism," 415). Similarly, Anna Snaith interprets La Trobe as an emblem for artistic struggle in reaction to the political situation from 1938 to 1941. As Snaith notes, La Trobe wants to engage members of the audience, and they want to be summed up by the pageant, but her pageant refuses fascist unity: "Holes mark the resistance to wholes" (*Public and Private*, 148). Others, such as Patricia Joplin and Bonnie Kime Scott, draw parallels between La Trobe and the figure of the dictator. Joplin observes that the troubling "proximity of artist to dictator" is revealed when La Trobe "succumbs to the temptation to treat meaning as 'hers'" ("Authority of Illusion," 89, 90). By the end of the play, La Trobe's totalitarian control of the audience, players, and meaning is finally relinquished when, as Scott remarks, "Miss La Trobe has been to Fascism and back" ("Subversive Mechanics," 105).

La Trobe is indeed an intriguing character. I would also agree with Catherine Wiley, who comments that La Trobe is more likely "all of these things: would-be dictator, would-be saviour . . . an artist with a vision" ("Making History," 15). Yet, what I find even more interesting is why La Trobe garners so much more scholarly attention than the other director and producer of a key performance in the novel who also overturns social and gender constructions—Mrs. Manresa. Both characters, after all, are captivating for the same reasons that fascism and Nazism are "fascinating"; they reveal that domination can be pleasurable—even for a woman. La Trobe seduces her audience into submission at the same time that Manresa plays the lead role of her own play, enticing spectators to participate in her act. In this way, Woolf draws the reader into observing the elements that attract individuals to the spectacle and dramaturgy of dictatorships. Even in *Three Guineas,* as Frost notes, "Woolf does recognize the figure of the dictator as seductive. When she describes Francisco Franco's dictatorship it is to present a picture that is exciting" (*Sex Drives,* 130). Although in her diary Woolf describes Hitler's "strangled hysterical sobbing swearing ranting" in much less appealing terms (*D,* 5: 245), her notebooks reveal that she was nevertheless exploring the public appeal of such a figure. As the novel insinuates, the relationship between dictator and public is not necessarily one of male domination versus female passivity and victimhood. Manresa, like La Trobe, is alluringly described in terms of a goddess, queen, dictator, and artist. Through both characters, Woolf reveals that sexual relationships are linked to political ones and simultaneously registers the complicated association of artistic production with mass manipulation.

Why, then, do critics love to shower attention on Miss La Trobe while giving Mrs. Manresa the brush-off? Although Manresa takes up as much "page space" as Isa, Giles, Dodge, and Lucy Swithin, for the most part she receives but a line or two of mention in the majority of analyses of the text. Moreover, while a number of critics have drawn connections between sex and violence in *Between the Acts,*[28] I wonder if it appears to be problematic for critics to read sex as being pleasurable in the novel. As the audience members of the pageant murmur, "why always drag in sex. . . . It's true, there's a sense in which we all, I admit, are savages still" (*BTA,* 179). Does sex, both hetero- and homosexual, necessarily have to be "savage," or insufferable and nasty? On balance, Mrs. Manresa is perhaps one of the most sexually charged characters in all of Woolf's canon, and yet, if mentioned at all, she is most often described in the most pejorative terms: as a sexual pariah, "the townee whose name is that of a Chelsea street as well as a pun on 'manraiser' or cock-teaser" (Beer, *Common Ground,* 143); a symbol of the "savage," "primitive" elements of nature, or "sexually voracious, uninhibitedly vulgar" (Jacobs, *Eye's Mind,* 233); or even as "a fraud" whose performance of class "solidifies power of those inside" (Johnston, "Class Performances," 65).[29] It is difficult not to notice how these descriptions of Manresa uncannily echo the stereotypical ways in which the Modern Woman is used to allude to the threat of modernity and its uncontrolled consumerism — both sexual and material.

One wonders if these interpretations of the text reflect Woolf's, the narrator's, or the critics' own prejudices. The text also positions Manresa as part of the urban masses who invade the genteel, respectable realm of Pointz Hall. As Andreas Huyssen points out, the association of the Modern Woman with mass culture was a political threat as well. The antagonism toward Mrs. Manresa conveyed in the novel could be interpreted as the bourgeois "fear of the masses," which Huyssen maintains was associated with "a fear of woman, a fear of nature out of control, a fear of the unconscious, of sexuality, of the loss of identity and stable ego boundaries in the mass" (*After the Great Divide*, 52). Even more disturbingly, because of Mrs. Manresa's association with Ralph Manresa's Jewishness, the parallels between her depiction as a sexually voracious gold digger and Nazi propagandist portrayals of the Modern Woman as seductive Jewess are especially distressing. Mrs. Manresa's materialism is not unconnected from her associations with her Jewish businessman husband.

Nevertheless, I find it difficult to read Mrs. Manresa as being as one-sided as all that. In my opinion, those who dismiss Mrs. Manresa as a promiscuous "tramp" neglect an opportunity to explore and negotiate the meanings around her character and the more complicated ways in which she is deployed to expose assumptions regarding gender relations and intolerance. Even the character's curious surname, Manresa, echoes a more complex association with a history (both recent and past) of oppression based on difference. Of course, the name "Manresa" easily puns with her effect on men. It could also be a sign of the arbitrariness of lineage: Ralph Manresa quite possibly named himself after a street in Chelsea, or purposefully adopted a so-called Christian name to assimilate into English society more easily. Nevertheless, Manresa has other historical and political connotations. It is most famously known as the town in Catalonia, Spain, where Saint Ignatius Loyola, founder of the Society of Jesus, stopped to pray in a cave for several months on his way back from Montserrat in 1522. Obviously, any connection between Mrs. Manresa and Catholic aestheticism or religious meditation is slim indeed, unless it is a gesture of irony. Farther back in history, however, Manresa was home to a thriving Jewish community, known for its prosperous involvement in manufacturing, trading, moneylending, and the cultivation of vineyards. Hostilities toward the Jewish community began in the fourteenth century when Christian inhabitants prevented Jews from baking Passover bread. By 1391 most Jews were forced to convert or flee, and by 1492 virtually no Jews were left in the Spanish city.[30] It would be tricky to ascertain whether Woolf knew the Jewish history of the town, but its chronicle of racism and intolerance undoubtedly has relevance in a European context in 1939, and especially in connection to the Spanish Civil War (1936–39).

Notably, the city of Manresa was also a stronghold of left-wing revolutionary activity during the civil war in Spain, where anticlerical mobs of the Popular Front destroyed nearly all the churches and convents (aside from the cathedral) in 1936. Allusions to Manresa, thereby, support the notion that the destructive forces of other forms of fascism are never far from the surface of *Between the Acts*. Woolf's diaries and reading notebooks in the late 1930s indicate that Spain, Franco, and the Spanish Civil War are a constant preoccupation. Woolf's diary records the Madrid massacres and the sight of Spanish children who were evacuated to London in June 1937, a "long trail of fugitives" (*D*, 5: 97). Only one month later, on July 20, 1937, she writes of "incredible suffering" upon receiving news of her nephew Julian Bell's death in the war in Spain (*D*, 5: 104). Brenda Silver's work on Woolf's notebooks reveals that Woolf regularly clipped newspaper articles and read information on the Spanish war. She also read Louis Delaprée's pamphlet *The Martyrdom of Madrid*, outlining the bombardment and massacre of Spanish civilians during November and December 1936, and she and Leonard signed a letter asking the English government to "take every legitimate opportunity" to help the Spanish people (Silver, ed., *Virginia Woolf's Reading Notebooks*, 285, 305).[31]

Important news from Spain, especially in *The Times*, as Emily Dalgarno observes, was nevertheless soon eclipsed by the abdication of King Edward VIII on December 10, 1936 (the same time as the Battle of Madrid), and the coronation of King George VI in May 1937, two weeks after the destruction of Guernica (*Visible World*, 160). Woolf's critique of the superficial pageantry and spectacle of English institutions of power such as royalty are made obvious in *Three Guineas*. The prominence of the abdication and coronation, however, is also alluded to in *Between the Acts* and linked to Mrs. Manresa. As the narrator wryly comments, although "gossip" surrounds Mrs. Manresa's former relationships, "surely with George the Sixth on the throne it was old fashioned . . . to go ferreting into people's pasts?" (*BTA*, 37). Mrs. Manresa's showiness and artifice also obscure the serious implications of oppressive politics and its connections to patriarchy. Perhaps for this reason it is hardly surprising that a character such as Mrs. Manresa is cast in a negative light. In essays such as *Three Guineas* and "Thoughts of Peace in an Air Raid" Woolf clearly blames women like Manresa for being catalysts for male oppression in their support of war and aggression. In "Thoughts of Peace in an Air Raid," for example, Woolf notes, "We can see women gazing; painted women; dressed up women; women with crimson lips and crimson fingernails. They are slaves who are trying to enslave. If we could free ourselves from slavery we should free men from tyranny. Hitlers are bred by slaves" (*DM*, 155). The description of "crimson fingernails" in the essay leaves no doubt of the parallel to Mrs. Manresa, who paints her fingernails "red as roses" (*BTA*, 36).

Mrs. Manresa undoubtedly represents the negative aspects of self-centered materialism, being the most "fake" and "unnatural" of characters in a novel that clearly opposes artifice and illusion. She wears glitzy rings on her fingers and polishes her nails, listens to popular music, reads romance novels, and goes out at midnight in silk pajamas. "We're all flesh and blood" is Manresa's motto (*BTA*, 36), pointing to a disregard for social propriety, as well as the intellectual, artistic, and moral facets of "civilized" social conduct. Moreover, Manresa is solely identified by her relationship with men — we never even learn if she has a first name — but what seems most disturbing to the residents of Pointz Hall is that she has no pedigree and her history is unknown. Rumor has it that she was born in Tasmania, that her grandfather was a convict, and that she had an uncle who was a colonial bishop where morals are lax: "They forgot and forgave very easily in the colonies" (*BTA*, 37). The narrator hints that she is a gold digger, having attained her diamonds and rubies from a previous "husband," and that she is with her current husband, a Jew, because he has "tons of money" (*BTA*, 37). She also has no children, making her role in society and relationship with Ralph Manresa perplexing. Compared with Isa, whose identity and social positioning are built upon her well-established roles within the patriarchal family—she is "Sir Richard's daughter" (*BTA*, 13) and the wife of Giles, who "is my husband" and "the father of my children" (*BTA*, 13, 44)— Mrs. Manresa's placement within a family structure is unclear. Even if Isa "loathed the domestic, the possessive; the maternal" (*BTA*, 17), she is still a dutiful wife and mother. Manresa, on the other hand, is a frivolous pleasure seeker, a "wild child of nature" (*BTA*, 38).

Yet, while it may be difficult to reconcile Mrs. Manresa's superficiality with Woolf's ardent antifascist ideology and concern with oppression, Manresa is not completely unlikeable. She is one of the few independent female characters with agency and autonomy who is willing and able to make decisions about how to use her body. Many readers, I suspect, would secretly confess they would rather spend an afternoon listening to jazz, eating bonbons, and weaving colorful baskets with gossipy Manresa than interacting with angst-ridden Isa, devout Swithin, morose Dodge, or bossy, short-tempered La Trobe. Moreover, I find myself skeptical of the view that Woolf, whose circle of Bloomsbury friends were known for their sexual liberalism, would find sex outside marriage that much of an issue. If Mrs. Manresa is "vulgar," "over-sexed," and "overdressed" (*BTA*, 37), there is nonetheless another way of viewing her. She allows people the liberty to "take advantage of the breach in decorum, of the fresh air that blew in, to follow like leaping dolphins in the wake of an ice-breaking vessel" (*BTA*, 37). Manresa tempts members of Pointz Hall with the freedom to break social boundaries because she has done it first. As the narrator comments, "A spring of feeling bubbled up through her mud. They had laid theirs with blocks of marble" (*BTA*, 41). Much like La Trobe, she disrupts conventions of bourgeois propriety. Manresa might be "primitive" or even "dirty" due to the anxiety associated with her "flood" of emotion, but she is also associated with a lack of restrictions from social constraints, and positive, natural elements such as earth and water. Building materials like marble, associated with cultural and social manners of Western "civilization," block the villagers from feeling passion. Manresa is repeatedly juxtaposed with the silent painting of the woman who is "not an ancestor" hanging opposite the window in the dining hall. As opposed to the image of a woman, which "looked at nobody" and "drew them down the paths of silence" (*BTA*, 42), Manresa is ebullient and loud; her voice is "fluty" as she bubbles over to articulate her sensations (*BTA*, 41). While the household members examine the lady in the portrait, who "looked over their heads, looking at nothing," leading spectators "down green glades, into the heart of silence" (*BTA*, 45), Mrs. Manresa interrupts the silence by drawing attention to the lady in the painting's construction as a picture, or cultural "image": "Said it was by Sir Joshua?" Manresa asks (*BTA*, 45).

Consistently, when viewers become captivated by the spectacle, whether it be the female spectacle or the pageant, Manresa undercuts the illusion by highlighting the constructed nature of all elements of the social web — identity, gender, history, art, sex, marriage, even nature. Noticeably, Manresa is the one character who never becomes drawn into the spectacle, or fascinated by it, because she is not tempted by the desire to participate in a fantasy of unity or belonging. She has her own fantasy — to be the "Queen" of the festival rather than spectator (*BTA*, 84). For example, while the audience members are mesmerized by the view, tempted to "let the view triumph, to reflect its ripple; to let their own minds ripple," Mrs. Manresa sees the view as just that. "What a view!" (*BTA*, 61). Hiding her desire to be either the center of attention, or alone reading a "picture paper" and eating sweets, she then "sighed, pretending to express not her own drowsiness but something connected with what she felt about views" (*BTA*, 61). Significantly, Manresa is the only member of the audience who does not experience extreme discomfort or indignation when La Trobe brings out the mirrors at the end of the pageant. The mirrors are meant to make the audience aware of its part as a "society" of the spectacle of "the Present Time." Manresa, however, never succumbs to the experience of mass spectatorship. As a "woman of action" (*BTA*, 99), Manresa is too busy manipulating her own image to be controlled by another.

While Manresa's narcissism is undeniably appalling, upon closer examination she also has numerous commendable qualities that the residents of Pointz Hall most definitely lack. By the familiar, considerate way she regards William Dodge, the reader acknowledges that, unlike the other characters, she does not "treat" his homosexuality in a stereotypical manner nor view him as anything other than a person. Her marriage to a Jew and her endearing comments regarding Ralph, her husband, indicate that despite her infidelities, she is not racist. Lastly, she is the only one who treats the manservant, Candish, "as if he were a real man, not a stuffed man" (*BTA*, 37). Unlike Bart Oliver, who completely ignores the fact that Candish is present when he states "Servants . . . must have their ghost," Manresa shows consideration in waiting until Candish leaves the room to say, "I'm on a level with the servants. I'm nothing like so grown up as you are" (*BTA*, 41). Furthermore, Manresa exhibits true kindness toward the village women by teaching them "*not how to pickle and preserve but how to weave frivolous baskets out of co-loured straw*" (*BTA*, 39). Surely a jab at the women who infantilize the villagers, taking it upon themselves as a "charitable" duty to teach the women home economics, Manresa recognizes that the village women, like anyone else, might want to indulge in a leisure activity in a rare respite from work and family.

Thus, there are two possible readings of Mrs. Manresa. One is that Woolf unwittingly participates in a discourse that links sexual desire in women with excessive materialism (possibly Jewishness), responsibility for shoring up patriarchy and, by extension, militarism. In this read-ing, Woolf refuses women the possibility of eroticism and enjoyment of material comforts since it mirrors masculine desire and maintains the existing system of economics. This reading would correlate with the way in which other representations of women in film and propa-ganda linked modern women with mass culture, excess, and artifice. For Woolf, being independent of family or financial obligations is also linked to the potential for creativity, an ideal that Manresa betrays. In *A Room of One's Own*, Woolf's main argument is that women have not been able to create great art because they have not had control over their own space and money. Since Manresa replaces "reproduction" (both biological and artistic) with "production," or what Mary Ann Doane calls "consumer vampirism" (*Desire to Desire*, 81), she also eschews the opportunity for true freedom of expression for women and relinquishes a possibility for creativity.[32]

Another reading is also feasible. Perhaps Woolf is setting up a different standard for representing women by giving her female character a moral choice and agency that is denied to her in both romantic fiction and in propaganda — and, I would add, even in current feminist readings of the text. Specifically, Manresa confounds categories of the sex-gender system by establishing herself in a new subject position; she undermines a male-female spectator-spectacle relationship because she presents herself as a spectacle to be seen. She *wants* to be viewed, and her overt control of the way in which she constructs herself as a subject subverts the subject/object, male/female divide. Manresa calculates her public exposure as a performance of what Liz Connor calls "appearing," thus challenging the appropriateness of narrower gender analyses of her character. Mrs. Manresa's desire to appear in public links her with the modern Flapper. As Connor notes, "The Flapper's practices of appearing were seen to be symptomatic of an excessive desire to be objectified by a heterosexual . . . gaze. This desire to attract sexualized, anonymous attention left her standing in the shadow of the street prostitute" (*Spectacular Modern Woman*, 13). Isa echoes this view when she describes Manresa as "that strumpet" (*BTA*, 87). In many ways, criticism of Manresa for drawing attention to herself as a sexual object reflects how she disturbs assumptions of spectatorship's usual processes. Much like Miss La Trobe, who creates the pageant as a spectacle to manipulate her audience, Manresa establishes a visual domain in which she, too, manipulates the gaze of viewers, thus challenging her status as an object of the gaze. This manipulation of viewers causes Manresa, like the "Modern Woman" or Flapper, to be conceived as a figure of both hate and love. Her identity is self-determined; she has agency and mobility, but she is also a figure linked with fraudulence. Woolf thus registers the discomfort associated with the shift in modernity from the "Angel in the House"—the Victorian view of women as meek, humble, and self-sacrificing—to modern female visibility, which challenged modes of looking "inciting display," self-expression, and mobility (ibid., 29).[33]

The contrast between Mrs. Manresa's agency and Isa's fixed positioning as the "Angel" counterpart is remarkable. Compared with Isa, who feels "prisoned" by her role as wife and mother (*BTA*, 61), Mrs. Manresa realizes a fantasy of social and economic freedom that was not possible for many women in the 1930s. Isa remains at home while Giles works in the city, dreams of love with the "gentleman farmer," and hides her poetry in budget books that manage Giles's wages. Manresa, in contrast, has complete flexibility, both economically and sexually. Her "great silver-plated" automobile is only one of the more obvious symbols of her mobility. Her childlessness allows her the flexibility to take trips; her two homes indicate that she can straddle both urban and rural environments; and her independence allows her to move easily among a variety of social strata in both private and public spheres. Manresa, similar to the Flapper or Modern Woman, is willing "to exploit the new technologies associated with mobility, leisure, and amusement, and she handled them adeptly" (Connor, *Spectacular Modern Woman*, 216). Needless to say, Manresa's mobility is due, in large part, to her disposable income attained through marriage and sexual exchanges with men. Nonetheless, in quite literal terms, Manresa drives her own car. She might be an outsider, or even a "party-crasher," but the cheeky manner in which she butts into the social rules of respectability is quite admirable. She is there, at the pageant, along with families who had been there for generations, pushing her way to tea at the pageant interval, "the first to drink, the first to bite" (*BTA*, 92). Undermining Pointz Hall's micro-oligarchy, she encourages villagers to follow her example in order to cross class barriers as well. By breaking through social barriers that impede the consideration of all people as equals, Mrs. Manresa's trail-blazing belief that "It's all my eye about democracy" (*BTA*, 92), and "we're all flesh and blood" (*BTA*, 36), allows villagers and "refeened" gentry to eat and mingle side by side (*BTA*, 92).

Like the Flapper, ever in pursuit of indulgence, Manresa is nevertheless associated with frivolous immaturity. As Connor notes, Flappers "retained 'not one, but a whole lot of sweet teeth'" (*Spectacular Modern Woman*, 216). In Manresa's pursuit of pleasure, it is difficult not to judge her lack of social responsibility that ignores, or even facilitates, the oppression of others. She is indeed justifiably blameworthy: not for being who she is but rather for failing to take notice of her impact on others. Even historically, the New Woman's and the Flapper's importance for women waned by 1939, a symbol of triviality that was inappropriate to a time of war. Moreover, "older" Flappers like Manresa were perceived as especially "conspicuous":

> The most pernicious threat posed by the older Flapper was that she might seduce young men through visually deceiving them about her age. . . . Because she constituted herself as spectacle, the Flapper was deceptive, illusory, and sexually manipulative of men. Her brazen comportment was sometimes seen as a new and rebellious configuration of womanhood, yet it could also give the smart Modern Woman a bad name — particularly if, despite her maturity in age, she displayed herself as still childishly enthralled by the modern spectacle. (ibid., 222)

This depiction describes Mrs. Manresa with uncanny accuracy; it also explains the moral apprehension conveyed by the "smart Modern Woman"—or smart woman writer—who dreads the impact of the aging Flapper on women's emancipation. Fear of her deceptiveness correlates with Huyssen's observations of the link between Modern Woman and the menacing aspects of mass culture. After all, when the Flapper was not busy seducing men, she was consuming mass cultural objects. Manresa, for example, reads trashy novels, listens to jazz, and is constantly drinking, eating, and smoking. It could also be said that Bart's and Giles Oliver's attraction to Manresa is similar to the allure of mass culture spectacles—these men can evade the reality of family responsibilities, loneliness, and the impact of war by escaping into the fantasy of Manresa's pageant, in which they play virile, chivalrous heroes to her jovial goddesslike Queen. As Giles Oliver observes, Manresa made him "feel less of an audience, more of an actor" (BTA, 97). Consequently, Mrs. Manresa competes with Miss La Trobe for narrative space off the stage, even if La Trobe more deliberately manipulates the "acts" themselves.

Because Manresa is so obviously a figure of irony, I would nonetheless argue that it is difficult to construe her as being overly threatening or menacing. Her tactics are *so* obvious, and the men who admire her so clearly clueless, that Manresa seems far from a dangerously deceptive or pernicious character linked with the threatening allure of the Nazi spectacle. She appears to be, rather, the butt of the narrator's jokes and an obviously satirical figure. In fact, if we read Manresa's performance in terms of satire and her act of femininity as parody, then her role in the novel also becomes a subversive challenge to Nazi pseudoscientific notions regarding sex, race, and gender. It is quite possible that Woolf read Joan Riviere's "Womanliness as a Masquerade," which had considerable cultural currency when it was published by The International Journal of Psychoanalysis in 1929.[34] In the essay, Riviere analyzes female identity in terms of performance or a "mask" which works to avert male fears that women possess masculine attributes. As Riviere observes, "womanliness [can] be assumed and worn as a mask, both to hide the possession of masculinity and to avert the reprisals expected if she was found to possess it—much as a thief will turn out his pockets and ask to be searched to prove that he has not the stolen goods" (38). As an alternative to Freud's theory of sexuality, which positioned female sexuality in terms of penis envy and the desire for children as the inverted wish for a penis, Riviere's argument reveals a less essentialized view of "feminine" nature. Of course, Riviere's theory still assumes masculinity as the primary trait, but it also provides a basis for perceiving gender as an act of self-construction.

A contemporary extension of "womanliness as masquerade" follows in postmodern theories of performativity and parody, whereby gender is interpreted as "manufactured through a sustained set of acts" (Butler, *Gender Trouble,* xv). In *Gender Trouble,* for example, Judith Butler argues that what members of society understand as "natural" or "normative" gender is in reality produced through acts and gestures that comply with social rules. The subject, therefore, is constituted and determined from within discourse, which is organized according to a gendered system. Rather than stemming from a predetermined, essential idea of gender, the feminine performs gender, a masquerade, to place itself within a logocentric symbolic order. As Butler posits, the way the subject can exercise agency is through repetitions, like parody, that draw attention to "the performative status of the natural itself" (*Gender Trouble,* 5, 143–46).[35] Although I would hesitate to presuppose that Woolf fully anticipates Butler's postmodern, antiessentialist argument, Mrs. Manresa's performance of womanliness is so over the top that it does draw attention to its own construction, undermining ideas of biologically determined femininity promoted in both Nazi ideology and in patriarchal England.

Manresa's positioning as a figure of subversive parody is enforced by the fact that her performance is only effective for male viewers. In parody the "mask" of the performer can be worn or removed — and the narrator notes that Manresa is aware of the need to remove her mask in front of women: "always when she spoke to women, she veiled her eyes, for they, being conspirators, saw through it" (*BTA,* 38). Manresa's overt sexuality creates a critical distance for female spectators, who are able to analyze and critique ways of thinking about gender. As Doane notes, for female viewers or spectators, masquerade is effective due to "its potential to manufacture a distance from the image, to generate a problematic within which the image is manipulable, producible, and readable by the woman" (*Desire to Desire,* 81–82). Manresa's femininity, then, rather than a negative representation of the dangers of mass culture, becomes subversive parody that wages war against the mind-numbing and ultimately harmful nondialogic myth of the maternal, modest, and virtuous woman. Like the painting of the woman in the Olivers' dining room, the maternal icon used in propaganda of the 1930s provides a fantasy, the result of which is numbing silence rather than a real engagement with the variety of human experience. Constantly and consistently, Manresa disrupts the myth "with blow after blow, with champagne and ogling," offering instead a "sample of her life" (*BTA*, 38). And yet, her subversive "act" nevertheless points to a problem: if the performer chooses to not remove the mask, or to disguise the interiority she does not want to reveal in performance, what happens to the "self"? Is there an ethics of the self that is neither essential nor performance, but part of a broader human condition that gets lost in conceptions of discourse and parody? Woolf hints that there is indeed an "I" that lies beyond the nature-culture divide through her narrative method of free indirect discourse.

Through her narrative technique, Woolf reinforces her parody of gender norms through critical distance, but she also emphasizes the multiple points of view that put those articulations into question. As a technique, free indirect discourse places public utterance and internal articulation — that is, the public and private realms — in a dialogical relation with one another. Snaith describes this narrative strategy as crossing the line between public and private voices to join the "internal and external" and purposefully convey ambiguity (*Public and Private*, 71).[36] For example, the narrator introduces Manresa as she invites herself and William Dodge to lunch at Pointz Hall in a manner that conflates both an observer's view and Manresa's own style of internal speech, reflecting how she would like to be perceived:

> Mrs. Manresa bubbled up, enjoying her own capacity to surmount, without turning a hair, this minor social crisis — this laying of two more places. For had she not complete faith in flesh and blood? and aren't we all flesh and blood? and how silly to make bones of trifles when we're all flesh and blood under the skin — men and women too! But she preferred men — obviously. (*BTA*, 35–36)

When Manresa is satirically slated as "prefer[ring] men — obviously," the narration is ambiguously caught between a public view of her character, her own private voice, and the reader's perception of the irony in the statement. Similarly, when Manresa is designated as "the wild child of nature," one might ask, whose point of view is this? The narrator's? Isa's? The general public's? The uncertainty relating to Mrs. Manresa's portrayal in free indirect discourse thus allows Woolf to ironically undercut the narrator and other characters' assumptions about Manresa's nature. It also belies that Mrs. Manresa conceals an aspect of herself that is unavailable to the narrator and the public.

Snaith probes a similar issue in the portrayal of Mrs. McNab, the housekeeper in *To the Lighthouse*. The depiction of Mrs. McNab appears to be condescending, classist, even stereotypical, and the narrator's reduction of her seems one-dimensional and simplistic. Snaith, however, argues that critics "often fail to distinguish between the narrator and the narrative. Woolf lets Mrs. McNab prove the narrator wrong" (*Public and Private*, 77). As Snaith posits, the narrative conjunctions that are reproduced in free indirect discourse allowed for the ambiguities and "indeterminacy" that are key to Woolf's work (71). The uncertainty produced by the device forces the reader to confront the fact that one interpretation, or absolute meaning, is impossible. This same strategy is evident in the portrayal of Mrs. Manresa. The narrator describes her as vulgar or the "wild child" (*BTA*, 41, 92), but Bart Oliver depicts her as "admirable" (*BTA*, 182), Isa as "a strumpet" (*BTA*, 87), Giles as "lust" and "goddess" (*BTA*, 89, 107, 182), and the public as "a breath of fresh air" (*BTA*, 84). Manresa's own point of view is that she is a "Queen" (*BTA*, 84). The range of perspectives, rather than consolidating Manresa's character, points to the way in which the public projects its own prejudices and judgments onto others. Just as the narrative parodies other obviously contradictory public utterances, such as "I thought it brilliantly clever. . . . O my dear, I thought it utter bosh" (*BTA*, 177), so readers have the opportunity to catch themselves in their narrow-mindedness with regards to Manresa. By extension, Manresa's character also allows the reader to register the text's uncertain assessment of the "Modern Appearing Woman"—who, on the one hand, exploits and bolsters the patriarchal system for her own benefit, but, on the other hand, is also an autonomous figure of change, self-determination, and individuality.

It would appear then that rather than being a symbol of shallow consumption (sexual and material), Mrs. Manresa serves as a moral compass for readers — past and present alike. How liberal are we? How willing are we to accept other ways of conceiving sexuality? Manresa is similar to La Trobe in that they both are invested in self-fashioning, in establishing alternatives that challenge their biological "destinies" and placement in society. As outsiders, newcomers, or exiles, they disrupt social hierarchies by creating their own fictions, but they cannot escape the consequences of their positioning within that system. Because Manresa substitutes fantasy and performance for communal responsibility and awareness, she neglects an opportunity to use that self-expression for a greater, more ethical purpose. In contrast, Miss La Trobe expands her role as performer and artist by using mirrors to reflect "the present time" to the crowd of onlookers, showing how they are complicit in passively allowing the current political spectacle to occur. Even so, she too is guilty of becoming swept up in her own self-absorbed goal to manipulate the audience. At the end of the novel, both women's plays are exposed as insufficient for the new ideological battlefield — an ethical and moral struggle against patriarchy and, by extension, the Nazi dictatorship as it gains in strength and support in Europe. Once the performance is over, Mrs. Manresa's makeup wears off: "plated it looked, not deeply interfused" (BTA, 181). Miss La Trobe, certain that her play was "a failure," goes to the pub to create yet another new work consisting of "Words without meaning" (BTA, 190–91). When politics is making a spectacle of itself, Woolf insists, the more urgent necessity is not only for women to free themselves from "private" social constrictions but also for women to "free ourselves from slavery" in order to "free men from tyranny" ("Thoughts," 155) This idealistic and perhaps overly burdensome responsibility for women is perhaps better in theory than in practice in the 1930s. Isherwood, who is observing the tyrannical nature of the Nazi spectacle and its effects up close, makes it more patent that it will take more than a personal attitude shift to "free men from tyranny." But he is also more severe in his castigation of women's roles on both sides of the ideological war.

## Vamps and Nazis: Goodbye to Women in Berlin

Similar to *Between the Acts*, female characters in *Goodbye to Berlin* serve as symbols for modern transformation, destabilizing gender identities and the fears associated with sexual and material consumerism. In Isherwood's novel, however, women also become metaphors for the ominous political atmosphere in Germany. As sexuality and sexual identification increasingly become key features in Nazi ideology, Isherwood registers the distortions, falsehoods, and twisted nature of Nazism through his representation of female characters. In fact, my reading of the novel suggests that the city of Berlin, and virtually all of the narrator's experiences of Berlin, are mirrored in Christopher's relationships with female characters. Most perceptibly, his relationship with Sally Bowles echoes his attraction to and disillusionment with Berlin as Nazi culture begins to encroach upon the everyday existence of the people living there. As opposed to the female spectacle in *Between the Acts*, an ambiguous image that both supports and subverts sexism, women in *Goodbye to Berlin* become more directly implicated in all that is false, artificial, and misleading in Hitler's Third Reich.

The notion that Isherwood would associate female characters with Berlin or represent the narrator's relationship with the city through women is not especially remarkable, given that historical and modernist traditions of using women's bodies as an allegory for the city is a well-worn trope.[37] Especially in the case of Weimar Berlin, which itself epitomized "the" modern city, the female figure often served as a symbol to evoke all that was both exhilarating and threatening about the new technological, intellectual, and social innovations that modern Berlin had to offer. As Patrice Petro observes, "Berlin . . . served as the decisive metaphor for modernity," and modernity was in turn signified by the female body (*Joyless Streets*, 40). The 1929 article by Harold Nicolson in *Der Querschnitt* (The Cross Section), a German magazine for "intellectuals," is but one example of many.[38] In the article, Berlin and the other European cities with which it is compared are described in terms of female bodies:

> London is an old lady in black lace and diamonds who guards her secrets with dignity and to whom one would not tell those secrets of which one was ashamed. Paris is a woman in the prime of life to whom one would only tell those secrets which one desires to be repeated. But Berlin is a girl in a pull-over, not much powder on her face, Hölderlin in her pocket, thighs like those of Atlanta, an undigested education, a heart which is almost too

ready to sympathize, and a breadth of view which charms one's repressions. . . . (quoted in Petro, *Joyless Streets*, 41–42)[39]

The image of Berlin closely resembles depictions of the Modern Woman or Flapper—young, naive, wild, and exhilarating. At the same time, however, Berlin could suggest all the negative aspects of the Modern Woman, a cruel, devouring city, whose vulgarity and deceitfulness was as alluring as it was odious. Playwright Carl Zuckmayer, for example, invokes a description of Berlin in the twenties in metaphors that reveal more about male perceptions of the highly desirable woman than anything to do with the city itself:

> People discussed Berlin . . . as if Berlin were a highly desirable woman, whose coldness and capriciousness were widely known. . . . We called her proud, snobbish, nouveau riche, uncultured, crude. But secretly everyone looked upon her as the goal of their desires. Some saw her as hefty, full-breasted, in lace underwear, others as a mere wisp of a thing, with boyish legs in black silk stockings. The daring saw both aspects, and her very capacity for cruelty made them the more aggressive. (quoted in Petro, *Joyless Streets*, 217)[40]

These descriptions reveal how the woman as allegory mediates between these male writers and intellectuals and the allure or anxiety toward their changing environment in modernity. One can observe a similar tendency in *Goodbye to Berlin*, where women manifest both the appeal and moral barrenness of life in the city. Although Isherwood does not come close to the overt misogyny of some modernists' works (Ezra Pound, T. S. Eliot, and Wyndham Lewis come to mind), his depiction of women is nevertheless disconcerting in the context of the thirties. Nazi propaganda, after all, was using similar strategies in Berlin at the same time. The narrator's experience of Berlin through women, most notably Sally Bowles, Frl. Schroeder, Frl. Mayr, Frau Nowak, and Natalia Landauer, covers a wide range of female types, but they are still archetypal in the aspects of Berlin to which they allude—Berlin's artifice (Sally Bowles), pride (Frl. Shroeder), intellectual Jewish snobbery (Natalia Landauer), and working-class antisemitism (Frl. Mayr and Frau Nowak). Aside from

Otto, there are few exceptional male characters in this book; for the most part, the narrator considers Berlin life in terms of women.

"Sally Bowles," the episode covering October 1930 to autumn 1931, provides the clearest example of the way the narrator's experience of the city is channeled through female characters. Much like the narrator, Sally is a foreigner in Berlin, living on a small allowance from her mother. In terms of sexual politics, Sally Bowles is strikingly similar to Mrs. Manresa in the way she overturns her role as passive object of the gaze through campy self-fashioning as *La Dame aux Camélias*. Sally is always "performing," constantly manipulating her audience's gaze in constructed acts of appearing. Like Manresa, her overblown, hypersexual nature also challenges Nazi ideology that emphasizes women's roles as mothers, nurturers, and helpmates. Throughout most of the episode, Sally's performance remains deliberately exaggerated and parodic, defying accepted heterosexual gender norms.[41] Repeatedly, the narrator emphasizes her theatricality. When he first meets Sally, he describes how "she cooed" on the telephone, "pursing her brilliant cherry lips as though she were going to kiss the mouthpiece. . . . I sat watching her like a performance at the theatre" (*GTB*, 35). Later he observes her "silvery little stage laugh" (*GTB*, 35). There are other occasions when the narrator draws attention to her ostentatious costume-like dress, her caked-on makeup, her self-conscious "poses," and her overt performance of the femme fatale. Nevertheless, in a novel that most clearly criticizes the perilous effects of illusion and artifice, Sally's performance also portends the ways in which Berliners will become swept up in illusion, slowly growing callous and blind to the cruelty of the Nazis. Much like Woolf's Mrs. Manresa, Sally becomes both an object of subversive comedy and at the same time a modernist symbol for the detestably shallow and crass aspects of materialism and mass culture.

There is little doubt that the narrator celebrates and is fascinated by Sally's playfulness, energy, and sexual agency. As Connor describes the Flapper, Sally seems to be "an allegory for spectacular modernity and its libidinized fascinations" (*Spectacular Modern Woman*, 13). Isherwood's portrayal of Sally's theatricality, however, is also a constructive example of self-determination and individualism at a time when the Nazis are increasingly limiting the liberties of women. Like Manresa's performance in *Between the Acts*, Sally's mask of "womanliness" can be interpreted as subversive parody, testing the entire political positioning of ideas of "femininity." Her nonconformity as a single, sexually available woman in Berlin is blatantly juxtaposed with National Socialism's strategy of "invisible propaganda" in film and other media encouraging women to become dutiful wives and mothers for the good of the country. Sally's way of life appears in such stark contrast with the ideal of the German film about a woman who "sacrifices her stage career for the sake of a Great Love, Home and Children" that she and Christopher "laughed so much we had to leave at the end" (GTB, 58). While the message of the film might seem absurd to Christopher and Sally, the film is representative of a type of propaganda that, according to Goebbels, worked effectively on the German population. Terri Gordon, for instance, quotes Goebbels's diary entry in March 1942, which records his idea of *unsichtbare Propaganda* (invisible propaganda):

> Even entertainment can be politically of special value, because the moment a person is conscious of propaganda, propaganda becomes ineffective. However, as soon as propaganda as a tendency, as a characteristic, as an attitude, remains in the background and becomes apparent through human beings, then propaganda becomes effective in every respect. ("Fascism and the Female Form," 170–71)

Susan Sontag also describes the allure of this type of Nazi aesthetics as "epics of achieved community, in which everyday reality is transcended through ecstatic self-control and submission" ("Fascinating Fascism," 87). The characteristic of the Nazi spectacle that the film underscores is the sacrifice of the individual and "the dissolution of alienation in ecstatic feelings of community" (ibid., 96). While the message of the film is not that dissimilar to the sentiments being expressed in American or British film, the implications of being apart from the greater image of the German *Gemeinschaft* (community) have more dire consequences.

The film sequence is soon followed by Sally's unwanted pregnancy and consequent abortion. The danger involved in obtaining an abortion and the seedy nature of her interaction with the abortionist who "kept stroking and pinching Sally's arm and pawing her hand" (GTB,

70) point to the highly illegal nature of abortion at the time, not only in Germany but also in England.[42] In her most candid moment, after being rebuffed by a reputable doctor, Sally asks him, "My dear man, what do you imagine would happen to the unfortunate child if it was born? Do I look as if I'd make a good mother?" (*GTB*, 69). Thus Isherwood draws a distinction between the actual experience of pregnancy and child rearing and "fascism's manipulation of those experiences in the service of the *patria*" (Carlston, *Thinking Fascism*, 7).[43] Sally's reaction to the film's message draws attention to her resistance of a more ominous form of fascist sexual politics that subjugated promiscuous women or "undesirables" while valorizing those women who supported the state by upholding family values. Sally clearly contradicts the *Kinder, Küche, Kirche* (Children, Kitchen, Church) image of woman promoted by Nazi propaganda. By using ideas of childbirth and maternity in an atypical manner in connection with her character, Isherwood daringly refutes those sexist ideologies.

For all these reasons, Sally's character, much like Mrs. Manresa's, is difficult to interpret as morally repugnant, particularly because her performance is entertaining and her sexual exploits constantly misfire. For the most part, she is the subject of irony — an unsuccessful gold digger who is consistently duped. And yet, perhaps part of her inability to be successful is due to the first-person narrator undermining her attempts to define her own character and sexuality. Christopher undercuts Sally's performance of the femme fatale with brutal bluntness:

> When you talk like that it's really just nervousness. You're naturally shy with strangers, I think: so you've got into this trick of trying to bounce them into approving or disapproving of you, violently. . . . Only I wish you wouldn't try it on me because it doesn't work and it only makes me feel embarrassed. If you go to bed with every single man in Berlin and come tell me about it each time, you still won't convince me that you're *La Dame aux Camelias*—because really and truly, you know, you aren't. (*GTB*, 47–48)

The narrator's words immediately put Sally in her place; however, his assessment of her character as shy and nervous is rather inappropriate and not altogether trustworthy. It would seem more acceptable for the narrator to think of Sally as bashful rather than outrageous or saucy since he can then maintain the upper hand. Even more ironically, when the narrator feels humiliated by Sally, he claims, "The awful sexual flair women have for taking the stuffing out of a man!" (GTB, 85). One can easily discern the misogynistic undertones of Christopher's outburst—especially considering he has no problem taking the "stuffing out" of Sally. Perhaps Sally's "sexual flair" is only tolerable when the narrator feels he is in control of the situation.

Notably, the ironic elements of Sally's performance become less amusing when she actually begins to attain success at her gold digging. Her artificiality is presented with more vehemence when it coincides with the crisis of Weimar politics that precipitates the emergence of the Third Reich. Suddenly, the playfulness with which the narrator treats Sally's vampishness is reversed and inscribed within a troubling historical framework through a series of antisemitic references. Her offensive remark, "there's an awful old Jew who takes me out sometimes" (GTB, 45), is certainly far from humorous. Even worse is her comment upon meeting Natalia Landauer, Christopher's Jewish friend: "I've been making love to a dirty old Jew producer" (GTB, 201). Isherwood would have been fully aware of Hitler's racial agenda against Jews, as is made clear in other references to antisemitism in Goodbye to Berlin, so one can only assume that Sally's comments are not placed there out of casual ignorance. The shift in attitude toward her character is paralleled by a transition in the narrator's relationship to Berlin. The headline Christopher observes in the newspaper that last morning he sees Sally reads, "Everything Collapses!" referring to the July 1931 financial debacle and closing of the banks in Berlin (GTB, 76). The other elements that collapse are the whimsical nature of Sally's performance as femme fatale and Isherwood's relationship with her. Sally is moving in privileged circles as Nazism is gaining power, hinting that in the rest of Berlin society, the illusion of unity and harmony that Hitler promotes has become indistinguishable from the "real" subjugation of rights and freedoms of Jews. Instead of challenging oppression, Sally's femme fatale act has become truly "fatal," marked by indifference to racism and discrimination.

The disintegration of Christopher's relationship with Sally runs parallel with the cessation of his friendship with another Modern Woman who clearly reflects Christopher's discomfort with bourgeois culture in Berlin — Natalia Landauer. Intellectual, ambitious, and slightly snobbish, Natalia is also kind and generous, and her opinions are distinctly progressive. She feels it is important to be independent and self-sufficient — to "be able to do all for myself," to earn a university degree or "go to Paris and study art," and she is also willing to "live with a man without that we were married" (GTB, 182). Moreover, Natalia is cultured, well read, and interested in Christopher's literary pursuits. One can deduce from the narrator's harsh treatment of her that, rather than being a sound judgment of Natalia's character, the text exposes Christopher's character flaws and stereotypical assumptions. For example, when Natalia takes him to a comedic film, although he is being hosted by her, he rather rudely shows his disapproval for her poor taste — he first "laughed exaggeratedly" and then "stopped laughing altogether" (GTB, 180). Christopher also purposefully insults her, telling her "Arguments bore me. . . . I like hearing the sound of your voice, but I don't care a bit what you're saying" (GTB, 185). Worst of all, his "experiment" to have Natalia meet with Sally is cruel, especially considering that, based on previous statements, it is likely Sally will say something antisemitic and offensive.

Christopher's insensitive and tactless conduct could be read as a projection of his own ambiguity toward his "snobby intellectual" side. The Sally-Natalia clash would then reflect a conflict between the narrator's warring inner selves, caught between a desire for seedy sexual liberation and aesthetic culture-worship. His corroding relationship with Berlin, therefore, predictably coincides with his rejection of both women — first Natalia and then, finally, Sally. Christopher's behavior also shows, however, a more common tendency in modernity to project ambivalence, materiality, immaturity, and fickleness onto both women and Jews. That Christopher thinks Natalia a "prude" for being horrified by Sally's comments and subsequently chooses to remain friends with Sally instead of Natalia also alludes to the troubling nature in which stereotypes regarding both women and Jews converge. While the chapter on Natalia and her family is undeniably meant to condemn Nazi antisemitism, all the Landauers, including Natalia, are featured with stereotypically "Jewish" character traits.[44]

Sander Gilman remarks that stereotypes are the way humans try to project a feeling of control in the world; they are "a crude set of mental representations of the world. . . . They perpetuate a needed sense of difference between the 'self' and the 'object,' which becomes the 'Other.' Because there is no real line between self and the Other, an imaginary line must be drawn" (*Difference and Pathology*, 20). Especially fascinating is the way Gilman notes how stereotypes become clustered and associated within various categories of Others: "The black, the proletarian, the child, the woman, and the avant-garde are all associated in a web of analogies" (ibid., 37). The intersection of race and gender in *Goodbye to Berlin* reveals how women from groups already marked by alterity are conceived of in codes that mark them as both racial and sexual outsiders. They are the "Other Other." The depiction of Natalia, the intellectual Modern Woman, as opposed to Sally, "the Flapper," is thus complicated by her characterization as a Jew. Similar to Mrs. Manresa, Natalia is a veritable caricature of the modern Jewish woman, an image not only inexorably linked to the emancipated Modern Woman but also related to the stereotype of the Jewish parvenu. In Isherwood's retrospective acknowledgment, Natalia is depicted as "a bossy bluestocking, desperately enthusiastic about culture, sexually frigid and prudish" (*CHK*, 64). She is overly aggressive, judgmental of other women, and overly concerned with money. As soon as Christopher is introduced to her, she asks him what he pays for rent and tells him that he could have gotten a better deal. "You should have asked me. . . . I should have found it for you myself" (*GTB*, 177). Reflecting on the portrayal of Natalia and her cousin Bernhard in the novel, Isherwood confesses that many of the segments were "callow and callous works" and they show the efforts of someone who was "twenty-four years old and in many respects very immature for . . . [his] age" (quoted in Shuttleworth, "Populous City," 150).

As Valentine Cunningham remarks, "Misogyny was rife in the writing of this period . . . even the determinedly womanizing and married found it hard to steer their texts clear of the prevailing hostility toward women and marriage" (*British Writers of the Thirties*, 152–53). Although Isherwood in no way comes close to the type of hateful sexism cited by Cunningham, his tendency to identify women with the narrator's ambivalence toward the city and to present female archetypes to the exclusion of actual women is noteworthy. Even the viciousness of Nazi anti-semitism and the blind adherence to National Socialism's racial policies become personified by women in *Goodbye to Berlin*. Aside from the

Nazi doctor portrayed on Reugen Island, for the most part it is German working-class women who reflect populist Nazi ideology or the voice of the *Volk*. Frl. Mayr, the Bavarian music-hall *jodlerin*, is the novel's most prominent Nazi. When Nazi gangs demonstrate against Jews in October 1930, the narrator notes how Frl. Mayr is delighted: "This town is sick with Jews. Turn over any stone, and a couple of them will crawl out. They're poisoning the very water we drink! They're strangling us, they're robbing us, they're sucking our life-blood" (*GTB*, 175). Frl. Mayr also conspicuously spoils her Jewish neighbor's chances for an engagement to a widowed butcher by spreading lies about her because she is "non-Aryan" and a "Jewess" (*GTB*, 21). Other female characters also speak the novel's most vicious expressions of antisemitism; notably, Sally Bowles, as described previously, and Frau Nowak, "who would sometimes say: 'When Hitler comes, he'll show these Jews a thing or two. They won't be so cheeky then'" (*GTB*, 148). Yet, when the narrator points out that Hitler intends to get rid of Jews completely, she takes it back, "Oh, I shouldn't like that to happen" (*GTB*, 148).

By the end of the novel, the narrator's association with women and with the city of Berlin becomes hollow and remote. In contrast with the female characters in *Between the Acts*, who reflect a wide range of human experience and fluctuating points of view, Isherwood's female figures remain specifically linked with the city. The narrator moves in and out of their space as spectator, while they remain part of the static photographic image, tied to his perception of Berlin. As the narrator describes in his last entry, "Berlin is a skeleton which aches in the cold: it is my own skeleton aching" (*GTB*, 230). It is no coincidence that Frl. Shroeder, the character who most directly personifies his memories of Berlin, is also cold and alone. The novel opens and closes with the portrayal of this kind-hearted, inquisitive, proud, middle-aged woman, the owner of the boardinghouse where Christopher lodges. "She is lonely, nowadays," Christopher tells the reader: "Sometimes she smokes a cigarette, sometimes she sips a glass of tea, but mostly she just sits, staring dully at the stove tiles in a kind of hibernation-doze" (*GTB*, 231). The city of Berlin, by this point, has become both desolate and unfeeling. Even Frl. Shroeder "is adapting herself, as she will adapt herself to every new regime" and "talking reverently about 'Der Fuhrer'" (*GTB*, 255).

As the narrator gloomily observes, "She is merely acclimatizing herself, in accordance with a natural law, like an animal which changes its coat for the winter. Thousands of people like Frl. Shroeder are acclimatizing themselves" (*GTB*, 255). Frl. Shroeder is compared to an "animal" who "changes its coat" to prepare for the cold. Instead of the "wild child of nature" of Mrs. Manresa and Sally Bowles, the woman has now become the beast.

## *Nightwood*: Monstrous Females and the Nazi Beast

If Isherwood's female characters reflect Berlin as "seductive, false, or weak," then the menacing threat of the city as the Nazi spectacle encroaches is emphasized to an even greater degree through the women portrayed in *Nightwood*. Is Barnes, then, like Isherwood, guilty of equating cultural and moral devastation with the seductive and cruel qualities of women? As some critics suggest, *Nightwood* blurs the boundaries of gender, satirizes characters and the ideas they represent, and engages in a form of subversive parody of sexism, much like Woolf's *Between the Acts*. Jane Marcus, for example, suggests that *Nightwood* is "Rabelaisian," a "feminist-anarchist call for freedom from fascism" ("Laughing at Leviticus," 221). Seen in this light, *Nightwood's* portrayal of monstrous, wretched, and pitiless women parodies the way in which all identities, sexual and racial, are images and illusions, constructed as ways of "appearing." Other, more critical interpretations of *Nightwood's* feminist content, however, are also plausible. Especially in the portrayal of Robin, Barnes evokes a trope of the depraved "masculine woman," or "invert," that colludes with both artistic and German media representations of emancipated women, androgynous women, and lesbians as objects of fear, mystery, and misery. Robin as an "image" and object of speculation draws the fascinated gaze of characters and readers alike in a manner that denies her autonomy and subjectivity. In some ways, as Shari Benstock suggests, by depriving Robin of a voice, *Nightwood* places her in the traditional role as "object" of a patriarchal text, "robbing" her of agency (*Women of the Left Bank*, 266).

I propose an interpretation that combines Jane Marcus's and Shari Benstock's readings of the novel, but I will make the bolder claim that the women in *Nightwood* are not simply resistant or objectified characters: they are allegories for the political climate. Similar to *Between the Acts* and *Goodbye to Berlin*, *Nightwood* undoubtedly undermines Nazi sexism by highlighting and thus undermining the way essentializing sexist ideologies such as *Kinder, Küche, Kirche* function. Barnes, like Woolf and Isherwood, underscores the ways in which gender identity is contingent upon performative acts and stylization. Throughout the novel, parodic and ironic performances that challenge hegemonic assumptions about race, gender, class, and heredity abound. Nevertheless, I am less certain that *all* the female characters demonstrate a parodic, "carnivalesque" atmosphere or that Barnes fully embraces an antiessentialist standpoint. Robin Vote, for instance, unlike a character such as Matthew O'Connor, or even Mrs. Manresa and Sally Bowles, lacks the over-the-top qualities of camp or parody. Instead, Robin hints at a more disquieting "essential" element of human nature — beyond gender — that lies beneath the masks, robes, and costumes that adorn the socially constructed body. As I argue, it is in the portrayal of Robin that *Nightwood* centers its most bleak and terrifying exposé of the nature of evil.

At a gathering of circus performers in Berlin at the home of Count Altamonte, circus performer Frau Mann, the Duchess of Broadback, articulates one of the novel's most prominent themes: "'*Herr Gott!*' said the Duchess, 'Am I what I say? Are you? Is the doctor?' She put her hand on his knee. 'Yes or no?'" (NW, 25). Needless to say, Frau Mann is a character whose costume is assimilated so closely with her body that any biological identification of her sex is completely masked. "She seemed to have a skin that was the pattern of her costume. . . . The stuff of the tights was no longer a covering, it was herself; the span of the tightly stitched crotch was so much her own flesh that she was as unsexed as a doll" (NW, 13). In a novel that links politics, sexuality, and identity with appearance, nearly every character is revealed as "a performer," defying notions of an ancestral, historical, racial, or gendered self. Sight and the visual — the idea of looking, being looked at, watching, gazing, and appearing — are all at the center of *Nightwood*. If identity is contingent on sight, in *Nightwood* characters roam in the dark, constructing images of themselves that elude scrutiny. It is a novel that discredits the reliability of the visible in an age when illusion, especially Nazi reliance on illusion, is paramount.

The focus on self-fashioning in all three novels joins them in a common concern with self and Other at a time when European concepts of belonging are decisive — soon to become matters of life or death. As a novel of resistance, *Nightwood* can be interpreted as being at war with identity. Monique Wittig argues that "it is quite possible for a work of literature to operate as a war machine, even 'a perfect war machine'" (*Straight Mind*, 59). Butler, explaining Wittig's quotation, adds to this remark by noting, "The main strategy of this war is for women, lesbians, and gay men — all of whom have been particularized through an identification with 'sex' — to pre-empt the position of the speaking subject and its invocation of the universal point of view." Barnes's novel is a "war text" because it gives voice to the marginal and dismantles the hierarchal division of gender "to establish the possibility of a new humanism" (Butler, *Gender Trouble*, 152). Barnes's concept of a "new humanism," however, includes a particular point of view of humans as exceptionally dangerous; and it also problematically excludes certain humans — in particular Jews — from that consideration. As a result, Barnes's work insinuates that self-fashioning is limited in its potential for positive subversion: firstly, if self-invention becomes too narcissistic, it risks overlooking a wider accountability toward humanity; and secondly, even then there are essential elements of humans that cannot be overcome.

My analysis of female representation as it relates to the political context of *Nightwood* focuses predominantly on Robin since she is the character who most clearly embodies the tensions among self-construction, ethical responsibility, and Nazi ideology. Like Mrs. Manresa and Sally Bowles, Robin challenges the way in which women are represented by forcing a reappraisal of the modern female spectacle. Robin can be understood as representing and resisting the most deviant and dangerous type of woman in Nazi propaganda and even before, in the sex reform literature of Weimar Germany. Grossman underscores affinities among misogyny, antisemitism, and homophobia in the 1920s, before the rise of Nazism. As she notes, the "unnatural" woman had "short, dark hair, dressed in a unisex shift, distinctly unmaternal — the image not only of the prostitute but also for the Jewess and the lesbian" ("New Woman," 167). Similarly, Robin is described as "a girl who resembles like a boy" (NW, 136); a "wild thing" (NW, 146); and a woman who rejects motherhood. It quite possible, then, that Barnes's depiction of Robin, in so closely resembling the most feared type of female, works to defamiliarize and critique cultural representations of the "unnatural" women. And yet Robin is an especially intriguing character because she functions on both sides of the spectacle—she is a spectacle that mirrors its subject (the spectator) to itself as object. For this reason, the narrator describes her as a "mirage" that magnetizes both male and female spectators. She overturns the entire hierarchy of gender categories to point to something, as the Mighty Matthew O'Connor observes, "outside the 'human type'—a wild thing" that lies beyond the categories and divisions of male or female, straight or queer, citizen or exile (NW, 146). It is through Robin that Barnes thus reveals the most pernicious aspects of the spectacle—how it erases the boundary between self and Other so that self-consciousness becomes impossible. Even more than that of Mrs. Manresa or Sally Bowles, Robin's narcissism becomes malevolent because she lacks the understanding that comes from perceiving the Other in the self.

Although O'Connor, Felix, Nora, and Robin all play central roles in the novel, Robin, because her identity is so difficult to pin down, is the object of fascination for characters of the novel, critics, and readers alike.[45] The 1961 book jacket cover ominously describes the novel as "the story of Robin Vote and those she destroys—her husband, the 'Baron,' their child Guido, and the two women, Nora and Jenny, who love her."[46] As the lurid cover suggests, and quite similar to the portrayal of Manresa and Sally, it is difficult to ascertain whether Robin's promiscuity is meant to be perceived as emancipatory or depraved and morally wrong. On the one hand, Robin's dress codes, like Sally Bowles's attire, emphasize her defiance of social norms for women (NW, 130). When Robin is first described lying unconscious in her hotel room, she is wearing "white flannelled trousers" (NW, 34), which, as Benstock notes, was especially subversive since it was against the law for women to wear trousers in public in Paris in the 1920s (Women of the Left Bank, 48). Her body and attire also point to her sexual and physical mobility. She is even described in terms of sensual movement—as a woman frozen, but still in motion, with her legs "spread as in a dance" and her "thick-lacquered pumps too lively for the arrested step" (NW, 34). Her "perfumed body" and "long and beautiful" hands also emphasize a "feminine" sensuality that overrides not only female stereotypes but also assumptions about the bisexual or lesbian "masculine woman."

Yet, because Robin's overt sexuality is far from over-the-top or "campy," as it is in the case of Sally and Manresa, it is difficult to read her as an ironic character. Nancy Levine argues that the portrayal of Robin as sexual predator and cold-hearted miscreant links Robin with the "cinema vamp" of post–World War I films; Barnes, according to Levine, uses the model of the cinema vamp to construct Robin as a symbol of female power ("Cinema Vamp," 272). The vamp was precursor to the Flapper, and similar in her rebelliousness and sexual availability, but more destructive and sinister as a femme fatale whose affinity for crime and perverse sex usually destroyed her male prey. Levine examines the various ways in which the cinema vamp becomes a trope in Barnes's journalism and fiction, pointing out that at just about the same time she was writing *Nightwood* in 1930, Barnes resurrected the famous vamp siren, Alla Nazimova, to study the actress's remarkable capacity to appear as "evil" (ibid., 274–75). In an almost uncanny coincidence with the depressing cabaret bar that Christopher visits at the end of *Goodbye to Berlin*, Nazimova is most famous for playing Salomé in Charles Bryant's 1923 film, roughly the same time in which *Nightwood* is set.[47] In line with the manner in which female archetypes function throughout *Nightwood*, Salomé, who for centuries represented the dangers of the seductive woman in the artistic and literary imagination, is depicted in both Oscar Wilde's play and Bryant's 1923 film adaptation as cruel, heartless, and deadly. Notably, George Mosse observes that Aubrey Beardsley's illustration of Wilde's play also depicted Salomé "as both androgyne and a *femme fatale*" (*Image of Man*, 104). Levine insists, however, that Barnes undermines the misogyny underlying the vamp's portrayal by "making her vamp a victim," invoking pity for Robin ("Cinema Vamp," 280). Her interpretation of Robin as a vamp is especially useful since it sheds light on the politics of the female spectacle and Robin's fascinating ability to project a fantasy of "invulnerability" and freedom that seduces her lovers. Nevertheless, I do not believe the reader is necessarily meant to feel that Robin is a victim. It is true that "Robin murders no one, steals nothing" (ibid., 279), but she is far from being free of guilt. She deserts her husband and child, psychologically abuses Nora, and purposefully seduces and torments a little girl, Sylvia, only to abandon the girl soon afterward (NW, 115–16). In other words, her culpability is due to a complete lack of human empathy.

Even Robin's rejection of motherhood, which could be considered a challenge to women's conventional role in society, is unsettling in its callousness. Ironically, with the exception of Frau Nowak in *Goodbye to Berlin* and Isa in *Between the Acts* (who "loathed . . . the maternal" [*BTA*, 17]), Robin is one of the few mothers from the three texts. It is almost as if Woolf, Isherwood, and Barnes promote a form of antifamily propaganda. Alice Kaplan posits an idea of fascism as "mother-bound," claiming that "fascism itself is a woman, a new mother" (*Reproductions of Banality*, 10). The refutation of the maternal role in *Nightwood* could then be interpreted as a seditious gesture against fascist ideology in both the figurative and literal senses. In preparation for birth, Robin attempts to associate with other "women that she had come to connect with women," such as "Louise de Vallière, Catherine of Russia, Madame de Maintenon, Catherine de Medici, and two women out of literature, Anna Karenina and Catherine Heathcliff" (NW, 47).[48] All of these historical women are queens, powerful mistresses of kings, or women who make tremendous sacrifices for love. Yet, they are also fictionalized images of women whose stories (even when taken from history books) are not based in the experience of "real" individuals. Robin's rejection of the experience of maternity is a denunciation of the cultural "image" of womanhood in the patriarchal paradigm; but it is nevertheless a ruthless way out since it coincides with violence, abuse, and an evasion of ethics and responsibility. Erin Carlston has a point when she maintains that the noticeable dearth of mothers is understandable "in a world where women especially struggle to escape their role in reproducing humanity and thus human pain" (*Thinking Fascism*, 52). Birth in *Nightwood*, as Carlston notes, is expressly connected with death and horror. The novel opens with Hedvig, Felix's mother, dying in childbirth: "With the gross splendour of a general saluting a flag, she named him Felix, thrust him from her, and died" (NW, 1). Robin, too, frantically cries out in despair, "looking about her in the bed as if she had lost something . . . she kept crying like a child who has walked into the commencement of a horror" (NW, 48). Nevertheless, Robin's rebuff of motherhood is not the same as Hedvig's, who dies; Sally's, who aborts; or Manresa's, who never has a child. Instead Robin comes distressingly close to committing infanticide, "holding the child high in her hand as if she were about to dash it down" (NW, 48), then changes her mind and abandons the sad, sickly boy as an admittedly preferable alternative. All the same, the desertion of her child comes with consequences that she conveniently evades.

In contrast to the 1920s Flapper, who, like Manresa and Sally, is frivolous and immature — the "wild child of nature"— Robin's paucity of human compassion affiliates her with the "wild beast of nature." By "beast," however, Barnes does not imply that Robin is "beastly" in terms of a monster or a fiend — Robin simply lacks self-consciousness and consideration, which makes her "inhuman." Her gaze is connected to that of a "wild beast" when Felix, after looking into Robin's eyes, "found himself seeing them still faintly clear and timeless behind the lids — the long unqualified range in the iris of wild beasts who have not tamed the focus down to meet the human eye" (NW, 37). She is also depicted as "carrying the quality of the 'way back' as animals do" (NW, 40) and has "temples like those of young beasts cutting horns" (NW, 134). When Nora meets her at the circus, even the animals find commonality with Robin. As they turn to look at her, "the orbit of light seemed to turn on her" as if only to them she is not "other," but one and the same (NW, 54). The novel concludes with Robin bizarrely "speaking in a low voice to animals" and "barking in a fit of laughter" (NW, 168, 170).

A number of critics have commented on Robin's correlation with animals. Most notably, Bonnie Kime Scott's interpretation of *Nightwood* centers on the relationship between animal and human: she construes the correlation between beast and human in Robin as a means for Barnes to challenge essentialisms such as "woman as nature." The link to the animal, according to Scott, is "the way we escape both otherness and essentialism" (*Refiguring Modernism*, 73). Diane Warren conceives of Robin's link to animals in similar terms, arguing that the entire cultural positioning of woman is "eternally located at the moment of transformation between animal and human" (*Consuming Fictions*, 128). Yet, if being affiliated with animals is a way to escape Otherness and identity, it is also a way to evade ethical responsibility toward others. In the context of *Nightwood*'s publication in 1936, this is an element that allows Nazi aggression and violence to flourish. As Zygmunt Bauman asserts, Nazi genocide was made possible by "apathy" and "indifference" rather than "outbursts of public violence" (*Modernity*, 31–32). Jenny Petherbridge tells Felix that Robin "always lets her pets die. She is so fond of them, and then she neglects them, the way animals neglect themselves" (NW,

115). But animals do not necessarily neglect their own — human "animals" do. *Nightwood* exposes that, in complete contrast to the exotically murderous and sinister cinema vamp, Robin's depravity hinges on the passivity of her character and the banality of the type of cruelty she exhibits. In point of fact, the brilliance of Barnes's analysis of evil in *Nightwood* is that it recognizes that evil is *not* Salomé or the femme fatale movie star. Levine is correct in noting that Robin does not kill or pilfer anyone's belongings ("Cinema Vamp," 279), but this does not mean she is guilt free. Instead, Barnes discloses that the surrender of humanity and lack of empathy is what lies at the center of evil and that this element of human nature can come out of "any animal" — male or female.

In many ways, Barnes's analysis of evil resembles Hannah Arendt's controversial observations on the "banality of evil." Arendt coined the term when covering the Adolf Eichmann trials in Israel in 1961 for *The New Yorker* (later published in 1963 as *Eichmann in Jerusalem: A Report on the Banality of Evil*). Arendt's observations speculate that Eichmann, despite being considered the "architect of the Holocaust" responsible for the organized deportation and extermination of the Jews, refuted what society usually perceives as villainous. According to Arendt, Eichmann was neither Iago nor Macbeth; as she sardonically states — "He *merely* never realized what he was doing" ("From *Eichmann in Jerusalem*," 379). The key to his character was wholesale self-deception, the blurring of reality and "truth." Eichmann, as Arendt depicts him (which so offended her Jewish colleagues as well as Holocaust survivors at the time), is somewhat of a clown, using stock and euphemistic phrases that muffle the horrifying and fantastic nature of the orders he was given. As Arendt insists, this is "the lesson of the fearsome, word-and-thought-defying *banality of evil*" (ibid., 365). In a letter justifying her view to Gershom Scholem, who, like other Jewish intellectuals, felt Arendt was belittling the nature of Nazi aggression, she explains the following:

> It is indeed my opinion now that evil is never "radical," that it is only extreme, and that it possesses neither depth nor any demonic dimension. It can overgrow and lay waste the whole world precisely because it spreads like fungus on the surface. It is "thought-defying," as I said, because thought tries to reach

some depth, to go to the roots, and the moment it concerns itself with evil, it is frustrated because there is nothing. That is its "banality." Only the good has depth and can be radical. (ibid., 396)

Russell Berman explains Arendt's theory of evil in terms that are strikingly similar to the way in which Robin's character is depicted. The key to Arendt's view of Eichmann, according to Berman, is that "he is not everyman but rather the individual who . . . surrenders individuality and thereby the ability to think, to make moral decisions, and to recognize the humanity of other individuals. . . . His evil is banal because it is predicated not on the decision to do bad but on the refusal to make any decisions at all" ("Wandering Z," xviii). The connection between Berman's explanation of the banality of evil and Robin is that she, too, surrenders her ability to think. Robin "held no volition for refusal" (NW, 43). As O'Connor describes her, "she can't 'put herself in another's place,' she herself is the only 'position'. . . she can't do anything in relation to anyone but herself" (NW, 146). Robin's character extends beyond the bounds of gender categories because she becomes a universal symbol that ignores the particular. She is an "enigma" because she is depicted as a figure outside the limits of an identifiable subject/object position (NW, 44). Her life, to use Arendt's terms, "possesses neither depth nor any demonic dimension" ("From *Eichmann in Jerusalem*," 396).

I would agree with Scott that the way Robin is connected with animals, or "beasts," underscores her placement in the novel as a symbol of nature. Nazi ideology, however, also linked itself to a "level of natural necessity" to justify German society's "loss of autonomy" (Berman, "Wandering Z," xvii). To quote Berman, "Perhaps more than any other motif, the desire for nature as guarantor of unchanging order—and as the alternative to the metropolis as the locus of individuality and democracy—marks the various fascist literary imaginations" (xvii). In contrast with the cities through which she roams, both the narrator and other characters time and again describe Robin in terms of nature and the primordial. When the doctor and Felix first see Robin unconscious in her hotel room, the narrator depicts her "faux" natural setting, almost as if placing her in a botanical or zoological study: "Her flesh was the texture of plant life, and beneath it one sensed a frame, broad, porous and sleepworn, as if sleep were a decay fishing her beneath the visible surface" (NW, 34). Robin's entire body appears subsumed by nature, but she is more closely linked with aspects of natural decay, fungus, and "luminous deteriorations" (NW, 34). Her positioning within a constructed, exotic, junglelike setting inside the urban metropolis of Paris alludes to the way she becomes an "illusion" of nature within the modern city. Like the *douanier* Rousseau painting, and like the painting of the lady in the yellow dress in *Between the Acts*, Robin is an inert image, lying in a room filled with "potted plants, exotic palms and cut flowers, faintly over-sung by the notes of unseen birds" (NW, 34). All of the "natural" elements in the room in actuality indicate a detention or even "annihilation" of the natural (NW, 35). Robin and her plants are taken from their natural settings to decorate the urban scene and thus facilitate an *appearance* of the exotic. Nevertheless, by definition their exoticism depends on not belonging.

Felix's, Nora's, and Jenny's attraction to Robin reveals more about the magnetism of evil than about Robin's character. As an exposé of human fascination with the depraved, *Nightwood* castigates those mesmerized by Robin even more than condemning Robin herself. Those who are drawn to watching Robin lose themselves in her gaze because they do not have to think — they use her as a mirror. In Woolf's *A Room of One's Own*, the narrator describes women as "looking glasses possessing the magic and delicious power of reflecting the figure of man at twice its natural size" (53). As she insists, "Whatever may be their use in civilised society, mirrors are essential to all violent and heroic action" (AROO, 54). The mirrors that La Trobe uses at the end of the pageant in *Between the Acts* are meant to show that violent aspect to the pageant audience. Robin similarly reflects, rather than projects, the vehement desire of her spectators. That gaze, however, melds feminine and masculine gender paradigms to gesture toward a universal or symbolic realm of human desire. For Felix, for example, Robin reflects the "newly ancient" destiny he so badly wants (NW, 42). The narrator tells us that "his love for Robin was not in truth a selection. . . . He had thought of making a destiny for himself, through laborious and untiring travail. Then with Robin it seemed to stand before him without effort" (NW, 42). Nora, too, sees in Robin a part of herself that is larger than life: "Thus the body of Robin could never be unloved, corrupt or put away" (NW, 56). Nora, even more than Felix, is described as being hypnotized: "Her mind became so transfixed that, by the agency of her fear, Robin seemed enormous and polarized" (NW, 56). Both descriptions indicate that encounters with Robin transform individuals into mesmerized spectators lacking autonomy and robbed of their own volition.

The crucial passage linking Robin to the particular threat of "spectacle" is in the novel's initial portrayal of her. Specifically, the text describes her effect on Felix, but it could well stand for any other character in the novel who is seduced by her allure — Nora, Jenny, O'Connor, or even the reader:

> The woman who presents herself to the spectator as a "picture" forever arranged is, for the contemplative mind, the chiefest danger. Sometimes one meets a woman who is beast turning human. Such a person's every movement will reduce to an image of a forgotten experience; a mirage of an eternal wedding cast on the racial memory; as insupportable a joy as would be the vision of an eland coming down an aisle of trees, chapleted with orange blossoms and a bridal veil, a hoof raised in the economy of fear, stepping in the trepidation of flesh that will become myth; as the unicorn is neither man nor beast deprived, but the human hunger pressing its breast to its prey. (NW, 37)

Initially, one would think that the narrator here is explicitly exposing the female spectacle as a threat. Yet, upon closer examination, one notices that the passage implies that it is also the "illusion" that is a threat. As Warren fittingly remarks, "The danger is not in the woman, but in the 'contemplative mind' which reads the scene, and seduces itself" (Consuming Fictions, 128). The spectator who succumbs to the allure of the spectacle is not passively manipulated — he or she is complicit in a relationship that can be perilous since the spectator's desire is insatiable and its goal too elusive to attain. This is the same type of mind that chooses to be seduced by the fascist and Nazi spectacles in Europe during that period. In the case of Nightwood, the woman who presents herself as a "picture" and the gazer are interconnected in their culpability. The cinema vamp, the Flapper, the literary heroines, the Madonna, or any female "mirage" for that matter is prey to an audience and cultural history that positions her as icon to fulfill its own needs — to reflect its "human hunger." Nevertheless, the particular woman who "arranges herself" as an object and is the "beast turning human" facilitates that fantasy, making it possible for the mythic violent past to continue into the present. The woman is thus culpable in the effects of the spectacle even if she is not directly responsible for the actions of the gazers.

This aspect of culpability makes the "image" of woman in Barnes's novel vastly different from the painting of the lady in the yellow robe in Woolf's *Between the Acts*. The lady hanging on the wall of Pointz Hall is just "a picture" without historical context. She is not "an ancestor" (*BTA*, 33). Barnes's woman, on the other hand, has an active and crucial role in the past and present. As the passage continues, the woman as "picture" takes on universal proportions, making it clear that she is an example of one of many "mirages." First the passage describes "the woman," then "such a person," who then turns into "a mirage," then "an eland," and lastly "a unicorn." The passage indicates how the woman becomes characterized as one object in a long, transmutable list of fantasies capable of seducing the generic "contemplative mind." Barnes's understanding of the aspects of illusion and fantasy that lead spectators to succumb to violence to satisfy their "human hunger" easily extends to the political context. Fascism, and the spectacle that Nazism promoted, glorified the mythic past to mirror how society wanted to see itself. Barnes's passage not only unveils this important aspect of its appeal but also eerily predicts the evil and tyranny that made this perfect image possible.

Conspicuously echoing the Nazi political and social fantasy taking over Europe, the *Nightwood* passage cited previously contemplates the very nature of myth, desire, and impossible satisfaction. As Linda Schulte-Sasse explains, Nazism promoted a fantasy of honor, strength, and unity to mask the impossibility of the ideals by which individuals identify themselves. "We are constantly subjected to demands by our reality but can never fully understand what this reality 'wants' of us; nor, of course, can we meet this demand. . . . Fantasy masks the fact that desire is by definition never satisfied" (*Entertaining the Third Reich*, 7–8).[49] To establish a genealogy for itself, Nazism used ancient symbols, such as the swastika, and associated its power with Greek and Norse myths and a racial heredity of legendary powers. Harmless as the eland (an animal featured in early cave paintings) or the unicorn may seem to *Nightwood*'s readers, a mythical and ancient past of "forgotten experience" can be dangerous when spectators are subsumed into believing that the myth is real. The image becomes "an eternal wedding cast on the racial memory" (NW, 37) because the significance of an ancient past and the power of myth are also wedded to produce an illusion of racial privilege. Only those who share in that "racial memory," like the gazer in the passage, can participate in the "unsupportable joy" of unity. Idealizing a history wherein humans are "married" to a myth of nature thus excludes all those who are not part of that history, which is why this marriage is also based on fear and damage, "a hoof raised in the economy of fear, stepping in the trepidation of flesh" (NW, 37).

Historical allegories linked with the figure of a woman, Barnes seems to imply, are a trap—a form of illusion that links us with patriarchal blood and violence that would consume the present entirely. Felix's attraction to the "picture" of Robin is just as misguided as his obsession for "Old Europe" and why he "felt that the great past might mend a little if he bowed low enough, if he succumbed and gave homage" (NW, 9). By succumbing to an illusion of the past that is ideal, and ultimately false, Felix is left with no future. Racially identified as Jewish in the text, he neither belongs to that racially constructed past, nor does the illusion he grabs on to to reinvent his past have any substance. Employing traditionally gendered symbols to depict the fantasy of a mythic past, the passage in *Nightwood* continues to bear out the danger of this illusion. As if staring at Eugène Delacroix's painting of Marianne in *Liberty Leading the People at the Barricades* (1835), we see the image of woman in her traditional role as national symbol, except that Barnes exposes how it is tainted by violence: "Such a woman is the infected carrier of the past: before her the structure of our head and jaws ache—we feel that we could eat her, she who is eaten death returning, for only then do we put our face close to the blood on the lips of our forefathers" (NW, 37). The desire to conceive of the present in terms of the past means continuing the violence of "our forefathers," the narrator insinuates. Likewise, those who idealize woman as myth assume a false sense of control over the present that can only end in terror. Both the women and the men who facilitate that fantasy, Barnes implies, are "infected" with malevolence.

Jenny Petherbridge's character and her association with history would buttress the argument that to surrender the self and construct an identity based on a mythic past is perilous for both the object and subject of that construction. Like Lucy Swithin in *Between the Acts,* who escapes to read H. G. Wells's *Outline of History* to support her fantasy of a utopian "oneness," Jenny's experience of the present is overshadowed by the prominence she awards to "history." The difference is that Jenny feeds her fantasy by escaping into people's lives rather than into books. The narrator relates that Jenny has "second-hand dealings with life," as she plunders other people's lives for their pasts (NW, 66). Described as wearing out four husbands "in an effort to make them historical" (NW, 65), she is characterized by a compilation of contradictions, "feeble and ferocious," "old, yet expectant of age," embodying two instincts "recoil and advance" (NW, 65). If Robin is a symbol of the Nazi spectacle, then Jenny is resonant with the "splitting and binding" of Nazi propaganda (Kaplan, *Reproductions of Banality,* 24). As the narrator describes her, "She had the fluency of tongue and action meted out by divine providence to those who cannot think for themselves. She was the master of the over-sweet phrases, the over-tight embrace" (NW, 68). Like the Nazi propagandist, Jenny empties human language of its meaning through clichés and repeated phrases, becoming "a dealer in second-hand and therefore incalculable emotions" (NW, 68). Barnes implies that, like the woman who arranges herself into a picture, Jenny is "wicked" because by turning people, places, and objects into stories for contemplation, she fails to feel emotions such as empathy or consideration. In Berman's terms, the evil of the Nazi is that she or he "surrenders . . . the ability to think, to make moral decisions, and to recognize the humanity of other individuals" ("Wandering Z," xviii). The narrator describes Jenny as "one of the most unimportantly wicked women of her time — because she could not let her time alone, and yet could never be a part of it" (NW, 67). Separated from her experience, Jenny can only fashion a fantasy life through the exploitation of others, much like the Nazis' exploitation of Norse myth excused violence toward those who were vulnerable.

When Jenny (Propaganda) meets Robin (Banality of Evil), the inevitable result, as the narrator tells us, is "catastrophe" (NW, 68). It would appear intentional that Robin and Jenny meet in 1927, the same year as the first Nuremburg Rally. The narrative effect of Robin, like the political rhetoric, becomes more brutal. Sylvia, the little girl whom Robin left in

Jenny's care, is left terrorized by Robin's manipulation of her; Nora, having been abandoned, becomes fanatically obsessed with Robin's image; and Jenny has "fallen apart" in Robin's wake, left between two tortures, "the past she can't share, and the present she can't copy" (NW, 124). Even Felix turns to drink to cope with his shattered destiny with his former wife. Because she has exposed their own desires to escape reality, Robin becomes the moment of dissolution for all the characters when she leaves them. She shatters their illusion of a unified self. According to Kaplan, the seductive nature of fascism "is not . . . a 'flight from freedom' but an imagined 'flight to freedom' in the collective will to breach all limits" (*Reproductions of Banality*, 35). Similarly, others see in Robin a reflection of their own desires to breach the limits of their own conceptions of themselves and their place in history. She becomes an Other for those who determine their identities against her. Nevertheless, once she leaves, the characters surrounding her catch sight of the terrifying abyss of the unknowable. As Nora finally figures out, "Only the impossible lasts forever" (NW, 139). Once the illusion of the Absolute image is broken, characters are exposed to their own finite and powerless realities.

As the range of female and male characters and their desires suggest, evil depends on social and cultural constructions, but it distills humanity to its most base, animal nature. O'Connor describes Robin as being "outside the 'human type'—a wild thing caught in a woman's skin, monstrously alone, monstrously vain" (NW, 146). Robin is "a girl who resembles a boy" (NW, 136)—a woman who overturns conventional stereotypes of female behavior by refusing to be contained within the myth of female domesticity, maternity, and self-sacrifice. Unlike the subversive females in *Between the Acts* and *Goodbye to Berlin*, however, she does not overturn her passive role as object of the spectacle. As object she is released from responsibility and has the option of refusing moral choice. Robin's character thus suggests that the monstrous is not limited to one sex. As the former priest tells O'Connor at the end of the novel, "Women can cause trouble, too" (NW, 164). Evil, after all, has no gender. It can hide under the image, mask, social attire, or civilized acts of any kind of animal. *Goodbye to Berlin* concludes with Frl. Shroeder changing her "coat" to prepare to embrace the Führer; *Between the Acts* ends with preparations for war "as the dog fox fights with the vixen" (BTA, 197).

Barnes's conclusions are similar to Isherwood's and Woolf's in suggesting that any animal can adapt to political conditions. In similar terms, Theweleit suggests the lesson of fascism in *Male Fantasies* as such:

> Fascism teaches us that under certain circumstances, human beings imprisoned within themselves, within body armor and social constraints, would rather break out than fill their stomachs; and that their politics may consist in organizing that escape. . . . The utopia of fascism is an edenic freedom from responsibility. (432)

In a novel that demonstrates "nothing is really as it looks," Robin signifies the characters' desire to be released from their "body armor and social constraints" and to dream that who they are and how they affect others does not matter. As the doctor sighs when contemplating Robin, "Ah . . . to be an animal, born at the opening of the eye, going only forward, and, at the end of the day, shutting out memory with the dropping of the lid" (NW, 134–35). Robin as an allegory for fascism implies that an illusion of freedom from responsibility opens the door for "the Nazi Beast." That, in the 1930s, is the "chiefest danger" of all.

## Conclusion

Walter Benjamin maintains that the spectacle shows masses to themselves as they want to be — it acts as a mirror. The female mirror in these three novels is nevertheless distorted. It is not the mirror of propaganda, reflecting an illusion of wholeness; it is a mirror that shows the reader a full range of human possibilities. *Between the Acts*, *Goodbye to Berlin*, and *Nightwood* portray female subjects who are often cruel, ignorant, silly, and malicious — as are all human beings. If Nazism attempts to unify an image of woman, the attempt to present women in all human capacities becomes vital. Not all women are good. Nor are narrative representations of them as less-than-virtuous necessarily antifemale if the text gives them a moral choice. And, of course, in the context of political resistance, the emphasis on moral choice is essential. To a greater or lesser degree, all three novelists, by using women as an allegory to represent a political message, nevertheless raise questions about how authors are implicated in the discourse around female identity, selfhood, and the ways that modern Western societies identified individuals according to assumptions that were determined as essential, "natural," and definitive. Their novels uncover how sexism, oppression, politics, and fictional resistance are interrelated throughout the political spectrum. Nevertheless, using the allegory of the Modern Woman, these authors also indicate that if self-fashioning becomes a way of evading responsibility toward others — an escape from reality — then it ultimately supports totalitarian ideologies and their oppression of Others.

## CHAPTER 3

# Seeing Jewish or Seeing "the Jew"? The Spectral Jewish Other

Where is the people which in the last two thousand years
has been exposed to so slight changes of inner dispositions,
character, etc., as the Jewish people?
—ADOLF HITLER, *MEIN KAMPF* (1925)

The Jew is evidently a scapegoat, though *for what* he is a
scapegoat we do not yet know.
—GEORGE ORWELL, *COLLECTED ESSAYS* (1945)

A joke circulated in the 1930s about a Jewish man who meets his friend Isaac sitting on a park bench reading *Der Stürmer* (a rabidly antisemitic Nazi newspaper).[1] "Have you gone crazy?" the man asks his friend. "Why are you reading that antisemitic trash?" "Well," Isaac answers, "when I read our newspapers I hear about Jews getting harassed and beaten, losing their jobs, their stores being boycotted, and families going hungry. I can't sleep at night! In *Der Stürmer* it seems we control all the money, own the banks, and are taking over the world. This is much better news, no?"

The anecdote came to mind in examining "the Spectral Jewish Other," since it so starkly marks the contrast between the lives of Jews in the 1930s, their own perspective of that life, and the discourses circulating around "the Jew" in the European public sphere. Of course, identification of the joke is with the victims, shared by victims, not with those whose gaze constructs the modern Jew in terms of money, power, and corruption. The joke is not terribly funny when one realizes the power those antisemitic discourses had in persuading the European public not to see real Jews behind stereotypical constructions of "the Jew." As I will argue in this chapter, it was specifically that "non-appearing" or "erasure" of the conditions of Jewish life that prepared the ground for the apathy toward National Socialism's policies against European Jewry, or, at worst, the active support of genocide.

## "The Jew" in Modernity

In the previous chapter, I examined representations of the "modern appearing woman" in Woolf, Barnes, and Isherwood. This chapter, in contrast, focuses on the "modern *nonappearing* Jew"—what Zygmunt Bauman calls the "conceptual Jew" or what I have termed the "spectral" Jewish other.[2] Parallel to the sexist attitudes toward women in modern society, the manner in which Jews were set out as pariahs in European discourse both mirrored and magnified Nazism's focus on masculinity, heredity, and the future of the German body politic (*Volkskörper*).[3] In many ways, the discourses surrounding antisemitism, misogyny, and homophobia in the 1930s were interconnected and inflected by one another. Jews, women, and homosexuals were all conceived as both physically and mentally inferior and thought to be consumed by emotion and sexual passion rather than reason. If not controlled or managed, their influence could spread and threaten the health of the Nazi body as a whole. National Socialism's Judeophobia and fear of contamination by Jewish "blood" nevertheless reached a delusional level that was distinctive in its nature and far more destructive than its sexism or homophobia.[4] There was no way to escape the deadly effects of racial antisemitism in Europe, even for those Jews who had assimilated, converted to Christianity, or were children or grandchildren of intermarriage.

Anti-Nazi writers and intellectuals in the 1930s clearly understood how central antisemitism was to Nazi ideology. By the time Barnes, Woolf, and Isherwood were writing, the Nuremberg Laws had been enacted (1935), Hitler's *Mein Kampf* had already been translated into English, and articles on Jewish persecution appeared widely and frequently in the English-language press. For this reason, it is not surprising that their works would feature Jewish characters to articulate the impending risk of a Nazi take-over. Like the Jew — an ultimate Other — female or gay writers or both could empathize with the Jew's alienation from "the nation" at a time when their own personal freedoms were at risk. As Maren Linett observes, "these writers see in their Jewish characters reflections of their own emotional pain and alienation from literary history" and thus identify with them (*Modernism,* 2). What is nonetheless disconcerting is the way in which they characterize Jews using the same damaging stereotypes that contribute to the Jew's alienation and persecution in the first place.[5]

A close examination of Jewish characters in *Nightwood, Between the Acts,* and *Goodbye to Berlin* importantly reveals not only the ways in which Jews were alienated through discourse but also how conceptions of "belonging" were articulated in 1930s Britain and Europe, even among liberal intellectuals. It is clear that Jewish characters in these texts are meant to function within the scope of political resistance, as do the female, lesbian, and homosexual characters in these three novels. The "Modern Woman" and "the homosexual" in Barnes's, Isherwood's, and Woolf's novels, similar to Jews, test the limits of accepted ideas regarding community, national character, and self-identity. Yet, there are some significant differences in the construction of Jews, as opposed to other marginal characters, that become inflected in these texts. For one thing, these Jews are typecast as foreign and alien, rather than a part of the society or community in which they live; they are inexorably linked with finance, commercialization, or the superficial and excessive aspects of modern urban culture. Moreover, the Jews in these texts do not look like other characters. They are, for the most part, physical caricatures whose differences are marked through various timeless and unchanging physical and psychological traits that identify "the Jew."

Even more intriguing, while the various Jewish characters come from different countries, backgrounds, and conditions, the most striking similarity in the various textual representations is that these Jews do not identify themselves with Judaism in any particular way, self-consciously "perform" their Jewishness, or engage in any acts of Jewish tradition. The only thing that identifies them as Jews is how the narrator and the other characters perceive their difference. Despite name changes, conversions, dress, fluency of language, even a non-Jewish parent, Jewishness is foisted upon characters conceived of as "Jewish" as a physical, class, gender, or psychological identification in the novels. Felix Volkbein in *Nightwood*, Ralph Manresa in *Between the Acts*, and the Landauers in *Goodbye to Berlin* are all either assimilated, intermarried, or trying to "pass" (if perhaps unsuccessfully) as ordinary citizens of their countries. They are "Jews" in quotation marks because they are racialized constructions of discourse, as opposed to a part of the multifarious group of men and women who identify themselves as Jewish or affiliate themselves with a Jewish community. As implied by the title of this chapter, writers such as Barnes, Isherwood, and Woolf might "see Jewish" in their texts by using "the Jew" as a concept or narrative inspiration. But this figure is based on an image that places the social reality of Jews outside the "we" of Western culture. This idea, I will argue, is not incidental or harmless. The opposition to political antisemitism that at the same time expressed prejudice against particular Jews (conceived of as alien, excessive, or "rich") normalized and legitimized stereotypes in a manner that was politically and psychologically damaging to Jews at the time.

In the past decade, numerous studies have drawn attention to the central role the figure of the Jew plays in modernist literature and in European modernism in general.[6] More often than not, as revealed by examinations of literary representations of "the Jew" in works by T. S. Eliot, Ezra Pound, James Joyce, Ernest Hemingway, F. Scott Fitzgerald, and Jean Rhys (among many others), Jewish characters become receptacles for a wide range of thematic, social, and political concerns: alienation, victimization, anxiety toward modernization, nostalgia, pity, and repulsion. And that is why, as Bryan Cheyette argues, analyzing Jewish representation in texts can provide "a key touchstone" for examining what European society considered "us" and what the cultural sphere considered "culture" (*Constructions*, 12). In my analysis of "the Jew" as textual "touchstone," I feel it is important to specifically draw attention to the implications of Jewish portrayal in the historical period leading up to the Holocaust. For this reason, I rely on Susan Shapiro's concept of "*écriture judaïque*" in my analysis of Jewish representation in the three novels. *Écriture judaïque* (a play on *écriture feminine*) identifies the way the Jew is used as a metonym for writing that is "displaced, exiled." It is a strategy that suggests a crisis of subjectivity within a narrative mode that "writes against representation," but it is also a device that "questions by a perpetual dismantling and displacing of its subject" (Shapiro, *Écriture Judaïque*, 183–84). The Jew in the text thus functions as a symbol for ambiguity, displacement, or uncertainty, while at the same time remaining outside the Western culture that analyzes him as such. Similar to Bryan Cheyette's term "semitic discourse," *écriture judaïque* identifies how "the Jew" is used as a subject of discourse rather than as a historical subject.[7] *Écriture judaïque*, however, avoids the somewhat problematic term "semitic," which points to the way in which Jewishness is conceived from an outside perspective (and only in terms of its opposite: Aryan). It also enables us to focus on a particular type of conceptualization of a universalized Jew that is linked to the way liberal intellectuals theorized the conditions of fascist ideology and Nazi persecution. Shapiro's concept specifically refers to the way in which the trope of "the Jew" is used in postmodern theory as a consequence of the "shattering of the telos" caused by the Holocaust.[8] I am extending her term to consider the years immediately preceding the Holocaust since the imminent destruction and persecution of Jews by the Nazis was already quite evident and had entered into public discourse. As I maintain, these factors certainly influenced how the metaphor of "Jew" was used in anti-Nazi fiction.

This nagging question remains, however: *why* does the Jew become so central in English and American modernist literature? Some scholars posit that in England it could be because such a large number of immigrants relocated from Eastern Europe in the wake of pogroms at the beginning of the twentieth century.[9] Linett, for example, notes that between the 1880s and World War I, 120,000–150,000 Eastern European Jews moved to Britain to escape persecution in Russia, Poland, and the Ukraine, increasing their visibility as a foreign Other (*Modernism*, 23). Although the influx of Jews to Britain dropped off following the Aliens Act of 1905 (which tried to limit the number of immigrants), Jews in Britain became one of the predominant topics of interest of literature and media from the 1890s through World War II.[10] The arrival of 60,000 Jewish refugees from Germany during the late 1930s increased British consciousness of Jewish issues (Kushner, *Persistence*, 12). *The Times Literary Supplement*, for example, between 1918 and 1939 published "roughly 200 short book notes and longer review articles about Jewish topics, with the number of longer articles (as well as the total number of articles) increasing as the time period proceeded" (Linett, *Modernism*, 25).[11] Even as early as 1933, *The Times* published four extracts of a one-volume English abridged version of *Mein Kampf* (entitled *My Struggle*), exposing English readers to Hitler's racial doctrine for the first time. Although the more crudely explicit expressions of antisemitism had been expunged in the abridgment, Hitler's racial agenda for the Jews was clear. By the end of 1933, more than 10,687 copies of Hitler's book had been sold, and virtually every major newspaper in England had reviewed it (thirty-six reviews in total); by 1938 the abridged version had sold close to 100,000 copies (Barnes and Barnes, *Hitler's "Mein Kampf,"* 8–9, 16). Interest was so significant that by March 1939 a full-text English edition of *Mein Kampf* was published in England, as were two competing American editions, to "mixed reviews" (ibid., 64, 68).[12] This interest did not necessarily mean that the average Brit was more sympathetic toward Jewish individuals, but it did contribute to the frequency of Jews as a topic. "Jews," as Tony Kushner observes, "were 'news' and antisemitism was common in daily discourse, literature and the press" (*Persistence*, 12).[13]

What is evident in the descriptions of assimilated Jews in these texts, however, is that more than an anxiety about immigration or fear of the foreign or "racial" Other, the acute interest in "the Jew" appears to be made up of the disarticulation of his difference. Jews could not easily be defined in categories of class, race, skin color, or gender; they therefore became emblems of the discomfort or the "uncanny" associated with slippage between self and Other.[14] This was evident in the United States, where Jews and Jewish issues became prominent topics of interest in the public sphere during the interwar period even in places where they were not the most significant or visible Other (African Americans and Asians were more visible as minorities). As Daniel Itzkovitz indicates, Jewishness and Jewish immigration from Europe tested the boundaries and notions of American identity and belonging, producing "a mountain of essays, abstracts, books, articles, songs, novels, and short stories . . . dedicated to the very mission of locating Jewish difference." "In fact," Itzkovitz remarks, "the more 'the same' the Jew was, the more there was to fear, and the more the Jew slipped across the line into otherness" ("Secret Temples," 178).

According to Bauman's analysis of "the Jew" in modernity, the conception of Jews was that they *were not just unlike any other nation; they were unlike any other foreigners.*" Jews were not outsiders to the nation because they came from somewhere else but because "they undermined the very difference between hosts and guests, the native and the foreign" (Bauman, *Modernity,* 52). The "fate of the Jews," as Bauman states,

> *epitomized the awesome scope of social upheaval and served as a vivid, obtrusive reminder of the erosion of old certainties....* Whoever felt thrown out of balance, threatened or displaced, could easily — and rationally — make sense of his own anxiety through articulating the experienced turbulence as an imprint of Jewish subversive incongruity. (*Modernity,* 45)

Since such an overdetermined symbol could not possibly exist in reality, the "conceptual Jew" becomes what Bauman calls "slimy" or "*visqueux*": he hovers between categories in a way that is fluid, ever-changing, and shifting (*Modernity,* 40). This "Jew" contains so many contradictory combinations of meaning that he could, in effect, stand in as any unacceptable element of modern society. For the Communist, "the Jew" became capitalist; for the fascist, he became Communist; for the traditionalist, modern; for the modernist, antimodern; for the intellectual, overly emotional; for the rural folk-worshiper, an urban parvenu. He was poor but rich, oversexed but effeminate — in sum, "the Jew" became the "bogeyman" of modern Europe.

Because modern conceptions of "the Jew" make it possible for a single figure to embody multiple types of often-conflicting discourses, racialized hostility toward Jews is often theorized as being distinct from other types of enmity toward the Other or the foreign. Bauman, for instance, differentiates among the concepts of: "xenophobia," the kind of hatred that results from fear of the stranger and the immigrant, common to every period; "contestant enmity," the fear that the alien may "penetrate" and change the native group; and "racism," a hatred that is based on declaring "a certain category of people endemically and hopelessly resistant to control and immune to all efforts at amelioration . . . [and] demands that the offending category ought to be removed" (*Modernity,* 64). Specifically, antisemitism as a racial hatred was particular to modernity because it relied on Jewishness being a biological difference rather than a cultural one. Even the term "antisemitism," as Sander Gilman contends, reflects nineteenth-century pseudoscientific discourse of ethnology and linguistics.[15] It is a term that specifically draws the dividing line between the binary of "Aryan" and "Semite" as linguistic terms. "The very choice of the label 'anti-Semitism,'" Gilman argues, "was to create the illusion of a new scientific discourse for the hatred of Jews and to root this hatred in the inherent difference of their language. . . . It has no validity except as a marker for the discourse of Jewish difference" (*Jew's Body*, 5).[16]

The more difficult it became to detect difference, as with regard to the assimilated Jew, the more those ambiguous, slippery lines of Jewishness were drawn, rearticulated, and insisted upon. As we see in the depiction of Ralph Manresa, the Volkbeins, and the Landauers in the texts I discuss later, assimilated Jews were conceived of in terms of excess, or "too much"—too rich, too sexual, too effeminate, too impassive, too emotional, too uncouth, too fake; in short, they exceed the categories of ordinary differences among other types of characters in the novels. Even more paradoxically, the nonacceptance of the assimilated Jew is directly linked with the presumed liberalism of modern society. As the novels reveal, liberal, modern European states — such as England, Germany, and France — promoted a double standard with regard to Jews that Barnes, Isherwood, and Woolf reiterate. The European nations encouraged a program of individualism, human rights, and toleration but demanded assimilation that "affirmed the dominance of the position in society from which the offer of toleration was made" (Feldman, "Was Modernity Good for the Jews?" 175). The incorporation of Jews into modern European society was based on diluting Jewish identity, but in return that dilution was not met with acceptance. This "double bind" of impossible assimilation is noted by a number of scholars. Alain Finkielkraut, for example, describes the attempt of Jews to assimilate in France using the metaphor of "a man running fast, hoping to leave his shadow behind" (*Imaginary Jew*, 82). In France, England, Austria, Germany, and other European nations, when modern Jews intermarried, they were accused of "race-mixing"; when they married each other, they were guilty of "inbreeding." As Ann Pellegrini observes, "At both poles . . . Jews were conceptualized as exceeding the norm. They were a 'people' too much of extremes" ("Whiteface Performances," 112). Since

Jewish difference was too broad to contain "distinctly Jewish traits" once Jews assimilated, the mark of difference became "the state of extremity itself" (Itzkovitz, "Secret Temples," 181).

Similar attitudes toward the assimilated Jew emerged in the United States in the 1930s, with some distinct differences. Unlike France, England, or Germany, there were few overtly antisemitic clubs, leagues, political movements, or newspapers (aside from those "imported" from Europe). Moreover, as mentioned previously, there was a more visible racial Other on which to project difference: the African American. Nevertheless, as Karen Brodkin observes, antisemitism and belief in a European hierarchy of races did take root in the late nineteenth and early twentieth centuries, mostly among the wealthy, Protestant elite. Such works as Madison Grant's *The Passing of the Great Race*, published in 1916 (notably read and quoted by Tom Buchanan in F. Scott Fitzgerald's *The Great Gatsby*), was highly influential, popularizing theories of the superiority of northern European races and the "native" white Americans who originated from there (Brodkin, *How Jews Became White*, 28).[17] Antisemitism especially flourished in institutions of higher education, where there were often quotas and blocked acceptance or promotions of Jews.[18] Until World War II, when Jews attained more economic prosperity and the fight against Nazi Germany somewhat altered conceptions of "whiteness" and racial hierarchies, Jews were considered part of a Euroethnic "off white" or "not quite white" (ibid., 36).[19] Even the American ideal of "tolerance," as Laura Levitt maintains, worked "both [to] regulate and maintain a deep ambivalence around Jews, Jewishness, and Judaism . . . even in the present" ("Impossible Assimilations," 807). Jews in America could not easily "fit" into a perception that they were "the same" but just "went to a different church." Thus, the Jew in America, as in Europe, produced a "complicated legacy of impossible assimilation — . . . The harder this subject tries to fit in, ironically, the more s/he differs. Instead of sameness, these efforts produce an excess that always marks the subject as other" (ibid., 809).

If in all of these various theories "the Jew" serves as a concept, an allegory, a universalism, or an overdetermined symbol or excess, where does the real Jew go? Within the discourse circulating around the conceptual Jew, the social reality of the actual Jew is placed in a void that virtually obliterates individual Jewish histories and experiences. The spectacle of

Jewishness is thus more precisely a *specter* of Jewishness — a fantasy that can inhabit contradictory and illogical explanations for any and all social and political ills. Phyllis Lassner posits that this "spectral" Jewish figure appears in many canonical British modern texts as a form of gothic terror, the "chameleon-like nature of these characters . . . demonstrated the tremulous relationships between myths of a unified British national character, economic uncertainty, and an influx of immigrants" ("Necessary Jew," 295). The mythical, occult figuration of the Jew, however, denies the possibility of Jewish self-determination and also obscures the variations and vibrancy of Jewish practices, beliefs, and cultural traditions.

Ultimately, the discourse surrounding the racialized, demonized, phantomlike Jew became essential to Nazism's understanding of itself. The image of wholeness upon which the Nazi spectacle depended required its flip side to ensure that a racially "pure" nation was possible. The categorization of "Jew" as Other and the erasure and dehumanization of the people who considered themselves Jewish facilitated the illusion and made it viable. In many ways, the Nazi spectacle exists *because* of the Jew. Linda Schulte-Sasse explains the central positioning of the Jew in Nazi ideology as such:

> [The Jew] embodies all obstacles to Nazism's harmonious corporatist society, yet, paradoxically, empowers the illusion that this harmony is possible. Since the social antagonism generated by modernity is displaced on the "Jew" and condensed in him, he is necessary for society to believe in itself, to disavow its internal contradictions. (*Entertaining the Third Reich*, 49)

In other words, the category of "Aryan" is only possible if it contains its opposite, "the Jew" — an entity composed of all the inconsistencies, antagonisms, and negations held within the ideology itself. Constantly and consistently, as Vivian Patraka contends, the spectacle of parades, films, and holidays reiterate, over and over, that binary of Aryan-Jew (*Spectacular Suffering*, 36). Thus the Jew is not only different and dangerous, but his *anti*-appearance in the Nazi spectacle is also necessary. This spectral Jew, moreover, made it possible for Germans, even when they did not feel particularly hostile toward Jews, to ignore the fate of individual Jewish people. Essentially, this produced the conditions for genocide that Bauman terms "co-operation by non-resistance" (*Modernity*, 32). Not only in Germany but also in other parts of Europe — and in England — the conceptual Jew replaced the real Jew in public discourse, resulting in an apathy that allowed the public to "resign themselves to ignorance" regarding the fate of millions of people (ibid.).

## The OTHER Other: Ways of Seeing Jewish

While "the Jew" might have been an imaginary, spectral figure that eluded boundaries of categorization, there were nevertheless also concrete ways in which the physical Jewish body was conceived and visualized in the modern Western European imagination. A complex set of codes characterizes the textual Jew in Barnes's, Woolf's, and Isherwood's novels that paradoxically link the tension between the subject and the object, and between the visible and the invisible. As Jay Geller, among others, notes, when modern social order began to crumble, identity became fixed on the body — "especially the bodies of those menacing others":

> The body remained inscribed with the natural markers of gender and sexuality, nation and race. Identity was read off these inextricably intertwined signs as these sciences provided a grammar of truth that treated that body . . . as the language by which "natural" difference was expressed. (*Freud's Jewish Body*, 7)

Anxiety around the hidden aspects of identity expressed itself as a need to make the invisible visible. Identifying the way the Jewish body looked, therefore, became key at a time when Jews were assimilating into mainstream culture. In particular, the Jewish body became a preoccupation for Western European scientists who were prompted to establish difference as a real, measurable, and visible category. Of course, there were certainly some realities to Jewish bodily difference (such as circumcision), but ideas about the Jew's body had more to do with perceptions of racial inferiority based on degeneracy and disease than on visible, biological traits or ritual practices.

In Sander Gilman's groundbreaking work *The Jew's Body*, he analyzes "how certain myths reflect basic cultural and psychological ways of dealing with the difference of the Jews" (4). Specifically, Gilman explores how the "vocabulary" of Jewish difference became part of Western culture through various myths, such as: the Jew's speech, or an idea that Jews "speak differently" because they have a "hidden language"; the Jew's feet and the Jewish "gait" (a disorder that supposedly revealed neurological imbalances); the Jew's nose and its connection to an aberrant sexuality; the Jew's gaze, eyes, or "look"; Jewish nervous disorders or other Jewish illnesses; and Jewish criminality, madness, and genius. Other persistent stereotypes include the relentless accusation that Jews are enmeshed with money, power, and corruption; that the Jew belongs to no country and is therefore a parasite who mimics other cultures; and that the Jew is "effeminate" or sexually deviant. Some of these myths will be discussed later as they emerge in the texts under examination.

The icon of the Jew as "wandering" and alien is an old and lasting notion that can be traced back to virtually the beginning of the Jewish Diaspora. Dating back to the thirteenth century (but revived in the sixteenth), the "Wandering Jew" is based on the Christian myth of Ahasver, or Ahasuerus, a Jew who taunted Jesus on his way to the Crucifixion and was thereby cursed to wander the earth. The figure has been the topic of countless poems, novels, works of art, plays, and films in Western culture. The myth, however, has also been used against the Jews to substantiate an essential Jewish "difference" that in the 1930s became linked with the image of the Jewish refugee (Kushner, *Persistence*, 115–16). Conceptions that Jews belong nowhere or that wandering is a fundamental part of their character became an integral part of their representation in Nazi Germany and one of Hitler's main indictments against them. In *Mein Kampf*, Hitler declares the Jew is "only and always a *parasite* in the body of other peoples . . . a sponger" (276–77). "The Jew of all times," as Hitler alleges, "has lived in the states of other peoples, and there formed his own state, which to be sure, habitually sailed under the disguise of 'religious community'" (277). Since the Jew is seen as a "borrower" and "imitator" of foreign cultures — "without any culture of its own" (275) — a "folkish culture" has no place for him. This notion is especially evident in the portrayals of Ralph Manresa in *Between the Acts* and Felix Volkbein in *Nightwood*, neither of whom can escape his foreignness or participate in "authentic" expressions of folk culture such as the pageant or circus.

Historically, Jews have also persistently been connected to a concept of money and "avarice," which is also reiterated in the three texts. Even medieval Christian Jew-hatred, for instance, was often based on the idea that Jews were greedy, characterized by "avarice for the possession of 'things,' of 'money,'" which, as Gilman explains, "signals his inability to understand (and produce) anything of transcendent aesthetic value" (*Jew's Body*, 124). In its modern manifestation, this image is linked with the image of the "international Jewish financier" and Jew as usurer, or Shylock.[20] This long-standing stereotype of Jews being ultimately uncreative and materialistic was also linked to a notion of corrupt sexuality and led to their expulsion from England (the Edict of Expulsion was in effect from 1290 to 1655) and other parts of Europe in the thirteenth to fifteenth centuries. Gilman summarizes:

> Canon law forbade the taking of interest. . . . [A]ccording to Thomas Aquinas, [it] was impossible, for money, not being alive, could not reproduce. Jews, in taking money, treated money as if it were alive, as if it were a sexualized object. The Jew takes money as does the prostitute, as a substitute for higher values, for love and beauty. And thus the Jew becomes the representative of the deviant genitalia, not under control of the moral, rational, conscience. (ibid., 124)

Much like the prostitute, the Jew played a critical role in society by functioning in a mediational relationship as a moneylender that allowed men to believe in a fantasy of "higher values," such as Christian virtue, love, and beauty. Societies required the services of moneylending, much as they supported but simultaneously condemned prostitution. Both Jews and prostitutes allowed men to imagine themselves, and their relationship to their property (including money and wives), as virtuous. By extension, Jews were depicted as "polluting" art and culture because they challenged a social order based on the separation of beauty (static, contained) and desire (infinite, out of control). Sexual desire was projected onto the Jew, and his money was conceived as circulating in a manner that destroyed a "pure" creative process linked with sexless birth and procreation.

The image of the avaricious Jew whose appetite for money, power, and sexual conquests knew no bounds persisted well into the twentieth century and even into the present. Especially in the nineteenth century, as Jews in Western Europe assimilated into mainstream culture, anxieties regarding sexual relations between Jewish males and gentile women and the corruption of a future generation of Christian children became clearly identifiable. Characters in popular novels, such as Fagin in Charles Dickens's *Oliver Twist* (1837–39) or Svengali in George du Maurier's *Trilby* (1894), depict Jewish men as evil, devilish, and in danger of violating and entrapping innocent Christian women or children.[21] Especially in Germany, at the forefront of scientific development, studies emerged legitimating concerns that Jews, having "uncontrolled sexual drive," were in danger of corrupting gentile women and preventing the regeneration of the Aryan race (Mosse, *Nationalism and Sexuality*, 140). Films and propaganda of the Third Reich often built on the fear and stereotype of the Jew's lecherous nature and "supersexualization" (Brod, "Some Thoughts," 92). The infamous antisemitic Nazi propaganda film *Jud Süss* (1941), for example, portrayed the Jew, Süss Oppenheimer, as someone consumed by greed and sexual rapaciousness who can only be stopped from polluting German virtue through death.[22]

While perceived as destroying Christian beauty and virtue through aberrant desire, "the Jew" was concurrently thought to be less virile than Christian men, prone to nervousness, weakness, and mental illness — like women (Mosse, *Nationalism and Sexuality*, 143). The Jew's body thus became a site of gender and sexual anxiety, a slate on to which identifiable "signs" of difference were inscribed. The feminization of the Jewish male body, in particular, became a prominent theme at the end of the nineteenth and early twentieth centuries with the publication of Otto Weininger's immensely influential 1903 study, *Sex and Character* (*Geschlecht und Charakter*). Described as a "self-hating" Jew from Vienna, Weininger proposed the idea that distinct male and female chemical elements existed in every person: the masculine element (*Arrheno*) was responsible for morality, decisiveness, and complex thinking; the feminine element (*Thelyplasma*) was composed of passion and emotion but lacked the sense of self and spirituality to control that emotion. For Weininger, only men could make up the moral and creative foundation of society, while "the woman of the highest standard is immeasurably beneath the man of the lowest" (*Sex and Character*, 302). The Jews, according to Weininger, were "saturated with femininity to such an extent that the most manly Jew is more feminine than the least manly Aryan" (ibid., 306). Jewishness, like femaleness, was not only a "negative" trait but also impossible to transcend because it was based in scientific truths. Especially in his thirteenth chapter, Weininger outlines how Jews, like women, have no capacity for reason or morality and are thereby unredeemably unfit for public life. Weininger, who committed suicide shortly after the book's publication, was significant not only for racist and misogynist thinkers like Hitler. His prominence also spread to intellectual circles, where his ideas were discussed widely among such writers and artists as Dorothy Richardson, August Strindberg, Gertrude Stein, Franz Kafka, Charlotte Perkins Gilman (who reviewed the book), D. H. Lawrence, and James Joyce. As Ritchie Robertson claims, the book "marked something of a watershed in expressing stereotypes whose crass explicitness seemed legitimated by scientific rhetoric" ("Historicizing Weininger," 35).[23]

Needless to say, in all of the aforementioned discussions of stereotypes of the Jew and *his* relationship to gender, sexuality, money, time, place, and race, there is an obvious lacuna. If the Jew's body is male, and onto this male body society projects various kinds of visual stereotypes, but this Jew is also imaginary, a phantom of real Jewishness, where does the female Jew fit in? Is she even a concept within the conceptualization of the Jew, or is she, in effect, a specter of a specter? As Ann Pellegrini asks, "What room does the intense, anti-Semitic identification of male Jews with 'woman' leave for Jewish women?" ("Whiteface Performances," 109). The consequence of separating Jewishness into a binary with race and masculinity on one side and feminine gender on the other, as Pellegrini emphasizes, is that "*All Jews are womanly, but no women are Jews*" (ibid., 118). It would seem that representation can be thought through the female Jewish body no less than through the male, yet this is not so obvious when one looks at Jewish stereotyping.

Important studies by Janet Hadda and Paula Hyman indicate that nineteenth- and twentieth-century notions of the female roles varied between Jewish cultures, but based on traditional roles they often offered more emancipation to women than their non-Jewish middle-class counterparts.[24] Hadda, in her analysis of Yiddish literature, for instance, exposes an image of the Jewish woman as willfully striving for independence (often unsuccessfully). Hyman offers a wider sociopolitical analysis of Jewish gender roles, proposing that notions of Jewish womanhood differed in Eastern and Western Europe. In Germany, France, and England, where civil liberties brought more opportunities for economic mobility and assimilation of (male) Jews into modern bourgeois society, gender roles reflected the wider European tendencies. Jewish women were mostly restricted to domestic roles and in charge of the spiritual life of the home (Hyman, *Gender and Assimilation*, 18–19). In contrast, Eastern European antisemitism restricted social and economic mobility of the Jewish communities, which gave rise to a modern Yiddish culture that tended toward Jewish community concerns and involvement in workers' rights (such as the left-wing General Jewish Labor Union of Russia and Poland, or "the Bund"). A greater proportion of women in these communities, as Hyman notes, were secularized; they held jobs, had access to education, and often dedicated themselves to education and activism (ibid., 75). In the context of the European *Männerbund*, however, the impression that Jewish women were "mannish" and would upset the natural social order prevailed. Daniel Boyarin, for example, points out that antifeminism expressed itself as hostility toward Jewish women. The German League for the Prevention of Women's Emancipation, in particular, criticized the "modern feminist movement" for being supported by "Jewesses" and other foreign elements (Boyarin, *Unheroic Conduct*, 255). The same rationale on the part of race science that assumed male Jews were "womanish" since they were lacking in sexual dimorphism also asserted that Jewish women had overly masculine characteristics. Political activism on the part of Jewish women was "evidence" for this, as was "Jewish men's pessimism, oversensitivity, and sympathy for feminism" (Robertson, "Historicizing Weininger," 35).

From the perspective of European conceptions of Jewishness as "queer," one can understand how figuring Jewish characters could provide an opportunity for writers to explore questions regarding identity (both sexual and gender), subjectivity, and belonging. Many of the characteristics attributed to Jews, even if conceptual or imaginary, could also be attributed to many of the era's most prominent modernist writers: sexual ambivalence, rootlessness, displacement, urbanity, modern alienation, and even mental illness. Certainly the Jew's perceived homelessness would speak to writers such as Barnes and Isherwood, who were self-exiled, or to Woolf, who expressed the conviction that "as a woman, I have no country" (TG, 125). Nevertheless, *Nightwood, Between the Acts*, and *Goodbye to Berlin* also participate in a type of *écriture judaïque* that uses the Jew in the function of their narratives while engaging the language of oppression and negative typecasting. Taking into consideration the repercussions, to which constructions of the imaginary Jew ultimately lead in the 1930s, how is one to judge the representation of "the Jew" in Barnes, Woolf, and Isherwood? Are their works antisemitic? Or, more pointedly, if the content of their works contains antisemitic elements, does this mean they themselves are antisemites? How does their construction of "the Jew" refute or impede one's perception of their writing as anti-Nazi resistance novels? Moreover, is it even possible to represent Jewish characters without characterizing them in identifiable ethnic or racial terms? It could be, after all, that all literary and artistic constructions of "the Jew" that deny Jewish diversity, specificity, subjectivity, and self-identity are antisemitic. Nevertheless, could not the same be said of any other caricature-like figure? How is the construction of the Jew in these texts distinct from the representation of other "Others"?

The term "antisemitism" itself is loaded with significance and somewhat of a blunt weapon with which to bludgeon the various types of problematic ways in which Jews are conceived and treated. In a post-Holocaust world the label of "antisemite," as Tony Kushner notes, "conjures up images of Nazi concentration camps" and skews distinctions between hurtful social animosity toward Jews and the Nazi death squads (*Persistence*, 2). As Jonathan Judaken aptly observes, "not all so-called antisemitism is the same," even if the term is often used "to cover everything from prejudices, biases, or stereotypes about Jews and Judaism to a causal factor in the genocide of European Jewry" (Judaken, "Between Philosemitism and Antisemitism," 26). Yet, to negate the harmful effects of social hostility toward Jews by refusing to call it antisemitism also normalizes and legitimizes discourse that alienates and marginalizes Jews so that more dangerous hostility *can* go unchecked. Zygmunt Bauman's influential article "Allosemitism: Premodern, Modern, Postmodern" suggests the more useful term "allosemitism" replace "antisemitism" for examining the figure of "the Jew" as a cultural production. "Allosemitism"—a term coined by the Polish-Jewish literary historian Artur Sandauer—is derived from the Greek word *allos*, or "other," and refers specifically to the construction of Jews as Others. Bauman defines the word as follows:

> "Allosemitism" refers to the practice of setting Jews apart as people radically different from all the others, needing separate concepts to describe and comprehend them and special treatment in all or most social intercourse — since the concepts and treatments usefully deployed when facing or dealing with other people or peoples, simply would not do. (143)

Allosemitism can be usefully employed to refer to the ways that Jews are represented in Barnes's, Isherwood's, and Woolf's novels. I nevertheless do not want to shy away from using *antisemitism* as a useful category for identifying prejudice in these works. However inadequate, the term still refutes the tendency to ignore the political implications of discourse, even if we as critics feel discomfort when those prejudices appear among our favorite authors. Following this premise, my analysis of Jewish characters and Jewishness as represented in Barnes, Woolf, and Isherwood will focus specifically on a number of issues. Through which mythic and stereotypical tropes is "the Jew" considered? What is the historical context for these stereotypes and how do they function textually, both formally and thematically? And lastly, how do their representations of "the Jew" inform or undermine Barnes's, Woolf's, and Isherwood's overall "anti-Nazi" strategies?

### "Everywhere from Nowhere": *Nightwood*'s Wandering Jews

To begin the textual examination of Jews with *Nightwood* seems fitting since the novel itself opens with a focus on Jews, their marginality, and their relationship to a history of oppression. The background of Felix Volkbein, and his "racial" legacy of Jewish alienation and suffering, inherited from his father, Guido, initiates this interwar saga, populated by displaced, expatriate characters estranged from the world of the day, the "normal." Barnes's Jews thereby emerge as the epitome of all stories of oppression and disaffection that begin in the past, bleed into the present day of the novel, and promise to stagger into a sickly future. In many ways, as Lara Trubowitz suggests, the story of Felix as "Wandering Jew" becomes a symbol for how the narrative functions as a whole. *Night-wood* is a narrative that wanders circuitously from a hostile history to a story of anguish and loss, and finally toward its own "undoing." The Jew becomes "a narratological category," and Jewish history and identity a "conceptual foundation, or analogy, for the art of storytelling, an art that in *Nightwood* is tantamount to self-erasure" (Trubowitz, "In Search," 313). This analysis of Barnes's particular form of *écriture judaïque* resonates with a number of recent claims, such as Linett's, that many modern feminist writers like Barnes rely on Jewishness as an "ingredient" or "shaping tool to tackle . . . crucial thematic and structural challenges" (Linett, *Modernism*, 189). What I nevertheless wonder is if the Jew is used as a thematic tool, how do we as readers undo the erasure of the historical reality of Jewish experience in the 1930s? For this reality not only is missing from the novel but also is reinforced, as Linett points out, by the lingering critical assumption that feminist authors were "'politically correct' across the board" (ibid., 10). There is, moreover, a tendency in literary scholarship to consider issues pertaining to Jews and their cultures as belonging solely to the field of Jewish studies rather than literary criticism.[25]

A number of critics, most notably Jane Marcus and Shari Benstock, have insisted that Barnes's opposition to fascism is explicitly articulated in the novel's identification with outsiders, and especially with Jews. Marcus, for example, claims *Nightwood*'s "antifascism is apparent only when its [*sic*] triumphs over its own anti-Semitism, when we realize that all its characters — Jews, homosexuals, lesbians, transvestites, gypsies, blacks, and circus performers — were all to perish in the Holocaust" ("Laughing at Leviticus," 229). Similarly, Benstock posits that *Nightwood* "concerns society's outsiders — Jews, homosexuals, the mentally and physically weak — those whom Hitler would define as *Untermenschen.*" As she argues, "*Nightwood* records their suffering and foreshadows their ultimate destruction, the specter of Fascism casting a long shadow over its landscape" (*Women of the Left Bank*, 424). While I agree with those who interpret *Nightwood* as a novel that is resistant to fascist ideology and its reliance on spectacle, I would nevertheless like to trouble the claim that Barnes could in any way foresee the Nazi genocide and complicate the notion that all "Others" are treated in the same manner in the novel. As I have argued in the previous two chapters, there are clear indications that *Nightwood* challenges the Nazi spectacle by exposing its workings and its oppressive policies toward gender and sexual difference. Yet, as an alternative to the view of *Nightwood* as apocalyptic prophecy of the Holocaust — and rather than interpreting Barnes as a postmodern antiessentialist — I propose that Barnes's novel more accurately reveals troubling attitudes toward the Jew that are particular to liberal conceptions of aesthetic modernism conceived of in terms of Jewishness. At the same time these attitudes are linked to medieval Christian and scientific racial anti-Jewish discourse of the 1920s–30s.

To suggest a more nuanced reading of the textual Jew, I will examine the roles that Guido, Felix, and little Guido play in Barnes's approach to history, story, and representation. As I will illustrate, although Barnes's Jew is a key metaphor for her narrative strategy, ultimately her method of using "the Jew" as symbol becomes complicit in eliminating the "real" Jew from both official history *and* his own subjective Jewish story. In this regard, my analysis of "the Jew" in *Nightwood* is in line with some of the recent critics who problematize how "the Jew" in *Nightwood* is erased or becomes solely contingent upon the history of others. My close reading, however, more explicitly argues that Barnes's portrayal obliterates considerations of Jewish history and, more problematically, distorts Jewish traditions, cultures, and beliefs in service of her narrative experiment at a time when Nazism is threatening Jewish culture using disturbingly similar devices.[26]

Even if the characters in *Nightwood* are interrelated in their "outsidership," readings that elide important distinctions among the various types of "Others" miss an opportunity to examine the specific ways each functions formally and thematically in Barnes's text, and the way each group functioned within Nazi ideology. The representation of women and homosexuals, for example, is poles apart from Barnes's textual Jew. Firstly, it is more difficult to see how the Jew functions positively to challenge fascist ideology in Barnes's text because the ambiguous, negatively racialized discourse associated with the Volkbein men appears to go unchallenged. As Meryl Altman asks, "How much sympathy can we discern in her stance when she draws on the same storehouse of images as do some of the most virulent attacks on Jews and lesbians in the twentieth century, and when she discusses them so clearly from the outside looking in?" ("A Book of Repulsive Jews?" 161). "The Jew" is inevitably portrayed as rich, physically repulsive, sexually ambiguous, and inescapably foreign — typical markers that racialize and marginalize Jews. Secondly, a crucial difference between Guido, Felix, and little Guido, and the other "Others" in the text is that these Jews do not define themselves as Jewish. Guido senior is a convert; Felix is only half Jewish (and, according to traditional Jewish law, not Jewish at all, since Judaism is matrilineal); and little Guido is one-quarter Jewish, a category that did not even exist until twentieth-century racial laws were introduced.[27] What, then, makes these characters Jewish?

Biologically, sex can be discerned through physical distinctions between males and females, so that women do quite clearly fall into a visible category of difference, even if arguably cross-dressing can obscure the gender of either. As for differences in sexuality and sexual desire, whether one is born or becomes gay or lesbian, and the political implications of such labeling, are topics of numerous theories and viewpoints, but at least in the text, the characters do practice activities that fall into the category of same-sex desire — Nora and Robin are undoubtedly lovers, and O'Connor, who self-identifies as an "invert" or the "bearded lady," makes obvious allusions to sexual acts in the pissoirs of Paris. Guido and Felix, on the other hand, do not practice any Jewish customs, engage in any Jewish-oriented activities, or self-identify themselves as Jewish. The only thing that makes them Jewish is that the text, the narrator, and other characters identify them as Jewish. In this way, the spectral Jew in Barnes's text falls outside the category of outsiders. In reference to Bauman's theory of "allosemitism," Felix and the two Guidos are represented not in terms of "heterophobia," the resentment or fear of difference, but *"proteophobia"* — "the apprehension and vexation related to something or someone . . . that does not fall easily into any established categories." Jews, as represented in Barnes's text, "explode the very categories meant to service the defining business" (Bauman, "Allosemitism," 144).

*Nightwood* itself is a novel characterized, like Felix the Wandering Jew, as distinctive in its inability to "fit" into accepted norms of narrative structure, order, and categorization. Donna Gerstenberger contends that Barnes's novel is marked by "a pattern of desire and deferral, absence not filled by presence" ("Radical Narrative," 133). Both Felix and his father long to fit into an "official" history, yet at the same time their failure to truly belong points to the impossibility of any story to serve as a basis for individual identities. "History" and "story" become blurred in Barnes's text—especially histories and stories of individuals who cross national, class, and racial borders to create their own fictions of self. The novel, after all, is replete with self-initiated Barons, Counts, Dukes, Duchesses, and doctors whose "real" stories are as difficult to decipher as the text itself. For this reason, Felix's birth at the start of the novel may seem somewhat baffling if one considers *Nightwood* to be the story of Robin and Nora, but if he symbolizes Barnes's narrative and aesthetic project as a whole, the beginning makes complete sense. The birth of Felix, the Jew-as-text, "seven days" after the doctor predicted his mother would be taken, initiates the novel as a creation narrative.[28] Yet, unlike the Bible, the narrative wanders toward decay and suffering instead of salvation, meandering its way through people's lives, observing misery and tragedy, and coming to its final end in incomprehensibility.[29]

By presenting the identity of Felix as contingent on an unclear historical narrative or lineage, however, the novel does fall into an accepted norm that uses the Jew metonymically as a symbol for crisis, or *écriture judaïque*. Felix's instability as a character characterizes the instability of the narrative itself. This becomes even clearer when the "exact history" of Felix's birth and family is exposed as a somewhat unreliable story told to Felix by his aunt, who "combing her long braids with an amber comb, told him what she knew, and this had been her only knowledge of his past" (NW, 7). In the context of Nazism's reliance on racial "truths" about Jews' inferiority based on their past history, one could deduce that Barnes is putting forth a powerful and extremely prescient antiessentialist argument against the fascist illusion of a "pure" Aryan race. Even more so, however, if the story of his past is called into question, and the past is the only thing that links Felix to Jewishness, then *all* identities can be called into question. Nevertheless, even if Barnes is drawing attention to the way that identities and histories are myth, "the imaginary is not without its effects" (Smith, "A Story Beside(s) Itself," 198). By alluding to the fact that Felix's Jewishness is only a representation, and that all histories and identities are only representations conceived and "told" by others, Barnes in effect marks the Jew in a manner in which he has historically been marked—only in terms of a relationship between self as teller and the Other as the told.

Since part of the Jew's "essential" character is his indeterminacy, an argument for Barnes's antiessentialism is not all that clear. Both Mairéad

Hanrahan and Lara Trubowitz convincingly argue that at the same time as transforming the Jew into an aesthetic mode for the text, Barnes denies Guido and Felix self-determination and ownership of their own history.[30] I would complicate this notion even further to argue that Barnes participates in a discourse that was pervasive and harmful in the 1920s and '30s because it ignored the particular subjective experiences of those who considered themselves Jews, and denied freedom to self-identify for those who did not. A common allegation against Jews, which was reiterated in Hitler's *Mein Kampf,* was that they mimicked other cultures by "borrowing" their histories, languages, and identities. If the Jew and his practices in *Nightwood* is replaced by the metaphoric and symbolic "spectral Jew," and even supplied with a mysterious, imaginary history (that is told by someone else, not Jewish), then the actual Jew falls into the same double bind of "impossible assimilation" into which he or she has consistently been placed. Doomed always to be on the verge of disappearing and yet still serving as a symbol of difference.

A closer look at how "the Jew," his history, and his "essence" are represented in the novel can shed some light on the problematic erasure of a Jewish living culture in service of its function as a symbol of erasure and absence. The novel begins as follows:

> Early in 1880, in spite of a well-founded suspicion as to the advisability of perpetuating that race which has the sanction of the Lord and the disapproval of the people, Hedwig Volkbein — a Viennese woman of great strength and military beauty . . . gave birth, at the age of forty-five, to an only child, a son, seven days after her physician predicted she would be taken. . . . [S]he named him Felix, thrust him from her, and died. (NW, 1)

Initially, the reader does not know for certain that Felix has any connection with Jewishness. It is only hinted at in the words "that race," but the structure of the sentence makes "which" race difficult to ascertain. The continuation of the passage, however, makes it quite clear that the "chosen" race ostensibly refers to Jews — a people not "advisable" to perpetuate for unmentioned reasons:

> The child's father had gone six months previously, a victim of fever. Guido Volkbein, a Jew of Italian descent, had been both

a gourmet and a dandy, never appearing in public without the ribbon of some quite unknown distinction tinging his button-hole with a faint thread. He had been small, rotund, and haughtily timid, his stomach protruding slightly in an upward jutting slope that brought into prominence the buttons of his waistcoat and trousers, marking the exact centre of his body with the obstetric line seen on fruits — the inevitable arc produced by heavy rounds of burgundy, schlagsahne, and beer. (NW, 1)

These lines depicting Felix's Jewish heritage could be read with purposeful skepticism. Yet, it is more obvious that the "suspicion as to the advisability of perpetuating" the Jewish race appears to be "well-founded" because this is a race that is physically unappealing, is psychologically damaged ("haughtily timid" and drunk), and falsifies its connections to "distinctions" it does not deserve. It is, of course, possible to read this passage as a parody of popular perceptions of Jews, but it has been well noted for being "unambiguously" problematic. Firstly, the depiction resonates with common racist caricatures of Jews as dwarfish, ugly, or fat (the last trait reflecting their avaricious or consuming nature).[31] Secondly, Guido Volkbein is typecast as effeminate and lacking in masculine traits. Moreover, to quote Karen Kaivola, he is "portrayed as the antithesis of desire" in a text that is primarily focused on desire and passion ("'The 'beast turning,'" 180). These traits are recognizably "Jewish" because they operate in a repetitive fashion, reiterating the signs of a discourse of "truths" about Jews that lie outside the text. All the Jews are unattractive "consumers" in the novel, even death-addicted little Guido, and this view of the repulsive Jew remains unchallenged throughout the rest of the narrative.

Specifically, these are some of the racialized stereotypes that characterize Guido: his eyes, with "thick eyelids quivering over thick eyeballs, black with the pain" (NW, 2); his walk, as he tries to imitate his wife's "goose-step stride," and instead becomes "dislocated and comic" (NW, 3); and his "sweeping Cabalistic line of nose" (NW, 7). All of these features, as Gilman details, operated as typical Jewish markers in the pseudoscientific discourse of the late nineteenth and early twentieth centuries. The Jewish "gaze" or "eyes" were often identified by racial scientists as a sure way to recognize hidden Jewishness, especially "heavy and bulging" eyelids and a gaze that reveals madness, nervous disorders, or psychological inferiority (Gilman, *Jew's Body*, 71–72). The foot or walk of the Jew also indicated difference. In the Middle Ages, Jews were thought to be associated with the cloven-hoofed devil, their shoes concealing a corrupt corporeality. In the nineteenth century, Gilman explains, flat feet and the "limping Jew's" gait were interpreted as a neurological disorder: "the Jew's foot is read . . . as the structure of the Jewish mind, the pathognomic status of the Jew's body as a sign for the Jew's inherent difference" (ibid., 53).[32] Guido's "Cabalistic" nose is obviously a sign of negative difference as well. The adjective "cabalistic" alludes to a cryptic or secret nature; the nose was often perceived as a "hidden sign of his sexual difference, his circumcised penis" (ibid., 189). Even more prominently, Guido's "virility" is called into question. When contrasted with his wife, who is "strong" and "militaristic" like a "general saluting a flag," Guido appears as a vain, short, and round "dandy" whose waist is marked by an "obstetric line" (NW, 1–2). The gender-bending Guido is a "fruit" who becomes, like a pregnant woman, "heavy with impermissible blood" when he prepares for a child, while his wife's pregnant belly is depicted in phallic terms as "the promise that hung at the Christian belt" (NW, 3). Even Guido's "sir name," far from being a Jewish Italian name, is quite possibly taken on from militaristic Hedvig or arbitrarily adopted when he converts and thereby, like a devoted wife, "marries" a new religion and culture.

Notably, even when Guido tries to "pass," his Otherness is given away by his excess. It is almost as if he performs a campy patriarchal role in a theater of make-believe. He pays "remorseless homage to nobility" (NW, 2), speaks too "highly of royalty," laughs "too heartily when in the presence of the lower order of title," and shakes with trepidation when faced with figures of authority or power (NW, 4). As Itzkovitz observes of assimilated Jewishness, Guido's main Jewish trait is that he is identified by "the state of extremity" ("Secret Temples," 181). His house becomes "a fantastic museum" with "long rococo halls, giddy with plush and whorled designs in gold," copies of paintings, not one but "three massive pianos," and a "thick dragon's-blood pile of rugs from Madrid" (NW, 5). Three full pages of excessively overwrought description are devoted to the spectacle of his richly curtained and plumed abode. As the narrator states, "The whole conception might have been a Mardi

Gras whim" (NW, 7). As if to compensate for the absences that mark Guido's Jewishness, the narrator fills the void of Jewish substance with a spectacle of overcompensation and excess. Perhaps this too is why the "suspicion" that it is inadvisable to perpetuate the Jewish race is "well-founded." The Jewish race, in Barnes's conception, is always straddling self-annihilation and excess, not quite virile enough to perpetuate, but still bowing and groveling to be an Other to "the people." Thus "the Jew" becomes marked not only by "self-erasure" in the narrative, as Trubowitz argues ("In Search," 313), but also by *excessive* erasure. All that is left of the character is the overspill, or trace, of Jewishness rather than any of its substance.

Guido bequeaths these same traits down to Felix, also a parvenu and a culture worshiper who desires to pass on a false connection to a patriarchal lineage that is not his. Similar to Guido's, Felix's stereotypical traits center on overcompensation and excess. He is described as being "heavier than his father," with a receding hairline and "heavy" features (NW, 8). He strives to be "properly garbed; wishing to be correct at any moment" (NW, 8). His distinctive trait of excess is denoted by his "bowing, searching, with quick pendulous movements, for the correct thing to which to pay tribute: the right street, the right café, the right building, the right vista" (NW, 8). Although he masters seven languages, no one knows where he is from, how he gets his money, or where he belongs. Reminiscent of Hitler's claim in *Mein Kampf*, Felix's character epitomizes "the Jew who can speak a thousand languages and nevertheless remains a Jew" (*Mein Kampf*, 283).

If one considers Guido's and Felix's exaggerated performances of class within European patriarchy as "camp," then the text presents an ironic parody of those hierarchies and calls into question racist and masculinist categories of identification. It draws attention to the artifice inherent in the constructions of class, gender, race, and "Europeanness." On the other hand, if the irony is not perceived, the text suggests that Guido's difference is impossible to transcend. All attempts to dilute it by discontinuing the patriarchal lineage through race-mixing, by procreating with the Aryan-Christian Hedvig, fail. While any form of birth in the text (including the birth of the text itself) ends in disaster, race-mixing emerges as particularly ill-fated. In marrying Hedvig and mixing the ancestry of both races, Guido launches a corrupted text, a *Mischling* (child of miscegenation, or mixed race), Felix, who suffers from his own painful alienation and difference until he marries Robin. Felix then continues the line of "degeneracy" by perpetuating a patriarchal lineage through another mixed-race child, little Guido. The latter, who is not only sickly but also mentally deficient, ends the entire story of procreation and miscegenation by preparing to enter the Church — assuming he makes it to adulthood.

Thus, the Jewish race in *Nightwood*, like the text itself, ultimately ends in dissolution — celibacy, illness, and hysteria — much as the race discourse concerning the *Mischling* in Nazi ideology describes. As Hitler professed, "The result of all racial crossing is . . . (a) Lowering the level of the higher race; (b) Physical and intellectual regression and hence the beginning of a slowly but surely progressing sickness. To bring about such developments is, then, nothing else but to sin against the will of the eternal creator" (*Mein Kampf*, 260). Even in late nineteenth-century racial science, as Gilman explains, "Mischling" came to refer to the offspring of a Jewish and a non-Jewish parent to describe degeneration through the practice of "exogamy." Mixing the Aryan race with Jew, instead of making the Jew "stronger," was thought to cause negative Jewish traits, racialized as "black," to appear even more profoundly. "So even when the Jew wished to vanish by marrying out of the 'race,'" as Gilman remarks, "his or her blackness was not diminished. Indeed, it was heightened" (*Jew's Body*, 175). As a less-than-virile patrilineal heritage, Guido's "fruit" shape thereby results in "fruitlessness," and his false "barony" ultimately ends in "barrenness." Once again, "the Jew" is signaled in the impossible and irrational terms of appearing only to disappear.

Jewish "presence in absence" in the novel occurs not only due to physical degeneration, however. Another way Jewishness functions as "excessive erasure" is the manner in which a culturally specific Jewish history is replaced by a history contingent on persecution and solely based in a negative relationship to "the people." In other words, the text depicts a history of Jews that is always already on the verge of being annihilated. To give Barnes credit, her most powerful anti-Nazi gesture surfaces in the part of the text that focuses on Jewish history. In that passage, Guido is connected to a Jewish "racial memory" that functions in a critical manner to uncover the painful history of Jewish persecution, as described by the narrator:[33]

The autumn, binding him about, as no other season, with racial memories, a season of longing and of horror, he had called his weather. Then, walking in the Prater he had been seen carrying in a conspicuously clenched fist the exquisite handkerchief of yellow and black linen that cried aloud of the ordinance of 1468, issued by one Pietro Barbo, demanding that, with a rope about its neck, Guido's race should run the Corso for the amusement of the Christian populace. (NW, 2)

By sympathetically presenting the history of Jewish persecution in medieval Rome, Barnes "unmasks" a story through a critique that is silenced under Western Christian discourse. To agree with Julie Abraham's contention, in this way Barnes "incorporates" a history of victimization that is "excluded" from the record of dominant history ("Djuna Barnes and History," 259). Significantly, however, it also neglects that Jewish culture, which by the 1920s and '30s had its own rich and significant literary tradition composed of hundreds of accounts of Jewish history, scholarly contributions, and traditions in Yiddish, Modern Hebrew, Ladino, as well as in English, German, French, Italian, and Russian, among many other languages.

Corroborating the view that Guido's "racial memory" in this section is nevertheless meant to symbolically resist European claims to a single, unequivocal, and unified view of "history" is an intriguing biographical detail concerning Barnes's research. It appears that Barnes applied in 1930 for a Guggenheim Memorial Foundation Fellowship to "make a study of pre-war conditions, intrigues and relations then existing between the Jews and the Court . . . for a book in progress whose chief figure is an Austrian Jew" (quoted in Trubowitz, "In Search," 311).[34] True to her application, telltale signs in Nightwood hint at the sources of Jewish history she must have consulted. The biggest clue is found in the passage cited previously, pointing to her use of The Jewish Encyclopedia. Published in twelve volumes between 1901 and 1906 in the United States, it was the first source of its kind to attempt a comprehensive, scholarly, and "scientific" account of Jewish history, customs, and literature. It proclaimed to be a "faithful record of . . . multifarious activity" in "all branches of human endeavour" of the Jewish people throughout the ages (1: vii).[35] What leads me to suggest that Barnes consulted this particular resource is that it seems to be the only source in English containing a historical note on Italy resembling the one to which she refers in the passage. Specifically, the article on "Rome," by Joseph Jacobs and Schulim Ochser, states the following:

> For the amusement of the people Paul II introduced foot-races during the carnival week, with costly mantles as prizes; on one day the Jews were compelled to join in the sport, arrayed in their red cloaks. . . . [T]he sports, however, were probably abolished shortly after, for in 1468 a plague that carried off fifty victims a day raged in Rome. (10: 452)

Although Pope Paul II, formerly known as Pietro Barbo (pontiff from 1464 to 1471), was often depicted in early twentieth-century sources as fair, generous, and supportive of the arts and learning (he was lauded as a patron of scholars and was known for being the founder of the first printing presses in the Palace of St. Mark), the article provides a viewpoint that diverges from the standard European history-book version of Rome and the Catholic Church. Only more recent accounts have recognized Paul II as being vain, autocratic, often cruel and suspicious, and a lover of pompous display. *Nightwood* highlights an alternative aspect of European history that includes oppression and cruelty toward Jews.[36]

The yellow-and-black handkerchief that Guido holds also alludes to an alternative history of medieval Europe linked with marginalization. Although some scholars have connected this inference in the novel to the Nazi badge,[37] Guido's handkerchief only eerily anticipates the yellow-and-black Jewish star inscribed with the word *"Jude"* that Jews were forced to wear under the Nazi regime during World War II. The ordinance to wear the yellow star in Germany was not officially issued until September 1941 (although a few places in Poland ordered Jews to wear badges in 1939), making it impossible for Barnes to connect the yellow-and-black kerchief with the yellow Star of David when she wrote *Nightwood*.[38] Nevertheless, it does clearly allude to a legacy of forbidding Jews to mix with Christians. Likely, Guido's kerchief is an inference to the medieval ordinances forcing Jews to wear a yellow hat or yellow badge (often called a *rota*, or Jewish ring) to distinguish them from Christians. *The Jewish Encyclopedia* article on the Jewish badge notes that the fourth

Lateran Council of 1215, at the instigation of Innocent III, ordered Jews to bear a badge ostensibly to "prevent illicit intercourse between Jews and Christian women" (2: 425).[39] "In the fourteenth and fifteenth centuries," the entry explains, "local injunctions are found in Venice, Verona, Parma, Rome, Asola, and Genoa. It was known as the 'O' from its shape" (2: 426). Similar injunctions appeared throughout England, France, Germany, Austria, as well as in Muslim countries, where Jews were forced to wear a yellow hat, a badge, or a cloth.

If Guido's yellow-and-black handkerchief does not directly refer to the Nazi badge, then it still points to a history of separation and persecution based, in part, on a fear of miscegenation. The racial laws of the 1930s were already in place when *Nightwood* was published. The Nuremberg Laws, for instance, which were announced at the party rally at Nuremberg in 1933 and were passed in September 1935, included the "Law for the Protection of German Blood and German Honor." This legislation prohibited marriages and illicit sexual intercourse between Jews and non-Jews to prevent the perpetuation of *Mischling*. It also stripped Jews — which would include half (Felix) and quarter (little Guido) Jews — of their citizenship and rights. Guido holds the yellow-and-black cloth in a "conspicuously clenched fist," which could be seen as either hiding his Jewishness, or clenched in fear for transgressing both Jewish laws and medieval injunctions preventing Christians and Jews from mixing. Or, it could also be clenched in anger at the continuation of policies that limit the freedoms of Jews and serve as justification for his persecution.

Considering the allusion to race laws and miscegenation in Guido's yellow-and-black handkerchief, the next part of the passage could suggest a parallel to the Nuremberg rallies, or even perhaps the Italian National Fascist Party's "March on Rome" in 1922, the coup d'état that established Benito Mussolini as "Il Duce," leader of the Italian people. In the novel's opening paragraphs, a scene that contains all the elements of the fascist spectacle is described:

> The ladies of noble birth, sitting upon spines too refined for rest, arose from their seats, and, with the red-gowned cardinals and the Monsignori, applauded with that cold yet hysterical abandon of a people that is at once unjust and happy, the very Pope

himself shaken down from his hold on heaven with the laughter
of a man who forgoes his angels that he may recapture the beast.
(*NW*, 2)

Undoubtedly, to anyone who had attended or heard of the fascist rallies,
the "hysterical abandon" of the "unjust and happy" people using Jews
for entertainment bears an uncanny resemblance to the mesmerized
crowds of the fascist spectacle. Even if Barnes did not physically see the
crowd of spectators, it is quite possible that by then she had read about
them, had seen photographs, or perhaps had watched Leni Riefenstahl's
1933 documentary of the Nuremberg rally in *Der Sieg des Glaubens*
(*Victory of Faith*), or her more famous 1935 film *Triumph des Willens*
(*Triumph of the Will*), which chronicled the 1934 Nuremberg rally and
won awards in both the United States and France.

The "beast" in the phrase "the laughter of a man who forgoes his
angels that he may recapture the beast" also evokes the Nazi "beast" as
suggested by the "red" gowns and red color of the Nazi flag. The ruddy
cloaks also insinuate that the result of the spectacle is bloody. With the
same orgiastic terminology that Hitler uses in *Mein Kampf* for the mass
meeting, Barnes depicts the allure of the abandonment, relinquishment,
and relief from individual responsibility that occurs at a large demonstra-
tion. As Hitler describes the individual in the mass meeting, "he is swept
away by three or four thousand others into the mighty effect of suggestive
intoxication and enthusiasm, when the visible success and agreement
of thousands confirm to him the rightness of the new doctrine"; finally
he "succumb[s] to the magic influence of what we designate as 'mass
suggestion'" (*Mein Kampf*, 435). With prescient insight, Barnes brings
to light the workings of the spectacle, whereby the individual is able to
abandon rationality and "forgo his angels" in favor of the release that
comes with belonging to the crowd.

In light of the spectacle of violence and persecution of the Jew, the
fact that Guido engages in an almost excessive abnegation of his Jewishness might be understandable. Yet, at the same time that the kerchief
binds him to past persecution, his clinging to an identity based only on
that persecution keeps him in a throttlehold in his present. The ring,
or "rota," might be a rope that holds "Guido's race" back from running
with or to the "Christian populace," but it constructs an identity that is

solely related to that Christian populace. The absent presence of Jewish culture is hinted at in the referral to the season of autumn, when Guido is "bound" by "racial memories" (NW, 2). Although Trubowitz interprets it as a season of decay ("In Search," 316), in Jewish tradition it is significantly a time of renewal. Fall is the time of the High Holidays, comprising Rosh Hashanah, the Jewish New Year (also known as the "Day of Remembrance"), and Yom Kippur, the "Day of Atonement." The remembering and atonement in the holidays are meant to start the new year with a "clean slate" following communal rituals of prayer, confession, and repentance. It would take an extremely assimilated Jew indeed to forget the most important days in the Jewish calendar. Nevertheless, while Jewish persecution is present in the text, Jewish experience, tradition, and practice are distinguished precisely by their absence.

Notably, the "binding" in the passage that links Guido to his racial memories of the rope around the neck of the Jews in the Corso also links the text to the binding of Isaac (Genesis 22), an event that occurred, according to tradition, on the first day of the month of Tishrei, the date Rosh Hashanah is celebrated. A parable of extreme faith and devotion, the story of how Abraham was asked by God to sacrifice his son is read on the holiday, and a ram's horn is blown, commemorating the ram that was sacrificed in Isaac's stead when an angel stopped Abraham from killing his son.[40] The "binding of Isaac," or *Akedah*, became a common trope for Jewish martyrdom in traditional Jewish literature, especially in the Middle Ages. It also has resonance and significance in Christian faith and theology since it foreshadows God's sacrifice of his own son to atone for the sins of the people (Hebrews 11:17–19, New King James Version). In the novel, the biblical allusion links Guido, Felix, and little Guido to a history of sacrifice, while also pointing to the double-bind, or choiceless choices that are presented in the text. Similar to Abraham, who must choose between either disobeying God or murdering his son, Guido seems bound either to abandon his religion or to sacrifice his own sons to persecution. His leap of faith results in an outcome that is the same either way — the annihilation of the Jew. This predicament is emphasized in Barnes's writing: "This memory and the handkerchief that accompanied it had wrought in Guido (as certain flowers brought to a pitch of florid ecstasy no sooner attain their specific type than they fall into decay) the sum total of what is the Jew" (NW, 2). One must nevertheless ask, is that all there is to being a Jew? A "sum total" of sacrifice and persecution?

Since "the binding of Isaac" could be both a parable for Jewish faith and obedience, and a parable of Christian sacrifice, the history of oppression of the Jew can be interpreted in two ways: as a "story" that opposes Western fascist dominant discourse or as a confirmation of Christian dominant discourse. Either way, representing the "story" of the Jew only in terms of Christian sacrifice or conversion distorts Jewish practice, supporting what Hanrahan refers to as "the cruci-fiction of the Jew." If one reads *Nightwood* as a predominantly Christian text (as numerous critics have), the view that the Jew functions metonymically as a symbol for a narrative based in a particular form of "self-negation" is convincing because it correlates with one of the theological functions of Christian sacrifice.[41] Jewishness needs to exist in order for Christian salvation to exist and for Christ to be sacrificed and then resurrected (thereby leaving a presence in his absence). *Nightwood* could even be read as a narrative reeling toward the "end of days," supporting Hanrahan's contention that "the Jew's past is only anchored in time, becomes history, insofar as it is mediated by the Christian" ("Djuna Barnes's *Nightwood*," 37).

A reading of "the Jew" in terms of sacrifice is certainly plausible when one considers how many Jewish references in the novel are tied to Christian allusions of martyrdom. The incident in Rome in the paragraph describing the persecution of Guido's ancestors, for instance, could also evoke the ancient Roman games in which Christian martyrs suffered degradation, humiliation, and execution. Felix's name points to the Latin term *felix culpa,* or the "fortunate fall" (also "happy fault"), referring to medieval theologian Saint Thomas Aquinas's notion that God allows evil to happen in order to bring salvation (specifically, although Adam and Eve's "fall" from grace in Eden brings "original sin" into the world, it also instigates Christ's redemptive sacrifice).[42] Felix is also called the "Wandering Jew," based on the thirteenth-century Christian myth of the Jewish sinner who is doomed to wander the earth until the end of the world because he taunts Jesus walking with the cross (discussed previously).[43] Even more notably, little Guido appears to be born without any hint of sexual intercourse. Felix demands, "Why is there no child," and as a result Robin "prepared herself for her child with her only power: a stubborn cataleptic calm, conceiving herself pregnant before she was." Shortly thereafter, instead of delivering a child, "Robin was delivered" (NW, 45, 48). Guido, like Isaac, is almost sacrificed when Robin "hold[s] the child high in her hand" as if performing a ceremonial rite (NW, 49). An emotional boy with "a mature heart" who is not "cruel or savage" (NW, 115), little Guido clings to his medallion of the Madonna and dreams of entering the Church while Felix worries if his son will be "chosen" or if he is "damned" (NW, 109, 121). All these examples point to a "spectral Jew" that is determined in terms of Christian rather than Jewish ideology, myth, and cultural references. Jewish storytelling, on the other hand, is erased.

In point of fact, the novel gives the distinct impression that no Jewish myth or legend can exist at all without the intervention of the Christian — the only view of Judaism possible is the one from the "outside in":

> A race that has fled its generations from city to city has not found the necessary time for the accumulation of toughness which produces ribaldry, nor, after the crucifixion of its ideas, enough forgetfulness in twenty centuries to create legend. It takes a Christian, standing eternally in the Jew's salvation, to blame himself and to bring up from that depth charming and fantastic superstitions through which the slowly and tirelessly milling Jew once more becomes the "collector" of his own past. His undoing is never profitable until some *goy* has put it back into such shape that it can again be offered as a "sign." (NW, 10)

This quotation from *Nightwood* is one of the most distressing in its implications. It appears to illustrate that the identity and past of "the Jew" is indeterminate: it is timeless, lacks introspection enough to create legend, and moreover is unable to "accumulate" toughness from wandering around. These traits are impossible to transcend because the text portends that Christian identity depends on the Jew remaining in that position for its own identity of salvation to come to fruition. The narrator suggests that the Jew must "collect" his past rather than write it himself because the history of his undoing is not interesting unless it comes from the perspective of the *goy*.[44] This is puzzling, since at its worst, this passage seems to justify the persecution of the Jews and their oppression as a condition of Christian history that is both essential and inevitable. A racialized Jewish difference is affirmed by the text in a manner that is unsettling in its similarity to Nazi thinking, which claims that the stereotypical Jew's homelessness and lack of identity prove his degenerate difference. Jews are also identified as a people who do not even have the possibility of flourishing since their identity is constantly on the verge of "undoing." At its best, the passage is a self-referential or metatextual gesture that signals Barnes's own function as the "goy" who makes "profit" on the novel by using the Jew as a "sign." She could be conceding that her own story is turned into a "commodity"—the book that crucifies his identity and history, and exploits him to create her own version of history. She then admits her collusion in the exploitation of the Jew but still uses him to signal exploitation in general. Thus, in Barnes's conception, the Jew may have traits but no substance.

A history of the Jews that would not involve persecution or sacrifice throughout the ages would look very different indeed. Yet, one quick scan through the thousands of pages of that very same 1906 edition of *The Jewish Encyclopedia* used by Barnes clearly indicates that Jewish history is also made up of the cultural diversity, experiences, and contributions of Jewish men *and* women (even if the latter's stories had to wait to be told in later editions). As an example of other types of histories, some of the subentries on Rome include "legends and traditions," "authors of the fourteenth century," "physicians of the fifteenth and sixteenth centuries," and lists of scholars and great works. Even under "Recent Conditions," the article comments that at the end of the nineteenth century, "a new era dawned" for the 7,000 Jews of Rome. It was also an era that ended with 1,000 of those Jews, mostly women and children, being sent to Auschwitz with little protest from the Catholic Church.[45] The tragedy is not only in the persecution itself but also in the loss of the rich culture and individual stories that became silenced.

The monocle that Felix wears (it covers up his blind eye) constantly falls off, fogs up, or needs to be wiped clear, much like the unifocal view of Jewish experience that denies those histories and experiences of individual Jewish men and women. In the last chapter of *Nightwood* in which Felix appears, entitled "Where the Tree Falls," O'Connor tells Felix, "A man is whole only when he takes into account his shadow as well as himself. . . . Guido is the shadow of your anxiety, and Guido's shadow is God's" (NW, 119–20). It is quite plausible that Barnes presents here an implied criticism of the assimilated Jew who abandons and ignores his own history, his shadow; but it is also possible that Barnes is so ambivalent about Jewish characterization that she converts her Jewish characters and thus participates in the sinister component of a Jewish past of enforced Christian conversions and persecution. The line anticipates Alain Finkielkraut's quotation on the impossible assimilation of "the Jew" as "the useless struggles of a man running fast, hoping to leave his shadow behind" (*Imaginary Jew*, 82). No matter which path the Wandering Jew takes in *Nightwood*, his eternal, unchanging Jewishness follows him, indelibly marked on his body and in his psyche.

If the text depicts society in the 1930s as "whole" only when it takes into account its shadow, and if that shadow is the space the "spectral" Jew occupies, then living people who are Jews are left with no physical or visual substance to reflect and refract their own light, vision, and perspective. Felix tells O'Connor that he believes "To pay homage to our past is the only gesture that also includes the future" (NW, 39). By honoring a past and a present constructed around his erasure, however, Felix ensures that his future will disappear. The outcome of Guido's and Felix's gestures is a son whose will it is to emulate Christ. Felix, in the end, realizes that "in accepting his son . . . he must accept the demolition of his own life" (NW, 108). The Jew here is thus annihilated — not through persecution but rather at the hands of a narrative technique that universalizes the Jew's experience and thus robs him of self-determination to create his own stories.

## Woolf's Jews: Outside the Society of Outsiders

If "the Jew" in *Nightwood* is constantly and excessively on the verge of dissolution, at least he is in the text as an entity with which to grapple. In contrast, what identifies the Jewish character in *Between the Acts*, as Phyllis Lassner has shown, is that he is present only in his complete absence ("Milk of Our Mother's Kindness," 137). Ralph Manresa is not even in the margins — he is virtually outside the borders of the text itself. A figure who is noticeably not in attendance at Pointz Hall on the day of the pageant, Manresa, as a conceptual entity, features prominently. Along with the airplanes, rumors of invasion, and newspaper snippets,

Ralph haunts the text, threatening to invade the private sphere of Pointz Hall and destroy the tranquillity of English country life perhaps no less than the German bombs. He epitomizes the typecasting that associates "the Jew" with the urban, the "slimy," and the commercially corrupt. Other works by Woolf in the 1930s, particularly *Three Guineas*, *The Years*, and her lesser-known short story "The Duchess and the Jeweller" (published at the time that she was writing *Between the Acts*), all point to this same concern: "the Jew," for Woolf, is significant as an idea, as a concept, and as a discourse, but is notably absent as a thinking, feeling, experiencing character.[46]

Lassner points out that although many female writers between the two world wars identify with Jews as victims of oppressive politics, and often plea for sympathy for the plight of European Jewry, in many instances they also "recapitulate and reinforce" that history of marginality (*British Women Writers*, 20). A case in point is Virginia Woolf's *Three Guineas*, a text in which women and Jews are united as outsiders "fighting the same enemy together"—the "tyranny of the patriarchal state" and "the tyranny of the Fascist state" (*TG*, 118). Woolf associates both groups as victims of the "Tyrant, Dictator" who "is dictating how you shall live; he is making distinctions not merely between the sexes, but between the races." Woolf explains to her readers: "The whole iniquity of dictatorship, whether in Oxford or Cambridge, in Whitehall or Downing Street, against Jews or against women, in England or in Germany, in Italy or in Spain is now apparent to you" (*TG*, 118). Woolf's strategy to connect the various types of oppression in a single, vigorous argument against fascism and patriarchy is a powerful one. Passionately she insists that since both are based in iniquity, the key to preventing war is to oppose injustice at home, "to protect liberty" (*TG*, 119). If patriarchy is anathema to freedom and lies at the root of racism, imperialism, and antifeminism, then the logical outcome of that rhetoric of exclusion is the despotism of fascist dictatorships.

As Lassner, Frost, and others have convincingly argued, unifying the victims of patriarchy in this way is nevertheless problematic. For one thing, the correlation between patriarchal oppression in Oxford or Cambridge and the systematic torture and murder of Jews is, to put it mildly, offensive. Yet, even if one refuses the "backshadowing"[47] that occurs in a post-Holocaust reading of the text and assumes that the oppression of

Jews is a conceivable outcome of the impulse toward misogyny, conflating both groups as passive victims of European society's construction of them is still troubling. Joining the various victims of patriarchal society in an "Outsiders' Society" (*TG*, 122) may work theoretically as a political strategy to provide all members with additional power in the collective, but the oversimplification that results in the elision obscures the particular histories and conditions of each of the oppressed groups.

In many ways, Woolf's strategy reinscribes the kind of typecasting that marginalizes these groups in the first place. To adapt Lassner, Woolf disrupts belief in "individuality and the word and names used to protect this dignity" ("Milk of Our Mother's Kindness," 138).[48] For both women and Jews, the impact of Woolf's "farsightedness" results in significant omissions. For the former, the result is that *Three Guineas* presents a particularly narrow conception of female desire based in falsely assumed stereotypes about women as victims, weakly complicit in patriarchy and war.[49] For Jews, however, it is even more complicated. Woolf's Jew, in *Three Guineas*, is conceived as both the victim of patriarchal fascism *and* the patriarchal subject, and thus is neither part of nor outside the Outsiders' Society. Once again, the Jew is characterized in a manner that is only based in difference. In *Three Guineas*, Woolf not only reduces all Jews, from anywhere, to a category of Otherness, but also sees this Jew as epitomizing the negative aspects of patriarchy. Woolf thereby reiterates the discourse that places Jews in the ambivalent position of being "boundary-defying"—a patriarchal entity in a "feminine" category of victims—and by extension she also inadvertently "shuts out" half of that category: namely, the female Jew. As Woolf contends, "You are feeling in your own persons what your mothers felt when they were shut out. . . . Now you are being shut out, you are being shut up, because you are Jews, because you are democrats, because of race, because of religion" (*TG*, 118). Jews are thus a distinctly male "you," and yet this claim is subsequently complicated by her assertion that "The whole inequity of dictatorship . . . against Jews *or* against women . . . is now apparent to you" (*TG*, 118, my emphasis). These passages deny that a *Jew*dith Shakespeare could exist—the category of "Jews" is not the "we" of the daughters of educated men, nor the "you" of the "because you are Jews, because you are democrats," and he is certainly not the "He" of the Tyrant. "The Jew" is thereby once again identified in terms of allosemitism — a murky "not belonging," where the Jew becomes the "site of ambivalence" for whom subjective responses to history are impossible (Bauman, *Modernity*, 146).

Textual ambivalence toward Jews becomes apparent in *Between the Acts* by the way in which Ralph, the only Jewish character, is set apart from the others in his impossible attempt to cross borders successfully. As a Jew, Ralph Manresa defies concrete categories of English society such as class, sex, or gender.[50] Again, like Guido and Felix, his assimilation and border-crossing is made impossible by being marked out by difference in excess. Ralph is associated with vulgarity: he spends too much, dresses too well, and tries too hard to fit in. Most disconcertingly, especially for those scholars who admire Woolf for the exceptionality of her writing and for her liberal and outspoken political views, "the Jew" in Woolf's text is depicted with caricature-like revulsion. Her writing discloses a social prejudice that pits "Jew" against art, culture, creativity, authenticity, dignity, and, most notably, "Englishness."

Woolf was married to a Jew for twenty-five years, was vocal in her support of Jewish refugees, and was both disturbed and personally affected by the threat of a Nazi invasion, even to the point of planning to commit suicide with her husband, Leonard, if Hitler invaded.[51] Nevertheless, Woolf's personal prejudices against Jews are made patent in a number of her diary entries and letters. As Natania Rosenfeld points out in *Outsiders Together*, when Virginia announced her engagement to Leonard, all her letters described him first as "a Jew" (59). In a note to her friend Madge Vaughan, she remarks, "How am I to begin about Leonard? First he is a Jew; second he is 31. . . ." (L, 1: 503); in her note to Violet Dickinson she begins with the words, "I've got a confession to make. I'm going to marry Leonard Wolf [*sic*]. He's a penniless Jew" (L, 1: 500).[52] Many years later, in a frequently quoted letter to Ethel Smyth, Woolf admits this:

> How I hated marrying a Jew — how I hated their nasal voices, and their oriental jewellery, and their noses and their wattles — what a snob I was: for they have immense vitality, and I think I like that quality the best of all. They can't die — they exist on a handful of rice and thimble of water — their flesh dries on their bones, but still they pullulate, copulate, amass (a Mrs. Pinto, fabulously wealthy came in) millions of money. (L, 4: 195–96)

Other letters in which Woolf often forgets to name individuals she meets at dinners or teas except to label them as "a Jew" also expose her prejudiced viewpoint. Thus, a birthday party at her in-laws' in 1932 becomes a scenario of "eating birthday cake with silent Jews at 11pm" (*L*, 5: 23). A list of examples from diary entries gathered by Leena Kore Schröder includes that Woolf read the French novel *Et Cie* "by a Jew" instead of by Jean-Richard Bloch (*D*, 1: 134); she remembered the famous conductor Bruno Walter as "a swarthy fattish man . . . a little Slav, a little semitic" (*D*, 4: 153); and called journalist and political activist Rita Hinden, who had visited Monk's House (and whose name she forgets as soon as Hinden leaves), "a cheap hard Jewess" (*D*, 5: 264–65). Her most vicious attacks are aimed at her mother-in-law, whom she categorizes as "vampire like & vast in her demand for my entire attention & sympathy, while she sits over the fire, in her dreary furs & ugly bonnet & large boots, with her pendulous cheeks & red nose & cheap earrings, talking about Worthing every year. . . ." (*L*, 2: 320–21).

Granted, the view disclosed in the diaries and letters reflects what is normally understood as the typical British upper-middle-class attitude toward Jews between the two world wars. Many antifascist writers like Woolf, who abhorred Germany's racist policies and vehemently protested against Oswald Mosley's British Union of Fascists (BUF), still considered Jews — especially those who had emigrated from Eastern Europe to escape persecution — vulgar or ill-bred. As Tony Kushner suggests, antisemitism in Britain was not violent, and the fascist movement was not particularly virulent, but "government policy toward Jewish refugees from the Nazis in the 1930s was not as generous as has been suggested" ("Paradox," 79). While the majority of Britons did not support violent action against Jews, as espoused by the BUF, Jews were popularly perceived as being "un-British" or a threat to British culture. A survey by the social research organization Mass Observation in 1942 revealed that "up to one-tenth of the population was actually worried about the supposed Jewish power in society," and British culture in general maintained toward Jews "a tradition of intolerance in society" (Kushner, "Paradox," 79, 84). The hypocrisy of British intellectuals' "antisemitism of exclusion" prompted George Orwell to write an essay entitled "Antisemitism in Britain" (1945), in which he criticizes the popular tendency to "draw a distinction between 'antisemitism' and 'disliking Jews'" (334).

British antisemitism, as Orwell contends, "does not take violent forms (English people are almost invariably genteel and law-abiding), but it is ill-natured enough" (333). As he describes it:

> There has never been much feeling against intermarriage, or against Jews taking prominent part in public life. Nevertheless, thirty years ago it was accepted that a Jew was a figure of fun and — though superior in intelligence — slightly deficient in "character". In theory a Jew suffered from no legal disabilities, but in effect he was debarred from certain professions. . . . Wealthy Jews tended to disguise themselves under aristocratic English or Scottish names, and to the average person it seemed quite natural that they should do this, just as it seems natural for a criminal to change his identity if possible. (337)

Orwell's description suggests the limits of sympathy that British intellectuals had for Jewish refugees and Jews in general. They were sympathetic to what was happening to Jews abroad and did not openly admit that they would want Jews gone, but they were far from accepting them as equals.

Critics such as Jane Marcus and David Bradshaw have argued that in her fiction Woolf is confronting and challenging prejudices by shedding light on British conceptions of the Jew.[53] It might be possible that Woolf is exposing the genteel type of antisemitism in Britain by revealing the hypocrisy and harm of what Orwell observed among educated people as "a widespread awareness of the prevalence of antisemitic feeling, and an unwillingness to admit sharing it" (335). Yet, such optimistic defenses of her work would perhaps be more credible if they did not ignore the fact that there is no alternative to this view of Jews in any of Woolf's works. Interrogating the way "the Jew" functions in a more critical manner can shed light on how this discourse functions within the larger context of her literary project. Ralph Manresa in *Between the Acts*, for example, is an especially interesting case since his nonappearance in the text occurs specifically at a time in Britain when Jews and their persecution are so clearly the focus of the media, opinion, and literature. Ralph's absence — and his phantomlike existence in the margins of the novel alongside issues such as war and the Nazi threat — is even more peculiar than his presence. Most notably, his body is missing, but all the metaphoric elements that represent the Jew's intrusion into English life are present. Moreover, Ralph paradoxically appears in the ambivalent position of being *in collusion* with fascism, through association with patriarchy and consumerism, rather than a victim of it.

Similar to Felix in *Nightwood*, Ralph comes from no place, his name is false, and his past is a fabrication. The only information the reader receives about him is that "Ralph, a Jew, got up to look the very spit and image of the landed gentry, supplied from directing City companies — that was certain — tons of money" (*BTA*, 37). Additionally, Ralph has no possibility of continuing into the future since he and Mrs. Manresa "have no child" (*BTA*, 37). His key role in the novel, however, is alluded to by his possessions — car and wife — and the list of associations that describe him: his Jewishness, his false pretense of class, and his money. All of these aspects directly correlate with some of the major themes in the text — patriarchy, desire, Englishness, old families, and the threat of commercialism to creativity. Linett points out that as a parvenu, Ralph represents the threat of "rupturing modernity" to "meaningful unity" (*Modernism*, 88). It could well be argued that while Miss La Trobe's pageant represents the possibilities of modernity to introduce a "new script" that disrupts the dominant patriarchal discourse, Ralph epitomizes the bleak, destructive side of modernization. As a conceptual figure, he corresponds with the anxiety connected to the urban, the material, and the superficial that is encroaching upon the English countryside. In Bauman's terms, the Jew is "a natural lightning rod to divert early discharges of the anti-modernist energy" (*Modernity*, 42). Despite his name change, marriage to a Christian, and "image" of landed gentry, Ralph, like Felix, cannot "pass" for reasons that fail categorization. The unadorned repetitiveness of these "slippery" markers of Jewish excess identify Ralph as a typical conceptual or spectral Jew: his country house, the rubies on his wife's hand "dug up, so people said, by thin Ralph Manresa in his ragamuffin days" (*BTA*, 181), and the "silver-plated car . . . with the initials R. M. twisted so as to look at a distance like a coronet" (*BTA*, 42) are all examples of the perceptible ways in which the narrative sets "the Jew" apart in his desperate, "twisted" determination to belong.[54]

Historically, aside from trading, mercantilism, and money-exchange, numerous professions were denied to Jews; as a result, many would cross class borders to attain their living. Trespassing class boundaries, however, as Bauman explains, "met with social disdain, moral condemnation and aesthetic disgust" (*Modernity*, 46). Linked with commercialization and the destruction of order and security, the conceptual Jew became tainted with a sordidness connected to the "selling out" of class birthrights for economic gain. Gilman links this aspect of Jewish "bordercrossing" to representations of the Jew's body in terms of prostitution and disease (*Jew's Body*, 124). The depiction of Ralph corresponds with these suspicions. Linett points out that in an earlier draft of the novel, Ralph is present at Pointz Hall, although only as a figure of contemplation. In one passage, Mrs. Manresa, in assessing the crowd, observes how they view her husband with a certain amount of distrust:

> Everyone was a thorough good sort; had money in the savings bank; didn't she know it? She was their pal; though as she knew, they regarded thin Ralph Manresa, her husband, with suspicion. It was partly his clothes. But the wild child they felt one of themselves; coming down from town with a boxful of goodies; and a boy or two to keep her company. . . . (*PH*, 115)

Linett appropriately observes that "Woolf does not enumerate the reason those gentry regard Ralph 'with suspicion'" (*Modernism*, 90). One wonders, if the problem is "*partly* his clothes" (my emphasis), which are somehow too perfect, what is the other part? In the final typescript, the rumors (or "so people said") are that Manresa's rubies "were dug up" (*BTA*, 181), intimating that Ralph scrounged for his fortune, digging up gems from the dirt or "gold digging." His wealth and person is thereby linked with grime and crudity. The Jew, trading values such as love and beauty for money, becomes the symbol of the aggressor, violating the land and consuming its contents for desire and profit. Unlike the local landowners, gentleman farmers, and villagers, Ralph is not "refined" and his money is tainted with disgrace. Yet, since his actions are not dissimilar to England's imperialist project and capitalist patriarchy in general, the villagers' suspicions expose that Ralph is indeed the "bogeyman" for their modernism. After all, his actions are not that different from Bart Oliver's in India, or young men like Giles Oliver who leave their country estates to move to the city and become stockbrokers.

Mrs. Manresa assumes that if everyone has "money in the savings bank," they cannot blame her for making sure she has her own financial assurances—but they do, as evidenced by Isa's comment that she is a "strumpet" (*BTA*, 87). A promiscuous Mrs. Manresa would mirror Ralph's avarice, but in her case, consumerism functions in a metaphor of sexual desire. In the passage cited previously, the lines following the "suspicion" with which people view Ralph point to Mrs. Manresa's appetite for "goodies" and "a boy or two to keep her company." This could also intimate suspicions concerning Ralph's masculinity, since he obviously cannot keep his wife satisfied. George Mosse asserts that "it was a racist commonplace that Jews were aggressive toward the female sex, lecherous, and given to corrupting Christian girls. Yet despite the putative masculine aggression, the accusation of confusing genders leveled against the Jews remained intact as well" (*Nationalism and Sexuality*, 144). Quite obviously, Mrs. Manresa is no easily corrupted Christian "girl," but Ralph is implicated as both pimp and dupe: he provides her with the house and car to entertain men but is either too obtuse or too greedy to stop working long enough to notice her infidelities or to "keep her company" himself. Like Felix Volkbein, Ralph's border-crossing is ultimately uncreative, because he does not have children and also because, as the embodiment of consumerism, his body, like his money, circulates in a manner outside the real. His profession, directing City companies, is as vague an occupation as his physical being. It is not based in anything concrete, material, or of aesthetic value aside from making more money.

Both Ralph and Mrs. Manresa participate in a relationship of exchange that is criminalized as a type of prostitution, while their bodies circulate in a manner that is detached from the concreteness of English rural life, including home, family, and history. In the earlier typescript, Ralph is present at the end of the pageant. La Trobe's megaphone monologue exposes his suspicious criminality:

> "Let's break the rhythm and forget the rhyme. And calmly consider ourselves. Ourselves. Bony of fat." (The looking-glasses kept rough pace with the words, [illustrating] <illuminating>them.) "Liars and thieves." (<Ralph Manresa.> [Manresa was here exposed to view.]) "The poor are as bad as the rich. Don't hide among rags; or let our cloth protect us." (The Rev. Streatfield faced the cheval glass from the rectory.) (*PH*, 162)

Alluding to the present state of affairs, the text, as Linett duly argues, "uses" Ralph to critique the corruption of modern consumerism (*Modernism*, 92–93). This connection is emphasized in the final draft of La Trobe's loudspeaker monologue. Among the "gun slayers, bomb droppers" that Miss La Trobe asks the audience to "Consider," she lists crimes such as "Mr M's bungalow. A view spoilt for ever. That's murder. . . . Or Mrs E's lipstick and blood-red nails. . . . A tyrant, remember is half a slave" (*BTA*, 168). Although it is not certain, one can assume that "Mr M" could well be Mr. Manresa — a Jewish travesty whose modernized country house is mentioned earlier — and that "Mrs E" would refer to Mrs. Manresa, the only person there who appears to paint her fingernails "red as roses" (*BTA*, 36). Mrs. Manresa's makeup, superficiality, and promiscuity, and even her adoption of Ralph's surname, associate her with "blood-red" blood spilled in the name of patriarchy as well as Jewish excess. But it is Ralph's "spoiled view" that is murderous. Because it threatens to destroy a way of life, it is connected with the Nazi airplanes that fly above. The view Ralph truly obscures, then, is the image of what does and does not belong in the English countryside.

Ironically, in the *Outline of History*, the book that Lucy reads throughout the novel, H. G. Wells espouses the argument that for Jews to be accepted, they need to be absent. In the section of Wells's text describing the beginnings of Christianity, he depicts two types of Jews: those who assimilate, like the ancient Sadducees, who "share God and his promise with all mankind"; and Jews who remain exclusive, like the Pharisees, who are identified as "greedy and narrow" (282). Bryan Cheyette shows how this idea of assimilation is represented in Wells's other works and how it influenced his outlook on antisemitism in the 1930s. As Cheyette maintains, Wells "was able to associate the latter exclusivist tradition of Judaism with a degenerate, contemporary world" ("H. G. Wells," 29). Just by being physically present, the Jews hindered a universalist world state in which everyone could be one; indeed, they embodied its failure (ibid., 30). Wells's utopian viewpoint also puts "the Jew" in a double-bind of impossible erasure — as a negative Other who can only be accepted by not being present. In the 1930s, Wells continued to promote the idea that Jews themselves "had caused 'Gentile intolerance'" by "diverting mankind from its universalist morals" and maintaining their own difference (ibid., 29–31). In both his journalism and *Experiment in Autobiography* (1934), Wells argued that if Jews had acted as they were supposed to, by assimilating, Europe would not have "a Jewish question"; thus the problem of Jewish refugees and antisemitism cannot "be dealt with by itself or in any way except as a part of the general human problem" (Wells, *Experiment*, 353).[55]

In *Outline of History*, where Lucy reads the historical account of "when we were savages," Wells also famously outlines the Races of Man, linking the financial and commercial traditions of the Semitic peoples with those of the ancient Phoenicians, an extinct race of maritime traders that demonstrated "the peculiar and characteristic gift of the Semitic peoples . . . trade and exchange." As Wells asserts, "The Semitic peoples, we may point out here, are even to this day *counting peoples* strong in their sense of equivalents" (*Outline*, 108). According to Wells, the Phoenicians in Spain and Africa converted to Judaism after the fall of Tyre and Carthage, and it is to them "that the financial and commercial tradition of the Jews is to be ascribed" (*Outline*, 281). Perhaps it is no coincidence, then, that Ralph's last name is Spanish in origin and his link to mercantilism is the only heritage accounted for in the novel. In chapter 2, I examined some of the associations of the Spanish town Manresa with the history of Jewish persecution and its role in evoking Woolf's concern with the Spanish Civil War. In addition, Spain is a country known for its *conversos*—Jews who converted to Catholicism and changed their names during and after the Spanish Inquisition (1478–1834) to avoid persecution—and "crypto-Jews" known as *marranos*, or converts who retained Jewish identities, performed rituals in private, or both. Ralph, the "image of landed gentry" who is "said" to be a Jew, may attempt to assimilate, but his "racial" associations to commerce, like those of Felix Volkbein, appear impossible to shake off.

It is important, however, to stress that Woolf also exposes that prejudice and suspicion against Jews is narrow-minded. One could assume that Woolf might agree with some of Wells's beliefs, especially his strong lifelong condemnation of nationalism and racial and cultural elitism, but because Lucy Swithin is most closely associated with the *Outline of History*, and she is a figure who appears to be criticized for clinging to an obtuse utopianism, Woolf's ambiguity once again comes to the fore.[56] I would argue that the Jew in Woolf's text also disrupts and challenges false illusions of unity and harmony inherent in the spectacle—whether in Germany, rural England, or Wells's utopian vision of the world. As a character whom no one actually sees, Ralph demands an examination of what differences truly exist between "Aryan and Semite" and between past and future. By the end of the pageant, public discourse, the disruption of order, and the dislocation of historical time lead the audience to ask, "And what about the Jews? The refugees . . . People like ourselves, beginning life again" (*BTA*, 109). Nevertheless, "the Jews" they speak of, who are "like ourselves," are not present in the mirror that reflects an "us." Moreover, the audience's comments imply that Jews are only sympathetic when they are indistinguishably "like ourselves." What if they are not? What about the Jews who did dress differently, had different traditions, or were poor, or had fled from different countries with different traditions? Does that, as Wells proclaims, justify their oppression? Considering Woolf's troubling portrayal of Jewish difference, one questions how she regards those "*not* like ourselves."

The audience's excuse for its indifference is a familiar one: "But it's always been the same. . . . My old mother, who's over eighty, can remember . . ." (*BTA*, 109). It would seem that prejudice will always exist and "be the same" as long as "the Jew" remains the nameless victim, unidentified except for his inability to become part of the "dispersed we" or to act in a new role in the play that opens the curtain at the novel's close. While modernization, when it comes in the form of feminist "new plots," produces life in the shape of new works of art and new types of relationships, modernization by the patriarchal Jew only reproduces more difference or complete erasure. For this reason, perhaps, Ralph's physical body is inconsequential. As Lassner insists, "Woolf's novel acknowledges the Jew's rescue as necessary, but she cannot tolerate the Jew's presence in her fiction of English history" ("Milk of Our Mother's Kindness," 137). The way "the Jew" functions in Woolf's work thus echoes the Orwell quotation with which this chapter began: "the Jew is evidently a scapegoat, though *for what* he is a scapegoat we do not yet know" (Orwell, "Antisemitism in Britain," 340). Upon examining Woolf's text, it seems plausible that while Jews as a group are recognized as victims of oppression, "the Jew" as a concept becomes symbolic of Woolf's anxieties concerning patriarchy, commercialization, miscegenation, and consumption. It is quite possible that her portrayal of Ralph Manresa is supposed to resist Nazism's racial ideology and expose and confront her own and British society's prejudices. Nevertheless, there appears to be too much evidence that suggests otherwise. Even if her portrayal of Ralph is part of Woolf's strategy of ambiguity, one thing that an antifascist writer should *not* want to be morally ambiguous about in the 1930s is antisemitism. Since there are no individual Jewish male or female characters whose interiority would convey the diverse ways in which Jewishness is experienced in English society — or any reference to Jewish culture, history, or tradition, for that matter — it becomes difficult to interpret *Between the Acts* as a challenge to, rather than a corroboration of, a perception of Jews based solely on negative difference.

## Images of the Modern Jewish Woman in *Goodbye to Berlin*

If the conceptual Jew for both Barnes and Woolf is a figure representing impossible assimilation due to excessive avarice, gender-bending, class-crossing, and boundary-blurring, and the gentile woman who associates with him sells her body in a relationship of exchange, what happens to the modern Jewish woman? How does she fare in the discourse of difference in the 1930s? Does she function in ways more similar to the Modern Woman or to the Jew? As Judith Lewin discerns, "Studies of Jewish women in literature have generally been a mere footnote under studies of 'the Jew' in Western literature — the appellation 'Jew' assuming a study of the Jewish man as representative of the Jewish community" ("Sublimity," 239). Indeed, few of the many essays on "the Jew" in modernist literature discuss female Jewish characters. Anne Pellegrini, whose work on the performance of female Jewishness broke ground for new considerations of Jews and gender, asserts that in most conceptions of Jewishness, the female Jew disappears. Even Gilman concedes, "Full-length studies of the actual roles of Jewish women in this world of representations and their own complex response are certainly needed" (*Jew's Body*, 5). Female Jewishness, however, is slightly complicated. Lewin notes this in her observations of Jewish stereotyping:

> The Jewish woman's image in literature cannot be captured in the formula "Jew" + "Woman," for she is somehow more than, less than, and beyond this summation. Conventional depictions of Jewish women rely on stereotypical codes that apply to each

of the separate groups. It is where these codes overlap that complexity is created. ("Sublimity," 239)

The advantage of examining the Jewish characters in Isherwood's *Goodbye to Berlin* is that it is one of the few novels in which Jewishness can be examined through the female body as well as through the male.

At the same time that Barnes was working on her portrait of Felix, and Woolf was writing *The Years*, Isherwood was more consciously and critically confronting Nazi racial policies and hostile attitudes toward Jews in Berlin. Explicitly, Isherwood highlights the casual antisemitism of ordinary Berliners, exposing how persecution was able to occur because of ignorance and apathy. German antisemitism, as Bauman points out, functioned mostly through "co-operation by non-resistance" (*Modernity*, 32). The Berlin that Isherwood portrays includes a Jewish population and way of life on the verge of disappearing in the "real" rather than the conceptual sense, and reveals some of the social and political conditions that are allowing that disappearance to happen. Germany, and especially Berlin (as historians such as Amos Elon have pointed out), were far from being the most antisemitic places in Europe at the turn of the twentieth century: Germany was a haven for Jewish intellectuals, artists, and writers, and had more Jewish professionals and academics than America, France, or Britain.[57] As mentioned previously, genocide was made possible by "the apathy with which most Germans viewed the fate of the Jews when they knew of it, or resigned themselves to ignorance." The callousness of the German populace toward Jews was due in part to the feeling made acceptable by the media and public discourse that Jews were different, "uncanny," or dangerous (Bauman, *Modernity*, 32). Isherwood's portrait of Berlin corroborates this idea, especially in the way he contrasts the official Nazi actions against Jews with the casual antisemitism of characters with whom the narrator associates.

Some examples of how Berlin becomes a hostile environment for Jews include a scene in which a Nazi tries to drag two Jews out of a car for picking up German women. A small crowd of spectators gathers to watch but does nothing (*GTB*, 236). Another incident describes a Jewish writer being hauled out of a café by the Nazis and taken away. The narrator observes how the reaction of onlookers is static: "Nobody moved a finger. You could have heard a pin drop, till they were gone"

(*GTB*, 251). These public displays of unspoken antisemitism are then contrasted with private expressions of hostility toward Jews, such as Sally Bowles's and Frau Nowak's seemingly casual statements. Sally remarks that she is making love to "a dirty old Jew producer" who might give her a role (*GTB*, 201), and Frau Nowak asserts that "When Hitler comes, he'll show these Jews a thing or two. They won't be so cheeky then" (*GTB*, 148). As antisemitism escalates in Berlin, so do the statements, such as Frl. Mayr's comment: "This town is sick with Jews. Turn over any stone, and a couple of them will crawl out. They're poisoning the very water we drink! They're strangling us, they're robbing us, they're sucking our life-blood" (*GTB*, 175).

The narrator's position is clearly in opposition to these overt expressions of antisemitism. When Christopher points out to Frau Nowak that Hitler intends to get rid of Jews completely, she admits, "Oh I shouldn't like that to happen." With the tragic irony that only today's readers can appreciate, she then adds, "You ask the people around here, Herr Christoph: they'd never turn out the Jews" (*GTB*, 148). In contrast, the narrator places himself as a somewhat ambiguous defender of Jews. When Frl. Mayr blames big department-store owners like the Landauers for being "Filthy thieving Jews," Christopher retorts, "The Landauers are personal friends of mine," which he admits, "wasn't strictly true" but was said for the effect (*GTB*, 175). Granted, Christopher sets out to make his statement true by using a letter of introduction from England to meet them and become personal friends of theirs. It is nevertheless slightly questionable if his "perverse" reaction to Frl. Mayr's antisemitic remark results in a friendship or a confirmation and reiteration of the stereotype that portrays Jews as being rich, snobbish, and slightly overbearing.

While the representation of Jewish characters such as the Landauers or the Bernsteins does not even approach the kind of typecasting endemic to Woolf's or Barnes's texts — for the most part Isherwood portrays Jews, both men and women, as people who happen to be Jewish — the language of difference and economy used in their portrayal still engages in timeworn stereotyping. In relation to the threatening political problem that is the subtext to *Goodbye to Berlin*, the portrayal of Jewish characters is clearly meant to draw attention to the lives of individual human beings who are threatened by Nazism. These characters are not the spectral Jews of Barnes's and Woolf's novels, nor of Frl. Mayr's and Frau

Nowak's reiterations of Nazi propaganda. Nevertheless, Isherwood draws on a type of *écriture judaïque* that prejudges Jewish characters in relation to common characteristics of difference and dissolution. As Jonathan Judaken stresses, portrayals of specific "Jewish qualities"—either good or bad—that rely on myths of Jewish Otherness, "are a part of a process of social and psychological identity construction" ("So What's New?" 29). Isherwood's depiction of Jewish characters fixes Jewish identity in a manner that emphasizes an ambiguous alterity that is, once again, featured as both dissipating and excessive.

The "some of my best friends are Jews" comment that the narrator uses to challenge private expressions of hostility, or perhaps to assuage his guilt and prove his broad-mindedness, launches a self-conscious appraisal of his encounter with Jewish families in Berlin. Yet one of the distinguishing factors between these Jews and the other characters is that money features prominently in their characterization. Christopher does not meet "regular" or financially struggling Jews among the artists and writers he associates with (of whom there were many in Berlin), but only extremely wealthy Jews whose overindulgence, culture-worship, and materialism are emphasized. Granted, as an English tutor, the narrator's access would be to those who could afford (or were interested in) his services. The portrayals, however, echo typical myths of the Jewish parvenu and his relationship to commercialism. The Bernsteins, for example, are nearly caricatures of the rich, overcompensating Jewish family, described in "their cosy, stuffy way" (*GTB*, 30). Herr Bernstein is "small, shaky, and sly," echoing assumptions that Jewish men are nervous, effeminate, and devious; his only concern or topics of conversation revolve around money. Upon hearing about Nazi rioting, for example, Herr Bernstein tells his wife to take the tram if going shopping so his "beautiful car" will not get ruined: "If they throw stones at you, I will buy you a sticking-plaster for your head. It will cost me only five groschen. But if they throw stones at my car, it will cost me perhaps five hundred marks" (*GTB*, 30). His joke to Christopher during the meal, "Not only do we give you a nice dinner but we pay you for eating it!" is crass. Frau Bernstein, too, "stout and placid," is shallow, especially when compared with the dynamic, "salt of the earth" working-class women with whom Christopher shares his home (*GTB*, 29). The Bernsteins' house, much like Guido Volkbein's and Ralph Manresa's, is excessively overdone, modern, and ugly, "like a power-station which the engineers have tried to make comfortable with chairs and tables from an old-fashioned, highly respectable boarding-house" (*GTB*, 26).

More notable, however, is the portrayal of Hippi, "a fat pretty girl" whom Christopher tutors: along with "big cow-eyes" she has "a lazy, jolly, self-indulgent laugh and a well-formed bust" (*GTB*, 26). The difficulty involved in examining Hippi as a particularly Jewish typecast is that her portrayal could also be attributed to stereotypes of women in general. Hippi, oddly enough, is strikingly similar to Mrs. Manresa — sensuous and indulgent but completely lacking in substance — alluding to the disconcerting way in which gender and race intersect in stereotypes regarding both women and Jews. Like Mrs. Manresa, Hippi has numerous boyfriends and is mainly interested in eating "goodies," dating, and gossip. The codes that apply to her as a Modern Woman or Flapper, however, overlap with those of the Jewish woman during the interwar era in Europe. Unintelligent, lazy, and lacking in critical skills, the attributes of the indulgent "wild child" become even more prominent when combined with the economic and commercial materialism of the racialized Jew. Like her father's money and car, Hippi's body circulates in a form of excessive sexuality. She plies Christopher with chocolate, coffee, and fruit, pumps him for information about "German women" and sex until he blushes, and smiles lazily as she watches him. Christopher comments that she "has a great many boy friends. . . . One has a wonderful car. Another has an aeroplane. Another has fought seven duels" (*GTB*, 29). Comparable to the way Mrs. Manresa uses men and cars for sexual mobility, Hippi exploits her many boyfriends, whose cars and airplanes provide her accessibility to the public sphere, and in return she allows them accessibility to her body.[58]

Typical stereotypes of Jewish women in literature, as Lewin illustrates, follow the virgin/whore model that links "a 'positive' image of moral virtue to a 'negative' image of sensuality and deceit'" ("Sublimity," 242–43). Especially in fin-de-siècle European literature, for example the novels of Henry James or Marcel Proust, Jewish women feature as "exotic and erotic spectacles" (Pellegrini, "Whiteface Performances," 110). The *belle juive*, as Pellegrini notes, was an especially "deceptive" femme fatale whose "stereotypically dark hair and black eyes" conceal her "powers of destruction" and "perverse masculinity" (ibid., 129). To give credit where credit is due, this type of representation does not resonate with Isherwood's portrayal. Nevertheless, Isherwood portrays the two main Jewish women on opposing sides of a more subtle virgin/whore dichotomy — boy-crazy, indulgent Hippi and prudish Natalia Landauer.

If Hippi is voluptuous, self-indulgent, and pleasure-seeking, Natalia, at the other end of the spectrum, is typecast as the cold, masculine Jewish nouveau riche woman.[59] She shakes hands "straight from the shoulder" (*GTB*, 176) and says good-bye by slamming the door (*GTB*, 183) — both actions bordering on the aggressive rather than the assertive. Even her looks are distinctly unfeminine and "Jewish," as she is described with "dark fluffy hair" looking like "a young fox" (*GTB*, 176). Jay Geller quotes German literary historian and antisemitic polemicist Otto Hauser in this regard:

> By no other people do you find so many effeminate men [*Weibmänner*] and masculine women [*Mannweiber*] as by Jews. That's why so many Jewesses push their way into male professions, study everything possible, from law [and] medicine to theology, become social organizers. It's clear that a good two-thirds of these Jewish women bear ambiguous secondary gender traits. Clear traces of beard growth are frequent, while their breasts are underdeveloped and their hair short. These women made . . . the pageboy cut [*Bubikopf*] fashionable. (quoted and translated by Geller in *Freud's Jewish Body*, 9)

Natalia is not quite as "masculine" as Otto Hauser's depiction of the Jewish New Woman, but she is still depicted as being loud, aggressive, and decidedly "unfeminine." She goes out of her way in conversation to compare herself with Hippi and allude to her unfavorable "faults" (*GTB*, 184). Her cold manner is emphasized when she shirks from any physical contact with Christopher: "She preferred always, I noticed, to have a table between us if we sat down. She hated me to help her into her coat." When one evening he offers her the spoon from his coffee cup, "she refused it with an expression of slight distaste. She declined even this indirect contact with my mouth" (*GTB*, 183). In her broken English she also makes sure to emphasize that "I do not admirate the women who is going always from one man to another — that is all so . . . so degenerated,

I find" (*GTB*, 183). Natalia's prudishness is expressly highlighted when she is contrasted with Sally (Christopher has them meet for coffee in a rather "cruel" experiment). Natalia looks "dowdy" and wears a "long townified dress she'd put on that didn't suit her" (*GTB*, 200). She arrives early, "flurried," then seems increasingly insecure, manipulative, and then "indignant," until she finally yells at Christopher, "Imbecile! I do not ask for compliments!" (*GTB*, 200). Sally, on the other hand, comes late, moves languidly, "cooing" that she's "been making love to a dirty old Jew producer. I'm hoping he'll give me a contract. . . ." (*GTB*, 201), prattling on about film, adultery, and how "this one drank and that one took drugs" (*GTB*, 202). Finally, Natalia leaves in a huff.

When contrasted with decadent Hippi Bernstein or vampy Sally Bowles, Natalia clearly falls on the preceding side of the virgin/whore equation. Yet, if her body does not circulate in a form of sexual exchange as does Hippi's or Sally's, then the discourse of excess connected to Natalia still links her to conceptions of "the Jew" in regard to economy and difference. Natalia's coldness toward sex is so excessive that one could conceive of her as overcompensating, covering up a "true" racial character by trying too desperately to be something else. Natalia is the female version of the Jewish culture-worshiper. She aspires to study art history in Paris; she and Christopher talk "as usual, of art, music, books" (*GTB*, 203). One of the first outings she and Christopher enjoy is a Mozart concert, where the audience's (including Natalia's) "taut, devotional enthusiasm oppressed [him] like a headache" (*GTB*, 184). Mostly, she is depicted as being loud and pushy, associated with money, overeager culture worship, and "dealing." Stephen Spender, in contrast, describes Gisa (Gise) Soloweitschik, on whom the character is based, as being "very passionate." In a letter to Isherwood, Spender criticizes Isherwood's depiction, remarking, "The essential fact to me about your relationship with Gisa is that you talked to her continually about Otto [Isherwood's boyfriend at the time]. When you did this, tears of sympathy started in Gisa's eyes" (*CHK*, 65). Spender also reproached Christopher for his sneers at Natalia's culture worship: "After all, the Nazi attitude towards concerts and culture and Jews is in some respects like yours" (*CHK*, 65).[60]

The discourses that construct the Jewish woman as "manly" inevitably pair her with the "effeminate" male Jew. In this case, Bernhard Landauer, Natalia's cousin, is depicted with the distinct gender and sexual ambiguity of allosemitic discourse. The narrator describes Bernhard as "oriental" and "soft, negative . . . yet curiously potent, with the static potency of a carved ivory figure in a shrine" (*GTB*, 194). His face, too, is "over-civilized, finely drawn, beaky" (*GTB*, 193), and he is described as "poking his delicate beak-like nose into everything" (*GTB*, 194). Bernhard mockingly calls himself a "cross-breed" and "poor barbarian," even "constitutionally incapable of bringing myself to the required pitch of enthusiasm" (*GTB*, 199). His unnatural or inorganic quality is emphasized as the narrator stresses how Bernhard hides his true feelings and remains "curiously remote," his gestures conveying "the arrogant humility of the East" (*GTB*, 197). Furthermore, the text suggests that Bernhard is romantically interested in the narrator, which Isherwood himself later believed was "offensive" since Wilfrid Israel, the character upon whom Bernhard is based, was neither homosexual nor in love with Isherwood. Isherwood later admitted, "I am embarrassed to know that Wilfrid read it" (*CHK*, 71).[61] While the depiction of Bernhard is not in and of itself antisemitic, Isherwood's portrayal very directly participates in popular European discourses that link Jewishness to ambiguity, foreignness, alienation, effeminacy, and fragility (while at the same time possessing sexual potency).

In Isherwood's portrayal of "typical" Jewish family life, the Landauers fare slightly better, although still marked by discernibly "Jewish" traits. Frau Landauer, a virtual replica of Frau Bernstein, is characterized by her large figure and "placidity." She is "a large pale woman . . . seated placidly at the dining-room table" who provides equally "placid" replies to questions (*GTB*, 176, 177). Herr Landauer, like Herr Bernstein, is "small," but at least he is lively, intelligent, with "boot button eyes twinkling with benevolence" (188). He adores his family in a less stuffy way than Herr Bernstein and is extremely considerate of Christopher at the table. Still, the Landauer household is conspicuously bourgeois, excessive in its worship of Western culture in a manner that is uncannily reminiscent of Felix Volkbein. Herr Landauer, like Guido and Felix, is a man who speaks many languages and travels to numerous countries. In Natalia's account, even when he loses all his money, he magically "can start with one pfennig and work and work until he gets it all back" (*GTB*, 182). Their house, too, is overstuffed: "the few available wall-spaces between pictures and cupboards were decorated with eccentric life-size figures, maidens with flying hair or oblique-eyed gazelles" (*GTB*, 177). The sexual ambiguity (and rapaciousness) of Herr Landauer is insinuated as the dinner conversation moves from foreign travel and languages to Byron, Oscar Wilde, Shakespeare, and Isherwood's own book. In a parallel manner, the conversation is in reality shifting from prostitutes (travel) to incest (Byron) to gay sex (Wilde) to romance (Shakespeare) and then criminal romance (what Landauer thinks *All the Conspirators* to be about). In other words, the discussion moves from one sexual topic to another, causing Christopher to become "quite red as a lobster" (*GTB*, 191). Herr Landauer is a modern intellectual whom Christopher admires, but he is also extreme in every category and therefore conspicuously Other.

While in retrospect these depictions are unsettling for the way they typecast Jewishness, it is important to emphasize that Christopher's compassion and concern in respect to the predicament of Bernhard and the other Jewish characters prevail over his "outsider looking in" stance. Isherwood's purpose, it would seem clear, is to emphasize that these are real people and that their way of life is on the verge of destruction. Like other Berliners, however, the Landauers and the Bernsteins remain in denial, believing in the validity of their citizenship in a German nation of intellectual depth and power. The unreality of their predicament becomes too difficult to face. In contrast to the "Jew" in Barnes and Woolf, this is a disappearing Jew who feels rooted and secure in his place in German society but whose disappearance is looming. Hippi, for example, "never worries about the future. . . . She means to go to the university, travel about, have a jolly good time and eventually, of course, marry" (*GTB*, 29). Natalia, even while she claims, "I await always the worst will come," continues to make plans for studies in Paris and for love: "I shall go away with the man I love and I shall live with him" (*GTB*, 182). Only the narrator, outside the predicament, hints that while no one imagines what can happen, the unimaginable is imminent. As a British subject, however, he can more easily escape the spectacle of Nazism in Berlin.

Antisemitic rhetoric and boycotts, escalating violence, and the progressively unreal quality of life in Berlin become the focus of the last two sections of the text. The gap between living Jewish characters and "the Jew" as it functions within the Nazi spectacle becomes progressively larger as the text emphasizes the sinister atmosphere of the Nazi street.

The extravagance of Nazi bravado is almost too overblown to be taken seriously — which in many ways "fools" some of the characters. One can see this in Bernhard's response to the menacing letter that he receives:

> Bernhard Landauer, beware. We are going to settle the score with you and your uncle and all other filthy Jews. We give you twenty-four hours to leave Germany. If not, you are dead men. (*GTB*, 221)

The letter is couched in so many clichés, a veritable parody of a gangster movie, that Bernhard's sole response is to laugh. The narrator is the one to point out that "The Nazis may write like schoolboys, but they're capable of anything. That's why they're so dangerous. People laugh at them, right up to the last moment. . . ." (*GTB*, 221).

Perhaps Bernhard's reaction to the Nazi spectacle is the only understandable one in the entire novel. He perceives that fighting against Nazism might be "sane" or "healthy" but ultimately hopeless in a place where reality has itself become a hallucination. Bernhard recognizes that as a Jew he has already been transformed into an unreal object in Germany's illusion of wholeness: "I have had an unpleasant feeling, such as one has in a dream, that I myself do not exist. . . . One evening, I was so much troubled by this hallucination of non-existence of Landauers' that I picked up my telephone and had a long conversation with one of the night-watchmen" (*GTB*, 222).[62] Antony Shuttleworth observes that "Landauer witnesses his own disappearance from the aesthetic sanctuary of the flat over which he presides" ("Populous City," 160). But even more than vanishing from his own created world, he foresees the obliteration of all individuals who fall under the category of "spectral Jew" in Germany. When Bernhard tells Christopher that Natalia has left Germany and is married to a French doctor, he foreshadows the demise of all of Berlin's marginal characters, including himself: "It's pleasant to think of one's friend being happy, isn't it? . . . Especially in another country. . . ." (*GTB*, 222). If Bernhard's death at the hands of the Nazis at the end of the novel is tragic, it is not only because he dies but because he epitomizes the bleakness and sense of futility that envelop the ending of the novel — and the entire city of Berlin. As Christopher observes despairingly, "whatever government is in power, [the people] are doomed" (*GTB*, 255).

## Conclusion

The passive audience of spectators that allows Jews to be terrorized in *Goodbye to Berlin* is the same group that the narrator observes "could be made to believe in anybody or anything" (*GTB*, 235). Being part of the Jewish spectacle, the conceptual Jew renders the real Jew invisible except as a barrier to a utopian, united body politic. The boundary-breaking, excess, and "slipperiness" that mark the Jews in these three novels reveal that all identities are contingent not on who one "is" but rather who one "is not." This is true of the Landauers in Berlin but also of Ralph Manresa, who ruptures the community of "we" at Pointz Hall, and of the Volkbeins, whose dissolution is deemed necessary as a condition of Barnes's modernism. Collusion in the fantasy on the part of the spectators in all three novels allows them to ignore intolerance, hostility, violence, and discrimination toward the Jew. At the same time, however, in their problematic construction of "the Jew" as an imagined entity that exceeds the boundaries of rationality, subjectivity, and self-determination, Woolf, Barnes, and Isherwood become complicit in that intolerance, as well as in the historical and cultural erasure of the multiple experiences of men and women of Jewish ancestry living in Europe. "Wittingly or not," to quote Lassner and Trubowitz, they treat Jewishness "as if it were always and only a representation" (*Antisemitism and Philosemitism*, 7).

Anthony Julius makes the claim for the antisemitism he discerns in T. S. Eliot's work that while "bad politics" do not mean "bad art," the substance of a work should not be overlooked. The kind of discourse that is hostile to Jews "is a discourse that intends harm" (Julius, *T. S. Eliot, Anti-Semitism, and Literary Form*, 11). Barnes, Woolf, and Isherwood perhaps do not "intend harm," but negative portrayals of Jews do contribute to a harmful discourse. As Gilman asserts, "no one who identifies, whether positively or negatively, with the label 'Jew' is immune from the power of such stereotypes. It reflects the relative powerlessness of the Jew in the Diaspora and the hostility which Christian society (even in its most secularized form) has against the Jews" (*Jew's Body*, 3). Unless these stereotypes are examined and critiqued by current readers, we risk ignoring important considerations of the way prejudice works and the impact that these types of prejudices had on Jews living in Europe in the 1930s, and continue to have on Jews today. So-called liberal attitudes that expressed sympathy for the universal idea of the Jewish refugee or alien but retained hostility toward Jews or connected them with money, greed, and power alienated Jewish individuals living in England. This mindset also contributed to apathy toward the fates of men and women who at that time could still be saved from Nazi persecution. Anti–Jewish prejudice in the 1930s and *écriture judaïque*, therefore, must be read within that context. The tendency to ignore the implications of characterizing "the Jew" only in terms of casual typecasting — whether it be corruption, money, and power, or eternal victimhood — ends in distorting and silencing the achievements, experiences, culture, practices, traditions, and contributions of the thousands upon thousands of individuals who lived, worked, and raised families as Jews in Europe before the Holocaust.

Historically, the reaction of some of the "real Jews" to the double-bind of imaginary representation and impossible assimilation resulted in a "counterpressure" to exert control over their own self-determination and inclusion in culture. Without that counterpressure, as Jonathan Freedman maintains, influential figures such as Einstein, Proust, Freud, Benjamin, Adorno, Arendt, Kafka, and others who are "virtually synonymous with our understanding of modernity" would never have achieved such prominence (*Temple of Culture*, 19). Nevertheless, what Orwell wrote in 1945 still applies today: "The point is that something, some psychological vitamin, is lacking in modern civilization, and as a result we are all more or less subject to this lunacy of believing that whole races or nations are mysteriously good or mysteriously evil" ("Antisemitism," 340). Alain Finkielkraut, in his acceptance speech for the *Prix Européen de l'Essai Charles Veillon* in 1984, asserts that "Culture, and perhaps European culture" should be understood as the expression of "the life of a people, group, or collectivity but which escapes the limits of a collective being" (*Imaginary Jew*, xii). A collective, of course, does not mean seeing everyone as "the same." It means viewing society as a diverse group of individuals who can live and belong together with equal consideration — rather than being fixed with identities of "like ourselves" or "not like ourselves."

**CHAPTER 4**

# Eventually We're All Queer:
# Fascism, Nazism, and Homosexuality

There is a great deal of the intellectual snob about the invert:
but since he converts what he borrows from the intellect for
the purpose of sex, he is a great enemy of the intellect.

—WYNDHAM LEWIS, *THE ART OF BEING RULED* (1926)

Unfortunately, we don't have it as easy as our forefathers
[the Teutons]. The homosexual, whom one called "Urning,"
was drowned in a swamp. . . . That wasn't a punishment,
but simply the extinguishment of abnormal life. It had to be
got rid of, just as we pull out weeds, throw them on a heap,
and burn them.

—HEINRICH HIMMLER, *SPEECH TO THE SS-GRUPPENFÜHRER*

(FEBRUARY 18, 1938)

In every human being a vacillation from one sex to the other
takes place, and often it is only the clothes that keep the male
or female likeness.

—VIRGINIA WOOLF, *ORLANDO: A BIOGRAPHY* (1928)

"Eventually we're all queer," drawls Christopher's friend Fritz as he and
the narrator sit in a bar watching a drag show toward the end of *Goodbye
to Berlin* (238). In this way, the text positions characters and readers

alike as "queer" outsiders, observing the Nazi spectacle through the inverted lens of the camera obscura that is the text. The idea that "we're all queer" or even *could be* all queer was diametrically opposed to an ideology such as National Socialism, which emphasized moral order, clear sexual boundaries, and the sanctity of the family as crucial principles. Isherwood's, Barnes's, and Woolf's texts foreground sexual anxieties that were present not only in Nazi Germany but also in their own countries. Especially in their portrayal of gay and lesbian characters, the novels highlight the way gender, sexual politics, and textual politics are decisively linked in all oppressive political ideologies. The main difference with sexual regulation in the Third Reich, however, was that defining and policing sexual expression often led to arrest, incarceration in concentration camps, and death.

As I demonstrate, homosexuality in the texts, like Jewish identity, demands questions from that "collective being" concerning self-determination, desire, and who belongs or who does not. The discourse of homophobia, along with that of antisemitism, was challenged by Isherwood, Woolf, and Barnes. Like Jewish representation, however, the construction of same-sex desiring bodies is complicated by scientific assumptions about eugenics, sexuality, and deviance. I will therefore investigate the various degrees to which these writers "queer" their texts to critique and unmask how the performance of sexuality functions in defiance of the spectacle of the Nazi *Männerbund* (the masculine public sphere) and draw attention to some of the predicaments involved in this portrayal.

For Isherwood, Woolf, and Barnes, portraying homosexual, lesbian, and queer characters becomes a strategy of resistance that confronts the prevailing homophobia and sexual anxieties of the era while also undermining the binary logic upon which the myth of stable identities relies.[1] Expressions of resistance to homophobia, however, presented particular problems in the 1930s. For one thing, similar to the depictions of emancipated women and Jews, in representing homophobia these texts can fall into the trap of using the same oppressive discourse of "deviance" and difference that they aim to undermine. Then again, one wonders if it is even possible to expose the processes of oppression without reproducing the discourse and ideology on which they are based. As Vivian Patraka notes, "If the polarity of fascist ideology underscores the difference of homosexuality from heterosexuality, fixates on it with a violent homophobia," then it is not an "erasure" of difference that could serve as the best antidote (*Spectacular Suffering*, 48). Representing homophobia, as she contends, while in danger of reproducing Nazi propaganda, at least provides an opportunity for the reader "to recognize how prejudice works" (ibid.). But even if these writers could effectively represent the oppression of gay men and women — and unlike literature that was antifascist, feminist, or sympathetic to Jews — exposing homosexuality incurred risks, such as censorship, career sabotage, and, especially for Isherwood, possible arrest.

How, then, do these writers evade the predicament of articulating homosexual desire to resist homophobia in their texts? As I propose, one method is by using camp, drag, parody, cross-dressing, and performative tropes. By featuring characters who challenge the idea of a "natural" gender, these texts expose that identity itself — national, racial, and sexual — is perpetually unstable. Another strategy is by "queering" their texts; manipulating the textual potential of the "unrepresentable." There are important ways in which analyzing these texts and writers as "queer" can be useful in understanding how they interrogate both sexual identity and representation in general. Queer, according to Eve Kosofsky Sedgwick, "happen[s] across lines that divide genders, discourses and 'perversions'" (*Tendencies*, ix). As she defines it, queer "hinges . . . radically and explicitly on a person's undertaking particular, performative acts of experimental self-perception and filiation" (*Tendencies*, 9). In its indefiniteness, the term "queer" points to the contradictory nature of defining sexual desire and the multiple possibilities it entails. Common to the texts of Isherwood, Barnes, and Woolf is the facility to exploit the potential of the visible/invisible nature of sexuality through ambiguity, elisions, and vacillation. Their method of "queering" thus allows them simultaneously to articulate and evade the sexual, textual, and legal regulations that would keep their texts from circulating.

## Historical Context: The Textuality of Sexuality

The big cities at the center of *Goodbye to Berlin*, *Nightwood*, and *Between the Acts* — Berlin, Paris, and London, respectively — were constantly being characterized by moral conservatives as havens for homosexuals and sexual deviants. The gay bars in Weimar Berlin, the flamboyant dandies and Sapphic cross-dressers of *belle époque* Paris,[2] and the London-based gay intellectuals and artists from Oscar Wilde to the Bloomsbury group were often the subject of attacks by nationalists and conservatives alike. In London, as Florence Tamagne notes, homosexuals were commonly arrested, and frequent police raids meant that "homosexual life . . . was primarily restricted to the night" or private establishments (*History of Homosexuality*, 45). More tolerant than London, Paris still "made fine distinctions in the ways in which female and male homosexuals were regarded, distinctions that reveal something of the moral and political priorities of the society. . . . Same-sex love was part of the 'mad gaiety' of *belle époque* life," but "discretion was required" (Benstock, *Women of the Left Bank*, 47). Likewise, in Weimar Berlin, known as a center for gay men and homosexual emancipation, "moral purity" movements reacted against the "moral decay" of the city (Fout, "Sexual Politics," 39). Throughout modern societies in Europe and the United States, fear that homosexuality would somehow ruin the strength of the nation still held sway.[3]

Late nineteenth- and early twentieth-century sexual scientific studies, such as those by Karl Westphal, Richard von Krafft-Ebing, Karl Heinrich Ulrichs, and Havelock Ellis, bolstered views that deviations from sexual norms ("norms" being heterosexual sex within the confines of marriage) were based on either pathological drives or biological/hereditary perversion. Krafft-Ebing and Ellis, both touted by homosexual emancipation movements for promoting an understanding of homosexuality, supported the decriminalization of homosexual activities based on a theory that homosexuals were unfortunate "victims of nature"— women trapped in men's bodies, and men trapped in women's. Yet, their versions of "inversion" bolstered the view that homosexuality was essentially tainted, abnormal, and, like any somatic or mental congenital disease, should be treated through institutionalization. Among the stereotypes that "proved" an individual was homosexual, based on sexology and pseudoscientific observations, were hypersexuality, neurasthenia, fatigue, emotional disorders, insanity, and, most predominantly, effeminacy (Fout, "Sexual Politics," 404). In other words, they were stereotypes of such a vague and inconclusive nature that, like Jewishness, any "disturbance" that negated the middle-class image of respectability and "manliness" could be categorized as homosexual. The homosexual was also perceived to be consumed with sex, and as such, unfit to serve the nation. As Krafft-Ebing insists, "Episodes of moral decay always coincide with the progress of effeminacy, lewdness, and luxuriance of the nations" (3–4). The most acute anxiety, however, was that "the homosexual" blurred the boundary between male and female, a threat to the hierarchical sex divisions of bourgeois society. Otto Weininger, for example, proposed that unmanly men and "mannish" women were a sign of civilization's decay. For Weininger, as Jay Geller notes, "the lack of gender differentiation was a sign of primitivity" (*Freud's Jewish Body*, 8).

Lesbianism, although far from tolerated, was thought to be so rare as to hardly exist at all.[4] Since female intimacy was not considered aberrant, and same-sex relationships were more easily concealed, it was easy to pretend that lesbianism was invisible (Benstock, *Women of the Left Bank*, 50). Still, the medicalization of sexuality, like the Westphal study in 1869, or Havelock Ellis's second volume of *Studies in the Psychology of Sex*, entitled *Sexual Inversion* (1897), forced conceptions of normal and abnormal behavior onto women's sexual relationships. Ellis, in *Sexual Inversion*, described the "female invert" as having "one fairly essential character: a more or less distinct trace of masculinity. . . . [S]he makes advances to the woman to whom she is attracted and treats all men in a cool, direct, manner, which may not exclude comradeship, but which excludes every sexual relationship" (*Psychology of Sex*, 54). The "mannish" lesbian may not have been named as a criminal, but as George Mosse notes, "a woman who dressed like a man could now find herself in an insane asylum" (*Nationalism and Sexuality*, 105). Distinct from the aversion to male homosexuals, stereotypes of the lesbian also conflated with the more general fear of female emancipation. Examining the lesbian culture of Paris in the early twentieth century, Benstock asserts, "The same ignorant fear that attaches to more generalized images of women defines the lesbian as a social misfit, a pariah" (*Women of the Left Bank*, 50). Nevertheless, while laws restricted cross-dressing, and "lesbian practices" were outlawed in all public institutions (schools, hospitals, and prisons), in general there was a "dormant indulgence" toward same-sex desire for women in France (ibid.). Class structure also clearly marked how women's homosexuality was handled: women in the upper classes were often protected by their social status but were "expected to be discreet about their sexual preferences"; middle- or working-class women, who often met in more public locations (such as bars), faced greater risk of exposure and were more vulnerable to legal prosecution (ibid., 47, 48).

Particularly in Weimar Germany, where the most discourse and literature on sex was produced, that same discourse was used for control over the sexuality of its citizens. As Michel Foucault points out, by the end of the nineteenth century "whole series of discourses on the species and subspecies of homosexuality, inversion, pederasty, and 'psychic hermaphrodism' made possible the strong advance of social control into this area of 'perversity.'" On the other hand, "it also made possible the formation of a 'reverse' discourse: homosexuality began to speak in its own behalf, to demand that its legitimacy or 'naturality' be acknowledged, often in the same vocabulary, using the same categories by which it was medically disqualified" (*History of Sexuality*, 1: 101). The influence of sexologist Magnus Hirschfeld's Institute for Sexual Research in Berlin, and his efforts on behalf of the emancipation and decriminalization of homosexual acts, are crucial examples. In 1895, Hirschfeld petitioned the Reichstag to amend the legal code criminalizing homosexuality, known as "Paragraph 175" (enacted in 1875): "A male who indulges in criminally indecent activities with another male or who allows himself to participate in such activities will be punished with jail." Hirschfeld's "third sex" theory, built on an essentialist view of gender, promoted the idea that homosexuals belonged to a distinct gender somewhere between "man" and "woman." A true homosexual, being born that way (and manifesting physiological signs to prove it), is not "at fault" for being who he is and therefore should be treated with compassion rather than be criminalized.[5] Another homosexual emancipation group that was able to establish itself in Berlin due to the increased discourse on sexuality was Adolf Brand and Benedict Friedländer's *Gemeinschaft der Eigenen* (Community of the Special). Founded in 1902, it distinguished itself from Hirschfeld's movement by promoting an idea of "manly" male friendship and love. According to Stefan Micheler, the interest in same-sex desire in Germany was so great that from 1919 to 1933 there were approximately twenty periodicals oriented toward homosexuals. Although subject to censorship and often confiscated, "according to their own sales figures, some of these were mass publications with a circulation of over 100,000 . . . [and] most were published regularly, without interruption" (Micheler, "Homophobic Propaganda," 102).

All this would change, however, as the "will to know" under Nazism "crossed the border into violence" (Herzog, *Sexuality and German Fascism*, 2). Germany's humiliating loss in World War I, a drop in population growth, and a shattered economy triggered public anxieties and shifted government and media focus toward how to build up the German nation. For nationalists and moral purists, the attention given to sexuality afforded additional opportunities to assert that homosexuality and the emancipation of women together were contributing to Germany's declining birthrate and would plunge the country into ruin. Inadvertently, the emancipation movements confirmed stereotypical beliefs that homosexuals "were not really men" (Plant, *Pink Triangle*, 34). Paradoxically, the efforts to elicit more understanding for homosexuals also forced a publicity and vocabulary for discussing sex that resulted in an increased demand for criminalization (Fout, "Sexual Politics," 389). The more talk there was of sex, the more ardent the attempt to control sexuality. The influence of the moral Right finally led to even stricter legal controls over sexuality. In 1935, Paragraph 175 sanctions against "sodomy" were expanded to include masturbation, touching, or even looking at another man with sexual intent. Criminalizing lesbianism was proposed but eventually rejected. Nevertheless, the regime's larger vision for women, as Elizabeth Heineman notes, meant lesbians could be deemed "asocial" or mentally ill, sterilized, and, in worst cases, institutionalized or sent to labor camps ("Sexuality and Nazism," 44).

Increasingly under the Nazi regime, homosexuality was portrayed as an "epidemic" that would spread and destroy the nation. Geoffrey Giles reveals the extent of the paranoia and obsession to which the Nazi leadership succumbed:

> On the eve of World War II, there were fewer than a quarter-million Jews in Germany. In 1934 the police believed there to be at least two million homosexual men in the country. By 1939

the army's chief psychiatrist was suggesting as many as three million, or four percent of the population. At the end of 1942 the figure of four million was being discussed. ("Why Bother," 2)

Convictions for homosexual acts rose as well. John Fout's study reveals that before World War I relatively few convictions were ever made under Paragraph 175—the highest was in 1905, when 605 convictions were made, 316 of which were for bestiality, 289 for sodomy (compared with a German population of more than 65 million). Generally, acts of "indecency" were difficult to prove. After the Nazi regime came to power, especially under Heinrich Himmler, prosecution increased considerably: from 1,091 cases brought to trial with 948 convictions in 1934 to 9,479 cases brought to trial with 8,562 convictions in 1938 (Fout, "Sexual Politics," 395). All in all, Himmler was personally responsible for 90,000 arrests for sodomy between 1937 and 1939. By 1940, men arrested for homosexual activities were automatically transferred to concentration camps and sentenced to hard labor as "pink triangle" prisoners or "175-ers"; by 1941, anyone who was deemed to "threaten the health of folk" was put to death (Plant, *Pink Triangle*, 116–17).[6] Approximately 2,100 castrations of both actual and "supposed" homosexuals were carried out by mid-1941. The survival rate for those men who were sent to concentration camps under Paragraph 175 was extremely low due to both the harsh conditions and brutal treatment by other prisoners (Giles, "Why Bother," 10).[7]

Nazism, nevertheless, did not "repress sex." Contrary to popular beliefs that Nazism negated sexuality altogether, it is clear, as Dagmar Herzog argues, that it could never have garnered as much public support as it did by suppressing sexual desire. "The distinctive innovation of Nazi sexual politics was the attempt to harness popular liberalizing impulses and growing preoccupation with sex to a racist, elitist, and homophobic agenda" (Herzog, *Sexuality and German Fascism*, 4). Sexual activity was not problematic — it just had to be the "right kind of sex." The persistent image of Nazism itself as "sexually deviant" is nevertheless enduring. Constructed as either a "sadomasochistic encounter between male fascist and subservient female," or as "repressed homosexuality," the image of the Nazi is one that consistently conflates sadistic cruelty with sexual repression or aberrant sexual desire (Frost, *Sex Drives*, 121).[8] In what

Andrew Hewitt calls the "homosexualization of fascism," the scenario of fascist power and the homophobia of the Nazi regime is readily imagined by critics and historians both of the time and now as being perpetrated *by* homosexuals rather than victimizing them (*Political Inversions*, 3). Prominent theorists such as Wilhelm Reich, Theodor Adorno, and Maria Antonietta Macchiochi, among others, conflate fascism, or the "homoerotic" aspects of Nazism, with an idea of sadomasochistic homosexual desire.[9] In Reich's widely popular *The Mass Psychology of Fascism* (1933), for example, Reich maintains that German fascism is most easily accepted by the middle-class masses because they are the most sexually repressed, which "leads to the development of pathological, emotionally tinged notions of honor and duty, bravery and self control" (54–55). In his opinion, by inculcating an antisexual atmosphere, Nazism distorted "natural sexual strivings toward the other sex" and replaced them with "homosexual and sadistic feelings" (192). Adorno and Horkheimer, like Reich, describe the masses as "feminized" by being influenced by masochistic tendencies. Exposing both his misogyny and homophobia, Adorno, in *Minima Moralia*, claims "the tough guys are the truly effeminate ones who need the weaklings as their victims in order to admit that they are like them. Totalitarianism and homosexuality belong together. In its downfall the subject negates everything which is not of its own kind" (46). The "(il)logic" of these arguments, as Hewitt surmises, is roughly summed up by the idea that heterosexual sadism is a manifestation of latent homosexual masochism; repressed homosexuals express self-loathing as homophobia; thus the Nazis are homosexuals, "and their persecutions of homosexuals 'proves it'" (*Political Inversions*, 12). In this tautological reasoning, "the homosexual" becomes the unfortunate victim of scapegoating for fascist and antifascist discourses alike.[10]

It would seem unnecessary to point out that the myth of Nazi sadism as closeted homosexuality is not only untrue but also harmful and cruel. As Sedgwick has noted, "The fantasy of Nazi homosexuality is flatly false; according to any definitions of homosexuality current in our culture, only one Nazi leader, Ernst Roehm, was homosexual, and he was murdered by the SS on Hitler's direct orders in 1934" (*Tendencies*, 49).[11] Nevertheless, the homosexualization of Nazism reveals how persistently the discourse of sexuality remains geared toward a normalization and moralization of heterosexuality and concomitant homophobia.

"Conceptions of homosexuality are so diffuse," Klaus Theweleit insists, "so much a product of defensive processes — even among analysts themselves — that we are forced to assume that the concept provides anything but a real understanding of what homosexuality is. It sets in motion a series of prejudices, false ideas, and personal-defense mechanisms to reach the strained-but-safe conclusion that homosexuals are first and foremost the *others*" (*Male Fantasies*, 54–55). It is exactly the diffuseness of the term "homosexual" that allows it to be conflated with the equally diffuse concept of fascism, according to Hewitt. "The allegorical press-ganging of homosexuality as a vehicle for articulating a historically reticent fascism relies on the fact that neither homosexuality nor fascism speaks in its own name" (*Political Inversions*, 9). In other words, the trope of homosexuality can stand in for all that is feared and unknowable. The homosexual thus becomes the figure for that unknowable *other* in oneself.

Resisting homophobic Nazism without participating in the "will to know" that defined, labeled, and oppressed the person known as "the invert" was no small task for Isherwood, Barnes, and Woolf. For the most part, their texts either elide or obscure (through bizarre or covert references) overt sexual encounters, and they especially avoid identifying themselves or their novels as "homosexual" bodies of work. Their "queer" characters, therefore, become ambiguous sites of unrepresentability — hinting at the infinite possibilities within those entities that refuse naming. Of course, there were also practical reasons for their cryptic treatment of same-sex desire — censorship. The trials of Oscar Wilde from April 3 to May 25, 1895, were still a warning of the risks of exposure — as was the more recent obscenity trial of Radclyffe Hall's *The Well of Loneliness* (1928). Wilde's books were not banned as a consequence of his trials, yet as Lesley Higgins and Marie-Christine Leps contend, the trials introduced a distinct relationship between text and identity that was consistently drawn by the court. The "act of writing" *The Picture of Dorian Gray*, for instance, "was considered first as proof of 'posing as a sodomite,' then as proof of 'gross indecency.'" As Higgins and Leps pointedly ask, "What does it mean when a judge allows the opinions, emotions . . . of fictional characters to be introduced in court as evidence of the writer's criminal immorality?" ("Governmentality Getting Wilde," 105).[12]

One could ask the same of the evidence used in the 1928 obscenity trial of Radclyffe Hall's *The Well of Loneliness*. Hall was a modestly successful novelist who self-identified as an "invert." She completed *The Well of Loneliness*, her first novel to deal with lesbian themes, in 1928. The bildungsroman of born invert Stephen Gordon, with its sexological introduction by Havelock Ellis, soon became the subject of a trial that drew writers like Woolf, Vita Sackville-West, and E. M. Forster to rally behind her to support her freedom of expression. Although lesbianism was not illegal in England at the time, and the novel eschews explicit depictions of sexual encounters, the text's pronounced and earnest plea for tolerance and acceptance of lesbianism resulted in the book being banned in England until 1949. It was the potential effect of the book to corrupt, not the intention of the author, that was judged as obscene. Hall's polemical stance, endorsing Havelock Ellis's theory of the "invert" in *Studies in the Psychology of Sex* (which was also banned), was denounced as a risk to those who might be tempted to stray from path of heterosexuality and be corrupted.[13] By linking sexuality and textuality, the law on what could be printed thus extended to assumptions about identity — *who* could be represented was as important as what could be circulated (Gilmore, "Obscenity, Modernity, Identity," 605).

The degree to which these novelists self-censored would be difficult to ascertain. Certainly, *Goodbye to Berlin* and *Between the Acts* could be interpreted as "performing" resistance by "the speech act of silence," which, in Sedgwick's terms, is "not a particular silence, but a silence that accrues particularity by fits and starts, in relation to the discourse that surrounds and differentially constitutes it" (*Epistemology*, 3). Noisy *Nightwood* could in no way be called "silent," but, as I discuss later, it masks its politics (sexual and social) behind poetically allusive language, drag, parody, and fragmentation. The texts thus become queer in that they all similarly expose the tension between the hidden and exposed, representation and reality, and self and other. If Nazism based itself on the myth of a unified and harmonious national identity, then works that expose identity as an illusion undermine the belief in myth itself (Hewitt, *Political Inversions*, 17–18). In other words, once that myth of identity is called into question, other binaries on which Nazi ideology relies begin to unravel. The queer characters Isherwood, Woolf, and Barnes depict, and their expressions of love and desire, offer an ambiguous and elusive alternative to both sexological discourses and the artificial, idyllic romance plot of the Nazi spectacle. The question is, does their strategy of ambiguous representation of that "love that dare not speak its name" (to use Wilde's defense in his 1895 trial),[14] resist or collude with banishing homosexuality (and homosexuals) from the public sphere altogether or risk being so obscure that it evades meaning completely?

## Of Doctors and Deviants: *Goodbye to Berlin*

The history of the interwar period and people's attitudes toward sexuality is coded in each of the six sections of Isherwood's text as antisemitism, sexual anxieties, and homophobia become paramount in the novel. The lens of the narrator's "camera," however, only reveals fragments of the stories that make up Berlin life, refusing the imposition of a single point of view or perspective. Gaps and lacunae in the text point to the impossibility of any narration that attempts to encompass a clear, whole picture of the political crisis present in Weimar Berlin society. Like *Between the Acts* and *Nightwood, Goodbye to Berlin* is a novel that exposes, rather than tells, the social and political conditions that could lead a nation to succumb to Hitler and the power of the Nazi Party.

The modes of narrative resistance in *Goodbye to Berlin* are obviously not solely influenced by the political atmosphere but are also informed through Isherwood's experiences as a homosexualized, and thus politicized, body in Nazi Germany.[15] As Erin Carlston aptly points out, "the 'private' realm of sexuality is inherently political" (*Thinking Fascism,* 180). Looking back at this time forty years later, Isherwood explains how homosexuality embodied his rebellion to the imposing power structure of "the State and the Law and the Press and the Medical profession":

> Girls are what the State and the Law and the Press and the Medical profession endorse, and command me to desire. My mother endorses them, too. She is silently, brutishly willing me to get married and breed grandchildren for her. Her will is the will of Nearly Everybody, and in their will is my death. *My* will is to live according to my nature, and to find a place where I can be what I am. . . . But I'll admit this — even if my nature were like theirs, I should still have to fight them, in one way or another. If boys didn't exist, I should have to invent them. (*CHK,* 17)

From this quotation, it is evident that for Isherwood, as for Woolf and Barnes, not only sexuality but also writing about sexuality—"inventing" boys—becomes a mode of resistance to patriarchy, nationalism, and subjugation early on in his career.[16] By disrupting the artifice of the Nazi spectacle and presenting what is left out of representations of the "State and the Law," Isherwood challenges Nazi suppression of both sexual and artistic freedom. Nevertheless, in *Goodbye to Berlin*, exposing a "will to live according to nature" becomes an act of resistance that is more serious in its implications.

Homophobia and censure (both personal and textual) were obviously difficult and very real fears for Isherwood. Considering the history of the Wilde trials, Hall's recent obscenity trial in England, and the fact that John Lehmann at the Woolfs' Hogarth Press refused to print the Sally Bowles story unless the abortion scene was cut, it is small wonder that Isherwood depicts the narrator's sexual orientation ambiguously and avoids emphasizing the Berlin gay "scene" that was central to his own experience of the city.[17] E. M. Forster, with whom Isherwood was in correspondence, chose not to publish his overtly homosexual novel *Maurice* for this same reason, circulating it privately among friends instead (including Isherwood, who was invited to read it in the spring of 1935).[18] In a letter to Isherwood, Forster names "the millions of beasts and idiots who still prowl the darkness" as one of the main reasons for withholding publication (*Letters*, 2: 119). Isherwood similarly felt compelled to destroy the detailed diary he kept in Berlin, from which *Mr. Norris Changes Trains* (1935) and *Goodbye to Berlin* stemmed. Despite his regret that "the Berlin novels leave out a great deal which I now want to remember," the cost of exposure was clearly too high. The diary, he admitted, "was full of details about [my] sex life and [I] feared that it might somehow fall into the hands of the police or other enemies" (*CHK*, 41). Only one year before *Goodbye to Berlin* was published, Isherwood's lover, Heinz Neddermeyer, was denied entry into England due to his "suspicious" relationship with Isherwood; he was sent back to Germany, charged, tried and found guilty of "homosexual acts," and sent to do hard labor before being drafted into the army. As Isherwood recalls, Neddermeyer received a "light" sentence and was saved from a concentration camp by chance, the court being "relatively unhysterical, un-Nazi" (*CHK*, 286).[19]

Eliding overt references to homosexuality in the novel was not solely due to legal constraints, however — it was a key narrative device in Isherwood's fictional experimentation. To reiterate the point made in the first chapter: a novel is not a life. A "snapshot" of Berlin will always leave out what is beyond the borders of the photograph. Only through *Goodbye to Berlin*'s novelization can the tensions and interplay between private and public, sexual and political, and reality and representation be exposed. Nowhere is this more evident than in the section "On Reugen Island." While there are a number of "hints" at homosexuality in various parts of the novel (including the fact that the names of all the bars Christopher visits are titles from Oscar Wilde plays, such as *Lady Windermere's Fan* and *Salomé*), "On Reugen Island" is the section that most clearly foregrounds and challenges the "homosexual panic" of interwar Europe. The importance of including the segment in the novel, despite protests by his publisher, is noted by Isherwood's biographers. Based on his own experience with his young lover Walter (*CHK*, 41–46), the episode reveals what Lisa Schwerdt astutely observes is "the most obscure yet the most unclouded look at Isherwood's sexual nature" and the danger involved in exposing it (*Isherwood's Fiction*, 85).

While Schwerdt, along with other critics, considers this section "the weakest in the novel" (*Isherwood's Fiction*, 85), I would disagree. For one thing, being the only segment that offers a detailed outsider's perspective of a particularly emotionally fraught and tense same-sex relationship, it is particularly intriguing from a perspective of queer identity and "the closet." It is also the only section in which the central relationship does *not* revolve around Christopher and another character (Frl. Shroeder, Sally, Natalia, or the Nowaks). Instead, the historically based Isherwood is represented by "Peter," a high-strung, nervous, and unmistakably queer Englishman, while Christopher stands by observing as Peter's relationship with his German lover, Otto, unfolds. Thus, by placing Christopher in the closet, so to speak, Isherwood produces additional opacity but also creates a new space for border-crossing that blurs the line between self/other and insider/outsider within the relationship of Peter and Otto. As Judith Butler insists, "The closet produces the promise of a disclosure that can, by definition, never come" ("Imitation," 309). The narrator, by being both inside and outside the "outed" relationship, becomes a queer "third" who exceeds the limits of either observer or participant, producing both disclosure and deferral of that disclosure simultaneously.

Even more interestingly, however, is the fact that "On Reugen Island" is the only section of the novel, other than the last, that is written in a diary-like present tense. This temporal disruption in the middle of the book lends a jarring immediacy to the observations that are revealed therein. The section begins, "I wake early and go out to sit on the veranda in my pyjamas" (*GTB*, 99), and then goes on to describe "the two people staying in this house, besides myself"; one being "an Englishman, named Peter Wilkinson, about my own age," and the other "a German working class boy from Berlin, named Otto Nowak" (*GTB*, 100). The only disruptions to the present-tense narration are made to relate extensive details of Peter's history that somewhat explain his "condition" as a "delicate" boy whose mother "coddled him into a funk" (*GTB*, 102), and to situate temporally recent observations on the island, such as "Yesterday was chilly" (*GTB*, 107) or "This morning we were all together in my room" (*GTB*, 111). The immediacy of the narration, and the contrast of the atmosphere of the island with Berlin — especially seeing as the chapter is thrust between the Berlin stories of Sally Bowles and the Nowaks — initiates the reader into a queer time, suspended somewhere between past and present. It is simultaneously an ahistorical *and* a modern moment. Stephen Barber and David Clark, in their introduction to *Regarding Sedgwick: Essays on Queer Culture and Critical Theory*, define a "queer moment" as "ongoing," a time that is "at once indefinite and virtual but also forceful, resilient and undeniable." Queer moments, in their conception, are always ambivalent since they are identified by the "temporal disorientation" and the "twists" they give to other temporalities (Barber and Clark, 2, 5, 4).[20] Similarly, the events that occur on Reugen Island force the reader into an encounter with both a past and a present look at concepts of nationalism, belonging, the politics of sex, and their intersections.

The manner in which the section renounces both Nazi homophobia and the "homosexualization of fascism" also has much to do with how Isherwood juxtaposes the romantic German pastoral landscape with violence and subjugation. Nostalgia for an idyllic past promoted by Nazi propaganda is consistently contrasted with the Other bodies it suppresses. In this way, Isherwood anticipates the element of Nazi aesthetics that Saul Friedländer identifies as "kitsch death." Kitsch stands for that which mass culture considers beautiful, harmonious, and nostalgic — landscapes that resemble postcards, families by the fireside, virile young men and women climbing mountains. What Friedländer names as a specifically Nazi aesthetic, however, is "kitsch death": a juxtaposition of "kitsch aesthetic and of the themes of death," which he maintains is "the bedrock of Nazi aesthetics" (*Reflections on Nazism*, 26–27). Notably, Stuart Christie calls "On Reugen Island" a "queer pastoral" that "marks the entry of violent social, sexual, and political histories onto the pastoral scene of Isherwood's desires and explodes the pastoral mode . . . in his fiction" (Christie, "A Further Reservation," 816).[21] While I would not venture to presume or speculate on "Isherwood's desires," the link between the pastoral and Nazi kitsch on Reugen Island is clear from the beginning of the episode:

> The wood casts long shadows over the field. Birds call with sudden uncanny violence, like alarm-clocks going off. The birch-trees hang down laden over the rutted, sandy earth of the country road. A soft bar of cloud is moving up from the line of trees along the lake. A man with a bicycle is watching his horse graze on a patch of grass by the path. . . . A woman in a shawl comes walking with a little boy. The boy wears a dark sailor suit; he is very pale and his neck is bandaged. They soon turn back. A man passes on a bicycle . . . [h]is voice rings out, quite clear yet unintelligible, in the morning stillness. A cock crows. (*GTB*, 99)

The narrator's initial depiction of the island places it squarely within the nostalgic, nature-worshiping mode of Nazi propaganda that valorized the idyllic German countryside for being harmonious, quiet, and pure, its farmers and traditional way of life untainted by urbanization. Undermining that pastoral scene, however, is the hint of violence: the "long shadows" of the wood appear ominous, as does the "uncanny violence" of the bird call, and the bandaged neck of the boy. The crowing cock ominously alludes to the betrayal of the German people, who sacrifice individuals like Christopher, Peter, and Otto for their illusion of unity. The price of nostalgia for a romantic national past is high — it supports that "unintelligible" voice that leads the public to oppress Others.

The portrayal of the separate beaches on the island, and forts decorated in swastikas and flags in Nazi colors, is an additional reminder of the frightening ideology of exclusion that accompanies an illusion of national unity. The text juxtaposes the rabbits, adders, and deer in the woods that surround the village with the warriorlike summer vacationers on the beach, their forts and chairs resembling "a medieval camp" (*GTB*, 110). Like ancient armies, they stake their claim to their territory with clear indications of nationalist identifications:

> Each chair flies a little flag. There are German city-flags — Hamburg, Hanover, Dresden, Rostock and Berlin, as well as National, Republican and Nazi colours. Each chair is encircled by a low sand bulwark upon which the occupants have set inscriptions in fir-cones: *Waldesruh. Familie Walter. Stahlhelm. Heil Hitler!* (*GTB*, 110)

The detail of the description makes it clear that the narrator wishes to remember every facet of the scene in the Weimar Republic in which, to quote Christie, "race, family, regional and political markers read as a list of different imaginings of the German nation" ("A Further Reservation," 818). In the present tense, these anecdotes and events in Christopher's life are etched into the ever-present moment of the photograph — a crime scene before the crime occurs.

To an even greater degree, the Nazi kitsch-death aesthetic is witnessed in the depictions of the neighboring village, Baabe: "[Baabe's] single sandy street of low-roofed houses among the pine-trees has a romantic, colonial air; it is like a ramshackle, lost settlement somewhere in the backwoods, where people come to look for a nonexistent goldmine and remain, stranded, for the rest of their lives" (*GTB*, 95). It is specifically in this nostalgic "lost" and timeless place where most "of Baabe boys are Nazis" (*GTB*, 95). The narrator relates how two Nazi boys tell him and Peter about their "field exercises and military games," to which Peter indignantly remarks, "You're preparing for war." The boy answers, "That's quite wrong. The Führer does not want war. Our programme stands for peace, with honour. All the same . . . war can be fine, you know! Think of the ancient Greeks!" (*GTB*, 121).

The boy's fantasy of the romantic past makes the destruction and devastation in the present seem removed, honorable, and "fine." An effortless belief in the enthrallment with war and destruction, however, is exactly what the narrator tries to undermine throughout the story. Similar to Friedländer's observations, Isherwood appears to recognize that the "ancient legends and bucolic countryside" are the hallmarks of Nazi kitsch; and, as Friedländer notes, in the context of Nazism, if "kitsch was there, Death could not be far off" (*Reflections on Nazism*, 29). Ever critical of the vainglorious nationalistic fervor toward war, the narrator sardonically informs the boy, "The ancient Greeks . . . didn't use poison gas" (*GTB*, 121)—to which one of the Nazi boys answers loftily, "That's a purely technical question" (*GTB*, 122). The honor of ancient Greek war, as the narrator points out, is based in a myth that precludes the agony of individual victims. Isherwood thus undercuts the impulse of kitsch nostalgia, of the ahistorical pastoral, by consistently drawing attention to the price of that illusion: the dangerous process by which Nazism romanticizes a utopian vision while ignoring the "technicalities" of destruction in the present.

Isherwood queers and contradicts the illusion of a harmonious Nazi *Volksgemeinschaft* (people's community) by foregrounding the "non-disciplined" male bodies that are obliterated from the ideal picture of the Nazi *Männerbund*. The self-reflexive stance of the narrator and his nonjudgmental depiction of Peter and Otto's relationship register a silent counter-discourse to the unifying kitsch sentimentality of the Third Reich. What is *not* said about sexual desire—Peter and Otto's or the narrator's—has even more potential to upset the division between homo/heterosexual identities than what *is* said. The vexed relationship of Peter and Otto provides a markedly unromantic look at desire, bodies, sex, and class conflict, but it clearly contradicts the homo/heterosexual binary of perversion/health that circulated in the medicalized discourse of the time. Otto, for one thing, defies categorization since he is depicted as neither homosexual nor heterosexual, yet notably he is described as the most "natural" of the characters. The almost mythical blond Aryan alpha male appears to walk straight out of a Wagner opera: "Otto is his whole body . . . his gestures have the savage, unconscious grace of a cruel, elegant animal" (*GTB*, 101). Peter, while in some ways typecast as the nervous, mentally unstable, unhealthy, "inverted" male, is nevertheless portrayed as choosing homosexuality rather than being a victim of the perversion-heredity-degeneracy model. That he blames his "weakness" on his mother, who "coddled him into a funk" (*GTB*, 102), is a different matter altogether. Moreover, the painful relationship of

Peter and Otto, as each strives to humiliate and control the other, rather than specifically characterizing the sexual nature of their relationship, reflects more general societal tensions among money, power, physical desire, class, and intellect.

Another strategy that Isherwood uses to confront the romantic, kitsch sentimentality of Nazism is through camp. Both Dennis Denisoff and Linda Mizejewski examine aspects of camp in Isherwood's work, mostly in relation to Sally Bowles and her campy performance of gender. I maintain that the caricature-like behavior of the little Nazi doctor "On Reugen Island" also falls into the category of camp. As mentioned previously, while the Nazi myth relies on adherence to the myth of identities, camp exposes illusion and artifice. Through "gestures of inclusion," camp performances also "unite and empower people who have frequently been isolated and disempowered," as Denisoff explains (*Aestheticism and Sexual Parody*, 124). In this case, we as readers do not identify with the camp performer, the Nazi doctor in *Goodbye to Berlin*, but we do identify with the creator of the textual performance of parody — the narrator.

Because the narrator, Peter, and Otto situate themselves on a part of the beach that is outside the "public" summer spectacle, they are targeted by the Nazi doctor's missionary zeal to observe, discipline, and cure them. In an almost comic fashion, the physician incessantly attempts to "teach" them how to be normal and belong, asserting his "knowledge" of human nature. He tries to persuade them to "come round to the other beach," where there are "nice girls" and "Nordic types" (*GTB*, 110), to which Peter sardonically retorts, "I'm afraid I should be out of place. I had a grandmother who was partly Spanish" (*GTB*, 111). The doctor's expertise as a medical professional is consistently mocked. He "knows" (1) about girls, "as a doctor I know how to appreciate them" (*GTB*, 110); (2) about sports, "You hold yourself stiff. . . . That is an error" (*GTB*, 109); (3) about politics, "my work at the clinic has convinced me that communism is a mere hallucination. I can tell you this as a doctor" (*GTB*, 111); and, evidently, (4) about "degenerate boys," as he informs Christopher, "my work at the clinic has taught me that it is no use trying to help this type of boy" (*GTB*, 114).

Quite obviously, the Nazi doctor's irrationality is a comment on the irrational psychosexual discourse and eugenic policies of Nazism as a whole. Instead of the romantic figure of the handsome, intelligent man of science, the doctor, like the rest of the pastoral setting, is a sham. Using the pseudoscientific discourse typical of the time, the doctor observes Otto and makes these remarks to Christopher:

> "He has a criminal head!"
>
> "And you think that people with criminal heads should be left to become criminals?"
>
> "Certainly not. I believe in discipline. These boys ought to be put into labour camps."
>
> "And what are you going to do with them when you've got them there? You say that they can't be altered, anyhow, so I suppose you'd keep them locked up for the rest of their lives?"
>
> The doctor laughed delightedly. . . . "You are an idealist! Do not imagine that I don't understand your point of view. But it is unscientific, quite unscientific. You and your friend do not understand such boys as Otto. I understand them. Every week, one or two such boys come to my clinic, and I must operate on them for adenoids, or mastoid, or poisoned tonsils. So you see, I know them through and through!" (*GTB*, 114–15)

The number of times the doctor claims to "know" and "understand" highlights the absurdity of his claims, thus destabilizing the credibility of all Nazi discourse and knowledge about "health" and sexuality. "Why," as Denisoff asks, does "Isherwood cho[o]se something so seemingly flip as camp as his way of publicly reacting to [Nazi homophobia]?" (*Aestheticism and Sexual Parody*, 134). One reason could be the opportunity for the counter-discourse that is always present in camp performance. The parodic humor is a form of revolt against suffering; it recasts and empowers the victims of the minority culture as subjects rather than objects of a discourse. That is, until one realizes that the reality of Nazi pseudoscientific discourse is even more overblown than the campy performance of the doctor. As the novel unfolds, one wonders how many of the boys whom the doctor has treated will live to adulthood after being "disciplined." Even more troubling, however, is the question of how a modern and purportedly advanced society such as that in Germany could adopt the irrational logic that the doctor proposes.

This same point is emphasized in the drag performance depicted in the final section of the novel, when Christopher and his friend Fritz are at the Salomé club. Similar to "On Reugen Island," the last section of the novel is framed in the present tense of a diary entry—the narrator witnesses the hostile political atmosphere that sees difference only to eradicate it. In this revealing exchange with an American foreigner, Christopher, more than in any other place in the novel, exposes his sexual identity. The incident in the Salomé happens in the immediacy of "last night," a time that could be any night in "Winter 1932–33":

> "Say," he asked Fritz, "what's going on here?"
>
> "Men dressed as women," Fritz grinned.
>
> The little American simply couldn't believe it. "Men dressed as *women*? As *women* hey? Do you mean they're queer?"
>
> "Eventually we're all queer," drawled Fritz solemnly, in lugubrious tones. The young man looked us over slowly. . . .
>
> "You *queer*, too, hey?" demanded the little American, turning suddenly on me.
>
> "Yes," I said, "very queer indeed." (*GTB*, 238)

Despite Christopher's cheeky retort to the American's disbelief that there could be *anything* but a solid division between sexes, the drag show at the end of the novel lacks its "transgressively self-conscious" playfulness when contrasted with fascist delusion and violence (Shuttleworth, "Populous City," 159). Like the doctor's campy performance, and Sally Bowles's artifice in the previous chapter, camp fails, as Mizejewski aptly observes, because "exaggeration has been out-parodied by the far-from amusing Nazis" ("Camp Among the Swastikas," 244).

Christopher describes the Salomé as being "expensive and even more depressing than I had imagined" (*GTB*, 237). The audience members are voyeurs, "respectable middle-aged tradesmen and their families, exclaiming in good-humoured amazement: 'Do they really?'" (*GTB*, 238). Oddly enough, the scene at the Salomé uncannily echoes a similar scene in Wyndham Lewis's *Hitler* (1931), when Lewis describes the "Eldorado of the Motzestrasse" in the "Perverts' Paradise" of western Berlin (21–22). Unlike the "good-humoured" tradesmen and their families, however, the narrator in *Hitler* looks down on the cabaret of cross-dressers with scornful disdain. Lesley Higgins grimly observes that through Lewis's homophobic gaze, the narrator "enjoys vicariously the violent way in which a 'young german [sic] politician' would want to destroy the Eldorado and all its patrons by rolling this 'luxury spot up like a verminous carpet'" (Higgins, *Cult of Ugliness*, 87, quoting Lewis, *Hitler*, 28). In *Goodbye to Berlin*, the narrator cannot help but draw attention to this very real potential. The belligerent American young man at the Salomé wonders whether "he ought not to hit [the narrator] in the face" but instead runs off yelling "some kind of wild college battle-cry" (*GTB*, 238). Isherwood thus inverts the "perversion" model to pinpoint what is truly perverse in a violent, hypermasculine, and homophobic society.

## *Nightwood*: "All queer in a terrible way"

To an even greater degree than *Goodbye to Berlin*, *Nightwood* "subverts" rather than "inverts" the binary relationship between male/female and homo/heterosexual by excluding completely the symbolic "other side of the beach." Barnes destabilizes the terms by which desire is constructed — not by shifting the viewpoint toward recognizing one side as more "perverse" than the other but by repositing the idea of "perversion" altogether. "Perversion," when it is self-consciously recognized as a legitimate part of human fantasy, can be desirable, even preferred. Thus *Nightwood* delves into the nature of desire, exposing the allure of the obscene, and divulging the secret attraction for that which is transgressive. Of course, as I have argued in the previous chapters, in so doing Barnes problematically reiterates Nazi ideology and aesthetics — in this case, the sadomasochist fantasy that numerous theorists have identified as a Nazi theme. The distinction Barnes insists upon, however, is between erotic *fantasy* and Nazi violence. Laura Frost locates a link between the crisis of modernism and the erotics of sadomasochism, specifically, "the oppositional compulsions of restraint and release, the building of tension, the creation of scenarios in which pain and pleasure are pushed to their extreme." According to Frost, "perversion" in literature has sociopolitical significance "that extends far beyond sexuality itself" and is often exploited by "writers who seek to unsettle dominant paradigms of politics and sexuality" (*Sex Drives*, 13). Interpreting *Nightwood* in this light, the various examples of sexual boundary-breaking, such as

O'Connor's cross-dressing, Nikka's tattoos, or Nora's and Robin's obsession with control and submission, become destabilizing forces that push the limits of physical, philosophical, psychic, national, and narrative boundaries to the extreme. And yet, as I would argue, not all fantasies are the same. Barnes's experimental ambiguity underscores the difference between self-conscious performances of the "perverse"—situations in which individuals participate democratically and willingly—and the fascist domination-submission scenario that ends in death: kitsch death.

A number of feminist critics have examined the ways in which *Nightwood* disrupts gender binaries and challenges the essentialisms upon which scientific discourses regarding gender, sexuality, and identity were based.[22] As I have argued previously, especially in her portrayal of Jewish essentialism, Barnes's work cannot be clearly situated on either side of the nature-culture divide. It is her skepticism, her vacillation between the two poles, that appears more accurately to define her work. Likewise, I am doubtful that Barnes's text either clearly celebrates and valorizes lesbianism and homosexuality or, conversely, contributes to a homophobic typecasting. Her depiction of queer sexuality, as I interpret it, is instead meant to probe and challenge ideas of human nature, identity, action, fantasy, and the forms of categorization and definition into which these fall.

Referring to her relationship with Thelma Wood, on whom Robin in *Nightwood* is based, Barnes is often quoted as saying, "I'm not a lesbian. I just loved Thelma" (Broe, *Silence and Power*, 16). Of course, there is little doubt that Barnes belonged to the lesbian circles in Paris and had affairs with women, but it is the proliferation of possibilities in the "I just [*insert verb of choice*]" rather than "I am" that Barnes highlights in her work. As Judith Butler insists, "The 'I' exceeds determination, and even produces that very excess. . . . In the act which would disclose the true and full content of that 'I,' a certain radical concealment is thereby produced" ("Imitation," 309). On the other hand, "the *pleasure* produced by the instability of those categories [is what] sustains the various erotic practices" (ibid., 308). Barnes practices a pleasurable, perverse, even obscene "gender trouble" by resisting classification—to the sexual-scientific and homophobic discourse, and to all types of identity politics. *Nightwood* thereby reveals a queer politics of nonrepresentation. Needless to say, the lack of clarity of *Nightwood* and Barnes's refusal for her or her work to be categorized or politicized as specifically lesbian had practical consequences. Despite overt homosexual nuances, and being replete with profanity, fetishism, and "perversion" (mostly uttered by O'Connor), the novel, strangely enough, managed to evade censors. As Dianne Chisholm notes, what modernist works banned for obscenity in the same period had in common (among them James Joyce's *Ulysses*, D. H. Lawrence's *Lady Chatterley's Lover*, and Henry Miller's *Tropic of Cancer*) was that they were all "made visible through the legal spectacularization of 'obscene' sexuality'" ("Obscene Modernism," 168). Leigh Gilmore, in her comparison of the public response to Hall's *The Well of Loneliness* and *Nightwood*, attributes Barnes's "non-case" of obscenity to the way *Nightwood*'s poetic style obscured its perversity. Hall's novel, along with its introduction by Ellis, affirmed how closely the novel's main character conformed to homosexual typology, placing it squarely within the discourse of identity rather than aesthetics. In other words, Hall's novel visibly linked textuality with sexuality; if lesbian sexuality could not be contained under law, at least lesbian textuality could. Barnes's "deviance," on the other hand, "was strictly a matter of literary style" (Gilmore, "Obscenity, Modernity, Identity," 623).[23]

That *Nightwood* was perceived to be "poetic" rather than "polemic," to use Gilmore's terms, was in no small part due to the role T. S. Eliot played in helping provide "expert witness" as to its literary merit in the introduction to *Nightwood* and to his prudent editorial "suggestions" (backed by Emily Coleman).[24] Eliot, for example, specifically edited out every word that had to do with homosexuality and "used the preface for the first American editions to set the work as a philosophical examination of universal human nature, leading away from its homosexual theme" (Plumb, NWOV, xxiv). Textual notes to the manuscript, published in *Nightwood: The Original Version and Related Drafts*, indicate that Eliot changed words and lines like the doctor's — "'You see before you, madame,' he said 'one who, in common parlance is called a "faggot," a "fairy" a "queen." I was created in anxiety'" — to "'You see before you, madame,' he said, 'one who was created in anxiety'" (NW, 74; NWOV, 64–65). Eliot also cut out the line, "You can lay a hundred bricks and not be called a bricklayer; but lay one boy and you are a bugger!" (NWOV, 132). Most notably, Eliot's blue pencil excised a section at the end of the first chapter in which O'Connor relates to Frau Mann his own obscenity trial after having been caught by police in an alley with a man's hand on "Tiny" (NWOV, 26–28).[25] In sum, it would appear that what "Eliot does and does not say helped to seal the fate of *Nightwood* for many years," as Gerstenberger points out ("Radical Narrative," 129).[26]

This does mean, however, that *Nightwood* is not an "obscene" novel in the artistic sense. Nor does it mean that it is not a novel that pointedly resists the discourse of homophobia. As Chisholm suggests, what *Nightwood* proved was that "'obscene art' does not derive from its illegality alone."[27] *Nightwood* deploys the kind of obscenity or erotics of transgression that, to quote Chisholm, "shocks and disperses the reactive forces of the sexual status quo while mobilizing radical, historical and political insight." It self-consciously draws attention to the potential of the dichotomies within the perverse to explode the limits of possibilities and nuances of sexual desire. Unlike Isherwood, Barnes does not hide lesbianism or male homosexuality in cryptic evasions; rather, she confounds the entire "ontological and epistemological claims" on which sexual discourse is based (Chisholm, "Obscene Modernism," 167, 170, 172).

In Barnes's investigation of the nature of representation, sexuality, and identity, O'Connor's cross-dressing and campy performance of "the invert" features most prominently. As Sarah Henstra points out, frequently O'Connor adopts a female subject position when speaking of himself, thus dramatizing a "transgressive mimicry of 'womanhood' on a textual stage" ("Looking the Part," 130–31). For example, he refers to himself as "the girl God forgot" (NW, 73), the "bearded lady" (NW, 100), or even "the Old Woman who lives in the closet" (NW, 138). But it is Nora's visit to his bedroom that introduces a more comprehensive exegesis of perversion. The narrator describes Nora's reaction when she finds O'Connor lying in bed in "costume" in "a woman's flannel nightgown," blond wig, and rouge as such:

> The doctor's head, with its over-large black eyes, its full gunmetal cheeks and chin, was framed in the golden semi-circle of a wig with long pendent curls that touched his shoulders. . . . He was heavily rouged and his lashes painted. It flashed into Nora's head: "God, children know something they can't tell; they like Red Riding Hood and the wolf in bed!" (NW, 79)

Similar to Sally Bowles's campy role-playing as the *Dame aux Camélias* or Mrs. Manresa's performance as the Flapper described in chapter 2, O'Connor highlights that gender identity exists only "as a masquerade — a pose or façade one dons like a costume" (Henstra, "Looking the Part," 131). A number of critics, however, have read this scene as an attempt by O'Connor either to "imitate" a woman or take from her what is not his. Andrea Harris, for instance, contends that "Matthew [O'Connor] regards cross-dressing . . . as a means of capturing and claiming true femininity for himself" ("Third Sex," 240). Benstock insists he "parodies woman's language, steals her stories and her images to teach her about herself. Gossipy and garrulous, he renders Nora mute" (*Women of the Left Bank*, 266). These interpretations nevertheless fail to recognize the transvestite as a figure in and of itself; O'Connor is not *trying* to copy the other sex.

Butler insists that "drag is not an imitation or a copy of some prior or true gender. . . . [D]rag enacts the very structure of impersonation by which *any gender* is assumed." In other words, drag implies that there is no notion of a true or original gender; it is all "impersonation and approximation" (Butler, "Imitation," 313).[28] Nora's reaction to O'Connor, that children "like Red Riding Hood and the wolf in bed," contradicts any notion that this scene is simply "about" gender inversion or even male dominance and patriarchy. After all, no child is naive enough to think that the wolf has fooled anyone by putting on Grandmother's clothes. While traditional versions of fairy tales insist that order be preserved, O'Connor's drag reveals that the fantasy of border-crossing and perversion is *likeable*. The wolf wants to devour the little girl, but the child knows that Red Riding Hood also wishes to be devoured. The scenario is similar to a dream that Nora has about her own grandmother, "dressed as a man, wearing a billycock and a corked moustache." Leering at Nora, the grandmother spreads her arms as if to devour her, calling out, "My little sweetheart" (NW, 63). Barnes thus explores the realm of border-crossing fantasies that breach the male/female, animal/human, child/innocence, homosexual/heterosexual, sacred/profane, and attraction/repulsion paradigms. From a psychoanalytic perspective, O'Connor's drag points to "the savage wildness that can only be hidden, never obliterated, in the forest of the night-wood that is sexuality" (Gubar, "Blessings in Disguise," 501). Barnes, as Susan Gubar observes, in this way "provides what might be called the anatomy of transvestism" in which "salvation is possible only through the sub-version preached and practiced by the invert" (ibid., 497). While I do not discern any "salvation" in the novel, especially not through O'Connor, the version of reality that the doctor provides at least attempts to induce other ways of thinking about human desire.

The simultaneously disconcerting and comical image of the doctor in a room so contrary to the clinical, sterile medical environments we expect from a "real" medical professional—like the depiction of the Nazi doctor in *Goodbye to Berlin*—clearly establishes a counter-discourse to psychoanalysis, sexology, and the scientific observation of "inversion" of the Nazi period. The room, filled with the evidence of discarded "medical books" and rusty instruments, is a virtual mockery of the medical establishment:

> A pile of medical books, and volumes of a miscellaneous order, reached almost to the ceiling, water-stained and covered with dust. . . . On a maple dresser, certainly not of European make, lay a rusty pair of forceps, a broken scalpel, half a dozen odd instruments that [Nora] could not place, a catheter, some twenty perfume bottles, almost empty, pomades, creams, rouges, powder boxes, and puffs. (NW, 78–79)

The disorder and ruined state of medical paraphernalia is juxtaposed with ribbons, lingerie, bottles of perfume, and creams, an obvious indication that medical discourse is insufficient to explain the multifarious expressions of gender, sexuality, and human desire. Instruments do not make O'Connor a doctor, just as "feminine finery" does not make him a woman. As Chisholm suggests, "gynecology is a poor instrument for servicing eros" ("Obscene Modernism," 191). The "catalogue" of the dresser's contents, however, also parodies the final lines of Canto I of Alexander Pope's mock-heroic poem "The Rape of the Lock," when the speaker describes the altar that is Belinda's "*toilet*":

> Here Files of Pins extend their shining Rows,
> Puffs, Powders, Patches, Bibles, Billet-doux,
> Now awful Beauty puts on all its Arms;

The Fair each moment rises in her Charms,
Repairs her Smiles, awakens ev'ry Grace,
And calls forth all the Wonders of her Face. (I: 137–42)

The intertextual gesture can be read as a send-up of Pope's misogyny and ridicule of women's superficiality, as he describes women who "shift the moving toyshop of their heart" from beau to beau (I: 100), and their excessive concern with dress and makeup. Pope, in the passage, parodies the epic style of listing military weapons and cavalry to disparage Belinda's shallow values as well as those of her upper-crust society; the amalgamation of sacred and profane "Powders, Patches, Bibles, Billet-doux" (I: 138) is one indication, among many, of Belinda's loose morals. *Nightwood*'s sexual/textual drag performance, however, exults in the muddle of sacred/profane and mocks gender conceptions based on a history of Western cultural texts and narratives: fairy tales, myth, Bible, epic poetry, works by the great poets, as well as historical, medical, and psychological treatises. O'Connor thus becomes not only a symbol that represents the failure of outside markers to define identity but also a figure who refutes the various ways gender and sexual desire have been culturally constructed throughout history.

Similar to the way Jewish characters such as Guido and Felix perform metonymic functions to symbolize Barnes's narrative method (see chapter 3), O'Connor functions metonymically as a "category crisis" (to borrow Marjorie Garber's phrase). According to Garber, the role of the transvestite in literature (or in society) is to signal "a failure of definitional distinction, a borderline that becomes permeable, that permits border crossing from one (apparently distinct) category to another: black/white, Jew/Christian, noble bourgeois." In other words, the transvestite not only blurs gender boundaries but also becomes an overdetermined figure that calls into question category crisis elsewhere — any "irresolvable conflict or epistemological crux." Not surprisingly, Garber observes that there are numerous transvestite figures in African American literature to highlight issues of "race conflict, miscegenation, and the mulatto/mulatta." In the same way, at a time of political crisis such as the 1930s, when race, nationality, and sexuality are at the forefront of Nazi discourse, the doctor introduces "trouble" into the paradigm of its false and enforced hierarchy, highlighting "cultural, social, or aesthetic dissonances" (Garber, *Vested Interests*, 16–17).

It is important, however, to distinguish between the fantasy and myth of gender as artifice that O'Connor represents, and the fantasy and myth of Nazi aesthetics. Drag and camp expose the myth of identity self-consciously; they are self-defining gestures in which the spectator colludes with the performer. Fascism, especially Nazism, is a myth that defines self and other. O'Connor's consistent blather, based on fabricated folk-wisdom and contradictory platitudes, articulates a "queer anti-discourse" (Chisholm, "Obscene Modernism," 186) because it disrupts and confounds the comfort of the myth with a constant reevaluation of "I." Like the campy portrayal of the little doctor in *Goodbye to Berlin*, whose "knowledge" of human nature, tonsils, and criminal heads is so ludicrous that it reduces all medical discourse to ironic parody, O'Connor's proclamations undercut not only pseudoscientific sexual discourse but also all ontological assumptions regarding human nature and desire. Barnes, however, also shows that the desire for an absolute truth and stable identity can be so compelling that individuals are prepared to give up their freedoms (as well as others) to keep the illusion intact.

I propose that Nora, who comes to O'Connor's room so he can "tell her of the night," clings to the romantic myth of the Absolute with such fervor that she knowingly relinquishes her grasp on reality in exchange for a predetermined and true destiny. Taken one step further, Nora can be seen as representing the same type of individual who desires the illusion of harmony so profoundly that she is willing to collude in a masochistic relationship that destroys her agency. Adorno and Horkheimer compare women like Nora, who "adore the unmoved paranoiac," to "nations [who] genuflect before totalitarian Fascism." As they propose, "in both cases the subject is extinguished" (*Dialectic of Enlightenment*, 191). Clearly the sexism in such a statement, which assumes women are more liable to be drawn to the supposed charms of psychopathic men, is reprehensible. Nevertheless, it is a view that fittingly correlates with Barnes's depiction of Nora in relation to Robin and the political atmosphere.[29] The dialogue (if one can call it that) between Nora and O'Connor, which takes up two full chapters — "Watchman, What of the Night" and "Go Down Matthew"—becomes a battle of two ideologies: one that desires absolute truth and one that tries to dismantle it. Nora, whose temperament is described as "early Christian" because "she believed in the word" (NW, 51), repeatedly seeks the nostalgic and mystical moment of certainty and assurance. Barging into his room unannounced, she demands of O'Connor, "Tell me everything you know about the night" (NW, 79). Instead of dispensing "doctrine or knowledge," however, the doctor "dispenses a radical heterodoxy" (Chisholm, "Obscene Modernism," 191). According to O'Connor, the night is a mode of thinking beyond binary logic that can discern that day and night are not opposites but are "related by their division" (NW, 80). As he tells Nora, the night is "not premeditated," but rather "every thought of the peculiar polarity of times and times" (NW, 80). The "night" is a conception of reality that blends opposites "bottom-out and wrong side up" and conflates sacred and profane: "The Bible lies the one way, but the night-gown the other" (NW, 80).

In an ideal world, O'Connor's counter-discourse, like the strategy of the avant-garde artist, would "shock" Nora out of believing that she can find any conviction in a "truth" about human nature. As Walter Benjamin proposes, the "shock effect" of art is essential to unsettle habit-forming patterns of sensory perception (*Illuminations*, 238). Disruption is a prerequisite for revolution. But the world Barnes exposes in *Nightwood* is one in which shock is not effective because the spectacle wins. Nora, described as one of the "people who love the people," is part of that spectacle society. Drag, camp, and the shock of the obscene may jolt the reader out of complacency, but for Nora the value of the disorderly "night" is eclipsed by the draw of the "paranoiac," the sacrifice, and the sentimental abnegation of the self. Nora has no sense of humor: "cynicism, laughter, the second hush into which the sucked man crawls, she seemed to know little or nothing about" (NW, 53). Deftly, Barnes reproduces the frustrating attempts by O'Connor to shift or refocus Nora's perspective, to challenge her way of thinking through story and fiction, but to no avail. Nora refuses to understand, because she "believes in the word" (NW, 51). Repeatedly, Nora interrupts O'Connor's long diatribe with platitudes: "I see that the night does something to a person's identity," she proclaims, miscomprehending that O'Connor is trying to articulate an idea that there *is* no identity (NW, 81). As he insists, "identity" (in quotation marks in the text) is only confused when one "Let[s] a man lay down in the Great Bed" of sexual identification. Only then does his identity become "no longer his own" (NW, 81). In vain the doctor tries to impress upon Nora, "We are but skin about a wind, with muscles clenched against mortality" (NW, 83). O'Connor recognizes that the "word" itself is what causes oppression: "Yes, we who are full to the gorge with misery should look well around, doubting everything seen, done, spoken, precisely because we have a word for it" (NW, 83). In asking her to think of the night, he asks her to break that binary: "think of the night the day long, and of the day the night through" he implores (NW, 84).

As an attempt to understand human nature, *Nightwood* refuses to judge Nora's appeal for certainty; nor, for that matter, does the novel belittle her desire to enslave herself to an obsession with an "enigma" — Robin. At the same time, the parallels between Nora and Robin's relationship (and O'Connor's analysis of it) can also be interpreted as a compelling examination of the political environment in 1930s Europe. As mentioned previously, numerous theorists have noted that Nazi aesthetics was particular in its ability to juxtapose contradictory ideas like harmony and battle, submission and control, terror and fascination — aspects of which are revealed in the relationship between Robin and Nora. The effect of the contradictions within Nazi dramaturgy is what critics such as Friedländer and Sontag, among others, identify as the concurrent desire for compliance, surrender, and abandon (Friedländer, *Reflections on Nazism*, xv; Sontag, "Fascinating Fascism," 91). As Patraka explains, "These effects were accomplished by yoking, on the one hand, love of death . . . nihilism, pessimism, primordial myth, blind destiny that leads to inevitable destruction, apocalypse, and universal conflagration . . . with, on the other hand, kitsch emotion" (*Spectacular Suffering*, 37). I propose that one of the ways *Nightwood* uncovers how individuals succumb to the dangerous allure of Nazism is through Nora's domination/submission relationship with Robin and her melodramatic obsession with Robin's love. Quite possibly, the fact that the fascist paradigm is illustrated by a same-sex relationship is not coincidental — an example of the "homosexualization of fascism." As Hewitt maintains, the conflation of homosexuality with fascism in literature sustains a homophobic image that links same-sex desire with masochism, narcissism, voyeurism, and sadistic pleasure (*Political Inversions*, 3). I think it is more plausible, however, that Barnes delves into the "dark night" that is *human* desire — the pleasure of submission and the fascination with nihilism that transcends the yearning for a specific sexual object.

Ultimately, O'Connor's efforts to transform Nora fail, just as the novel itself fails to rectify the nihilistic obliteration of sense and meaning. In

"Go Down Matthew," the duel of ideologies eventually evolves into language that more closely mimics the kitsch-death theme. Echoing the melodrama of a 1920s film-noir script, Nora introduces death into her obsession with Robin, surrendering herself to the concept of an inevitable, glorified destruction. "Once, when she was sleeping," Nora says of Robin, "I wanted her to die" (NW, 128). Nora's wish for Robin's death soon turns into certainty as she exalts in the inevitability of her sacrifice for love: "I can only find her again in my sleep or in her death" (NW, 129); "Love is death, come upon with passion; I know, that is why love is wisdom. I love her as one condemned to it" (NW, 137); and even, "we love each other like death" (NW, 139). Nora's image of love moves from fantasy — loving her "like" death — to a craving for kitsch-death: "I kissed her, holding her hands and feet, and I said: Die now, so you will be quiet, so you will not be touched again by dirty hands . . . — die now, then you will be mine forever" (NW, 145). The certainty of Nora's tone, and the overwhelming force of her yearning to abandon herself, finally convinces the doctor that he has lost his battle against the Absolute. O'Connor's counter-discourse becomes less coherent, however, when confronting the "fine and terrifying spectacle" of Nora's devotion to Robin (NW, 138). As if yelling out into the void of a nightmare, O'Connor shouts, "Stop it! . . . Robin is not your life, you are in her dream" (NW, 146). If the polarities between fantasy and self-consciousness become incommensurable, however, radical resistance is impossible. Nora revels in her fantasy of domination when she recognizes, "There's something evil in me that loves evil and degradation — purity's black backside!" (NW, 135). She chooses illusion due to its power, because "Only the impossible lasts forever" (NW, 139).

If anything, *Nightwood* indicates that drag, camp, profanity, shock, resistance, avant-garde art, shouting, and emancipation are engulfed by the draw of romance, myth, nostalgia, and the glorification of sacrifice and death. In Barnes's text, queer counter-discourse fails: "I've not only lived my life for nothing," O'Connor declares, "I've told it for nothing. . . . I know it's all over, everything's over, and nobody knows it but me" (NW, 166). The domination-enslavement scenario that writers and intellectuals such as Barnes believed enslaved the masses in the 1930s is a scenario in which one side always loses. This is confirmed by the pastoral, idyllic scene of complete nihilism that ends the novel — trees, wilderness, flowers, communion with animals, an Eliotic decaying chapel — and complete and utter annihilation of the self. O'Connor, who crosses the boundaries of stable gender and sexual categories, can be a figure of positive transformation; but his performance relies on sympathetic reception, self-reflexivity, humor, and critique. The reader, to whom T. S. Eliot appeals in his introduction to *Nightwood,* is asked to be that audience. As Eliot insists, "To regard this group of people as a horrid sideshow of freaks is not only to miss the point, but to confirm our wills and harden our hearts in an inveterate sin of pride" (xvi). In more than one sense, after 1936 the European audience O'Connor addresses is already lost: "What people! All queer in a terrible way. There were a couple of queer good people once in this world — but none of you" (NW, 161).

### *Between the Acts* and the Discourse of Dodging

In a far less shocking and outrageous manner than *Nightwood, Between the Acts* more subtly suggests that queer counter-discourse has the possibility of leading to transformation and new definitions of justice. In a footnote to *Three Guineas,* published two years before beginning *Between the Acts,* Woolf observes how the distinction between sexes in fascist dictatorships actually encourages men to fight:

> The nature of manhood and the nature of womanhood are frequently defined by both Italian and German dictators. Both repeatedly insist that it is the nature of man and indeed the essence of manhood to fight. . . . Nevertheless, a very strong movement is on foot towards emancipating man from the old "natural and eternal law" that man is essentially a fighter. (*TG,* 205 n. 48)

*Three Guineas* conveys an underlying message that fascist binary thinking "mak[es] distinctions between the sexes" (*TG,* 118), and its categorization of "normal" and "abnormal" leads to oppression of all types of difference, including those *within* the sexes. As mentioned in the previous chapter, recent critics have noted the problems in Woolf's refusal to distinguish between British patriarchy, Italian fascism, and Nazism — a strategy that distorts their vast differences. Her line of reasoning also assumes that fighting is always masculine and that all fighting is the same, whether it be self-defense, protecting those who are attacked, or the aggressive militarism of Germany. Many Woolf scholars concur that by 1940, her position regarding the need to fight against Nazism had somewhat altered as she recognized the more immediate danger to Nazi victims.

Woolf's representation of homophobia in *Between the Acts* functions within her analysis of fascism, nationalism, and its link with patriarchal ideas of "manliness" and "womanliness." That the novel speaks more to British views of sexuality than to Nazi oppression is most likely because knowledge of the Nazi persecution of homosexuals was not widespread and was less widely discussed in the media than the oppression of women and Jews. Nevertheless, her recognition that labeling and categorization of individuals prevents peace and mutual understanding emphasizes the wider, more dangerous implications of prejudice toward sexual difference. One wonders if, as in her portrayal of Jews, Woolf reiterates or challenges the prevailing stereotypes of homosexual men in her novel by using them as a universal category while ignoring the particular conditions that alienate them from the communal "we." Nevertheless, even the act of sympathetically representing overtly homosexual characters could be considered rebellious at a time when same-sex desire was considered unmentionable. The connections she makes in the novel among homophobia, ideas of national belonging, and suppression of freedom of expression are daring and courageous when considered within their historical context. But they are also telling in how they reveal prevailing attitudes toward homosexual men at the time.

Although a number of feminist scholars have focused on how lesbian desire functions in *Between the Acts* (in the context of Miss La Trobe and the text's opposition to patriarchy), few have specifically explored Woolf's reaction to homophobia and the psychosexual discourses of the time.[30] Among them, Stephen Barber interprets *Between the Acts* as being "distinctly queer" in the way it "vigilantly . . . train[s] its readers to perceive, map, and counter the homophobic and misogynistic force-fields within and by which the [novel's] characters' souls, their emotions, gestures and postures, are formed" ("Lip-Reading," 427). Annette Oxindine also elucidates how *Between the Acts* "expos[es] the ideologies that connect and perpetuate the violence of nationalism, sexism, and homophobia" ("Outing the Outsiders," 115).[31] Woolf's strategies in resisting fascist homophobia nevertheless deserve more scholarly attention within their historical context, and in a manner that distinguishes between her message about homophobia and that of misogyny. This section will analyze the specific ways in which Woolf draws parallels between "the textual" and "the sexual" by shedding light on the politics and effects of homophobic discourse, especially targeted toward the homosexual male, in both Nazi and British nationalist discourse.

For Woolf, as for Isherwood and Barnes, counter-discourse at the time became a complicated war of words. Woolf had attended the obscenity trial for Radclyffe Hall's *The Well of Loneliness* (along with Leonard Woolf, Vita Sackville-West, and E. M. Forster) and knew well what the consequences could be for a polemical work that made homosexuality too visible.[32] In *Between the Acts*, the blanks and elisions that evade clear terminology to describe same-sex desiring men and women such as William Dodge and Miss La Trobe also "dodged" the British and American censors. But the strategy of evasion serves another purpose as well. Through these lacunae Woolf delves into the effects of labeling to explore the implications, effects, and politics of words that define sexual desire. "Where people mistake," Woolf asserts, "is in perpetually narrowing and naming these immensely composite and wide-flung passions — driving stakes through them, herding them between screens. But how do you define 'Perversity'? What is the line between friendship and perversion?" (*L*, 6: 200). For Woolf, subverting definitions of so-called "perversion" allows her to blur the defining lines of human experience and "redraw parameters within which sexuality is define and suppressed" to expand meaning (Parkes, *Theater of Censorship*, 164).

According to Hewitt, in literary expressions of fascism often the body of the homosexual becomes a "trace": "that singular moment of representation that must be retained in order for the abstract to encode and represent antirepresentationalism. It both makes possible and precludes the absolute of abstraction" (*Political Inversions*, 217). In other words, the figure of the homosexual, which is always already only a representation, becomes a symbol not of the fascist myth of the Absolute, but of the impossibility of that myth. Much like the Jew, the homosexual figure is one that is present in his absence, constructed in the fantasy of what he is not. Moreover, as Klaus Theweleit points out, since there is no real concept of what homosexuality *means*—the various forms of behavior,

drives, love, activities, pleasure or "modes of thinking, feeling and acting" that make up "the homosexual"—it becomes a catchword for all that
fails categorization (*Male Fantasies*, 54). In *Between the Acts*, William
Dodge is a figure who epitomizes that "trace" in the text. Tagging along
with the flamboyant Mrs. Manresa, Dodge arrives uninvited at Pointz
Hall and spends most of the afternoon anxiously attempting (rather unsuccessfully) to sidestep assumptions about his sexuality in fear of being
subjected to the cruel repercussions of homophobia. As a character who
highlights the effects and processes of subjectification, he participates in
what Barber describes as Woolf's "queer textual practice" by functioning
as a force "of intervention in normalizing procedures" ("Lip-Reading,"
404). Homophobia and the medical discourse of sexual perversion, both
practices that oppress the Other through labeling, are brought to light
through the narrator and other characters' reactions to Dodge. Nevertheless, the fact that he does not "pass" as straight in *Between the Acts*,
and that as readers we recognize his stereotypical gestures, mode of behavior, and physical description as "that word," indicates that he is both
more and less than a "trace" for antirepresentationalism.

The way in which the narration both participates in and points to
all that exceeds Dodge's labeling is evident in his initial depiction. Oxindine points out that Woolf's characterization of Dodge is "more stereotypically effete than any other male homosexual to appear in her
fiction" ("Outing the Outsiders," 115). Sallow, effeminate, nervous, and
delicate, Dodge's body and demeanor situate him squarely within the
discourse of sexual science, thus pointing to the problematic construction and representation of "the homosexual" in the text. The narrator
describes Dodge as such:

> He was of course a gentleman; witness socks and trousers;
> brainy—tie spotted, waistcoat undone; urban, professional, that
> is putty coloured, unwholesome; very nervous, exhibiting a
> twitch at this sudden introduction, and fundamentally infernally
> conceited. (*BTA*, 35)

The portrayal of Dodge resonates with troubling homophobic indictments that homosexuality is unhealthy for the body and soul. It could be
argued, however, that this is specifically for the purpose of seeing how

others see him, "to expose the homophobia that informs the communal response to the homosexual characters" (Oxindine, "Outing the Outsiders," 115). Because Woolf uses free indirect discourse, the point of view from which Dodge is perceived remains ambiguous. It appears to be Isa's viewpoint, since immediately beforehand the narrator states, "there was an element of silence, supplied by Isabella, observing the unknown young man" (*BTA*, 35). Suspended between Isa's perception, the public view, and the reader's perception of the irony in the narration, Dodge becomes a figure who is marked by vagueness. This vagueness, like the indeterminacy of the Jew, still participates in a typecasting that links homosexuals to weakness, suspicion, and concealment. Nevertheless, if in free indirect discourse points of view become blurred, then assumptions about Dodge's character are also put in question, leaving room to challenge other binary structures upon which homophobic assumptions are built.

The resulting uncertainty as to "who Dodge really is" on the one hand allows for multiplicity of meaning, but on the other hand it leaves him fair game for scapegoating. Considering the dangers of exposure epitomized by Giles Oliver and his hostile reaction toward "half-breeds," it is small wonder that William Dodge tries to avoid being identified as a homosexual. Isa clearly does not understand this when she asks, "Why's he afraid? . . . A poor specimen he was; afraid to stick up for his own beliefs — just as she was afraid, of her husband" (*BTA*, 46). Dodge is "convenient to hate," as Oxindine observes, "because (as his name applies) he does not fight back" ("Outing the Outsiders," 121). Still, Isa's and Dodge's fears of Giles are poles apart. Giles not only is disrespectful toward Dodge but also violently and aggressively aims his rage at Dodge — the epitome of homosexual panic. The young man's precarious position is even more patent in *Pointz Hall*, the earlier typescript of *Between the Acts*, when Dodge fears that Mrs. Manresa is "outing" him by her references to his delicacy and fine handwriting: "Didn't [Mrs. Manresa] see she was putting nails in his coffin with every word she spoke, hanging him with her fiddle-faddle" (*PH*, 81). All Giles needs to set him off in a rage is to pinpoint Dodge as a threat to normative manliness. Conveniently, when Isa drops her blue china coffee cup and Dodge recognizes the make, even the year, Giles's "proof" that Dodge represents the ruin of European society is provided.

Described as having "no command of metaphors," Giles duly finds a metaphor in Dodge:

> A toady; a lickspittle; not a downright plain man of his senses; but a teaser and a twitcher; a fingerer of sensations; picking and choosing; dillying and dallying; not a man to have straightforward love for a woman — his head was close to Isa's had — but simply a — —At this word, which he could not speak in public, he pursed his lips. . . . (*BTA*, 55)

Notably, all the descriptors in Giles's tirade are set in a relational positive-negative dichotomy. In sum, Dodge, whose name nobody remembers, is *not*. For there to be a coherence of "manliness," its opposite needs to exist as well. There can be no "hetero-" sexuality without the "homo-," just as there can be no such thing as Aryan without the Jew. Giles's vitriol reverberates with the type of rhetoric spouted in Wyndham Lewis's *The Art of Being Ruled* (1926), in which Lewis describes "the Nancyism of the joy-boy or joy-man — the over-mannered personality, the queer insistence on 'delicate nature' as enemy of the intellect" (235, 244). For Lewis, one of the most serious faults of the "invert" was that he "takes over the traditional idiosyncrasies of the feminine role; and certainly one of them has always been to be the 'enemy of the Absolute'" (*Art*, 275). Dodge is certainly portrayed as anything but "Absolute," although for Woolf this would clearly not be a fault. Giles's outpouring of rage is almost a parody of the rancorous schoolboy bully tone of the 1914 issue of *BLAST*: "CURSE WITH EXPLETIVE OF WHIRLWIND THE BRITANNIC AESTHETE CREAM OF THE SNOBBISH EARTH ROSE OF SHARON OF GOD-PRIG OF SIMIAN VANITY SNEAK AND SWOT OF THE SCHOOL ROOM" (12). Considering that Lewis blamed "feminism" and "the rashness ignorance and weakness of women" for creating unmanly men and the "homo" (*Art*, 215, 205, 244), as well as personally attacking Woolf in *Men Without Art* (1934), criticism of Lewis and his kind could feasibly lie at the heart of the novel's portrayal of Giles's misogyny and homophobia.[33] If this is Woolf's counterattack, she most certainly brings misogyny and homophobia down to size, as Isa proclaims, "as plainly as words could say it": "No, . . . I don't admire you . . . 'Silly little boy, with blood on his boots" (*BTA*, 100).[34]

Woolf elucidates the psychology behind Giles's panic when she makes it apparent that he covers up his own insecurities by directing his anger at homosexuals and women. Remembering "a child's game," Giles kicks stones in the dirt path: "The first kick was Manresa (lust). The second, Dodge (perversion). The third himself (cowardice)" (*BTA*, 89). If it is not clear enough that his resentment is infantile, the narrator makes it even more obvious a few pages later, when Giles casts doubt on Dodge's "civility": "It was a bit of luck — that he could despise him, and not himself" (*BTA*, 100). Similar to the Modern Woman and the phantasmatic Jew, Dodge functions as a negative fantasy that allows Giles to transpose his fear that the Other might lurk in himself. As a receptacle for all that cannot be contained in the borders of the "meaning," Dodge is the blank "— —" that is censored out of the public text of coherent identities.

Noticeably, Dodge's failure to "pass" and the external markers of his deviance are focused on his hands; people keep wondering what he *does* with "his hands, the white, the fine, the shapely?" (*BTA*, 47). Similarly, Giles "looked, once, at William. He knew not his name; but what his left hand was doing" (*BTA*, 100). Dodge's decidedly unmanly and "delicate" hands, aside from giving away his status as an urban professional, indicate that his body and sexuality cannot be "handled" or controlled. The insinuation is that his hands must be doing something hidden and perverse when he puts them in his pockets. As Lesley Hall's study of masturbation and "moral panic" in Great Britain reveals, "Men's attitudes toward masturbation were attitudes toward the nature of their own male sexuality, unmediated through the female" and "bound up with assumptions about masculinity" (Hall, "Forbidden by God," 366, 375).[35] George Mosse points out that "the homosexual" was often linked with "the masturbator" in nineteenth- and early twentieth-century German discourse as well. Both practices were believed to lead men to be consumed by sex, in direct opposition to the very essence of manliness — respectability and self-control (Mosse, *Nationalism and Sexuality*, 11). Common traits of both "masturbator" and "homosexual" included nervousness and twitches, much like Dodge demonstrates. These men were also inevitably depicted as "pale, hollow-eyed, weak of body and spirit," and, because of their secrecy, enemies to the security of the state (ibid.).

While Isa also detects Dodge's sexual identity from his "delicate" hands, for her they symbolize a corresponding sensitivity of spirit. Isa feels a bond with Dodge due to their shared oppression and entrapment within the confines of patriarchy. She sees he is "the word that Giles had not spoken. Well, was it wrong if he was that word? Why judge each other? Do we know each other? Not here, not now" (*BTA*, 56). The early typescript makes it clearer that Isa understands why Dodge is despised and is sympathetic:

> She knew at the moment that he was being made responsible, together with her Aunt Lucy, for all that her husband hated. She guessed the very word that Giles had not spoken. But was it true that William Dodge was that word? If so, how far was it wrong? Can you condemn people for their sexuality? the way they feel? How far are we responsible? Question circled from question. He was fond of pictures. Probably he had an old mother . . . Why do we all hate each other? (*PH*, 81)

The passage indicates that Dodge has the potential to be a figure who can make others (or at least Isa) feel and think differently. "He smiled. She smiled. They were conspirators" (*BTA*, 94). Isa, whose social identity is based upon her positioning within the patriarchal family, is in hiding too — she is "Sir Richard's daughter" (*BTA*, 13) and the wife of Giles, who "is my husband" and the "father of my children" (*BTA*, 44, 13). Loathing the domestic, she feels trapped in her role as a dutiful wife. Through mutual understanding, both Isa and Dodge attain a measure of freedom — to talk "as if they had known each other all their lives" (*BTA*, 103). Yet Isa too is guilty of typecasting Dodge in a role only to fulfill her own selfish need for an "other." After all, she asks him to come with her to the greenhouse to talk only to even the score with Giles for his infidelity with Mrs. Manresa. The narrative is unclear whether Dodge feels that he and Isa are "conspirators" as well. Dodge, it seems, knows the typical script of a gay male–straight female relationship: "They liked it. For then they could say — as she did — whatever came into their head. And hand him, as she handed him, a flower" (*BTA*, 102). Then they talked,

> which was odd, she said, as they always did, considering she'd known him perhaps one hour. Weren't they, though, conspira-

tors, seekers after hidden faces? That confessed, she paused and wondered, as they always did, why they could speak so plainly to each other. (BTA, 103)

The phrase "as they always did" suggests that although Isa believes Dodge, the "lip reader," is her "semblable" (BTA, 187), he does not reciprocate those feelings. Isa may feel that Dodge understands her, but does she understand Dodge? For her, he is still a figure that fills in "that word" rather than an agent of his own self-identity.

Only utopian Mrs. Swithin, naive, or perhaps unaware, manages to look beyond Dodge's otherness and the labeling that identifies him. She takes him away from the mesmerized crowd outdoors, staring at the stupefying, spectacular view, "'because I felt wound tight here . . .' She touched her bony forehead upon which a blue vein wriggled like a blue worm" (BTA, 67). Swithin's guided tour of the house covers her history by way of: art (the "not an ancestress" painting [BTA, 63]); culture ("the poets from whom we descend" [BTA, 63]); and identity ("I was born. In this bed" [BTA, 64]). The core message she conveys to Dodge is that the spirit, the essence of human beings, exists beyond the physical reality of their existence. "'But we have other lives, I think, I hope' she murmured. 'We live in others, Mr . . . We live in things'" (BTA, 64). Swithin's kindness toward Dodge stirs within him a heartbreaking desire to confess:

> At school they held me under a bucket of dirty water, Mrs Swithin; when I looked up, the world was dirty, Mrs Swithin; so I married; but my child's not my child, Mrs Swithin. I'm a half-man, Mrs Swithin; a flickering, mind-divided little snake in the grass, Mrs Swithin; as Giles saw; but you've healed me . . . (BTA, 67)

Dodge's silent confession reveals that sometimes the soul is limited by physical reality. The devastating effects of homophobia not only force individuals falsely to conform to heterosexual norms but also shame them into internalizing that hostility as self-hatred. As Barber observes, "In this never-quite-performed self-outing to Mrs Swithin . . . Dodge's initial recourse is to a logic and rhetoric of among the most authoritative of technologies for self-fashioning and self-knowledge: the psychoanalytic narrative of psychosexual development" ("Lip-Reading," 419). Dodge's identity becomes entrenched in his subjugation, believing that he is "a half man" as the sexologists, Giles, and the Church believe. He might not want to "live in others" when they have made his world dirty from oppression. Perhaps this is why Dodge does not "come out" to Mrs. Swithin out loud. Her utopian philosophy of universal love is beautiful, but for true freedom, Dodge would need to be in a society in which differences are accepted rather than overcome — where people willingly say his name and where he can speak out loud.

The one character who challenges Swithin's concept of a unified utopian ideal with the more pluralistic goal of recognizing and accepting otherness is Miss La Trobe. Like Dodge, Miss La Trobe spends much of her time in hiding, behind a tree. Ostracized by the community, as an outsider she nevertheless becomes the agent through which transformation is possible. Like Dodge, her sexual identity is not named, but it is perceived through the stereotypical traits of the "mannish" female "invert":

> Outwardly she was swarthy, sturdy and thick set; strode about the fields in a smock frock; sometimes with a cigarette in her mouth; often with a whip in her hand; and used rather strong language — perhaps, then, she wasn't altogether a lady? At any rate, she had a passion for getting things up. (BTA, 53)

Despite being an outcast, La Trobe is able to effect social change precisely because she is *not* "a lady." In contrast to Dodge, who allows himself be identified by others, La Trobe becomes a figure capable of using her outsidership for the purpose of transformation. Andrew Hewitt insists that "The homosexual . . . acknowledges the 'fascist within' in a way that the heterosexual subject cannot." This is not to say that the homosexual *is* a fascist but that he is a person who more easily recognizes or acknowledges that the self has within it aspects of the Other, that " 'within' is a mere function of the definitive 'without' " (*Political Inversions*, 208). La Trobe not only recognizes the Other in the self but also admonishes her pageant audience to do the same. She experiments with ideas of perception by presenting her viewers with double images, elisions, and mixed messages, thus leaving room for contemplation and critique. *"Let's break the rhythm and forget the rhyme,*" she tells her audience, and "*consider ourselves*" not as one, but as separate individuals together, "*Liars, most of us. Thieves too*" (BTA, 168). Only through acknowledging that Other, La Trobe seems to imply, can one create new ethical ways of seeing; only then can one say, "*here I change*" (BTA, 169).

Like O'Connor, La Trobe's passion and fearlessness stem from her ability to construct her own identity by "troubling" the gender binary and showing how sexual identities are "theatrically produced effects" (Butler, "Imitation," 313). In disrupting the mythic kitsch nostalgia of a history based on romance, heroes, and military conquests, her pageant, like O'Connor's stories, explores the multifaceted nature of power, patriarchy, love, and human desire. The ending of *Between the Acts* implies that there is also a third option — coming together in difference. "Peace was a third emotion. Love. Hate. Peace" (BTA, 83). Garber defines "the 'third term'" as "a mode of articulation, a way of describing a space or possibility. Three puts in question the idea of one: of identity, self-sufficiency, self-knowledge" (*Vested Interests*, 11). One wonders, however, if it is too late to speak about "peace" when the term itself is already an anachronism for Nazism's victims. If Woolf includes the diversity of all of the "*orts, scraps, and fragments*" in the "jangle and the din" of humanity in her fiction as a concept (BTA, 169, 165), is she willing to include it in her vision of Englishness? Woolf, Isherwood, and Barnes, by introducing "crisis" into the binary logic that oppresses Others, imagine a third way of knowing through ambiguity — the ultimate rejection of the Absolute. The novels do not all unambiguously represent gay men and women and same-sex desire without prejudice, or prejudgment of what determines "deviant" behavior. Nevertheless, by "queering" their texts they construct spaces where differences are brought to the fore, highlighted, and examined. A regime that tyrannizes men and women in the name of morality, that subjugates and oppresses them due to paranoia and fear, the novels indicate, must be resisted. We as readers are nevertheless required to fill in the meaning in those blanks to include the voices, differences, contradictions, and desires that are not articulated as part of human nature.

*Between the Acts*, *Goodbye to Berlin*, and *Nightwood* all suggest that human beings, and their heterogeneous ways of "being," exceed the limited — and limiting — terms defined by Nazi discourse. Their strategy is nevertheless risky: will the blanks, evasions, elisions, and vacillations exceed the capability of making meaning and become nihilistic? Is the desire for the Absolute on the part of the public too great? Comments from audience members in *Between the Acts* articulate the same doubt: "if you think, and I think, perhaps one day, thinking differently, we shall think the same?" (*BTA*, 180). This question, it seems, remains unanswerable. La Trobe wonders if her pageant is "A failure" (*BTA*, 188). It may well be. Even so, she begins a new artistic project: "She heard the first words" (*BTA*, 191). She even becomes intoxicated with the non-absolute of "Words without meaning—wonderful words" (*BTA*, 191). Perhaps the true task for the reader, then, is to make those words meaningful; to fill in those blanks and evasions and to examine not only how injustice and prejudice can be identified as a universal theme but also how we can read ethically to translate that knowledge into the particular.

# Can Fiction Make a Difference?
# Writing and Reading Resistance

The artist in the thirties was forced to be a politician. That
explains why the artist in the thirties was forced to be a
scapegoat.

—VIRGINIA WOOLF, *COLLECTED ESSAYS* (1940)

In *A Room of One's Own,* Virginia Woolf concedes, "How unpleasant it
is to be locked out; [but] it is worse perhaps to be locked in" (24). Upon
finishing a draft of *Between the Acts,* Woolf, ill with depression and no
doubt affected by the war's general devastation and the destruction of
her London home during the Blitz, committed suicide by drowning herself in the River Ouse on March 28, 1941. In a move that many of his
contemporaries interpreted as a betrayal, in January 1939, the same year
*Goodbye to Berlin* was published, Christopher Isherwood, along with
W. H. Auden, left Europe for America with the admission "it just doesn't
mean anything to me anymore . . . the anti-fascist struggle" (*CHK,* 248).
Djuna Barnes's novel *Nightwood,* after numerous rejections, was published in England in 1936. Although it received high critical acclaim
(encouraged by the support of T. S. Eliot), it never sold more than 2,000
copies at its most popular and was virtually ignored, if not disparaged,
by serious journals in America (Field, *Djuna,* 206, 215).[1] By the time
the German occupation of France began, Barnes was living in London.
In February 1939, she suffered an emotional breakdown and attempted

suicide. By 1940, she was back in New York, living the rest of her life in relative seclusion.

It is tempting for the contemporary reader to engage in apocalyptic readings of these writers' works, to study them in the shadow of the impending disaster of World War II and the Nazi Holocaust. After all, the Holocaust is an indelible part of our present, a genocide that brought racism to its furthest and most unimaginable conclusion. But no one could predict the concentration camps, the terror, or the mass murder that occurred in the 1940s — it was not yet in the realm of the imagination. As Zygmunt Bauman remarks, "For all they had known and believed, the mass murder for which they did not even have a name yet was, purely and simply, unimaginable. . . ." (*Modernity*, 85). Despite that which they could not know, the novels that Barnes, Isherwood, and Woolf wrote do reveal the historical, cultural, political, and social conditions in 1930s Europe that made the continent ripe for disaster. They expose the mentality, the discourses of exclusion, and the modern anxieties that led entire countries either to ignore or to facilitate the oppression, subjugation, and annihilation of Others. These are not, however, works that privilege victimhood or the oppressed. Instead they strive to point out how the "beast" lives within every person, whenever or wherever he or she becomes part of a herd that supports an illusion of harmony and unity at the expense of those who do not belong.

My goal in this book has been to examine the various ways in which aspects of Nazi culture are brought to light and challenged — both thematically and aesthetically — in modernist fiction of the 1930s. I have also highlighted the ways in which different kinds of oppression were interconnected in modern European discourse and the complex ways they are represented in novels such as *Nightwood, Between the Acts,* and *Goodbye to Berlin.* This is not to say that all oppressions are equal or that the vehemence with which the Nazis targeted each group was alike. As Barnes's, Isherwood's, and Woolf's works demonstrate, an "anti-Nazi aesthetic" serves a mode of novelization that intervenes into accepted notions of what it means to "belong" as a national, racial, gendered subject. The settings in *Nightwood, Goodbye to Berlin,* and *Between the Acts* become spaces that give voice to difference and expose the workings of the spectacle of fascism and Nazism as it begins to overtake Europe. They are novels that value ambiguity and uncertainty above the illusion and appeal of absolute harmony and unity that Nazism promotes. At their most radical, these texts encourage readers to rethink their sets of beliefs, to critique their values, and to transform their perceptions of their surroundings.

An "anti-Nazi aesthetic," however, can also backfire. As I have argued, the types of experimental modernist narrative strategies that rely on ambiguous typecasting to expose prejudices against Jews, homosexuals, and emancipated women also have the potential to confirm essential differences, alienate Others from the community, and even facilitate apathy toward the more urgent need to stand up and help those being persecuted. At worst, then, Woolf, Barnes, and Isherwood support a discourse of exclusion and their novels become intellectual exercises for readers privileged enough to access them. Especially in the case of Britain and the plight of Jewish refugees from Germany, feeling righteously empathetic for the persecuted allowed many intellectuals to avoid the more difficult decision to take them in. As we saw from the audience's response to the pageant in Woolf's *Between the Acts*, while they may ask, "And what about the Jews?" they do not accept their Jewish neighbors (*BTA*, 109).

This brings me to a crucial question that I hope this book suggests. Can an anti-Nazi aesthetic, or any fictional resistance for that matter, be an effective mode of opposition to political and social oppression? Even more importantly, what constitutes literary resistance? And, what are the right questions to even ask regarding the effectiveness of literature and writing to counter the many continuing forms of tyranny prevailing in our time? After all, as Bauman insists, "we know what we did not know in 1941; that *also the unimaginable ought to be imagined*" (*Modernity*, 84–85).

Perhaps what we should be asking is not whether resistance writing can *be* effective, but rather how we, as readers and critics, can *make* resistance writing viable. Understanding how the Nazi spectacle worked to encourage the public to believe in an ideal image of a strong and harmonious nation, for instance, encourages us to think more critically not only about the literature written in the years leading up to the war but also about the workings of totalitarian and tyrannical regimes today. Notions of mass psychology and the spectacle have also extended to revolutionary theories of consumer society and the role of mass media, including the ideas advanced in Guy Debord's *The Society of the Spectacle* (1967). In other words, while writing itself can be an act of rebellion when it questions meaning and demands new interpretations of social justice, it is only truly resistant if it is matched with a reader who can be enlightened and transformed by an understanding of the social plots we live by.

Woolf tells readers that their role is to "insist that writers come down off their plinths and pedestals, and describe beautifully if possible, truthfully at any rate, the spirit we live by" (*E*, 2: 33). As she asserts, "We can help England very greatly to bridge the gulf between the worlds if we borrow the books she lends us and if we read them critically. We have got to teach ourselves to understand literature" (*M*, 125). If anything, this study has tried to emphasize that it is up to the reader to fill in the writers' perspectives that are missing in the textual "gulf," to be critical, and to recognize rhetoric that is antisemitic, sexist, homophobic, or exclusionary within the cultural and historical context of the 1930s, and even today. Reading as an act of resistance also means reading with skepticism. This is not for the purpose of demoting the importance of these writers in the modernist canon, but neither is it to excuse the serious and harmful outcome of typecasting in the years leading up to the Holocaust. As Tzvetan Todorov insists, "discourses are also events. They make acts possible and they make it possible for these acts to be accepted" (*On Human Diversity*, xiii). Todorov's succinct argument applies directly to our reading of literature and to the reasons why it is crucial to engage modern literary criticism within its historical, political, and cultural context. Examining how Barnes, Isherwood, and Woolf articulate their positions vis-à-vis art and politics, and how resisting Nazism informs their works, can advance fruitful dialogues about identity, discrimination, ethical responsibilities toward others, and political activism against tyrannical regimes. Realizing how the complex matrices of oppression are brought to light in modernist cultural productions in the period when the Nazis came into power is an important task for current scholars.

Exposing prejudice in literary modernism, however, is often deemed the responsibility of the victim group rather than the perpetrator of that prejudice, or its analysis is left to specialized academic fields of "minority" or Other interests, where it frequently remains. And yet, transformation and, by extension, acts of resistance, may not always occur at the level of the storyteller, but it can occur by placing literature in a dialogical relationship with cultural and ethnic discourses. This is how we as readers can undo the erasure of the historical and represented experience of Jewish men and women living in the 1930s before Hitler's Final Solution, as well as draw attention to non-Jewish victims of Nazi persecution such as homosexuals, "asocial" women, the mentally and physically disabled, political adversaries, Roma, Sinti, and religious minorities.

What makes modernist writers like Barnes, Woolf, and Isherwood so exceptional is that they used writing and fiction to expand conceptions of what identity itself consists of. Despite falling into the trap of exclusionary discourse, they did attempt to challenge assumptions embedded in fascist and Nazi culture that dictated the rules of belonging and difference. It is that layered legacy of ethical responsibility and aesthetic innovation that can inform contemporary readings of their works. Experimental texts can be disruptive because reading them becomes an experience that can revolutionize ways of making meaning. The challenges of resistance are thus in the hands of those who receive that narrative and begin thinking and acting differently because of their broadened awareness of culture, politics, and history.

Introduction

1. In the last few years, the field of modernism has undergone revision and expansion of its temporal and theoretical boundaries. See Douglas Mao and Rebecca Walkowitz's review of the transformation of modernist studies in their essay "The New Modernist Studies," *PMLA* 123, no. 3 (2008): 737–48.

2. Patrick J. Quinn, *Recharting the Thirties* (Selinsgrove, Pa.: University of Susquehanna Press, 1996); Keith Williams and Steven Matthews, eds., *Rewriting the Thirties: Modernism and After* (London: Longman, 1997); Antony Shuttleworth, ed., *And in Our Time: Vision, Revision, and British Writing of the 1930s* (Lewisburg, Pa.: Bucknell University Press; Associated University Press, 2003); Gill Plain, *Women's Fiction of the Second World War: Gender, Power and Resistance* (Edinburgh: Edinburgh University Press, 1996); Phyllis Lassner, *British Women Writers of World War II: Battlegrounds of Their Own* (New York: Macmillan, 1998); Maroula Joannou, ed., *Women Writers of the 1930s: Gender, Politics and History* (Edinburgh: Edinburgh University Press, 1999); Judy Suh, *Fascism and Anti-Fascism in Twentieth-Century British Fiction* (New York: Palgrave Macmillan, 2009). Other important studies include these: Janet Montefiore, *Men and Women Writers of the 1930s: The Dangerous Flood of History* (London: Routledge, 1996); Karen Schneider, *Loving Arms: British Women Writing the Second World War* (Lexington: University Press of Kentucky, 1997); Elaine Martin, ed., *Gender, Patriarchy, and Fascism in the Third Reich: The Response of Women Writers* (Detroit: Wayne State University Press, 1993).

3. For more on British fascism, see Tony Kushner and Nadia Valman, eds., *Remembering Cable Street: Fascism and Anti-Fascism in British Society* (London: Valentine Mitchell, 2000); Martin Pugh, *Hurrah for the Blackshirts!* (London: Cape, 2005); and Richard Thurlow, *Fascism in Britain: From Oswald Mosley's Blackshirts to the National Front* (New York: Palgrave Macmillan, 1998).

4. In the past few decades, studies that explore the appeal of fascism — including those by Alice Yaeger Kaplan, Russell Berman, George Mosse, Zygmunt Bauman, Saul Friedländer, Slavoj Žižek, Dagmar Herzog, Renate Bridenthal, Atina Grossman, Marion Kaplan, and the many other scholars I discuss in the following chapters — challenge and complicate the idea that German citizens were mesmerized masses that could be easily controlled by Hitler. The studies instead offer theories that point to the participation, voluntary choice, and even pleasure that many Germans derived from their participation in Nazism, as well as the historical and cultural contexts that paved the way for so many individuals to choose to ignore or even to participate in persecution in service of the greater nationalist vision of the Nazi Party.

5. In this manner they distinguish themselves from other antifascist modernist writ-

ers of the period such as Naomi Mitchison, Storm Jameson, Phyllis Bottome, Rebecca West, and George Orwell.

6. Greenberg's famous essay was first published in the *Partisan Review* in 1939 as a political response to Nazi suppression of modernist and avant-garde art as well as a comment on capitalist consumer culture. In more recent years, kitsch has become associated with postmodernism and "camp" sensibility, which may be interpreted as a self-conscious mode of social critique. For more on kitsch and camp sensibility, see chapter 4.

7. For an especially lucid summary of the variety of approaches to avant-garde aesthetics, fascism, and the political Left and Right, see Erin Carlston, *Thinking Fascism: Sapphic Modernism and Fascist Modernity* (Stanford, Calif.: Stanford University Press, 1998), 8–9. See also Judy Suh's enlightening study on "middlebrow" fiction in relation to British fascist and antifascist movements.

8. Philip Rahv's review, "The Taste of Nothing," appeared in *The New Masses* (May 4, 1937): "It is not the doom of a world reeling to its destruction that Miss Barnes expresses, but those minute shudders of decadence developed in certain small in-grown cliques of intellectuals and their patrons, cliques in which the reciprocal workings of social decay and sexual perversion have destroyed all response to genuine values and actual things." See Carlston, *Thinking Fascism*, 56, for her reference to Rahv.

9. In *Christopher and His Kind*, Isherwood mentions that when he and Stephen Spender saw *Kameradshaft*, a film about trapped coalminers in 1932, he had thought, "'That makes Virginia Woolf look pretty silly.' Stephen replied that he had been thinking something similar, though not specifically about Virginia" (*CHK*, 90). Woolf, for her part, refers to the writing of Isherwood and his contemporaries (W. H. Auden, C. Day Lewis, Spender, Louis MacNeice)—whom she calls "leaning tower writers"—as "betwixt and between," exhibiting "discomfort" and "self-pity for that discomfort" and "anger . . . against society" (*M*, 115).

10. The extensive canon of criticism on Woolf requires me to name but a few of the many scholars who examine Woolf and fascism, among them Jane Marcus, David Bradshaw, Mark Hussey, Alex Zwerdling, Michele Pridmore-Brown, Natania Rosenfeld, Bonnie Kime Scott, Anna Snaith, Maren Linett, Phyllis Lassner, Erin Carlston, Laura Frost, and Judy Suh.

11. See Merry Pawlowski, ed., *Virginia Woolf and Fascism: Resisting the Dictator's Seduction* (New York: Palgrave, 2001), 6–7, for more on Woolf and propaganda. In his study *Modernism, Media, and Propaganda* (Princeton, N.J.: Princeton University Press, 2012), Mark Wollaeger also draws attention to the ways in which British modern writers engage with and resist modern propaganda. Although Wollaeger does not focus on *Between the Acts* specifically, he highlights Woolf's attention to, and ambivalence toward, propaganda from *The Voyage Out* (1915) to her later works. As he notes, Woolf "was inclined to view modernism as the antithesis of propaganda" but also recognized that modern art and propaganda are "complexly entwined" (Wollaeger, *Modernism, Media, and Propaganda*, 71).

12. Some recent critics who analyze *Nightwood*'s politics since Mary Lynn Broe's *Silence and Power: A Reevaluation of Djuna Barnes* (Carbondale: Southern Illinois University Press, 1991) are Jane Marcus, Cheryl Plumb, Erin Carlston, Donna Gerstenberger, Laura Winkiel, Bonne Kime Scott, Susan Hubert, Karen Kaivola, and Diane Warren (among others).

13. Woolf's 1938 diary entry, "Jews persecuted, only just over the channel" (D, 5: 189), and specific references to racial laws and violence against Jews in Isherwood's *Goodbye to Berlin*, show evidence that these writers were well aware of the implications of antisemitism in Nazi Germany.

14. See Hannah Arendt, Zygmunt Bauman, Susan Sontag, Russell Berman, Alice Yaeger Kaplan, and Vivian Patraka, among others, as examples of studies that have made such an assumption commonplace.

## Chapter 1

1. In the quotation, Wim Wenders is referring to contemporary German filmmakers and their (perhaps well-justified) distrust in images, as well as their misgivings toward their national stories and myths.

2. See, among others, Saul Friedländer, Zygmunt Bauman, Alice Yaeger Kaplan, Eric Rentschler, Linda Schulte-Sasse, Mary-Elizabeth O'Brian.

3. Andrew Hussey more specifically relates Nietzsche's concept of the "spectator" and "second spectator" to Guy Debord's situationist philosophy as outlined in his well-known 1967 work *The Society of the Spectacle*. See Andrew Hussey, *The Game of War: The Life and Death of Guy Debord* (London: Cape, 2001), 189–90.

4. Some of the well-known, politically active British writers included George Orwell, E. M. Forster, Phyllis Bottome, Harold Nicolson, Stevie Smith, W. H. Auden, Stephen Spender, Naomi Mitchison, C. Day Lewis, Louis MacNeice, Dorothy Sayers, and Storm Jameson (to name but a few). For an overview, see Valentine Cunningham, *British Writers of the Thirties* (Oxford: Oxford University Press, 1988); Maroula Joannou, ed., *Women Writers of the 1930s*; Janet Montefiore, *Men and Women Writers of the 1930s*; Gill Plain, *Women's Fiction of the Second World War*; Keith Williams and Steven Matthews, eds., *Rewriting the Thirties: Modernism and After*; Phyllis Lassner, *British Women Writers of World War II*; and Judy Suh, *Fascism and Anti-Fascism in Twentieth-Century British Fiction*. Notable American writers such as Dorothy Parker, John Steinbeck, and other prominent figures affiliated with the antifascist, left-leaning League of American Writers (established in 1935) were active in resisting fascism and Nazism and endorsed a clear statement against antisemitism in 1939. At its peak, the league had more than eight hundred members, including Ernest Hemingway, Theodore Dreiser, Thomas Mann, Nathanael West, Lillian Hellman, William Carlos Williams, and Langston Hughes. It was dissolved in January 1943. See Franklin Folsom, *Days of Anger, Days of Hope: A Memoir of the League of American Writers, 1937–1942* (Niwot: University Press of Colorado, 1994), which includes a list of members; and Judy Kutulas, "Becoming 'More Liberal': The League of American Writers, the Communist Party, and the Literary People's Front," *The Journal of American Culture* 13, no. 1 (1990): 71–80.

5. Woolf's notebooks indicate she read Freud's *Group Psychology and the Analysis of the Ego* in 1939. Brenda Silver specifies that Woolf recorded her reading as "Freud on Groups" on December 2 and 18, 1939 (*Virginia Woolf's Reading Notebooks*, ed. Brenda Silver [Princeton, N.J.: Princeton University Press, 1983], 115).

6. This menacing aspect of the culture industry is distilled even further in Adorno's 1967 essay "The Culture Industry Reconsidered," in *Critical Theory and Society: A Reader*, eds. Stephen Eric Bronner and Douglas MacKay Kellner, trans. Anson Rabinbach (New York: Routledge, 1989), 128–35. Referencing the United States rather

than fascist Europe, Adorno maintains that mass culture "intentionally integrates its consumers from above" and "cheats them out of the same happiness which it deceitfully projects" (Adorno, "The Culture Industry Reconsidered," 128, 134). This type of "mass deception" is thus "turned into a means for fettering consciousness," as Adorno claims: "It impedes the development of autonomous, independent individuals who judge and decide consciously for themselves" (134–35).

7. See Miriam Hansen's assessment "Benjamin and Cinema: Not a One-Way Street," in *Benjamin's Ghosts: Interventions in Contemporary Literary and Cultural Theory*, ed. Gerhard Richter (Stanford, Calif.: Stanford University Press, 2002), 41–73. Hansen bases a portion of her argument on Susan Buck-Morss's concept of "aesthetics and anaesthetics," which she identifies as the key to understanding Benjamin's "Work of Art" essay. As Hansen posits, for Benjamin the welcome decay of the "aura" has the potential to promote a future that allows the masses a voice and opinion, yet, in "On Some Motifs on Baudelaire" (1938–39), written closer to the rise of National Socialism and World War II, Benjamin's attitude toward the revolutionary potential of technology and media changes slightly. As Hansen convincingly makes the case, when Nazism becomes more of a threat, Benjamin "laments the decline of experience synonymous with 'the disintegration of the aura in the experience of shock.'" See Hansen, "Benjamin and Cinema," 44–47; and Susan Buck-Morss, "'Aesthetics and Anaesthetics': Walter Benjamin's Artwork Essay Reconsidered," *October* (1992): 3–41.

8. See, for example, Eric Rentschler, *Ministry of Illusion: Nazi Cinema and Its Afterlife* (Cambridge, Mass.: Harvard University Press, 1996); Terri J. Gordon, "Fascism and the Female Form: Performance Art in the Third Reich," in *Sexuality and German Fascism*, ed. Dagmar Herzog (New York: Berghahn, 2005), 164–200; Sabine Hake, *Popular Cinema of the Third Reich* (Austin: University of Texas Press, 2000); Mary-Elizabeth O'Brian, *Nazi Cinema as Enchantment: The Politics of Entertainment in the Third Reich* (Rochester, N.Y.: Camden House, 2004); Thomas Elsaesser, *Weimar Cinema and After: Germany's Historical Imaginary* (New York: Routledge, 2000); and Jo Fox, *Film Propaganda in Britain and Nazi Germany: World War II Cinema* (New York: Berg, 2007).

9. The idea that World War II was "a spectacle founded in the imagination of moviegoers" is reiterated in Hans-Jürgen Syberberg's eight-hour film and book entitled *Hitler: A Film Made in Germany* (*Hitler, ein Film aus Deutschland*), which more bluntly names the film phenomenon in Germany. As Syberberg maintains, Hitler was a type of filmmaker, and his grand project was Germany in the Second World War. Syberberg's film was actually entitled *Our Hitler* when it played in Germany, implying that every German was responsible for Hitler, and the only way to exorcise the collective guilt was to take a close and long look at what happened.

10. In September 1933, the National Chamber of Culture was also established, which set out "The Law for Author Leaders" (October 4, 1933) and the "Theatre Law" (May 15, 1934) to make sure that cultural leaders would "merge together the creative elements from all fields for carrying out, under the leadership of the state, a single will. . . ." (qtd. and trans. Robert A. Brady, *The Spirit and Structure of German Fascism* [New York: Viking, 1937], 84–85).

11. Kaplan, for example, asserts that the Nazi spectacle provided pleasure in the rewarding feelings of a fantasy of cohesion. Fascism (or, more specifically, Nazism) was truly "utopian" since it allowed individuals to lose themselves in the collective,

thereby giving the impression of being "not in one place" and at the same time "everywhere" (Alice Yaeger Kaplan, *Reproductions of Banality: Fascism, Literature, and French Intellectual Life* [Minneapolis: University of Minnesota Press, 1986], 35). In this manner, the Nazi spectacle served a double function—it provided a mirror in which spectators could see an image of themselves in an ideal form; and at the same time, it was a vehicle through which they could be seen.

12. Especially for Virginia Woolf, as Melba Cuddy-Keane points out, better access to media and a broader public sphere could proscribe new, more democratic subject positions for members of society previously excluded from "highbrow" cultural circles. See Melba Cuddy-Keane, *Virginia Woolf, the Intellectual, and the Public Sphere* (Cambridge: Cambridge University Press, 2003), 8, and especially chapter 1, "Democratic Highbrow: Woolf and the Classless Intellectual," 13–58.

13. This would change in the United States with the 1938 establishment of the House Committee on Un-American Activities (HCUA). Also known as the "Dies Committee" (after chairman Martin Dies Jr.), it became permanent in 1947. One of its main aims was to investigate Communist activity in America, and as such it became responsible for the infamous Hollywood blacklist (especially active in the forties and fifties), which boycotted screenwriters and other members of the film industry suspected of involvement with the Communist Party. The list included writers such as Lillian Hellman and Richard Wright who had been prominent in supporting anti-Nazi causes before the war. The HCUA was abolished in 1975.

14. The BBC, too, came under criticism by the working class and writers on the Left, who dubbed it the BFC, "British Falsehood Company." See Keith Williams, *British Writers and the Media, 1930–1945* (London: Macmillan, 1996); Brigitte Granzow, *A Mirror of Nazism: British Opinion and the Emergence of Hitler 1929–1933* (London: V. Gollancz, 1964); and Karin Westman, "'For her generation the newspaper was a book': Media, Mediation, and Oscillation in Virginia Woolf's *Between the Acts*," *Journal of Modern Literature* 29, no. 2 (2006): 1–18.

15. See Suh, *Fascism and Anti-Fascism*, 2–3. See also Pugh, *Hurrah for the Blackshirts!* and Thurlow, *Fascism in Britain*.

16. Woolf refers to the young writers of the thirties (W. H. Auden, C. Day Lewis, Stephen Spender, Christopher Isherwood, and Louis MacNeice) as "leaning-tower writers" because they belonged to ivory towers of education and middle-class privilege that were "no longer steady" and "were being thrown to the ground" as the writers realized that the foundation of that society was built on tyranny (*M*, 114).

17. To elucidate her point, Woolf uses the example of the German film *The Cabinet of Dr. Caligari* (*Das Kabinett des Dr Caligari*, 1919), which debuted in London in 1924. The film melds perceptions of the real and the imaginary by depicting the viewpoint of a mad doctor. Notably, it was denigrated by the Nazis for being too open to irrational forces. As Eric Rentschler contends, "Nazi cinema . . . shunned the extremes of Weimar's haunted screens . . . assuming a middle ground of historical period pieces, costume dramas, musical revues, light comedies, melodramas, and petty-bourgeois fantasies" (Rentschler, *Ministry of Illusion*, 216)—precisely the kind of films Woolf calls "parasites" (*E*, 4: 350).

18. The similarity of this concept to Walter Benjamin's observations in his "Work of Art" essay reveals how parallel notions entered into various cultural contexts of the period. As Benjamin notes, "even the most perfect reproduction of a work of art is

lacking in one element: its presence in time and space" (Benjamin, *Illuminations,* ed. Hannah Arendt, trans. Harry Zohn [New York: Schocken, 1969], 220). For other comparisons between Woolf and Benjamin, see Pamela Caughie, ed., *Virginia Woolf in the Age of Mechanical Reproduction* (New York: Garland, 2000). Recent critics have also noted the influences of film, photography, and other media on Woolf, who used photographs strategically in a number of her texts. See, for example, Brenda Silver, *Virginia Woolf Icon* (Chicago: University of Chicago Press, 1999); Diane Gillespie, "'Her Kodack Pointed at His Head': Virginia Woolf and Photography," in *The Multiple Muses of Virginia Woolf,* ed. Gillespie (Columbia: University of Missouri Press, 1993), 113–47; Helen Wussow, "Virginia Woolf and the Problematic Nature of the Photographic Image," *Twentieth-Century Literature* 40, no. 1 (1994): 1–14; Wussow, "Travesties of Excellence: Julia Margaret Cameron, Lytton Strachey, Virginia Woolf, and the Photographic Image," in *Virginia Woolf and the Arts,* eds. Diane Gillespie and Leslie Hankins (New York: Pace University Press, 1997), 48–56; Maggie Humm, *Modernist Women and Visual Culture: Virginia Woolf, Vanessa Bell, Photography, and Cinema* (New York: Rutgers University Press, 2003); and Emily Dalgarno, *Virginia Woolf and the Visible World* (Cambridge: Cambridge University Press, 2001).

19. In "Are Films Worth While?," the conclusion to *Footnotes to the Film,* Charles Davy claims that Woolf's method of writing could be directly translated into film: "The scenes she evokes are scattered through space and time: her total picture is of something which does not and cannot exist as an entity in the physical world. . . . It is from precisely similar selective approach to nature . . . that the cinema derives its own creative power." See Charles Davy, ed., *Footnotes to the Film* (London: Lovat Dickson/ Readers' Union, 1938), 286.

20. As Ian Kershaw contends, British propaganda built itself "upon the general acceptance of a just and necessary war in defence of existing values and one which, with all its setbacks, could be viewed with increasing optimism" as opposed to German propaganda which "set itself the task of educating the German people for a new society based upon a drastically restructured value system." See Ian Kershaw, "How Effective Was Nazi Propaganda?" in *Nazi Propaganda: The Power and the Limitations,* ed. David Welch (London: Croom Helm, 1983), 181–82.

21. Some examples of popular American films that dealt with Europe's positioning of Jewish Others, albeit in coded terms, included *The Life of Emile Zola* (1937), *Black Legion* (1937), *The Adventures of Robin Hood* (1938), and MGM's 1940 blockbuster *The Mortal Storm* (based on Phyllis Bottome's 1937 anti-Nazi novel). *Confessions of a Nazi Spy,* produced by Warner Bros. in 1939, was the first openly anti-Nazi film. For an example of the controversy around anti-Nazi films, see Alexis Pogorelskin, "Phyllis Bottome's *The Mortal Storm*: Film and Controversy," *The Space Between* 4, no. 1 (2010): 39–57.

22. See chapter 4 for a more detailed discussion on books and censorship in England.

23. Information on which films were censored and the comments that accompanied them appear in the British Film Institute (BFI) Special Collections, British Board of Film Censors (BBFC) Scenario Reports, 1938 and 1939. They are quoted in more detail in Jeffrey Richards, "The British Board of Film Censors and Content Control in the 1930s: Foreign Affairs," *Historical Journal of Film, Radio, and Television* 2, no. 1 (1982): 40. It is important to note, however, that American cinema in what is known as "The Golden Age of Hollywood" (1920s–50s) was extremely popular in both Germany

and England and had its own methods of censorship, such as the 1930 Motion Picture Production Code (1930–67; also known as the "Hays Code"). See Gregory Black, *Hollywood Censored: Morality Codes, Catholics, and the Movies* (Cambridge: Cambridge University Press, 1994).

24. The few exceptions are films that coded their anti-Nazi message, such as Leslie Howard's 1940 film *Pimpernel Smith*, about the rescue of artists and intellectuals from Nazi Germany. The film implies that those rescued are Jews, although it does not name them explicitly as such. See Estel Eforgan's biography *Leslie Howard: The Lost Actor* (Middlesex, U.K.: Vallentine Mitchell, 2010). In addition, Alfred Hitchcock's *The Lady Vanishes* (1938) is often recognized as an anti-Nazi film, even if the villains are not labeled as Nazis.

25. Woolf here alludes to Matthew Arnold's "Stanzas from the Grand Chartreuse," in which the speaker declares that he (and his society) are "Wandering between two worlds, one dead / The other powerless to be born" (lines 85–86). See *The Poems of Matthew Arnold*, ed. Kenneth Allot (London: Longmans, 1965), 288.

26. Mikhail Bakhtin, in "Discourse in the Novel," conceives of language "not as a system of abstract grammatical categories, but rather language conceived as ideologically saturated, language as a world view, even as a concrete opinion" (Mikhail Bakhtin, "Discourse in the Novel," in *The Dialogic Imagination: Four Essays*, ed. Michael Holquist, trans. Caryl Emerson and Michael Holquist [Austin: University of Texas Press, 1981], 271). This view of language is especially valuable in analyzing experimental novels that resist conventional use of language and plot.

27. Jane Marcus, Mark Hussey, Bonnie Kime Scott, Merry Pawlowski, Alex Zwerdling, Michele Pridmore-Brown, Natania Rosenfeld, Karen Schneider, Anna Snaith, Melba Cuddy-Keane, and Phyllis Lassner, among many others, interpret *Between the Acts* as a critique of the political atmosphere in Europe.

28. Edith Craig (Edy), daughter of Ellen Terry, was an actress, producer, and director of theater productions, as well as a friend of Virginia Woolf's. Critics such as Jane Marcus, Nina Auerbach, and Anna Snaith have remarked on the parallels between Craig and Miss La Trobe, especially in her dress (Craig smoked and often wore men's clothing or smocks in rehearsals), abrupt manner, and "bossy" directing methods. Woolf had reviewed Craig's production of *The Higher Court* with the Pioneer Players for the *New Statesman* in 1920 (Snaith, *Public and Private*, 150). For more on Edith Craig and *Between the Acts*, see Jane Marcus, "Some Sources for *Between the Acts*," in *Virginia Woolf Miscellany* 6 (1977): 1–3; and Snaith, *Public and Private*, 150–51.

29. One cannot help but notice the echoes of Walter Benjamin's description of the allure of fascism in this description of the pageant: "Fascism sees its salvation in giving these masses not their right, but instead a chance to express themselves" (Benjamin, *Illuminations*, 241).

30. According to Hutcheon, novels that practice "repetition with critical distance" challenge the structures of conventions from within. More important for this reading of Woolf is Hutcheon's insistence that this kind of parodic strategy "uses its historical memory, its aesthetic introversion, to signal that this kind of self-reflexive discourse is always inextricably bound to social discourse." In this way, as a form of resistance writing, parody can involve both artist and audience. See Linda Hutcheon, *The Politics of Postmodernism* (New York: Routledge, 1989), 26, 35, and her chapter on "The Politics of Parody," 95–117.

31. Snaith asserts that "The terms 'public' and 'private' were useful to Woolf and are useful in reading her, as they speak to so many concerns which were foremost in her mind" (*Public and Private*, 11). These concerns include the "movement between public and private matters, between writing and war, between privacy and the bombardment of public media" (138). For more on issues of public and private realms in Woolf's diaries in the 1930s, see ibid., especially 138–42.

32. Leonard Woolf's 1935 study of fascist ideology, *Quack, Quack!*, also examines the nature and tropes of propaganda, suggesting that propaganda has its basis in "savage instincts" and that Hitler's racial message and political practices are based in the psychology of the "savage" and "primitive mind" (Leonard Woolf, *Quack Quack!* [London: Hogarth, 1935], 84–85).

33. See chapter 3 for a further discussion on Wells's *Outline of History* in connection with Ralph Manresa and Wells's theory of Semitic origins and mercantilism.

34. See Storm Jameson's edited volume of essays, *A Challenge to Death* (London: Constable, 1934), as an example of then-current debates on issues of nationalism and internationalism. Contributors included well-known English writers such as Jameson, Vera Britain, Rebecca West, and Julian Huxley.

35. While living in London, Aldous Huxley associated with Lytton Strachey, John Maynard Keynes, and others in the Bloomsbury circle and was a personal friend of the Woolfs. By the time he wrote the essays in *The Olive Tree*, Huxley was fervently committed to pacifism, and by 1938 he had already moved with his wife to California to embrace Hindu Vedantism (as did Christopher Isherwood). *Oxford Dictionary of National Biography*.

36. For a more detailed analysis of *The Times* and its role in Woolf's work, see Karin Westman, "For her generation the newspaper was a book."

37. Critics such as Gillian Beer, Anna Snaith, and Karin Westman have noted that the rape occurred in April 1938 and was reported in *The Times* in a series of articles in June and July 1938 that Woolf's readers would have been familiar with. See Gillian Beer, *Virginia Woolf: The Common Ground* (Edinburgh: Edinburgh University Press, 1996), 138–39; Snaith, *Public and Private*, 143; and Westman, "For her generation the newspaper was a book," 7–8.

38. See also Natania Rosenfeld, "Monstrous Conjugations: Images of Dictatorship in the Anti-Fascist Writings of Virginia and Leonard Woolf," in *Virginia Woolf and Fascism*, ed. Pawlowski, 122–36, for a similar take on Woolf's change of attitude in relation to using force against Nazism.

39. Considering that *I Am a Camera* and *Cabaret*, the 1951 stage and 1972 film adaptations of the "Sally Bowles" sequence, became immensely popular forms of mass entertainment, one wonders if perhaps Isherwood anticipated his role as a creator of illusions and self-consciously examined the position of the author in that context.

40. Lisa Schwerdt provides an extensive overview of the different critics' responses to the "I am a camera" line in *Isherwood's Fiction: The Self and Technique* (London: Macmillan, 1989), 80–82. Virtually no critic has failed to comment on this famous quotation.

41. For more on Eugène Atget and examples of his photography, see Hans Christian Adam, ed., *Eugène Atget's Paris* (Köln, Germany: Taschen, 2001).

42. I would concur with Katherine Bucknell, who claims that Isherwood's use of his own name as narrator "highlights for his reader the implied view that the storyteller is

never entirely objective," in her essay "Why Christopher Isherwood Stopped Writing Fiction," in *On Modern Fiction*, ed. Zachary Leader (Oxford: Oxford University Press, 2002), 130.

43. Compare Samuel Hynes's claim, "The narrator is to be, not the photographer . . . but the camera, the photographic mechanism itself. The vision of the camera eye is a symbol of isolation," in *The Auden Generation: Literature and Politics in England in the 1930s* (Princeton, N.J.: Princeton University Press, 1972), 356. Hynes also maintains that the narrator is "the lonely, passive voyeur who desires love" (*The Auden Generation*, 357).

44. The resort, with space for 20,000 vacationers, was never completed. Construction slowed in 1939, when Germany invaded Poland, and the project was abandoned due to the expense of war. A section was used as a military convalescent home by East Germany, but after reunification it stood empty. In 2008 plans to rebuild it as a resort were underway. For the controversy surrounding the current rebuilding of the resort, see Tristana Moore, "Holiday Camp with a Nazi Past," *BBC News Europe*, posted December 13, 2008, http://news.bbc.co.uk/2/hi/7777866.stm; and Allan Hall, "Mein Summer Camp: How Hitler Wanted Nazis to Become the World's Largest Tour Operator with Butlins-Style Holiday Resorts," *Mail Online*, posted April 28, 2011, http://www.dailymail.co.uk/news/article-1381124/Mein-summer-camp-How-Adolf-Hitler-wanted-Nazi-Butlins-style-holiday-resorts.html.

45. For the full version of the poem, see W. H. Auden and Louis MacNeice, *Letters from Iceland* (London: Faber and Faber, 1937), 223–27. The poem is quoted to a greater extent and analyzed in terms of 1930s writers and the media in Williams, *British Writers*, 127.

46. In his 1933 letter to Spender, Isherwood unknowingly anticipates the role Charlie Chaplin would play in *The Great Dictator*. Released in 1940, Chaplin's film vehemently satirizes Hitler and the Nazis, entreating its audience to recognize the dangers of National Socialism.

47. Bob Fosse's film version of *Cabaret* earned a total of eight Oscars at the Academy Awards in 1972, including one for best director.

48. Linda Brengle's "Divine Decadence, Darling!: The Sixty-Year History of the Kit Kat Klub," *The Journal of Popular Culture* 34 (Fall 2000): 147–54, explores the metaphor of cabaret in Isherwood's *Goodbye to Berlin* and its subsequent adaptations. Brengle quotes Broadway director Hal Prince as attributing the prominence of cabaret metaphor in the stage adaptation of "Sally Bowles" to playwright Joe Masteroff, who envisioned "the life of the cabaret as metaphor for Germany" (qtd. in Brengle, "Divine Decadence, Darling!" 148).

49. The names of the bars, Lady Windermere and Salomé, are both titles of plays by Oscar Wilde. These and other allusions to Wilde and homosexual subtexts are scattered throughout the novel.

50. The unforgettable final image of a warped mirror in Fosse's film *Cabaret*, which reflects and morphs together the cabaret, its audience, and the swastika armbands of Sturmabteilung (SA) soldiers, epitomizes the merging of spectators, spectacle, and Nazism at the end of the novel. Fosse's image, indelibly etched into the minds of film viewers for the past thirty years, corresponds with the mirrors at the end of Woolf's pageant — a reminder that the audience, the viewers of the spectacle, are complicit in permitting Nazism to overtake Europe.

51. Jane Marcus's in-depth analysis of *Nightwood* as a political novel that functions as a critique of fascism and predicts the Holocaust has influenced numerous critics in the past decade and broken ground for analyses of the novel in its historical context. I agree with Marcus's view that *Nightwood* resists Nazi ideology, but I examine Barnes's text, and especially her ambiguous attitudes toward "Others," slightly more skeptically. See Marcus, "Laughing at Leviticus: *Nightwood* as Women's Circus Epic," in Broe, ed., *Silence and Power*, 221–50.

52. Donna Gerstenberger argues a similar point, stating that "the reader of *Nightwood* experiences O'Connor largely *as narrative*," in her essay "The Radical Narrative of Djuna Barnes's *Nightwood*," in *Breaking the Sequence: Women's Experimental Fiction*, Ellen Friedman and Miriam Fuchs, eds. (Princeton, N.J.: Princeton University Press, 1989), 136.

53. See Cheryl Plumb's introduction to *Nightwood: The Original Version and Related Drafts* (Normal, Ill.: Dalkey Archive Press, 1995), where she outlines the many interchanges among Barnes, Coleman, and Eliot with regard to O'Connor. Eliot did not find that O'Connor's conversation "flags," but he believed that the doctor "distorts the shape of the book" and "we don't want him to steal everything" (qtd. in Plumb, *Nightwood: The Original Version*, xiv). Emily Coleman thought the novel should focus more on unity and the "tragedy of Nora and Robin," and that not only O'Connor but also Felix distracted from the story (qtd. ibid., xviii). Barnes, it seems, stood her ground against both, suggesting that she had another idea in mind as to how the novel and these two characters would "disqualify" conventions.

54. Laura Winkiel provides an overview of Barnes's critique of public forms of entertainment, especially her interview of Arthur Voegtlin, artistic director of the Hippodrome in New York. By linking the Voegtlin interview with Barnes's use of the circus as a motif in *Nightwood*, Winkiel argues that Barnes suggests "a different kind of public culture" and "how that [modern] public had become homogenized," in "Circuses and Spectacles: Public Culture in *Nightwood*," *Journal of Modern Literature* 21, no. 1 (1997): 10.

55. Marc Blanchard goes on to specify the relationship between the tattooed subject and society: "Indeed, tattooing is not only properly a sign which denotes social distinction on the body or part of the body. It is also a sign of a sign: in addition to specifying differences of status and class, it has generally been variously interpreted in the West as illustrating the many facets of the social bond between individual and society, the self and the Other." See Blanchard, "Post-Bourgeois Tattoo: Reflections on Skin Writing in Late Capitalist Societies," in *Visualizing Theory: Selected Essays from V.A.R. 1990–1994*, ed. Lucien Taylor (New York: Routledge, 1994), 290. These themes clearly have significance for Barnes's work, in which the relationship among self, Other, and representation is consistently questioned.

## Chapter 2

1. A wide range of studies such as Nina Auerbach's *Woman and the Demon: The Life of a Victorian Myth* (Cambridge: Cambridge University Press, 1982); Sandra M. Gilbert and Susan Gubar's *The Madwoman in the Attic: The Woman Writer and the Nineteenth-Century Literary Imagination* (New Haven, Conn.: Yale University Press, 1979); Bram Dijkstra's *Idols of Perversity: Fantasies of Feminine Evil in Fin-de-Siècle Culture* (New York: Oxford University Press, 1986); Alice Jardine's *Gynesis: Configu-*

*rations of Woman and Modernity* (Ithaca, N.Y.: Cornell University Press, 1987); Eva Feder Kittay's "Woman as Metaphor," *Feminist Social Thought: A Reader,* ed. Diana Tietjens Meyers (New York: Routledge, 1997), 265–85; and Liz Connor's *The Spectacular Modern Woman: Feminine Visibility in the 1920s* (Bloomington: Indiana University Press, 2004) have traced how the female image was conceived, represented, mediated, and channeled in the nineteenth and twentieth centuries.

2. Suffrage was extended to women in Germany in 1919; in the United States in 1920; in the United Kingdom women older than 30 could vote by 1918, and in 1928 all women were granted the same right to vote as men; and in France, relatively later, the vote was extended in 1944. For more information on the suffrage movement in France, see Steven Hause and Anne Kenney, *Women's Suffrage and Social Politics in the French Third Republic* (Princeton, N.J.: Princeton University Press, 1984); for Germany, see Richard Evans, "German Social Democracy and Women's Suffrage 1891–1918," *Journal of Contemporary History* 15, no. 3 (1980): 533–57; for England, see Jane Purvis and Sandra Stanley Holton, eds., *Votes for Women* (London: Routledge, 2000); and for the United States, see Ellen Carol DuBois, *Woman Suffrage and Women's Rights* (New York: New York University Press, 1998).

3. See especially Dijkstra's introduction to *Idols of Perversity.* See also my discussion of both the possibilities and limitations of female representation further on in the chapter.

4. According to George Mosse, nationalism in Europe became linked to a Protestant idea of respectability and sexuality in the eighteenth and nineteenth centuries, articulated in terms of distinct "masculine" and "feminine" traits. The outcome of Nazi attitudes toward sexuality is simply an extension of what happens when a country tries to control the body and sexuality through what Mosse calls an "aesthetics of nationalism and respectability" in *Nationalism and Sexuality: Respectability and Abnormal Sexuality in Modern Europe* (New York: Fertig, 1985), 10. See also Mosse's exploration of women as national symbols in art (such as Marianne in Delacroix's famous 1835 painting, *Liberty Leading the People at the Barricades,* or Philipp Veit's 1835 *Germania*) in *Nationalism and Sexuality,* 90–100.

5. Alice Jardine traces the discourse of "the feminine, woman" to modernism's intrinsically "new and necessary modes of thinking, writing, speaking" (Jardine, *Gynesis,* 25). In this way, her theory is very similar to Susan Shapiro's concept of "the Jew" as trope in postmodern discourse in Shapiro's essay "Écriture Judaïque: Where Are the Jews in Western Discourse?" in *Displacements: Cultural Identities in Question,* ed. Angelika Bammer (Bloomington: Indiana University Press, 1994), especially 190–91. Jardine's analysis, however, is more closely connected with French poststructuralist thought and the crisis of the subject than the wider historical conditions of modernity in Europe and political crisis that I address.

6. In regard to women's new visibility and positioning within modernity, Liz Connor poses particularly intriguing questions: "Was the spectacle of the Modern Woman true to modern women? Or was it indeed the truth *of* modern women: Did spectacularization come to produce their identities as modern and as women?" I would concur with her response that it seems to be a little bit of both. Women were as much a part of their own construction — of making themselves visible — as they were objects of a fetishized spectacularization. The Modern Woman, as Connor convincingly argues, was defined by, but also self-identified *with,* her visibility. See Connor, *Spectacular Modern Woman,* 24–26.

7. In *The Crowd: A Study of the Popular Mind*, Gustave Le Bon notably remarks, "Among the special characteristics of crowds there are several — such as impulsiveness, irritability, incapacity to reason, the absence of judgment and of the critical spirit, the exaggeration of the sentiments, and others besides — which are almost always observed in beings belonging to inferior forms of evolution — in women, savages, and children, for instance." See *The Crowd* (London: T. Fisher Unwin, 1903), 40.

8. For Andreas Huyssen's analysis of the link between women and mass culture and its connotations for postmodernism and the feminist avant-garde, see *"After the Great Divide" in Modernism, Mass Culture, Postmodernism* (Bloomington: Indiana University Press, 1986), chapter 2, 44–62.

9. Theodor Adorno and Max Horkheimer compare women's passive and unthinking acceptance of male domination, "women adore the unmoved paranoiac," to the allure of fascist totalitarianism and nations' susceptibility to mass culture in *Dialectic of Enlightenment: Philosophical Fragments*, ed. Gunzelin Schmid Noerr, trans. Edmund Jephcott (Stanford, Calif.: Stanford University Press, 1987), 191. See also Laura Frost's commentary on the quotation in *Sex Drives: Fantasies of Fascism in Modernism* (Ithaca, N.Y.: Cornell University Press, 2002), 122.

10. See, for instance, Judy Suh's investigation of middlebrow fiction in *Fascism and Anti-Fascism*; Melba Cuddy-Keane's analysis of Woolf in *Virginia Woolf, the Intellectual*; and Phyllis Lassner's numerous works on modern female British writers and intellectuals, including *British Women Writers of World War II*.

11. The debasement of women in public space, Susan Buck-Morss points out, was clearly not obvious to Benjamin. In his work that refers to prostitution, the prostitute is a mute image: "As a dialectical image, [the whore] is 'seller and commodity in one.'" See Buck-Morss, *The Dialectics of Seeing: Benjamin and the Arcades Project* (Cambridge, Mass.: MIT Press, 1989); and Angelika Rauch, "The Trauerspiel of the Prostituted Body, or Woman as Allegory of Modernity," *Cultural Critique* 10 (1998): 77–88.

12. Such critics as Liz Connor, Patrice Petro, Adrian Bingham, and Laura Frost, among others, have challenged the division of spectatorship along sexual lines. See especially Connor's critique of Mulvey's theory in *Spectacular Modern Woman*, 34. Mulvey does address some of these problems in "Afterthoughts on 'Visual Pleasure and Narrative Cinema,'" inspired by King Vidor's *Duel in the Sun*, 1981, reprinted in Mulvey's *Visual and Other Pleasures* (Bloomington: Indiana University Press, 1989), 29–38.

13. A helpful overview and analysis of the various theories of female spectatorship is offered by Patrice Petro in *Joyless Streets: Women and Melodramatic Presentation in Weimar Germany* (Princeton, N.J.: Princeton University Press, 1989), 39–78, and Connor, *Spectacular Modern Woman*, especially 15–35. Their analyses of media images of men and women in popular culture in Europe during the interwar years convincingly illustrate that this era was a time of destabilizing identities — both masculine and feminine.

14. See Snaith, *Public and Private*, and Cuddy-Keane, *Virginia Woolf, the Intellectual*.

15. The term "Flapper" was first used in Britain in the early twentieth century to connote a young, somewhat reckless, woman or teenager. Both the 1920 film *The Flapper*, starring Olive Thomas, and F. Scott Fitzgerald in his collections of short stories *Flappers and Philosophers* (1920) and *Tales of the Jazz Age* (1922) popularized the term to allude to the wild postwar young woman who wore short skirts, smoked,

listened to jazz, and bobbed her hair. Although used with slightly different connotations, "Flapper" was a popular press catchword for the modern young women who challenged norms in both the United States and Britain.

16. The press, for instance, reported less on women's issues, fashion became more "feminine," and women were depicted in more traditional roles (Petro, *Joyless Streets*, 124; and Adrian Bingham, *Gender, Modernity, and the Popular Press in Inter-War Britain* [Oxford: Clarendon Press, 2004], 78). By examining the fashion layout of *Die Dame*, a popular German women's magazine, and other examples of photojournalism, Petro illustrates the mixed attitudes toward the Flapper and her androgynous clothing in Germany. Petro also demonstrates how fashion transformed from the twenties to the thirties as "female bisexuality was replaced by an excessive femininity in fashion" (*Joyless Streets*, 124, also 125, 131). According to Adrian Bingham's assessment, the "backlash" toward postwar "libertinism" was not as prominent in England. Arguing that the view of a conservative reaction to the postwar period is only one of many opinions, Bingham insists that although the British press reported women's issues less frequently, it was because women had already broken down so many barriers that emancipation was not as much an issue as it was in the twenties. As Bingham argues, it did not "seem like that there could be a return to older conventions of femininity." See Bingham, *Gender, Modernity*, 79–83.

17. See Klaus Theweleit, Gisela Bock, Atina Grossman, Dagmar Herzog, and the other scholars in *When Biology Became Destiny: Women in Weimar and Nazi Germany*, eds. Renate Bridenthal, Atina Grossman, and Marion Kaplan (New York: Monthly Review Press, 1984), who have revealed how closely linked conceptions of woman were to National Socialism's oppressive policies.

18. *Das Schwarze Korps* was free of charge and distributed to all members of the SS. The articles promoted "proper" Nazi family values while frequently castigating any group that threatened Nazi dominance, including Jews, Communists, Americans, the Catholic Church, emancipated or "Amazon" women, and homosexuals. It ran from 1935 to 1945. See William Combs, *Voice of the SS: A History of the SS Journal "Das Schwarze Korps"* (New York: Peter Lang, 1986).

19. See chapter 3 for a more detailed account of Weininger and conceptions of the "effeminate" Jewish male. See also Ritchie Robertson, "Historicizing Weininger: The Nineteenth-Century German Image of the Feminized Jew," in *Modernity, Culture, and "the Jew,"* Bryan Cheyette and Laura Marcus, eds. (Cambridge: Polity Press, 1998), 35–37; and Maren Linett, *Modernism, Feminism, and Jewishness* (Cambridge: Cambridge University Press, 2007), 6–8.

20. A label of lesbianism or promiscuity could also lead to a woman being deemed "asocial" and denied permission to get a "Mother's Cross" or to marry. In worst cases, these women were institutionalized or sent to labor camps, as Elizabeth D. Heineman notes in her essay "Sexuality and Nazism: The Doubly Unspeakable?" in Herzog, ed., *Sexuality and German Fascism*, 44.

21. According to Gisela Bock, post–World War I sterilization as a form of population control was considered to be a solution to numerous social problems: "shiftlessness, ignorance, and laziness in the workforce; deviant sexual behavior such as prostitution and illegitimate births; the increasing number of ill and insane; poverty; and the rising cost of social services" (Bock, "Racism and Sexism in Nazi Germany: Motherhood, Compulsory Sterilization, and the State," in Bridenthal, Grossman, and Kaplan, eds., *When*

*Biology Became Destiny*, 274). Recommendations for eugenic sterilization came from both Right and Left sides of the political spectrum as a way to control procreation effectively and also impose "proper" behavior on women and men so they would be seen as valuable members of society (Bock, "Racism and Sexism in Nazi Germany," 275).

22. Describing how Nazi sterilization policies from 1933 to 1939 were linked to racial policy—in what she calls *"racist sexism"*—Bock notes how mental health was judged in the same way as race. A schizophrenic episode—one's own, one's parent's, or even a grandmother's—similar to a Jewish bloodline, was categorized as a genetic defect that could only be prevented from contaminating the rest of society through sterilization (276).

23. In *Male Fantasies*, Klaus Theweleit specifically draws parallels between Nazi sexism and murderous aggression by relating the way in which women are represented in the diaries, letters, and memoirs of members of the *Freikorps* (the volunteer German army enlisted to fight Communist revolutionaries after World War I) to a misogynist pathology that would eventually lead to a will and desire to commit genocide. Theweleit's analysis suggests that the *Freikorps* members were motivated to create order by a fear of a "disorder" that was expressly feminine (and Communist). As Theweleit summarizes, "The men construct an image of a high-born woman ('white countess'). They then worship that image, which must be asexual. They persecute the sexuality of the low-born woman—proletarian, Communist, Jew (= whore)—by first making her a prostitute, then murdering her; meanwhile lack is maintained with their own (child-bearing and asexual) women through their exclusion (as nameless wives) from social productions and from the confraternities of men" (trans. Stephen Conway, 2 vols. [Minneapolis: University of Minnesota Press, 1987], 367).

24. As Claudia Koonz points out in her well-known study of German women during the Nazi period, *Mothers in the Fatherland: Women, the Family, and Nazi Politics* (New York: St. Martin's, 1987).

25. Those studies that claim that Nazism's attitudes toward women and sexuality were based only in an attempt to establish order, race purity, and respectability often assume that Nazism was inherently "sexually repressed," a notion that current German historians contest since it does not take into account the wider scope of fascist appeal. Although, as Elizabeth Heineman notes, "the regime was neither 'prosex' nor 'antisex,' the overall message was not that 'anything goes.' Rather, it was a coherent whole that simultaneously rejected Victorian prudery and the 'degenerate' sexuality associated with Weimar in favor of a 'clean' but distinctly sexual life" (Heineman, "Sexuality and Nazism," 32). For young women in German youth groups like the BDM (*Bund Deutscher Mädel*, or German League of Girls), for example, the Nazi Party provided adventure, excitement, freedom from parental authority, and even sexual freedom (Koonz, *Mothers*, 228). The league even made news when it was leaked to the press that 900 girls had become pregnant at the 1936 Nazi Party rally (Heineman, "Sexuality and Nazism," 29). Dagmar Herzog asserts that the tendency to link Nazism with a hostility toward sex, or to represent it in film and pop culture using lurid and salacious sadomasochistic tropes (Liliana Cavani's 1974 film *The Night Porter* being a prime example), makes it obvious that many fail to engage seriously with the important intricacies comprising German life under National Socialism (Herzog, ed., *Sexuality and German Fascism*, 1).

26. Alex Zwerdling, Natania Rosenfeld, and Phyllis Lassner, among others, all give examples of members of the Bloomsbury group and others who changed their pacifist

stance due to the specific circumstances of Nazism's antisemitic policies and their aggression toward political prisoners. These included Leonard Woolf, E. M. Forster, Duncan Grant, Storm Jameson, Rebecca West, Stevie Smith, and others. See Zwerdling, *Virginia Woolf and the Real World*, 288; Lassner, *British Women Writers*, 31; Rosenfeld, "Monstrous Conjugations," in *Virginia Woolf and Fascism*, ed. Pawlowski, 133–34.

27. La Trobe's character is often assumed to be inspired by actress and director Edith (Edy) Craig, who founded the Pioneer Players with her mother, Ellen Terry, and produced and acted in suffragist pageants. Woolf went to at least one of Edith Craig's plays, *The Higher Court*, and wrote about it in the *New Statesmen*. See chapter 1 for more on the pageant and its connection to Craig. See also Snaith, *Public and Private*, 148–52; and Marcus, "Some Sources for *Between the Acts*."

28. Gillian Beer, Bonnie Kime Scott, Karen Jacobs, Alex Zwerdling, Jane Marcus, to name but a few.

29. Georgia Johnston is one of the few critics who presents a thorough and comprehensive consideration of the complexity of Mrs. Manresa's character. In Johnston's estimation, Manresa's role is comparable to, and as crucial as, La Trobe's since they both draw attention to class politics and show how "ideologies of class and performance intersect" (66). See Johnston, "Class Performances in *Between the Acts*: Audiences for Miss La Trobe and Mrs. Manresa," *Woolf Studies Annual* 3 (1997): especially 62–65.

30. The account of the Jews of Manresa is in *The Jewish Encyclopaedia* (1901–6), widely available in London at the time. Considering Woolf's relatively unsympathetic portrayal of Jewish Ralph Manresa, and that her reading notebooks have no account of the encyclopedia entry, I doubt that Woolf would have read or considered this information. More on the connection between the Manresas and Woolf's attitude toward Jews is discussed in chapter 3.

31. For a discussion on Woolf's allusions to photographs of "ruined houses and dead bodies" in *Three Guineas* and the spectacle of the Spanish Civil War, see Dalgarno, *Virginia Woolf and the Visible World*, 149–78. Susan Sontag's "Looking at War: Photography's View of Devastation and Death" in *The New Yorker* (December 9, 2002), also refers to Woolf's use of these images in her essay on the spectacle of war and photography from the Spanish Civil War. See especially 82–84.

32. Mary Ann Doane analyzes how economic excess in films of the 1940s is linked to sexual desire or the "consumer vampire": "Economics and sexuality are inextricably linked in this algebra whereby a wartime economy of lack or scarcity is seriously threatened by excessive female sexuality" (Mary Ann Doane, *The Desire to Desire: The Woman's Film of the 1940s* [Bloomington: Indiana University Press, 1987], 81).

33. "The Angel in the House" is the title of a poem by Coventry Patmore (1823–96), an ode to his wife, Emily. Written in 1854 (rev. 1862), the poem depicts the ideally submissive and docile Victorian wife, describing her as meek, humble, compassionate, self-sacrificing, modest, and most importantly "pure." Woolf references Patmore's popular poem in "Professions for Women," blaming the Angel for impeding women's freedom of expression: "It was she who used to come between me and my paper when I was writing reviews. It was she who bothered me and wasted my time and so tormented me that at last I killed her" (*DM*, 150). Because the Angel inhibits women from having a mind of their own, Woolf insists, "Killing the Angel in the House was part of the occupation of a woman writer" (*DM*, 151).

34. While Woolf's notebooks reveal that she did read works with which Joan Riviere's theory was in dialogue, such as Freud and *The Psychology of the Sexes* by Cyril Burt (Silver, *Reading Notebooks,* 115, 283), there is no specific mention of Riviere's "Womanliness as Masquerade." I am indebted to Petro for her illuminating analysis and discussion of Riviere's essay, first published in *The International Journal of Psychoanalysis* 10 (1929), and reprinted in *Formations of Fantasy,* eds. Victor Burgin, James Donald, and Cora Kaplan. See Petro, *Joyless Streets,* 114–15.

35. See Eve Kosofsky Sedgwick's discussion of the nature/culture debate and the problems with notions that gender is a "cultural choice" in *Epistemology of the Closet* (Berkeley: University of California Press, 1990), 41–43. See also my analysis of parody and the performance of gender, especially "camp," in Isherwood and Barnes in chapter 4.

36. For more details, see Snaith, *Virginia Woolf,* 63–87.

37. Notably, biblical cities such as Jerusalem and Babylon are gendered, reflecting sexual ambivalence toward the virtuous (maternal Jerusalem) and the wicked (Babylon the "whore").

38. Harold George Nicolson (1886–1968) was a British diplomat, writer, and politician, married to the author and poet Vita Sackville-West (1892–1962). He was particularly active politically between the two world wars and acted as secretary to Eric Drummond, the first secretary-general of the League of Nations. Nicolson supported Sir Oswald Mosley's party in 1931 but withdrew support a year later when the British Union of Fascists was formed. He served as parliamentary secretary to the Ministry of Information under Winston Churchill's government and authored numerous books on European politics (*Oxford Dictionary of National Biography*). For an overview of his life between the two world wars, see Harold Nicolson's *Diaries and Letters, Vol. 1* (*1930–1939*), edited by his son Nigel Nicolson (London: Collins, 1966).

39. Petro's quotation is taken from the German version of Harold Nicolson's "The Charm of Berlin," *Der Querschnitt* (May 1929), originally published in English and reprinted in *Der Querschnitt: Das Magazin der aktuellen Ewigkeitswerte, 1924–1933* (Berlin: Ullstein Verlag, 1980), 261–63.

40. Carl Zuckmayer, *Als Wär's ein Stück von mir* (1966), reprinted in translation as *A Part of Myself.* The preceding work is quoted in Petro, *Joyless Streets,* 42.

41. For a more detailed description of the correlations between "camp" and Sally Bowles, see Mizejewski, *Divine Decadence: Fascism, Female Spectacle and the Makings of Sally Bowles* (Princeton, N.J.: Princeton University Press, 1992), 60–65, and her more recent article, "Camp Among the Swastikas: Isherwood, Sally Bowles, and 'Good Heter Stuff,'" in *Camp: Queer Aesthetics and the Performing Subject: A Reader,* ed. Fabio Cleto (Ann Arbor: University of Michigan Press, 1999), 237–53.

42. Mizejewski remarks that John Lehmann, who was responsible for publishing the story for the Woolfs' Hogarth Press, recalled he was "nervous whether our printers — in the climate of those days — would pass it" (qtd. "Camp Among the Swastikas," 242). Abortion in Great Britain had always been illegal, but more women had recently been reported dying from illegal abortion. Lehmann encouraged Isherwood to leave out the abortion sequence, to which Isherwood replied in 1937, "It seems to me that Sally, without the abortion sequence, would just be a silly little capricious bitch. Besides, what would the whole thing lead up to? And down from? The whole idea of the study is to show that even the greatest disaster leaves a person like Sally

essentially unchanged" (John Lehmann, *Christopher Isherwood: A Personal Memoir* [London: Weidenfeld and Nicolson, 1987], 28–29; Mizejewski, "Camp Among the Swastikas," 242).

43. Carlston aptly uses the term "matriotism" to describe the ideology of motherhood that "conceals gender inequality behind an idealization of maternity [that] harnesses women's (reproductive) labor in service of the State" (*Thinking Fascism*, 7).

44. This intersection of gender and race in the novel participates in a trend that has been well noted in studies such as Andrea Freud Lowenstein's *Loathsome Jews and Engulfing Women* (New York: New York University Press, 1993) and Maren Tova Linett's *Modernism, Feminism and Jewishness*. More detail on gender and Jews in *Goodbye to Berlin* will follow in chapter 3.

45. Diane Warren, in her overview of the critical context surrounding Barnes's works (1940s–present), lists some of the various critical opinions as to who is the "central character" of *Nightwood*. Among them, Warren cites Jane Marcus's "polycentric" view; T. S. Eliot's assertion that it is the doctor; biographically based opinions that it is Nora (Barnes's fictional double); and other readings that suggest that it is Felix. Robin, however, as Warren argues, "does occupy an emphasized structural position within the work." See Diane Warren, *Djuna Barnes' Consuming Fictions* (Aldershot, U.K.: Ashgate, 2007), 131, 1–24.

46. In the New Directions paperback, first published in 1961, cover design by Gilda Kuhlman.

47. The novel begins with Felix in Paris in 1920 and ends with Robin in the United States in 1927—just slightly following the period of the "vamp craze" in cinema.

48. Louise de Vallière (1644–1710) was a mistress of King Louis XIV of France from 1664. She was forced to remain in court as an official mistress to cover up Louis's affair with the married Marquise de Montespan. Vallière suffered years of humiliation until Louis granted her permission to retreat to a Carmelite convent in Paris in 1674, where she lived until her death. Catherine of Russia (1729–1796), also known as Catherine II or Catherine the Great, married the grandson of Peter the Great, but shortly after his accession to power she replaced him as ruler in a coup d'état with the support of the army and aristocratic society. Catherine was proclaimed Empress of Russia in 1762. Known for her liberal and "enlightened" views (despite supporting a system of serfdom for 95 percent of the Russian people), Catherine led the country to political and cultural greatness for 34 years. Madame de Maintenon (1635–1719), also known as Françoise Scarron, was the second wife of King Louis XIV of France. After loyally caring for Louis's illegitimate children by Montespan, Scarron married Louis XIV following the queen's death in 1683, and he remained devoted to her for thirty-two years. She encouraged piety at court and supported education for the poor. Catherine de Medici (1519–1589) married King Henry II of France (reigned 1547–59) and served as regent of France (1560–1574) following his death. Catherine gave birth to ten children, three of whom became kings of France for short periods. She struggled to reign through years of strife between religious factions in the Catholic-Huguenot wars. Anna Karenina is the tragic heroine of Leo Tolstoy's eponymous novel (1875–77) whose adulterous affair and consuming guilt upon abandoning her husband and child lead to her madness and eventual suicide. "Catherine Heathcliff" refers to Catherine Earnshaw, the main female character of Emily Brontë's *Wuthering Heights* (1846). Like Anna Karenina, Catherine feels passionate and all-consuming love that destroys

not only her and her childhood love, Heathcliff, but also devastates the lives of those around her.

49. Linda Schulte-Sasse bases her theory on Slavoj Žižek's *The Sublime Object of Ideology*. See Žižek, *Sublime Object* (London: Verso, 1989), 9–11.

## Chapter 3

1. *Der Stürmer* (The Stormer) was a weekly tabloid published between 1923 and 1945 by Julius Streicher. It contained some of the most virulent and obscene antisemitic accusations and caricatures geared to a wide circulation of mostly youth and working-class Germans. At the bottom of its title page was the motto, "*Die Juden sind unser Unglück!*" (The Jews are our misfortune!).

2. See Zygmunt Bauman's *Modernity and the Holocaust* (Ithaca, N.Y.: Cornell University Press, 1989), especially 39–40.

3. See Boaz Neumann's analysis of the importance of the German *Volkskörper* and the centrality of the body and politics in its worldview and in its attitude toward Jews in "Antisemitism and the 'Decline of Language,'" in *Varieties of Antisemitism: History, Ideology, Discourse*, eds. Murray Baumgarten, Peter Kenez, and Bruce Thompson (Newark, N.J.: University of Delaware Press, 2009), 60–68.

4. See David Biale's essay "Blood and the Discourses of Nazi Antisemitism," in Baumgarten et al., eds., *Varieties of Antisemitism*, 29–47, where Biale emphasizes the centrality of the rhetoric of blood and pollution in Nazi ideology and propaganda.

5. See Maren Linett's close readings of Jewish characters, where she more specifically examines how they are identified in terms of money, timelessness, and gender ambiguity, "sometimes a model for the author's art, and sometimes a foil against which her writing must be defined" (Linett, *Modernism, Feminism, and Jewishness*, 2).

6. See, for example, the special 2005 issue on Jewish modernism in *Modern Fiction Studies*, as well as Linett's *Modernism, Feminism, and Jewishness*; Phyllis Lassner and Lara Trubowitz, eds., *Antisemitism and Philosemitism in the Twentieth and Twenty-first Centuries: Representing Jews, Jewishness, and Modern Culture* (Newark, N.J.: University of Delaware Press, 2008); Lassner, *British Women Writers of World War II*; Esther Panitz, *The Alien in Their Midst: Images of Jews in English Literature* (Rutherford, N.J.: Fairleigh Dickinson University Press, 1981); Tony Kushner and Kenneth Lunn, eds., *Traditions of Intolerance: Historical Perspectives on Fascism and Race Discourse in Britain* (Manchester, U.K.: Manchester University Press, 1989); Bryan Cheyette, *Between "Race" and Culture: Representations of "the Jew" in English and American Literature* (Stanford, Calif.: Stanford University Press, 1996) and *Constructions of "the Jew" in English Literature and Society* (Cambridge: Cambridge University Press, 1993); Jonathan Freedman, *The Temple of Culture: Assimilation and Anti-Semitism in Literary Anglo-America* (New York: Oxford University Press, 2000); Jonathan Boyarin and Daniel Boyarin, eds., *Jews and Other Differences: The New Jewish Cultural Studies* (Minneapolis: University of Minnesota Press, 1997); Linda Nochlin and Tamar Garb, eds., *The Jew in the Text: Modernity and the Construction of Identity* (London: Thames and Hudson, 1995); and the myriad texts and articles on Jewish representation with regard to specific authors, such as Anthony Julius, *T. S. Eliot, Anti-Semitism, and Literary Form* (London: Thames and Hudson, 2003), and Leon Surette, *Pound in Purgatory: From Economic Radicalism to Anti-Semitism* (Chicago: University of Illinois Press, 1999), which have been published in the last fifteen years.

7. Semitic discourse is based on Bryan Cheyette's view that Jewish characters or

images are dependent upon their social contexts (as opposed to unhistoricized or de-politicized descriptions of antisemitic stereotypes in literature in general); "discourse" emphasizes the manner in which Jewish representation is ambivalent, unstable, contradictory, and nuanced rather than changeless and consistent. See especially Cheyette's introduction to *Between "Race" and Culture*, 1–15.

8. In her essay, Susan Shapiro uses the example of how "the Jew" functions in Jean-François Lyotard's *Heidegger and "the Jews."* Interestingly, her analysis is strikingly similar to Alice Jardine's observations on how "woman" functions in French theory to suggest a crisis of subjectivity in a process she names *gynesis.* See Susan Shapiro, "*Écriture Judaïque,*" in *Displacements*, ed. Angelika Bammer, chapter 2.

9. In other European countries, such as Germany and France, the flood of Jewish immigrants escaping persecution in the East in the first half of the century was prominent as well, creating a "space of difference." See Jay Geller, *On Freud's Jewish Body: Mitigating Circumstances* (New York: Fordham University Press, 2007), 7; Paula Hyman, *The Jews of Modern France* (Berkeley: University of California Press, 1998); and Amos Elon, *The Pity of It All: A Portrait of the German-Jewish Epoch 1743–1933* (New York: Picador, 2003).

10. The main purpose of the Aliens Act was to "stop the flow of East European Jews into Britain," as Tony Kushner notes in *The Persistence of Prejudice: Antisemitism in British Society During the Second World War* (Manchester, U.K.: Manchester University Press, 1989), 11. Under this legislation, 20,000 "aliens" were deported and 32,000 interned during World War I. More importantly for consideration in this study, "In the 1930s it would also be used against Jewish refugees from Nazi oppression" (Kushner, *Persistence of Prejudice,* 11).

11. These included Jewish involvement in Russian politics and Bolshevism, essays on Zionism, debates of establishing a Jewish homeland in Palestine (especially following the Balfour Declaration, signed in 1917), and articles on antisemitism and "the Jewish Question." See Linett, *Modernism,* 24–26.

12. The full-text edition was reviewed in *The Times* (March 24, 1939): 20; *The Times Literary Supplement* (March 25, 1939); *The Spectator* (March 24, 1939): 492; and *The Daily Telegraph* (March 23, 1939): 16. For other reviews, see James Barnes and Patience Barnes, *Hitler's "Mein Kampf" in Britain and America: A Publishing History 1930–39* (Cambridge: Cambridge University Press, 2008), 146 n. 17. Exact sales for the full-text English edition are not available since the royalty records were lost because of wartime bombing; sales are nevertheless estimated in the 150,000–200,000 range (Barnes and Barnes, *Hitler's "Mein Kampf" in Britain and America,* 68).

13. Kushner refers to a number of Mass Observation and opinion polls in 1939–42 that indicate that perceptions of Jews and refugees were linked with money and power: "In an opinion poll carried out in 1940, 38% of the comments on money-mindedness were connected to Jews. Exactly the same percentage of the sample saw Jews as predatory." The image of the refugees was also not as positive or sympathetic as one might think; it rather confirmed the "alien Jew stereotype." See Kushner, *Persistence of Prejudice,* 12, 112, 115.

14. See Susan Shapiro's analysis of Jean-François Lyotard's *Heidegger and "the Jews,"* in which she observes that the "Jew" is "figured as the *unheimlich,* the 'uncanny,' the 'un-homey'" (184). See also Lyotard, *Heidegger and "the Jews,"* trans. Andreas Michel and Mark Roberts (Minneapolis: University of Minnesota Press, 1988), 13, 17.

15. Antisemitism (*Antisemitismus*), a term coined by Wilhelm Marr in 1879 to re-

place "Jew hatred" (*Judenhetze* or *Judenhass*), marked the emergence of a scientific racial notion of Jews. See Jonathan Judaken, "Between Philosemitism and Antisemitism: The Frankfurt School's Anti-Antisemitism," in Lassner and Trubowitz, eds., *Antisemitism and Philosemitism*, 24; and the introduction to Baumgarten et al., eds., *Varieties of Antisemitism.*

16. For this reason, too, the spelling "antisemitism" rather than "anti-Semitism" has been used in recent scholarship to denote the lack of ethnic or cultural validity of the term "Semite."

17. For a broader overview on Jews, eugenics, immigration, and theories of Euroraces in the United States, see Karen Brodkin, *How Jews Became White Folks and What That Says About Race in America* (New Brunswick, N.J.: Rutgers University Press, 1998), especially 27–34. See also Lisa Marcus, "'May Jews Go to College?': Fictions of Jewishness in the 1920s," in *Antisemitism and Philosemitism*, eds. Lassner and Trubowitz, 138–53.

18. For example, Harvard University President Lawrence Lowell was known to oppose Jews at Harvard, and Columbia as well as Yale restricted admission of Jews, especially in the 1920s. See Jerome Karabel, *The Chosen: The Hidden History of Admission and Exclusion at Harvard, Yale, and Princeton* (Boston: Houghton Mifflin, 2005).

19. On the construction of Jewish "whiteness" in the United States, see also Michael Rogen, *Blackface, White Noise: Jewish Immigrants in the Hollywood Melting Pot* (Berkeley: University of California Press, 1996).

20. See Kushner's analysis of the ways in which images of the Jewish financier manifested itself in the popular British imagination in 1930s in *Persistence of Prejudice*, 106–13.

21. See Margaret Stetz's discussion of George du Maurier's *Trilby* and its film revision, "Esther Kahn: Antisemitism and Philosemitism at the Turns of Two Centuries," in *Antisemitism and Philosemitism*, eds. Lassner and Trubowitz, 119–37.

22. *Jud Süss*, an immensely popular film commissioned by Goebbels and directed by Veit Harlan in 1941, was based on German-Jewish Leon Feuchtwanger's 1925 novel about Joseph Süss Oppenheimer, a financial adviser to Duke Karl Alexander of Württemberg, who was executed in 1738 (guilty of transgressing a law prohibiting Jews from having sexual relations with gentiles). The German film is often thought to be a response to the 1934 British film *Jew Süss* (directed by Lothar Mendes), starring German actor Conrad Veidt, which openly condemned antisemitism and the persecution of Jews in Europe. The British 1934 version was banned in Vienna and did not play in England, where films that openly criticized Germany were censored because of appeasement policies.

23. Sander Gilman, Jean Radford, and Anne Pellegrini all discuss Weininger's popularity and influence on modernist writers. According to Radford, by 1922 the book had gone through twenty-four editions. She even claims that the three types of elements in Weininger's theory are models for Joyce's Stephen Dedalus (Male), Molly Bloom (Woman), and Leopold Bloom (Jew). See Radford, "The Woman and the Jew: Sex and Modernity," in Cheyette and Marcus, eds., *Modernity, Culture, and "the Jew*," 92; Gilman, *The Jew's Body*, 133–34; *Freud, Race, and Gender* (Princeton: Princeton University Press, 1995); and Pellegrini, "Whiteface Performances: 'Race,' Gender, and Jewish Bodies," in Boyarin and Boyarin, eds., *Jews and Other Differences*, 114. See also Ritchie Robertson, "Historicizing Weininger," in Cheyette and Marcus, eds., *Moder-*

*nity, Culture, and "the Jew,"* for a detailed analysis on the influence of Weininger on modern antisemitic and misogynist thinking; and Linett, *Modernism, Feminism, and Jewishness*, 6–8.

24. See chapter 2 for more on historical and cultural perceptions of female roles in nineteenth- and twentieth-century Western Europe.

25. As Phyllis Lassner has convincingly argued, "Even as some scholars are constructing a critical relationship to the modernist aesthetic . . . [t]he real Jew and Jewish culture, including Judaism as a religion, have not been considered in their expression as Jewish voices. . . . Jewishness constructed by Jews has not been claimed as a provenance of modernist critical practice except by scholars of Jewish modernism." See Lassner's chapter "The Necessary Jew" in Baumgarten et al., eds., *Varieties of Antisemitism*, 306. My reading attempts to fill this significant lacuna.

26. Compare, for example, readings of the Jew as a function of Barnesian aesthetics, such as Mairéad Hanrahan, Karen Kaivola, Lara Trubowitz, and Maren Linett to the way Lassner focuses on the need to include the historical context of antisemitism in "The Necessary Jew."

27. Possibly, Barnes is basing her racial conception of Jews on nineteenth-century American race designations quantifying the "impure" presence of "Negro blood" in a person of mixed race: mulatto (one nonwhite parent); quadroon (one nonwhite grandparent); and octoroon (one nonwhite great-grandparent). These categories were used to establish racial segregation based on the concept that anyone with African ancestry would be classified as black (also known as the "one-drop rule").

28. Mairéad Hanrahan similarly argues that the opening scene of the novel can even be read as "a parody of the opening of the Book of Genesis" in "Djuna Barnes's *Nightwood*: The Cruci-Fiction of the Jew," *Paragraph* 24, no. 1 (2001): 34.

29. See also Lara Trubowitz, "In Search of 'the Jew' in Djuna Barnes's *Nightwood*: Jewishness, Antisemitism, Structure, and Style," *Modern Fiction Studies* 51, no. 2 (Summer 2005): 320–21, for Trubowitz's interpretation of Felix's "Wandering Jew" traits.

30. As Mairéad Hanrahan points out, Barnes fails "to provide him with a distinct identity . . . [E]ven his Otherness does not belong to him" (Hanrahan, "Djuna Barnes's *Nightwood*," 32–33) Trubowitz proposes that *Nightwood's* representation of Jews in effect "erases the actual histories of Jews from which such traits are drawn" ("In Search of 'the Jew,'" 312). Both these critics draw attention to the important ways that Barnes erases the Jew's particularity in service of her narrative as a universal symbol. I have attempted to also draw attention to the aspects of that particularity that are left out.

31. The depiction of Guido Volkbein uncannily resembles the 1921 caricature of the Jewish art critic in *Kikeriki*, an antisemitic Viennese magazine depicted in Sander Gilman's *The Jew's Body*, 45.

32. See especially chapter 2 of Gilman, *The Jew's Body*, for an analysis of the role of the Jew's foot in representations of Jewish difference.

33. See Julie Abraham, "'Woman, Remember You': Djuna Barnes and History," in *Silence and Power: A Reevaluation of Djuna Barnes*, Mary Lynn Broe, ed. (Carbondale: Southern Illinois University Press, 1991), 253–54.

34. Lara Trubowitz cites the grant application in "In Search of 'the Jew.'" The application can be found in the papers of Djuna Barnes, housed in Special Collections in the University of Maryland libraries under copyright of the Authors League Fund (ibid., 311, 328 n. 1).

35. The full text of *The Jewish Encyclopedia* became available online in 2002, sponsored by the Kopleman Foundation.

36. Compare, for example, the 2009 *Encyclopaedia Britannica* article on "Paul II" that hints at his cruelty and paranoia to the entry in *The Catholic Encyclopedia*. Some have insinuated that Pope Paul II was homosexual; unsubstantiated rumors circulated that he died of a stroke in "compromising" circumstances with a page boy. Homophobic stereotypes that link the love of finery and the celibacy of priests with a predilection for boys and sadistic sexual practices could be responsible. For more on homosexual stereotyping between the two world wars, see chapter 4.

37. Mairéad Hanrahan's interpretation of the yellow kerchief, for example, states, "Yellow is the colour of the Star of David, with which the Nazis were beginning to mark out the Jews at the time of writing *Nightwood*" (Hanrahan, "Djuna Barnes's *Nightwood*," 36). While her argument is extremely compelling in its link to Nazism, it historically predates Nazi laws on Jewish badges by a few years.

38. See Bernhard Blumenkranz and B. Mordechai Ansbacher in the *Encyclopaedia Judaica* under "Jewish Badge" 3: 45–48; and "Badge," in *The Jewish Encyclopedia* 2: 425–27.

39. The exact terms of the order, as cited in a *Jewish Encyclopedia* article, reads as such: "*Contingit interdum quod per errorem christiani Judæorum seu Saracenorum et Judæi seu Saraceni christianorum mulieribus commisceantur. Ne igitur tam damnatæ commixtionis excessus per velamentum erroris hujusmodi, excusationis ulterius possint habere diffugium, statuimus ut tales utriusque sexus in omni christianorum provincia, et omni tempore qualitate habitus publice ab aliis populis distinguantur*" (2: 425); "it sometimes happens that by mistake Christians have intercourse with Jewish or Saracen women, and Jews or Saracens with Christian women. Therefore, lest these people, under the cover of an error, find an excuse for the grave sin of such intercourse, we decree that these people [Jews and Saracens] of either sex, and in all Christian lands, and at all times, shall easily be distinguishable from the rest of the populations by the quality of their clothes" (qtd. and trans. Steven F. Kruger, "Conversion and Medieval Sexual, Religious, and Racial Categories," in *Constructing Medieval Sexuality*, ed. Karma Lochrie, Peggy McCracken, and James Alfred Schultz [Minneapolis: University of Minnesota Press, 1997], 168). The article follows up the decree with the comment, "From this it would appear that the motive of the order was to prevent illicit intercourse between Jews and Christian women; but it is scarcely doubtful that this was little more than a pretext, the evidence of such intercourse being only of the slightest and doubtful" (*Jewish Encyclopedia* 2: 425).

40. According to Genesis 22: 1–24, God asks Abraham to sacrifice his son Isaac as an act of faith and to prove his devotion. Abraham prepares to do so, binding Isaac to the altar, when an angel sent by God stops him. Instead, Abraham sacrifices a ram found in the thicket nearby.

41. See, for example, Carlston, *Thinking Fascism*, 65–68, for readings of *Nightwood*'s Catholic content.

42. Thomas Aquinas, in *Summa Theologiae* III, 1, 3, ad. 3, cites the line which is read in traditional Latin Mass, and *Exsultet* of the Easter Vigil masses: "*O felix culpa quae talem et tantum meruit habere redemptorem*"; "O happy fault that earned us so good and great a Redeemer."

43. The most famous account of the Wandering Jew is from a 1602 German pam-

phlet, *"Kurze Beschreibung und Erzählung von einem Juden mit namen Ahasverus"* [A brief description and narration regarding a Jew named Ahasuerus]. The legend was the subject of paintings, plays, and books. It was probably best known in literature as the subject of Eugène Sue's romantic anti-Jesuit novel *Le Juif errant* (10 vols., 1844–45), whose Jew, Djalma, is the name whence Djuna's is derived (Marcus, "Laughing," 229; Hanrahan, "Djuna Barnes's *Nightwood*," 34). On the origins of the myth, see "Wandering Jew" in *The Jewish Encyclopedia* and the *Encyclopaedia Britannica Online*.

44. *Goy* is the Yiddish and Hebrew term for "gentile," literally translated from the Hebrew "stranger."

45. For more on Roman Jews and the Holocaust, and especially the controversial position of Pope Pius XII, noted for his failure to protect the Jews or adequately protest the Nazi atrocities, see Israel Gutman, ed., *Encyclopedia of the Holocaust* (New York: Macmillan, 1995), vol. 3, 1136–39, and John Cornwell, *Hitler's Pope: The Secret History of Pope Pius XII* (New York: Penguin, 1999).

46. An especially valuable analysis of "The Duchess and the Jeweller" is provided by Phyllis Lassner, "'The Milk of Our Mother's Kindness Has Ceased to Flow': Virginia Woolf, Stevie Smith, and the Representation of the Jew," in Bryan Cheyette, ed., *Between "Race" and Culture*, 131–34. See also Maren Linett's reading of the Jew in *The Years* in her essay "The Jew in the Bath: Imperiled Imagination in Woolf's *The Years*," *Modern Fiction Studies* 48, no. 2 (Summer 2002): 341–61; and Leena Kore Schröder, "Tales of Abject and Miscegenation: Virginia Woolf's and Leonard Woolf's 'Jewish' Stories," *Twentieth-Century Literature* 49, no. 3 (Fall 2003): 298–327.

47. "Backshadowing" is a term coined by Michael André Bernstein to describe the tendency to read literature of the *Shoah* as if the participants should have known what was coming: "Backshadowing is a kind of retroactive foreshadowing in which the shared knowledge of the outcome of a series of events by narrator and listener is used to judge the participants in those events *as though they too should have known what was to come.*" See especially chapter 2, "Backshadowing and Apocalyptic History," in Bernstein's *Foregone Conclusions: Against Apocalyptic History* (Berkeley: University of California Press, 1994), 9–41.

48. Max Silverman extends this critique to Jean-Paul Sartre's *Anti-Semite and Jew* and Edward Said's *Orientalism*. As Silverman states, in conflating difference into a single concept of Othering, "the other is presented as simply the object of an originary gaze, someone else's representation than having any active subject-status, mediatory power, or history of its own." See Silverman, "Re-Figuring 'the Jew' in France," in Cheyette and Marcus, eds., *Modernity, Culture, and "the Jew,"* 200.

49. Compare Frost's view of *Three Guineas* in *Sex Drives*, 21, and Lassner's analysis in *British Women Writers*, 4, both mentioned in chapter 2.

50. For another take on Woolf's "border-crossing," especially with regard to Jews and class, see Leena Kore Schröder, "Tales of Abjection and Miscegenation," and Rosenfeld, "Monstrous Conjugations," in *Virginia Woolf and Fascism*, Pawlowski, ed., 122–36.

51. In her diaries, Woolf records that she and Leonard "discussed suicide if Hitler land[ed]" (*D*, 5: 284); before her 1935 trip to Germany, she explains to Ethyl Smith that they have "to get a letter out of Prince Bismarck since our Jewishness is said to be a danger" (*L*, 5: 386).

52. In *Outsiders Together*, Natania Rosenfeld cites a number of letters as examples of

Woolf's ambivalent attitude to becoming engaged to Leonard. See Rosenfeld, *Outsiders Together: Virginia and Leonard Woolf* (Princeton, N.J.: Princeton University Press, 2000), 57–60.

53. David Bradshaw, for instance, in his introduction to *Carlyle's House and Other Sketches* — which contains a shockingly offensive sketch of a "fat Jewess" — claims "there are many indications that such attitudes were endemic among [the] English upper middle class in Woolf's time" but "Woolf was no dyed-in-the-wool anti-Semite" and would later on confront her antisemitism and "go out of her way in *The Years* to contest the anti-Semitism of the British Union of Fascists" (Bradshaw, *Carlyle's House and Other Sketches* [London: Hesperus, 2003], 45). Similarly Jane Marcus, in *Virginia Woolf and the Languages of Patriarchy* (Bloomington: Indiana University Press, 1987), discusses the problematic portrayal of Sara Pargiter's long lament against her neighbor, "the Jew in my bath," in *The Years* in terms of Woolf's exposure of British genteel antisemitism. Marcus argues that Sara overcomes her prejudice toward her Jewish neighbor to join with him in working "toward a better world" (64).

54. See Maren Linett's similar reading of Ralph as a "parvenu" as identified by his clothes and his car. Linett is one of the few critics, aside from Phyllis Lassner, who focuses on the important role of Jewish Ralph Manresa in *Between the Acts*. Linett, *Modernism, Feminism, and Jewishness*, 80–95.

55. See Bryan Cheyette, "H. G. Wells and the Jews: Antisemitism, Socialism and English Culture: Antisemitism, Socialism and English," *Patterns of Prejudice* 22, no. 3 (1988): 30–31.

56. For a more detailed discussion of Lucy Swithin's character, see chapter 2.

57. See Elon, *The Pity of It All*, 221–96.

58. This intersection of gender and race with regard to Jewish representation in literature participates in a trend that has been well noted in Freud Lowenstein, *Loathsome Jews and Engulfing Women*; Linett, *Modernism, Feminism and Jewishness*; Pellegrini, "Whiteface Performances"; and Judith Lewin, "The Sublimity of the Jewish Type: Balzac's *Belle Juive* as Virgin Magdalene *aux Camelias*," in *Jewishness: Expression, Identity, and Representation*, ed. Simon J. Bronner, *Jewish Cultural Studies*, (Portland, Ore.: Littman Library of Jewish Civilization, 2008), vol. 1, 239–71.

59. See also my analysis of Natalia Landauer in chapter 2.

60. In a 1977 interview with Studs Terkel, Isherwood admits, "I feel that this character more than any other does wrong to its original because Gise [Soloweitschik, on whom the character is based] was an altogether warmer and emotionally more responsive kind of person than Natalia, and I was rather driven into the position, for purely technical reasons, of making Natalia an opposite of Sally Bowles. Therefore, to some extent, the more Sally Bowles was outrageous, the more Natalia had to be sort of conservative, prudish, capable of being shocked" (James Berg and Chris Freeman, eds., *Conversations with Christopher Isherwood* [Jackson: University Press of Mississippi, 2001], 173). Isherwood's retrospective comment confirms that the virgin/whore dichotomy was purposeful rather than accidental.

61. In *Christopher and His Kind*, Isherwood relates Wilfrid's real-life story and how he was killed by the Nazis (but much later in the war). As Isherwood notes, "The timing of his death [in the novel], so early in the persecution, is unconvincing," especially since he was such an influential figure in the business world. Nevertheless, "In a novel such as this one, which ends with the outbreak of political persecution, one death is a must" (*CHK*, 71). Isherwood reports that Wilfrid settled in England and devoted him-

self during the war to helping his fellow refugees, paying for visas, and arranging for some of the younger refugees to immigrate to Palestine. In 1943, on a return trip from Portugal to London, Wilfrid's plane was shot down by Nazi fighter jets who believed Churchill might be on board (*CHK*, 72).

62. Oddly enough, in *Nightwood* Nora also appeals to the "night watchman" — Matthew O'Connor — to try to understand her own "hallucination of non-existence" in the chapter "Watchman, What of the Night?" See my examination of Nora and her exchange with O'Connor when he tells her "of the night" in chapter 4.

## Chapter 4

1. As inadequate as the terminology may be, in the chapter I will use "queer" to refer to the trope and style of experimentation in the texts that refuses definition for various nuances of sexuality; "homosexual" as a term when referring to same-sex-desiring men in the texts and in historical discourses; and "gay" or "gay and lesbian" as a general category of self-avowal.

2. Shari Benstock describes Paris's reputation as a haven for flamboyant homosexual dandies and same-sex-loving women, to the extent that it was sometimes called "Paris-Lesbos" (*Women of the Left Bank* [Austin: University of Texas Press, 1986], 47).

3. See, for example, Benstock's description of male homosexuality and lesbianism in *belle époque* Paris in *Women of the Left Bank*, 44–61; Florence Tamagne, *A History of Homosexuality in Europe: Berlin, London, Paris, 1919–1939* (New York: Algora, 2006), especially 45–50; and John Fout's description of gay emancipation in Weimar Berlin in "Sexual Politics in Wilhelmine Germany: The Male Gender Crisis, Moral Purity, and Homophobia," *Journal of the History of Sexuality* 2, no. 3 (1992): 388–421.

4. In the United Kingdom, for example, section 11 of the Criminal Law Amendment Act of 1885, called "The Labouchere Amendment" after MP Henry Labouchere, criminalized acts of "gross indecency" between men only: "Any male person who, in public or private, commits, or is a party to the commission of, or procures, or attempts to procure the commission of any male person of, any act of gross indecency shall be guilty of a misdemeanour, and being convicted shall be liable at the discretion of the Court to be imprisoned for any term not exceeding two years, with or without hard labour." See Caryn Neumann, "The Labouchere Amendment 1885–1967," *glbtq: An Encyclopedia of Gay, Lesbian, Bisexual, Transgender, and Queer Culture*, 2004, http://www.glbtq.com/social-sciences/labouchere_amendment.html. Tory MP Frederick Macquisten tried to expand the Labouchere Amendment in 1921 to include same-sex acts between women, or sapphism, but was unsuccessful. It was thought that criminalizing lesbianism would encourage women who otherwise had no clue that the practice even existed. See Tamagne, *History of Homosexuality in Europe*, 151–52.

5. Fout examines in detail Hirschfeld's petition for the abolition of §175, drawing attention to specific elements of the pamphlet "*Ursachen und Wesen des Uranisums*" (1903) and its problematic relationship to the moral purity movements at the time. Among other things, the pamphlet posited that homosexuality is a phenomenon that is inborn, innate, with no escape (and therefore could not be judged wrong, except in case of rape or prostitution). Moreover, Hirschfeld reasoned that given many artists were homosexuals, Germany would rob its nation of talent if they were persecuted. See especially Fout, "Sexual Politics in Wilhelmine Germany," 395–403; and Richard Plant, *The Pink Triangle: The Nazi War Against Homosexuals* (New York: Henry Holt, 1986), 30, 34.

6. The pink triangle was not used until 1939. Before that, homosexuals were often referred to as "175-ers." Geoffrey Giles outlines Nazi castration practices in more detail in "'The Most Unkindest Cut of All': Castration, Homosexuality and Nazi Justice," *Journal of Contemporary History* 27 (1992): 41–61.

7. The treatment of homosexuals during the Nazi regime is described in Frank Rector, *The Nazi Extermination of Homosexuals* (New York: Stein and Day, 1981); Plant, *The Pink Triangle*; John Fout, "Sexual Politics in Wilhelmine Germany"; Dagmar Herzog, ed., *Sexuality and German Fascism*; and Geoffrey Giles, "Legislating Homophobia in the Third Reich." Giles and others have noted how difficult it is to obtain an exact number of how many "pink triangle" prisoners died in concentration camps. "As a consequence of the obstructiveness of the International Red Cross," Giles maintains, "no detailed research into the overall dimensions of the pink triangle population in the concentration camps has been possible since 1977" ("Why Bother About Homosexuals? Homophobia and Sexual Politics in Nazi Germany" [J. B. and Maurice C. Shapiro Annual Lecture. Washington, D.C.: United States Holocaust Memorial Museum Center for Advanced Holocaust Studies, May 30, 2001], 21 n. 10).

8. See Laura Frost, *Sex Drives*, for her argument that there is an "insistence that fascism be construed as sexually deviant," 3. Her study, which examines eroticized images of fascism in literature, considers why dictatorships have been culturally linked with sexual fantasy.

9. Compare Andrew Hewitt, *Political Inversions: Homosexuality, Fascism, and the Modernist Imaginary* (Stanford, Calif.: Stanford University Press, 1996), chapter 2; and Elizabeth Heineman, "Sexuality and Nazism," in Herzog, ed., *Sexuality and German Fascism*, 26–27.

10. Hewitt's analysis of the "homosexualization of fascism" is particularly constructive in considering representations of "sexual deviance" and Nazism. One could nevertheless argue that fascist and Nazi imagery clearly does play a role in erotic fantasy in certain sexual subcultures (both gay and heterosexual) and especially in connection with sadomasochism and submission-domination scenarios, in a manner unrelated to homophobia. I would concur with Laura Frost, however, who argues that "erotic sadomasochism" is distinguishable from "fascist violence" (*Sex Drives*, 12). Notably, partners in the sadomasochistic drama have agency and an agreed-upon arrangement — both survive and gain some sort of sexual gratification from the encounter; the victims of Nazi brutality do not. To quote Frost, "The most relevant crime of fascism is not 'sexual sadism' but murder." See Frost, *Sex Drives*, 12, 27–34, and Hewitt, *Political Inversions*, x–xix and 9–12.

11. Ernst Röhm (Roehm) was an openly homosexual SA chief of staff who was assassinated in June 1934, along with other SA members believed to belong to a "homosexual clique." Originally, his sexual orientation was considered irrelevant as long as he was an effective leader (Hitler defended him by saying that the private life of SA leaders was their own affair), but he still elicited violent response among many in the party's upper ranks and the conservative "moral purity" movement. Röhm's assassination is generally regarded as a turning point in the National Socialist regime's treatment of homosexuals. The tendency to equate the Nazi elite with homosexuality also stems from the belief that because Röhm was homosexual, others shared his sexual preferences. For more on the Röhm purge, see Richard Plant, *The Pink*

*Triangle*, and Stefan Micheler, "Homophobic Propaganda and the Denunciation of Same-Sex-Desiring Men," trans. Patricia Szobar, in Herzog, ed., *Sexuality and German Fascism*, 105–7.

12. See Lesley Higgins and Marie-Christine Leps, "A 'Complex Multiform Creature' No More: Governmentality Getting Wilde," *College Literature* 35, no. 3 (2008): especially 105–10.

13. On the trial and reception of *The Well of Loneliness*, see Michael Baker, *Our Three Selves: The Life of Radclyffe Hall* (New York: William Morrow, 1985); Leigh Gilmore, "Obscenity, Modernity, Identity: Legalizing *The Well of Loneliness* and *Nightwood*," *Journal of the History of Sexuality* 4, no. 4 (1994): especially 608–9; and Adam Parkes, *Modernism and the Theater of Censorship* (New York: Oxford University Press, 1996), 144–62.

14. The opening line of Wilde's defense at his second trial for "gross indecency," "The love that dare not speak its name," is based on Alfred Douglas's poem "Two Loves." Wilde's speech at the trial began thus: "'The love that dare not speak its name' in this century is such a great affection of an elder for a younger man as there was between David and Jonathan, such as Plato made the very basis of his philosophy, and such as you find in the sonnets of Michelangelo and Shakespeare. It is that deep, spiritual affection that is as pure as it is perfect. It is in this century misunderstood, so much misunderstood that it may be described as 'the Love that dare not speak its name,' and on account of it I am placed where I am now" (Lucy McDiarmid, "Oscar Wilde's Speech from the Dock," *Textual Practice* 15, no. 3 [2001]: 453–54).

15. Shari Benstock describes the political rhetoric of Isherwood (and others in the "Auden Generation") as a "mask" for homosexuality. "W. H. Auden, Christopher Isherwood, and Stephen Spender developed poetic styles that simultaneously mapped and masked homosexuality." As she claims, their writing was "subversive" mainly in the way it "eluded readers who accepted the coded political rhetoric at face value." See Benstock, *Women of the Left Bank*, 398.

16. See also Erin Carlston, who draws similar parallels between Woolf (in *Three Guineas*, especially) and Isherwood's politics with the contention that both reveal that "the regulation of sexual expression is one of the critical functions of patriarchal structures of domination" (*Thinking Fascism*, 180).

17. One of the main reasons Christopher Isherwood was in Berlin was that he and many of his gay colleagues could openly practice homosexuality, which was illegal and still quite dangerous in England. As Isherwood notes in his memoir, "Berlin meant Boys" (*CHK*, 2).

18. Forster finished a draft of *Maurice* in 1914 but continued to revise it as late as 1960; it was published after his death in 1971. The following note was written on the cover of the 1959 copy of the transcript: "Publishable—but worth it?" (quoted in Philip Gardner's introduction to his edition of Forster's *Maurice* [London: André Deutsch, 1999], xlvii). Isherwood mentions reading *Maurice* in *Christopher and His Kind* and remained in correspondence with Forster until Forster died. Isherwood was instrumental in editing and publishing the posthumous *Maurice* (ibid., xxvii). On Isherwood's involvement with Forster, see ibid., xxxvi–xliii.

19. Isherwood claims that the other reason the narrator is not overtly gay is stylistic. In a 1973 interview with Winston Leyland, Isherwood remarks, "I'm often asked if I regret that I didn't say outright in *The Berlin Stories* that I was homosexual. Yes, I wish

I had. But I should have had to say it very casually, if I had said it; otherwise, I would have made the Christopher character too odd, too remarkable, and that would have upset the balance between him and the other characters. . . . To have made him homosexual, in those days, would have been to feature him as someone eccentric" (Berg and Freeman, *Conversations with Christopher Isherwood*, 100). In responding to the question of whether it would have been published, Isherwood answers, "Oh yes . . . if I hadn't gone into too many details about homosexual lovemaking" (ibid.).

20. See also Jamie Carr, *Queer Times: Christopher Isherwood's Modernity* (New York: Routledge, 2006), for an analysis of "queer time" as an anti-identarian strategy in Isherwood's later works.

21. Stuart Christie examines "On Reugen Island" as an answer to the English pastoral mode and, more specifically, in relation to E. M. Forster's *Maurice*. See Christie, "'A Further Reservation in Favour of Strangeness': Isherwood's Queer Pastoral in the *Mortmere Stories* and 'On Reugen Island,'" *Modern Fiction Studies* 47, no. 4 (Winter 2001): 816–24. My analysis of the segment situates the story more specifically in relation to the political environment and nostalgic mode of Nazi Germany, which Isherwood was observing at the time, rather than the English pastoral.

22. Jane Marcus, for instance, argues that in *Nightwood* "the carnival of cross-dressing destabilizes identity" and exposes theories of sexuality that try to "'civilize' and make 'normal' the sexually aberrant misfit" ("Laughing at Leviticus," 233). Similarly, Benstock maintains that Barnes shows that "definitions of gender and sexuality are . . . socially produced rather than biologically determined" (*Women of the Left Bank*, 262). Bonnie Kime Scott, too, claims, "Barnes breaks with binary traditions by calling attention to impositions of culture, including its rules of gender, upon nature" (*Refiguring Modernism: Postmodern Feminist Readings of Woolf, West, and Barnes* [Bloomington: Indiana University Press, 1995], vol. 2, 73). Although I do think Barnes disrupts accepted ideas of sexuality and gender, I am more skeptical than these critics that Barnes promotes a clear antiessentialist argument.

23. See Leigh Gilmore for her comparison of Hall's and Barnes's texts in relation to the censors. As she claims, "Radclyffe Hall was perceived as both the lesbian in the text and the lesbian writing the text. . . . Because Barnes's legal identity was primarily literary, her novel was not subject in the same way as Hall's to the intersection of literary and lesbian that identifies obscenity" ("Obscenity, Modernity, Identity," 623).

24. Cheryl Plumb, Leigh Gilmore, and Dianne Chisholm all point to Eliot's role in the editing of *Nightwood*. Eliot, then a director of the English publisher Faber and Faber, advised Barnes to cut out some of the most shocking parts of the book, especially those having to do with homosexuality. According to Plumb, "all in all the editorial hand was light; certainly because he anticipated potential difficulty with censors, Eliot blurred sexual, particularly homosexual, references and a few points that put religion in an unsavory light" (*Nightwood: The Original Version*, xxiii). The critical edition of *Nightwood* from the Dalkey Archive Press (abbreviated as NWOV) indicates his changes. See also Gilmore, "Obscenity, Modernity, Identity," 617–21; and Chisholm, "Obscene Modernism: Eros Noir and the Profane Illumination of Djuna Barnes," *American Literature* 69, no. 1 (1997): 170–72.

25. In this excised passage, the doctor tells Frau Mann the story of "the night I popped Tiny out to relieve him of his drinking, when something with dark hands closed over him as if to strangle the life's breath out of him and suddenly the other, less pleasing hand, the hand of the law, was on my shoulder and I was hurled into jail,

into Marie Antoinette's very cell." He is acquitted by a sympathetic judge (Barnes, NWOV, 25).

26. Gilmore notes how Faber and Faber went out of its way to "warn" optimists to "keep this novel from the hands of that over-protected child, the average reader, and themselves from the wrath of his governesses — the Mothers' Union and the Public Morality Council" ("Obscenity, Modernity, Identity," 618).

27. For more on Barnes and the concept of "obscenity" and the profane, especially in relation to avant-garde art and surrealism, see Chisholm, "Obscene Modernism."

28. See Susan Gubar's contradictory view of transvestism as "an imitation or artefact — not like a man, but like a mannikin [sic]" ("Blessings in Disguise: Cross-Dressing as Re-dressing from Female Modernists," Massachusetts Review 22, no. 3 [1981]: 499).

29. See Frost's analysis of Adorno and Horkheimer's gendered attitude in Sex Drives, 122.

30. Compare Jane Marcus, Virginia Woolf and the Languages of Patriarch; Julie Abraham, Are Girls Necessary? Lesbian Writing and Modern Histories (New York: Routledge, 1996); and Eileen Barrett and Patricia Cramer, eds., Virginia Woolf: Lesbian Readings (New York: New York University Press, 1997), especially the chapter by Lise Weil, "Entering a Lesbian Field of Vision: To the Lighthouse and Between the Acts," 241–52.

31. See also Abraham, Are Girls Necessary?, and David Eberly, "Talking It All Out: Homosexual Disclosure in Woolf," in Virginia Woolf: Themes and Variations, eds. Vara Neverow-Turk and Mark Hussey (New York: Pace University Press, 1992), 128–33.

32. Hall's essentialist views of "inverts" and her earnest plea for understanding their predicament as "hapless freaks of nature" nevertheless clearly diverged from Woolf's own (Parkes, Theater of Censorship, 156). Woolf described Hall's book as "meritorious" and "dull" (D, 3: 193); as she wrote to Vita Sackville-West, "And no one read her book; or can read it. . . . So our ardour in the cause of freedom of speech gradually cools, and instead of offering to reprint the masterpiece, we are already beginning to wish it unwritten" (L, 3: 120).

33. For more on Lewis's disparaging attitudes toward gay men and women, see Lesley Higgins, The Modernist Cult of Ugliness: Aesthetics and Gender Politics (New York: Palgrave Macmillan, 2002), 84.

34. Lewis's chapter criticizing Woolf and Bloomsbury, titled "Virginia Woolf: 'Mind' and 'Matter' on the Plane of a Literary Controversy," caused Woolf much anxiety. In a diary entry on October 11, 1934, she writes, "In today's Lit. Sup., they advertise Men without Art, by Windham Lewis: chapters on Eliot, Faulkner, Hemingway, Virginia Woolf. . . . Now I know by reason & instinct that this is an attack; that I am publicly demolished; nothing is left of me in Oxford & Cambridge & places where the young read Wyndham Lewis. . . . & then there is the queer disreputable pleasure in being abused — in being a figure, in being a martyr. & so on" (D, 4: 250–51).

35. See also Thomas Laqueur, Solitary Sex: A Cultural History of Masturbation (New York: Zone Books, 2003).

## Conclusion

1. According to Andrew Field, Barnes's first half-yearly royalties were only £430 in England and $350.23 in the United States (Djuna [Austin: University of Texas Press, 1985], 206).

# WORKS CITED

**Primary Sources**

Barnes, Djuna. *Nightwood.* 1937. New York: New Directions, 1961.

———. *Nightwood: The Original Version and Related Drafts.* Edited by Cheryl Plumb. Normal, Ill.: Dalkey Archive Press, 1995.

Isherwood, Christopher. *Christopher and His Kind: 1929–1939.* New York: Farrar, Straus and Giroux, 1976.

———. *Goodbye to Berlin.* 1936. London: Minerva, 1989.

Woolf, Virginia. "'Anon' and 'The Reader': Virginia Woolf's Last Essays." Edited by Brenda Silver. *Twentieth-Century Literature* 25, nos. 3–4 (1979): 356–441.

———. "The Artist and Politics." In *The Moment and Other Essays,* 180–82. London: Hogarth, 1964.

———. *Between the Acts.* 1941. London: Oxford University Press, 1992.

———. *Carlyle's House and Other Sketches.* Edited by David Bradshaw. London: Hesperus, 2003.

———. "The Cinema." In *The Essays of Virginia Woolf, Volume 4, 1925–1928.* Edited by Andrew McNeillie, 348–53. London: Hogarth, 1994.

———. *The Diary of Virginia Woolf.* Edited by Anne Olivier Bell. 5 vols. New York: Harcourt Brace Jovanovich, 1977–84.

———. "The Duchess and the Jeweller." In *The Complete Shorter Fiction of Virginia Woolf.* Edited by Susan Dick, 248–53. London: Hogarth, 1989.

———. "The Leaning Tower." In *The Moment and Other Essays,* 105–25.

———. *The Letters of Virginia Woolf.* Edited by Nigel Nicolson and Joanne Trautmann. 6 vols. New York: Harcourt Brace Jovanovich, 1975–80.

———. *Orlando: A Biography.* 1928. New York: Harcourt Brace Jovanovich, 1953.

———. *Pointz Hall: The Earlier and Later Transcripts of "Between the Acts."* Edited by Mitchell A. Leaska. New York: University Publications, 1983.

———. "Professions for Women." In *The Death of the Moth and Other Essays,* 149–54. London: Hogarth, 1942.

———. *A Room of One's Own.* London: Hogarth, 1929.

———. "Thoughts of Peace in an Air Raid." In *The Death of the Moth and Other Essays,* 154–57.

———. *Three Guineas.* 1938. London: Hogarth, 1991.

———. *The Waves.* 1931. London: Hogarth, 1990.

———. *The Years.* 1937. London: Hogarth, 1992.

**Secondary Sources**

Abraham, Julie. *Are Girls Necessary? Lesbian Writing and Modern Histories.* New York: Routledge, 1996.

———. "'Woman, Remember You': Djuna Barnes and History." In *Silence and Power: A Reevaluation of Djuna Barnes*, edited by Mary Lynn Broe, 252–68. Carbondale: Southern Illinois University Press, 1991.

Adorno, Theodor W. *Aesthetic Theory*. Edited by Gretel Adorno and Rolf Tiedemann, translated by Christian Lenhardt. London: Routledge, 1984.

———. "The Culture Industry Reconsidered." Translated by Anson Rabinbach. In *Critical Theory and Society: A Reader*. Edited by Stephen Eric Bronner and Douglas MacKay Kellner, 128–35. New York: Routledge, 1989.

———. *Minima Moralia: Reflections from Damaged Life*. Translated by E. F. N. Jephcott. London: New Left Books, 1974.

Adorno, Theodor W., and Max Horkheimer. *Dialectic of Enlightenment: Philosophical Fragments*. Edited by Gunzelin Schmid Noerr and translated by Edmund Jephcott. Stanford, Calif.: Stanford University Press, 1987.

Albrecht, Gerd. *Nationalsozialistische Filmpolitik: Eine soziologische Untersuchung über die Spielfilme des dritten Reiches* [National Socialist film politics: a sociological examination of feature films in the Third Reich]. Stuttgart: Ferdinand Enke, 1969.

Altman, Meryl. "A Book of Repulsive Jews? Rereading *Nightwood*." *The Review of Contemporary Fiction* 13, no. 3 (1993): 160–71.

Arendt, Hannah. "Antisemitism." In *The Jewish Writings*, edited by Jerome Kohn and Ron H. Feldman, 46–111. New York: Schocken, 2007.

———. "From *Eichmann in Jerusalem*." 1963. In *The Portable Hannah Arendt*, edited by Peter Baehr, 313–88. New York: Penguin, 2000.

———. *The Origins of Totalitarianism*. San Diego: Harcourt Brace Jovanovich, 1973.

Arnold, Matthew. "Stanzas from the Grande Chartreuse." In *The Poems of Matthew Arnold*, edited by Kenneth Allot, 285–94. London: Longmans, 1965.

Atget, Eugène. *Eugène Atget's Paris*. Edited by Hans Christian Adam. Köln, Germany: Taschen, 2001.

Auden, W. H. "Letter to William Coldstream, Esq." In *Auden and Louis MacNeice, Letters from Iceland*, 223–27. London: Faber and Faber, 1937.

Auerbach, Nina. *Woman and the Demon: The Life of a Victorian Myth*. Cambridge: Cambridge University Press, 1982.

"Badge." In *The Jewish Encyclopedia*, edited by Isidore Singer. New York: Funk and Wagnalls, 1901–6.

Baker, Michael. *Our Three Selves: The Life of Radclyffe Hall*. New York: William Morrow, 1985.

Bakhtin, Mikhail M. "Discourse in the Novel." In *The Dialogic Imagination: Four Essays*, translated by Caryl Emerson and Michael Holquist and edited by Michael Holquist, 259–300. Austin: University of Texas Press, 1981.

———. *Rabelais and His World*. Translated by Helen Iswolsky. Cambridge, Mass.: MIT Press, 1968.

Barber, Stephen. "Lip-Reading: Woolf's Secret Encounters." In *Novel Gazing: Queer Readings in Fiction*, edited by Eve Kosofsky Sedgwick, 400–443. Durham: Duke University Press, 1997.

Barber, Stephen, and David Clark, eds. *Regarding Sedgwick: Essays on Queer Culture and Critical Theory*. New York: Routledge, 2002.

Barnes, James, and Patience Barnes. *Hitler's "Mein Kampf" in Britain and America: A Publishing History 1930–39*. London: Cambridge University Press, 1980.

Barrett, Eileen, and Patricia Cramer, eds. *Virginia Woolf: Lesbian Readings*. New York: New York University Press, 1997.

Bartov, Omer. *The "Jew" in Cinema: From "The Golem" to "Don't Touch My Holocaust."* Bloomington: Indiana University Press, 2005.

Bauman, Zygmunt. "Allosemitism: Premodern, Modern, Postmodern." In *Modernity, Culture, and "the Jew,"* edited by Bryan Cheyette and Laura Marcus, 143–56. Cambridge, U.K.: Polity Press.

——. *Modernity and the Holocaust*. Ithaca, N.Y.: Cornell University Press, 1989.

Beegle, Mary Porter, and Jack Randall Crawford. *Community Drama and Pageantry*. New Haven, Conn.: Yale University Press, 1916.

Beer, Gillian. *Virginia Woolf: The Common Ground*. Edinburgh: Edinburgh University Press, 1996.

Benjamin, Walter. "Central Park" [Zentralpark]. Translated by Lloyd Spenser. *New German Critique* 34 (1985): 39–40.

——. *Illuminations*. Edited by Hannah Arendt and translated by Harry Zohn. New York: Schocken, 1969.

Benstock, Shari. *Women of the Left Bank*. Austin: University of Texas Press, 1986.

Berg, James, and Chris Freeman, eds. *Conversations with Christopher Isherwood*. Jackson: University Press of Mississippi.

Berman, Russell. "The Wandering Z: Reflections on Kaplan's *Reproduction of Banality*." Foreword to Alice Yaeger Kaplan, *Reproduction of Banality: Fascism, Literature, and French Intellectual Life*, xi–xxiii. Minneapolis: University of Minnesota Press, 1986.

Bernstein, Michael André. *Foregone Conclusions: Against Apocalyptic History*. Berkeley: University of California Press, 1994.

Bernstein, Sidney. "Walk Up! Walk Up!—Please." In *Footnotes to the Film*, edited by Charles Davy, 221–37. London: Lovat Dickson/Readers' Union, 1938.

Bhabha, Homi K. "Joking Aside: The Idea of a Self-Critical Community." Foreword to *Modernity, Culture, and "the Jew,"* edited by Bryan Cheyette and Laura Marcus, xv–xx.

Bingham, Adrian. *Gender, Modernity, and the Popular Press in Inter-War Britain*. Oxford: Clarendon Press, 2004.

Black, Gregory. *Hollywood Censored: Morality Codes, Catholics, and the Movies*. Cambridge: Cambridge University Press, 1994.

Blanchard, Marc. "Post-Bourgeois Tattoo: Reflections on Skin Writing in Late Capitalist Societies." In *Visualizing Theory: Selected Essays from V.A.R. 1990–1994*, edited by Lucien Taylor, 287–300. New York: Routledge, 1994.

*BLAST: Review of the Great English Vortex*, nos. 1–2 (1914–15). New York: Kraus Reprints, 1974.

Bluemel, Kristin. "Not Waving or Drowning: Refusing Critical Options, Rewriting Literary History." In *And in Our Time: Vision, Revision, and British Writing of the 1930s*, edited by Antony Shuttleworth, 65–94. Lewisburg, Pa.: Bucknell University Press; Associated University Press, 2003.

Blumenkranz, Bernhard, and B. Mordechai Ansbacher. "Badge, Jewish." *Encyclopaedia Judaica*. Edited by Michael Berenbaum and Fred Skolnik. 2nd ed., 3:45–48. Detroit: Macmillan Reference, 2007.

Bock, Gisela. "Racism and Sexism in Nazi Germany: Motherhood, Compulsory Sterilization, and the State." In *When Biology Became Destiny: Women in Wei-*

*mar and Nazi Germany*, edited by Renate Bridenthal, Atina Grossman, and Marion Kaplan, 271–96. New York: Monthly Review Press, 1984.

Boxwell, D. A. "In the Urinal: Virginia Woolf Around Gay Men." In *Virginia Woolf and Communities*, edited by Jeanette McVicker and Laura Davis, 173–78. New York: Pace University Press, 1999.

Boyarin, Daniel. *Unheroic Conduct: The Rise of Heterosexuality and the Invention of the Jewish Man*. Berkeley: University of California Press, 1997.

Boyarin, Jonathan, and Daniel Boyarin, "Diaspora: Generation and the Ground of Jewish Identity." *Critical Inquiry* 19, no. 4 (1993): 693–725.

———, eds. *Jews and Other Differences: The New Jewish Cultural Studies*. Minneapolis: University of Minnesota Press, 1997.

Bradshaw, David. Introduction to *Carlyle's House and Other Sketches*, by Virginia Woolf, xiii–xxv. London: Hesperus, 2003.

———. "Hyams Place: *The Years*, the Jews and the British Union of Fascists." In *Women Writers of the 1930s: Gender, Politics and History*, edited by Maroula Joannou, 179–91. Edinburgh: Edinburgh University Press, 1999.

Brady, Robert A. *The Spirit and Structure of German Fascism*. New York: Viking, 1937.

Brewer, Mary F. *Race, Sex, and Gender in Contemporary Women's Theatre*. Eastbourne, U.K.: Sussex Academic Press, 1999.

Bridenthal, Renate, Atina Grossman, and Marion Kaplan, eds. *When Biology Became Destiny: Women in Weimar and Nazi Germany*. New York: Monthly Review Press, 1984.

Brod, Harry. "Some Thoughts on Some Histories of Some Masculinities: Jews and Other Others." In *Theorizing Masculinities*, edited by Harry Brod and Michael Kaufman, 82–96. Thousand Oaks, Calif.: Sage, 1994.

Brodkin, Karen. *How Jews Became White Folks and What That Says About Race in America*. New Brunswick, N.J.: Rutgers University Press, 1998.

Broe, Mary Lynn. *Silence and Power: A Reevaluation of Djuna Barnes*. Carbondale: Southern Illinois University Press, 1991.

Bronner, Stephen Eric, and Douglas MacKay Kellner. Introduction to *Critical Theory and Society: A Reader*, edited by Bronner and Kellner, 1–21. New York: Routledge, 1989.

Buck-Morss, Susan. "'Aesthetic and Anaesthetics': Walter Benjamin's Artwork Essay Reconsidered." *October* (1992): 3–41.

———. *The Dialectics of Seeing: Benjamin and the Arcades Project*. Cambridge, Mass.: MIT Press, 1989.

———. "The Flaneur, the Sandwichman and the Whore: The Politics of Loitering." *New German Critique* 39 (1986): 99–140.

Bucknell, Katherine. "Why Christopher Isherwood Stopped Writing Fiction." In *On Modern Fiction*, edited by Zachary Leader, 126–48. Oxford: Oxford University Press, 2002.

Bürger, Peter. *Theory of the Avant-Garde*. Translated by Michael Shaw. Minneapolis: University of Minnesota Press, 1984.

Burns, Christy L., "Re-Dressing Feminist Identities: Tensions Between Essential and Constructed Selves in Virginia Woolf's *Orlando*." *Twentieth-Century Literature* 40, no. 3 (Autumn 1994): 342–64.

Burt, Ramsay. *Alien Bodies: Representation of Modernity, "Race" and Nation in Early Modern Dance*. London: Routledge, 1998.

Butler, Judith. *Bodies That Matter: On the Discursive Limits of Sex.* London: Routledge, 1994.

———. *Gender Trouble: Feminism and the Subversion of Identity.* New York: Routledge, 1999.

———. "Imitation and Gender Insubordination." In *The Lesbian and Gay Studies Reader,* edited by Henry Abelove, Michele Aina Barale, and David M. Halperin, 307–20. New York: Routledge, 1993.

*Cabaret.* Screenplay by Jay Presson Allen. Directed by Bob Fosse. Featuring Liza Minnelli, Michael York, and Joel Grey. ABC Pictures, 1972.

Carlston, Erin G. *Thinking Fascism: Sapphic Modernism and Fascist Modernity.* Stanford, Calif.: Stanford University Press, 1998.

Carr, Jamie. *Queer Times: Christopher Isherwood's Modernity.* New York: Routledge, 2006.

Casillo, Robert. *The Genealogy of Demons: Anti-Semitism, Fascism and the Myths of Ezra Pound.* Evanston, Ill.: Northwestern University Press, 1988.

Caughie, Pamela, ed. *Virginia Woolf in the Age of Mechanical Reproduction.* New York: Garland, 2000.

Cheyette, Bryan, ed. *Between "Race" and Culture: Representations of "the Jew" in English and American Literature.* Stanford, Calif.: Stanford University Press, 1996. See especially the introduction by Cheyette, 1–15.

———. *Constructions of "the Jew" in English Literature and Society.* Cambridge: Cambridge University Press, 1993.

———. "H. G. Wells and the Jews: Antisemitism, Socialism and English." *Patterns of Prejudice* 22, no. 3 (1988): 22–35.

Cheyette, Bryan, and Laura Marcus, eds. *Modernity, Culture, and "the Jew."* Cambridge, U.K.: Polity Press, 1998.

Chisholm, Dianne. "Obscene Modernism: Eros Noir and the Profane Illumination of Djuna Barnes." *American Literature* 69, no. 1 (1997): 167–206.

Christie, Stuart. "'A Further Reservation in Favour of Strangeness': Isherwood's Queer Pastoral in the *Mortmere Stories* and 'On Reugen Island.'" *Modern Fiction Studies* 47, no. 4 (Winter 2001): 800–830.

Cockburn, Claud. *The Devil's Decade.* London: Sidgwick and Jackson, 1973.

Cohen, Derek, and Deborah Heller. *Jewish Presences in English Literature.* Montreal: McGill-Queen's University Press, 1990.

Combs, William. *Voice of the SS: A History of the SS Journal "Das Schwarze Korps."* New York: Peter Lang, 1986.

Connor, Liz. *The Spectacular Modern Woman: Feminine Visibility in the 1920s.* Bloomington: Indiana University Press, 2004.

Cooke, Alistair. "The Critic in Film History." In *Footnotes to the Film,* edited by Charles Davy, 238–63.

Cornwell, John. *Hitler's Pope: The Secret History of Pius XII.* New York: Penguin, 1999.

Cramer, Patricia. "Notes from the Underground: Lesbian Ritual in the Writings of Virginia Woolf." In *Virginia Woolf Miscellanies,* edited by Mark Hussey and Vara Neverow-Turk, 177–88. New York: Pace University Press, 1991.

Cuddy-Keane, Melba. *Virginia Woolf, the Intellectual, and the Public Sphere.* Cambridge: Cambridge University Press, 2003.

Cunningham, Valentine. *British Writers of the Thirties.* Oxford: Oxford University Press, 1988.

Dalgarno, Emily. *Virginia Woolf and the Visible World*. Cambridge: Cambridge University Press, 2001.

Davy, Charles, ed. *Footnotes to the Film*. London: Lovat Dickson/Readers' Union, 1938. See especially the conclusion by Davy, "Are Films Worth While?" 279–302.

Day Lewis, Cecil. "Revolution in Writing." In *A Time to Dance: Noah and the Waters and Other Poems: With an Essay, Revolution in Writing*, 61–96. New York: Random House, 1936.

Debord, Guy. *The Society of the Spectacle*. Translated by Donald Nicholson-Smith. New York: Zone, 1994.

Denisoff, Dennis. *Aestheticism and Sexual Parody 1840–1940*, Cambridge Studies in Nineteenth-Century Literature and Culture. Cambridge: Cambridge University Press, 2001.

Des Pres, Terence. *Writing into the World. Essays: 1973–1987*. New York: Viking, 1991.

Diamond, Elin. Introduction to *Performance and Cultural Politics*, 1–12. New York: Routledge, 1996.

Dijkstra, Bram. *Idols of Perversity: Fantasies of Feminine Evil in Fin-de-Siècle Culture*. New York: Oxford University Press, 1986.

Doane, Mary Ann. *The Desire to Desire: The Woman's Film of the 1940s*. Bloomington: Indiana University Press, 1987.

——. "Film and the Masquerade: Theorizing the Female Spectator." *Screen* 23, nos. 3–4 (1982): 74–87.

DuBois, Ellen Carol. *Woman Suffrage and Women's Rights*. New York: New York University Press, 1998.

Eberly, David. "Talking It All Out: Homosexual Disclosure in Woolf." In *Virginia Woolf: Themes and Variations*, edited by Vara Neverow-Turk and Mark Hussey, 128–33. New York: Pace University Press, 1992.

Eforgan, Estel. *Leslie Howard: The Lost Actor*. Middlesex, U.K.: Vallentine Mitchell, 2010.

Eksteins, Modris. *Rites of Spring: The Great War and the Birth of the Modern Age*. New York: Doubleday, 1990.

Ellis, Havelock. *Studies in the Psychology of Sex*. 2 vols. New York: Random House, 1942.

Elsaesser, Thomas. "Primary Identification and the Historical Subject: Fassbinder and Germany." In *Narrative, Apparatus, Ideology*, edited by Philip Rosen, 535–49. New York: Columbia University Press, 1986.

——. *Weimar Cinema and After: Germany's Historical Imaginary*. New York: Routledge, 2000.

Evans, Richard J. "German Social Democracy and Women's Suffrage 1891–1918." *Journal of Contemporary History* 15, no. 3 (1980): 533–57.

Farfan, Penny. "Writing/Performing: Virginia Woolf *Between the Acts*." *Text and Performance Quarterly* 16, no. 3 (1996): 205–15.

Feldman, David. "Was Modernity Good for the Jews?" In *Modernity, Culture, and "the Jew,"* edited by Bryan Cheyette and Laura Marcus, 171–86.

Field, Andrew. *Djuna*. Austin: University of Texas Press, 1985.

Finkielkraut, Alain. *The Imaginary Jew*. Translated by Kevin O'Neill and David Suchoff. Lincoln: University of Nebraska Press, 1994.

Finney, Brian. *Christopher Isherwood: A Critical Biography*. New York: Oxford University Press, 1979.

Folsom, Franklin. *Days of Anger, Days of Hope: A Memoir of the League of American Writers, 1937–1942.* Niwot: University Press of Colorado, 1994.

Forster, E. M. *Maurice.* Edited by Philip Gardner. London: André Deutsch, 1999.

——. *Selected Letters.* 2 vols. Cambridge, Mass.: Harvard University Press, 1983–85.

Foucault, Michel. *The History of Sexuality, Vol. I: An Introduction.* Translated by Robert Hurley. New York: Vintage, 1980.

Fout, John C. "Sexual Politics in Wilhelmine Germany: The Male Gender Crisis, Moral Purity, and Homophobia." *Journal of the History of Sexuality* 2, no. 3 (1992): 388–421.

Fox, Jo. *Film Propaganda in Britain and Nazi Germany: World War II Cinema.* New York: Berg, 2007.

Fox-Genovese, Elizabeth. "Culture and Consciousness in the Intellectual History of European Women." *Signs* 12, no. 3 (1987): 529–47.

Freedman, Jonathan. *The Temple of Culture: Assimilation and Anti-Semitism in Literary Anglo-America.* New York: Oxford University Press, 2000.

Freud, Sigmund. *The Standard Edition of the Complete Psychological Works of Sigmund Freud.* Edited by James Strachey et al. Vol. 10, *Analysis of a Phobia in a Five-Year-Old Boy:* 5–149. London: Hogarth and the Institute of Psycho-Analysis, 1955.

——. *The Standard Edition of the Complete Psychological Works of Sigmund Freud.* Edited by James Strachey et al. Vol. 18, *Group Psychology and the Analysis of the Ego:* 67–143. London: Hogarth and the Institute of Psycho-Analysis, 1955.

Friedländer, Saul. *Reflections on Nazism: An Essay on Kitsch and Death.* New York: Harper and Row, 1984.

Friedman, Ellen, and Miriam Fuchs, eds. *Breaking the Sequence: Women's Experimental Fiction.* Princeton, N.J.: Princeton University Press, 1989.

Friedman, Jonathan. *Speaking the Unspeakable: Essays on Sexuality, Gender, and Holocaust Survivor Memory.* New York: University Press of America, 2002.

Frost, Laura. *Sex Drives: Fantasies of Fascism in Modernism.* Ithaca, N.Y.: Cornell University Press, 2002.

Froula, Christine. *Virginia Woolf and the Bloomsbury Avant-Garde.* New York: Columbia University Press, 2005.

Fuss, Diana. *Essentially Speaking: Feminism, Nature and Difference.* New York: Routledge, 1989.

Garb, Tamar. "Modernity, Identity, Textuality." In *The Jew in the Text: Modernity and the Construction of Identity,* edited by Linda Nochlin and Tamar Garb, 20–30. London: Thames and Hudson, 1995.

Garber, Marjorie. *Vested Interests: Cross-Dressing and Culture Anxiety.* New York: Routledge, 1992.

Gardner, Philip. Introduction to *Maurice,* by E. M. Forster, vii–lv. London: André Deutsch, 1999.

Gättens, Marie-Luise. *Women Writers and Fascism: Reconstructing History.* Gainesville: University Press of Florida, 1995.

Geller, Jay. *On Freud's Jewish Body: Mitigating Circumstances.* New York: Fordham University Press, 2007.

Gerstenberger, Donna. "The Radical Narrative of Djuna Barnes's *Nightwood.*" In

*Breaking the Sequence: Women's Experimental Fiction.* Edited by Ellen Friedman and Miriam Fuchs, 129–39.

Gilbert, Sandra M., and Susan Gubar. *The Madwoman in the Attic: The Woman Writer and the Nineteenth-Century Literary Imagination.* New Haven, Conn.: Yale University Press, 1979.

———. *No Man's Land 2: Sexchanges.* New Haven, Conn.: Yale University Press, 1989.

Giles, Geoffrey J. "Legislating Homophobia in the Third Reich: The Radicalization of Persecution Against Homosexuality by the Legal Profession." *German History* 23, no. 3 (2005): 239–54.

———. "'The Most Unkindest Cut of All': Castration, Homosexuality and Nazi Justice." *Journal of Contemporary History* 27 (1992): 41–61.

———. "Why Bother About Homosexuals? Homophobia and Sexual Politics in Nazi Germany." J. B. and Maurice C. Shapiro Annual Lecture. Washington, D.C.: United States Holocaust Memorial Museum Center for Advanced Holocaust Studies, May 30, 2001.

Gillespie, Diane, ed. *The Multiple Muses of Virginia Woolf.* Columbia: University of Missouri Press, 1993. See especially "'Her Kodack Pointed at His Head': Virginia Woolf and Photography" by Gillespie, 113–47.

Gilman, Sander. *Difference and Pathology: Stereotypes of Sexuality, Race, and Madness.* Ithaca, N.Y.: Cornell University Press, 1985.

———. *The Jew's Body.* New York: Routledge, 1991.

Gilmore, Leigh. "Obscenity, Modernity, Identity: Legalizing *The Well of Loneliness* and *Nightwood.*" *Journal of the History of Sexuality* 4, no. 4 (1994): 603–24.

Glendinning, Victoria. *Leonard Woolf: A Life.* London: Simon and Schuster, 2006.

Gordon, Terri J. "Fascism and the Female Form: Performance Art in the Third Reich." In *Sexuality and German Fascism,* edited by Dagmar Herzog, 164–200. New York: Berghahn, 2005.

Granzow, Brigitte, *A Mirror of Nazism: British Opinion and the Emergence of Hitler 1929–1933.* London: V. Gollancz, 1964.

Greenberg, Clement. "Avant Garde and Kitsch." *Partisan Review* 6, no. 5 (1939): 34–39.

Grossman, Atina. "The New Woman and the Rationalization of Sexuality in Weimar Germany." In *Powers of Desire: The Politics of Sexuality,* edited by Ann Snitow, Christine Stansell, and Sharon Thompson, 153–71. New York: Monthly Review Press, 1983.

Gubar, Susan. "Blessings in Disguise: Cross-Dressing as Re-dressing from Female Modernists." *Massachusetts Review* 22, no. 3 (1981): 477–508.

Gutman, Israel, ed. *Encyclopedia of the Holocaust.* Vol. 3. New York: Macmillan, 1995.

Hadda, Janet. *Passionate Women, Passive Men: Suicide in Yiddish Literature.* Albany, N.Y.: SUNY Press, 1988.

Hake, Sabine. *Popular Cinema of the Third Reich.* Austin: University of Texas Press, 2000.

Hall, Alan. "Mein Summer Camp: How Hitler Wanted Nazis to Become the World's Largest Tour Operator with Butlins-Style Holiday Resorts." *Mail Online,* posted April 28, 2011, and accessed November 30, 2011. http://www.dailymail.co.uk/news/article-1381124/Mein-summer-camp-How-Adolf-Hitler-wanted-Nazi-Butlins-style-holiday-resorts.html.

Hall, Lesley A. "Forbidden by God, Despised by Men: Masturbation, Medical Warnings, Moral Panic, and Manhood in Great Britain, 1850–1950." *Journal of the History of Sexuality* 2, no. 3 (January 1992): 365–87.

Hall, Radclyffe. *The Well of Loneliness.* New York: Anchor Books, 1990.

Hanrahan, Mairéad. "Djuna Barnes's *Nightwood:* The Cruci-Fiction of the Jew." *Paragraph* 24, no. 1 (2001): 32–50.

Hansen, Miriam. "Benjamin and Cinema: Not a One-Way Street." In *Benjamin's Ghosts: Interventions in Contemporary Literary and Cultural Theory,* edited by Gerhard Richter, 41–73. Stanford, Calif.: Stanford University Press, 2002.

Hardy, Forsyth. "Censorship and Film Societies." In *Footnotes to the Film,* edited by Charles Davy, 264–78.

Harris, Andrea L. "The Third Sex: Figures of Inversion in Djuna Barnes' *Nightwood.*" In *Eroticism and Containment: Notes from the Flood Plain,* edited by Carol Siegel and Ann Kibbey, 233–59. New York: New York University Press, 1994.

Hause, Steven, and Anne Kenney. *Women's Suffrage and Social Politics in the French Third Republic.* Princeton, N.J.: Princeton University Press, 1984.

Heineman, Elizabeth D. "Sexuality and Nazism: The Doubly Unspeakable?" In *Sexuality and German Fascism,* edited by Dagmar Herzog, 22–66.

Hekman, Susan. "Truth and Method: Feminist Standpoint Theory Revisited." *Signs* 22, no. 3 (1997): 341–65.

Heller, Deborah. "The Outcast as Villain and Victim: Jews in Dickens's *Oliver Twist* and *Our Mutual Friend.*" In *Jewish Presences in English Literature,* edited by Derek Cohen and Deborah Heller, 40–60.

Henstra, Sarah. "Looking the Part: Performative Narration in Djuna Barnes's *Nightwood* and Katherine Mansfield's 'Je Ne Parle Pas Francais.'" *Twentieth-Century Literature* 46, no. 2 (2000): 125–49.

Herf, Jeffrey. *Reactionary Modernism: Technology, Culture, and Politics in Weimar and the Third Reich.* Cambridge: Cambridge University Press, 1984.

Herzog, Dagmar, ed. *Sexuality and German Fascism.* New York: Berghahn, 2005. See especially Herzog's chapter "Hubris and Hypocrisy, Incitement and Disavowal: Sexuality and German Fascism," 1–21.

Hewitt, Andrew. *Political Inversions: Homosexuality, Fascism, and the Modernist Imaginary.* Stanford, Calif.: Stanford University Press, 1996.

Higgins, Lesley. *The Modernist Cult of Ugliness: Aesthetics and Gender Politics.* New York: Palgrave Macmillan, 2002.

Higgins, Lesley, and Marie-Christine Leps. "A 'Complex, Multiform Creature' No More: Governmentality Getting Wilde." *College Literature* 35, no. 3 (2008): 96–119.

Himmler, Heinrich. "Speech to the SS-Gruppenführer." Bad Tölz, Germany. February 18, 1937. Translated by Michael Burleigh and Wolfgang Wippermann. In *The Racial State: Germany 1933–1945,* by Burleigh and Wippermann, 192–93. Cambridge: Cambridge University Press, 1991.

Hitler, Adolf. *Mein Kampf.* Translated by Ralph Manheim. London: Hutchison and Co., 1969.

———. *The Speeches of Adolf Hitler, April 1922–August 1939.* 2 vols. Translated and edited by Norman Baynes. London: Oxford University Press, 1942.

Hoberman, J. *Vulgar Modernism: Writing on Movies and Other Media.* Philadelphia: Temple University Press, 1991.

Holland, Merlin. *Irish Peacock and Scarlet Marquess: The Real Trial of Oscar Wilde.* London: Fourth Estate, 2003.

Hubert, Susan. "The Word Separated from the Thing: *Nightwood's* Political Aesthetic." *Midwest Quarterly* 46, no. 1 (2004). 39–50.

Humm, Maggie. *Modernist Women and Visual Culture: Virginia Woolf, Vanessa Bell, Photography, and Cinema.* New York: Rutgers University Press, 2003.

Hussey, Andrew. *The Game of War: The Life and Death of Guy Debord.* London: Cape, 2001.

Hussey, Mark, ed. *Virginia Woolf and War.* Syracuse: Syracuse University Press, 1991.

Hutcheon, Linda. *The Politics of Postmodernism.* New York: Routledge, 1989.

Huxley, Aldous. "Writers and Readers." In *The Olive Tree and Other Essays,* 1–45. London: Chatto and Windus, 1936.

Huyssen, Andreas. *After the Great Divide: Modernism, Mass Culture, Postmodernism.* Bloomington: Indiana University Press, 1986.

Hyman, Paula E. *Gender and Assimilation in Modern Jewish History: The Roles and Representation of Women.* Seattle: University of Washington Press, 1995.

———. *The Jews of Modern France.* Berkeley: University of California Press, 1998.

Hynes, Samuel. *The Auden Generation: Literature and Politics in England in the 1930s.* Princeton, N.J.: Princeton University Press, 1972.

Itzkovitz, Daniel. "Secret Temples." In *Jews and Other Differences: The New Jewish Cultural Studies,* edited by Jonathan Boyarin and Daniel Boyarin, 176–202.

Jacobs, Joseph, and Schulim Ochser. "Rome." In *The Jewish Encyclopedia,* edited by Isidore Singer.

Jacobs, Karen. *The Eye's Mind: Literary Modernism and Visual Culture.* Ithaca, N.Y.: Cornell University Press, 2001.

Jardine, Alice. *Gynesis: Configurations of Woman and Modernity.* Ithaca, N.Y.: Cornell University Press, 1987.

Jelavich, Peter. *Berlin Cabaret.* Cambridge, Mass.: Harvard University Press, 1996.

Joannou, Maroula, ed. *Women Writers of the 1930s: Gender, Politics, and History.* Edinburgh: Edinburgh University Press, 1999.

Johnston, Georgia. "Class Performances in *Between the Acts*: Audiences for Miss La Trobe and Mrs. Manresa." *Woolf Studies Annual* 3 (1997): 61–75.

Joplin, Patricia Kindliest. "The Authority of Illusion: Feminism and Fascism in Virginia Woolf's *Between the Acts*." *South Central Review* 6, no. 2 (1989): 99–104.

Judaken, Jonathan. "So What's New? Rethinking the 'New Antisemitism' in a Global Age." *Patterns of Prejudice* 42, nos. 4–5 (2008): 531–60.

———. "Between Philosemitism and Antisemitism: The Frankfurt School's Anti-Antisemitism." In *Antisemitism and Philosemitism in the Twentieth and Twenty-First Centuries: Representing Jews, Jewishness, and Modern Culture,* edited by Phyllis Lassner and Lara Trubowitz, 23–46. Newark, N.J.: University of Delaware Press, 2008.

Julius, Anthony. *T. S. Eliot, Anti-Semitism, and Literary Form.* London: Thames and Hudson, 2003.

Kaivola, Karen. "The 'Beast Turning Human': Constructions of the 'Primitive' in *Nightwood*." *The Review of Contemporary Fiction* 13, no. 3 (1993): 172–88.

———. *All Contraries Confounded: The Lyrical Fiction of Virginia Woolf, Djuna Barnes, and Marguerite Duras.* Iowa City: University of Iowa Press, 1991.

Kaplan, Alice Yaeger. *Reproductions of Banality: Fascism, Literature, and French Intellectual Life*. Minneapolis: University of Minnesota Press, 1986.

Karabel, Jerome. *The Chosen: The Hidden History of Admission and Exclusion at Harvard, Yale, and Princeton*. Boston: Houghton Mifflin, 2005.

Kershaw, Ian. "How Effective Was Nazi Propaganda?" In *Nazi Propaganda: The Power and the Limitations*, edited by David Welch, 180–205. London: Croom Helm, 1983.

Kittay, Eva Feder. "Woman as Metaphor." In *Feminist Social Thought: A Reader*, edited by Diana Tietjens Meyers, 265–85. New York: Routledge, 1997.

Koonz, Claudia. *Mothers in the Fatherland: Women, the Family, and Nazi Politics*. New York: St. Martin's, 1987.

Kracauer, Siegfried. *From Caligari to Hitler: A Psychological History of the German Film*. 1947. Princeton, N.J.: Princeton University Press, 1971.

———. "The Mass Ornament." In *The Mass Ornament: Weimar Essays*. Translated and edited by Thomas Y. Levin, 75–88. Cambridge, Mass.: Harvard University Press, 1995.

Krafft-Ebing, Richard von. *Psychopathia Sexualis: With Especial Reference to the Antipathic Sexual Instinct: A Medico-Forensic Study*. 12th ed. Translated by Franklin S. Klaf. New York: Stein and Day, 1965.

Kruger, Steven F. "Conversion and Medieval Sexual, Religious, and Racial Categories." In *Constructing Medieval Sexuality*, edited by Karma Lochrie, Peggy McCracken, and James Alfred Schultz, 158–79. Minneapolis: University of Minnesota Press, 1997.

Kushner, Tony. "The Paradox of Prejudice: The Impact of Organised Antisemitism in Britain During an Anti-Nazi War." In *Traditions of Intolerance: Historical Perspectives on Fascism and Race Discourse in Britain*, edited by Tony Kushner and Kenneth Lunn, 72–90. Manchester, U.K.: Manchester University Press, 1989.

———. *The Persistence of Prejudice: Antisemitism in British Society During the Second World War*. Manchester, U.K.: Manchester University Press, 1989.

Kushner, Tony, and Nadia Valman, eds. *Remembering Cable Street: Fascism and Anti-Fascism in British Society*. London: Valentine Mitchell, 2000.

Kutulas, Judy. "Becoming 'More Liberal': The League of American Writers, the Communist Party, and the Literary People's Front." *The Journal of American Culture* 13, no. 1 (1990): 71–80.

Langmuir, Gavin. *Toward a Definition of Antisemitism*. Berkeley: University of California Press, 1990.

Laqueur, Thomas. *Solitary Sex: A Cultural History of Masturbation*. New York: Zone Books, 2003.

Lassner, Phyllis. *British Women Writers of World War II: Battlegrounds of Their Own*. New York: Macmillan, 1998.

———. "'The Milk of Our Mother's Kindness Has Ceased to Flow': Virginia Woolf, Stevie Smith, and the Representation of the Jew." In *Between "Race" and Culture: Representations of "the Jew" in English and American Literature*, edited by Bryan Cheyette, 129–44.

———. "The Necessary Jew: Modernist Women Writers and Contemporary Women Critics." In *Varieties of Antisemitism: History, Ideology, Discourse*, edited by

Murray Baumgarten, Peter Kenez, and Bruce Thompson, 292–314. Newark, N.J.: University of Delaware Press, 2009.

Lassner, Phyllis, and Lara Trubowitz, eds. *Antisemitism and Philosemitism in the Twentieth and Twenty-First Centuries: Representing Jews, Jewishness, and Modern Culture*. Newark, N.J.: University of Delaware Press, 2008.

Le Bon, Gustave. *The Crowd: A Study of the Popular Mind*. London: T. Fisher Unwin, 1903.

Lee, Hermione. *Virginia Woolf*. London: Chatto and Windus, 1996.

Lehmann, John. *Christopher Isherwood: A Personal Memoir*. London: Weidenfeld and Nicolson, 1987.

Levine, Nancy. "'I've Always Suffered from Sirens': The Cinema Vamp and Djuna Barnes' *Nightwood*." *Women's Studies* 16 (1989): 271–81.

Levitt, Laura. "Impossible Assimilations, American Liberalism, and Jewish Difference: Revisiting Jewish Secularism." *American Quarterly* 59, no. 3 (2007): 807–32.

Lewin, Judith. "The Sublimity of the Jewish Type: Balzac's *Belle Juive* as Virgin Magdalene *aux Camelias*." In *Jewishness: Expression, Identity, and Representation*, edited by Simon J. Bronner. *Jewish Cultural Studies*. Vol. 1, 239–71. Portland, Ore.: Littman Library of Jewish Civilization, 2008.

Lewis, Wyndham. *The Art of Being Ruled*. London: Chatto and Windus, 1926.

———. *Hitler*. London: Chatto and Windus, 1931.

———. *Men Without Art*. London: Cassell, 1934.

Linett, Maren Tova. "Introduction. Modernism's Jews/Jewish Modernisms." *Modern Fiction Studies* 51. no. 2 (2005): 249–57.

———. *Modernism, Feminism, and Jewishness*. Cambridge: Cambridge University Press, 2007.

Lowenstein, Andrea Freud. *Loathsome Jews and Engulfing Women*. New York: New York University Press, 1993.

Lyotard, Jean-François. *Heidegger and "the Jews."* Translated by Andreas Michel and Mark Roberts. Minneapolis: University of Minnesota Press, 1988.

"Manresa." In *The Jewish Encyclopedia*, edited by Isidore Singer.

Mao, Douglas, and Rebecca Walkowitz. "The New Modernist Studies." *PMLA* 123, no. 2 (2008): 737–48.

Marcus, Jane. Introduction to *Three Guineas* by Virginia Woolf, edited by Mark Hussey, xxxv–lxxii. Orlando, Fla.: Harcourt, 2006.

———. "Laughing at Leviticus: *Nightwood* as Women's Circus Epic." In *Silence and Power: A Reevaluation of Djuna Barnes*, edited by Mary Lynn Broe, 221–50.

———. "Some Sources for *Between the Acts*." *Virginia Woolf Miscellany* 6 (1977): 1–3.

———. *Virginia Woolf: A Feminist Slant*. Lincoln: University of Nebraska Press, 1983.

———, ed. *Virginia Woolf and Bloomsbury: A Centenary Celebration*. Bloomington: Indiana University Press, 1987.

———. *Virginia Woolf and the Languages of Patriarchy*. Bloomington: Indiana University Press, 1987.

Marcus, Lisa. "'May Jews Go to College?': Fictions of Jewishness in the 1920s." In *Antisemitism and Philosemitism in the Twentieth and Twenty-First Centuries:*

*Representing Jews, Jewishness, and Modern Culture*, edited by Phyllis Lassner and Lara Trubowitz, 138–53.

Martin, Elaine, ed. *Gender, Patriarchy, and Fascism in the Third Reich: The Response of Women Writers*. Detroit: Wayne State University Press, 1993.

McDiarmid, Lucy. "Oscar Wilde's Speech from the Dock." *Textual Practice* 15, no. 3 (2001): 447–66.

Micheler, Stefan. "Homophobic Propaganda and the Denunciation of Same-Sex-Desiring Men." Translated by Patricia Szobar. In *Sexuality and German Fascism*, edited by Dagmar Herzog, 95–130.

Mizejewski, Linda. "Camp Among the Swastikas: Isherwood, Sally Bowles, and 'Good Heter Stuff.'" In *Camp: Queer Aesthetics and the Performing Subject: A Reader*, edited by Fabio Cleto, 237–53. Ann Arbor: University of Michigan Press, 1999.

———. *Divine Decadence: Fascism, Female Spectacle and the Makings of Sally Bowles.* Princeton, N.J.: Princeton University Press, 1992.

Montefiore, Janet. *Men and Women Writers of the 1930s: The Dangerous Flood of History*. London: Routledge, 1996.

Moore, Tristana. "Holiday Camp with a Nazi Past." *BBC News Europe*, posted December 13, 2008, and accessed November 10, 2011. http://news.bbc.co.uk/2/hi/7777866.stm.

Morrison, Paul. *The Poetics of Fascism*. Oxford: Oxford University Press, 1996.

Mosse, George. *The Image of Man: The Creation of Modern Masculinity*. New York: Oxford University Press, 1996.

———. *Nationalism and Sexuality: Respectability and Abnormal Sexuality in Modern Europe*. New York: Fertig, 1985.

———. *Nazi Culture: Intellectual, Cultural, and Social Life in the Third Reich*. New York: Grosset and Dunlap, 1966.

Mulvey, Laura. *Visual and Other Pleasures*. Bloomington: Indiana University Press, 1989, especially Mulvey's chapter "Afterthoughts on 'Visual Pleasure and Narrative Cinema,'" 29–38.

———. "Visual Pleasure and Narrative Cinema." *Screen* 16, no. 3 (1975): 6–18.

Neumann, Caryn E. "The Labouchere Amendment 1885–1967." *glbtq: An Encyclopedia of Gay, Lesbian, Bisexual, Transgender, and Queer Culture*. glbtq: 2004. http://www.glbtq.com/social-sciences/labouchere_amendment.html.

Nicolson, Harold. *Diaries and Letters, Vol. 1 (1930–1939)*. Edited by Nigel Nicolson. London: Collins, 1966.

Nietzsche, Friedrich. *The Birth of Tragedy in the Spirit of Music*. Translated by Walter Kaufman. New York: Random House, 1992.

Nochlin, Linda, and Tamar Garb, eds. *The Jew in the Text: Modernity and the Construction of Identity*. London: Thames and Hudson, 1995. See especially Nochlin's introduction, "Starting with the Self: Jewish Identity and Its Representation," 7–19.

Nolte, Ernst. *Three Faces of Fascism: Action Française, Italian Fascism, National Socialism*. Translated by Leila Vennewitz. New York: Holt, Rinehart and Winston, 1966.

O'Brian, Mary-Elizabeth. *Nazi Cinema as Enchantment: The Politics of Entertainment in the Third Reich*. Rochester, N.Y.: Camden House, 2004.

Orwell, George. "Antisemitism in Britain." In *The Collected Essays, Journalism and Letters of George Orwell*, edited by Sonia Orwell and Ian Angus, Vol. 3, *As I Please*, 332–41. London: Secker and Warburg, 1968.

———. *Collected Essays*, edited by Sonia Orwell and Ian Angus, Vol. 2. Harmondsworth, U.K.: Penguin, 1971.

Oxindine, Annette. "Outing the Outsiders: Woolf's Exploration of Homophobia in *Between the Acts*." *Woolf Studies Annual* 5 (1999): 115–31.

Page, Judith. *Imperfect Sympathies: Jews and Judaism in British Romantic Literature and Culture*. New York: Palgrave, 2004.

Page, Norman. *Auden and Isherwood: The Berlin Years*. New York: St. Martin's, 1998.

———. *Modern Novelists: E. M. Forster*. New York: St. Martin's, 1987.

"Pageants." *Macmillan's Magazine* 92 (1905): 452–58.

Panitz, Esther. *The Alien in Their Midst: Images of Jews in English Literature*. Rutherford, N.J.: Fairleigh Dickinson University Press, 1981.

Parkes, Adam. *Modernism and the Theater of Censorship*. New York: Oxford University Press, 1996.

Patraka, Vivian. *Spectacular Suffering: Theatre, Fascism, and the Holocaust*. Indianapolis: Indiana University Press, 1999.

"Paul II." *The Catholic Encyclopedia*. Vol. 11. New York: Robert Appleton Company, 1911. Accessed April 15, 2009. http://www.newadvent.org/cathen/11578a.htm.

"Paul II." *Encyclopaedia Britannica Online*. Accessed March 30, 2009. http://www.britannica.com/EBchecked/topic/446940/Paul-II.

"Paul II." *The Oxford Dictionary of Popes*, edited by J. N. D. Kelly. Oxford University Press, 2006. *Oxford Reference Online*. Accessed April 2, 2009. http://www.oxfordreference.com/pages/Subjects_and_Titles__2E_H10.

Pawling, Christopher. "Revisiting the Thirties in the Twenty-First Century: The Radical Aesthetics of West, Cauldwell, and Eagleton." In *And in Our Time: Vision, Revision, and British Writing of the 1930s*, edited by Antony Shuttleworth, 45–64. Lewisburg, Pa.: Bucknell University Press; Associated University Press, 2003.

Pawlowski, Merry M., ed. *Virginia Woolf and Fascism: Resisting the Dictator's Seduction*. New York: Palgrave, 2001, especially Pawlowski's introduction, "Virginia Woolf at the Crossroads of Feminism, Fascism, and Art," 1–10.

Paxton, Robert O. *The Anatomy of Fascism*. New York: Knopf, 2004.

Payne, Stanley G. *A History of Fascism, 1914–1945*. New York: Routledge, 1996.

Peach, Linden. "No Longer a View: Virginia Woolf in the 1930s and the 1930s in Virginia Woolf." In *Women Writers of the 1930s*, edited by Maroula Joannou, 192–204.

Pellegrini, Ann. "Whiteface Performances: 'Race,' Gender, and Jewish Bodies." In *Jews and Other Differences: The New Jewish Cultural Studies*, edited by Jonathan Boyarin and Daniel Boyarin, 108–49.

Peskowitz, Miriam. "Engendering Jewish Religious History." In *Judaism Since Gender*, edited by Miriam Peskowitz and Laura Levitt, 17–39. New York: Routledge, 1997.

Petro, Patrice. *Joyless Streets: Women and Melodramatic Presentation in Weimar Germany*. Princeton, N.J.: Princeton University Press, 1989.

Pick, Daniel. "Powers of Suggestion: Svengali and the *Fin-de-Siècle*." In *Modernity, Culture, and "the Jew,"* edited by Bryan Cheyette and Laura Marcus, 105–25.

Plain, Gill. *Women's Fiction of the Second World War: Gender, Power and Resistance.* Edinburgh: Edinburgh University Press, 1996.

Plant, Richard. *The Pink Triangle: The Nazi War Against Homosexuals.* New York: Henry Holt, 1986.

Plumb, Cheryl, ed. *Djuna Barnes' Nightwood: The Original Version and Related Drafts.* Normal, Ill.: Dalkey Archive Press, 1995, especially Plumb's introduction, vii–xxvi.

Pogorelskin, Alexis. "Phyllis Bottome's *The Mortal Storm:* Film and Controversy." *The Space Between* 4, no. 1 (2010): 39–57.

Pridmore-Brown, Michele. "1939–40: Of Virginia Woolf, Gramophones, and Fascism." *PMLA* 113 (1998): 408–21.

Pugh, Martin. *Hurrah for Blackshirts! Fascists and Fascism in Britain Between the Wars.* London: Cape, 2005.

Purvis, June, and Sandra Stanley Holton, eds. *Votes for Women.* London: Routledge, 2000.

Radford, Jean. "The Woman and the Jew: Sex and Modernity." In *Modernity, Culture, and "the Jew,"* edited by Bryan Cheyette and Laura Marcus, 91–104.

Rauch, Angelika. "The Trauerspiel of the Prostituted Body, or Woman as Allegory of Modernity." *Cultural Critique* 10 (1998): 77–88.

Rector, Frank. *The Nazi Extermination of Homosexuals.* New York: Stein and Day, 1981.

Reese, Dagmar. *Growing Up Female in Nazi Germany.* Translated by William Templar. Ann Arbor: University of Michigan Press, 2006.

Reich, Wilhelm. *The Mass Psychology of Fascism.* Translated by Vincent Carfagno. 3rd ed. New York: Farrar, Straus and Giroux, 1970.

Renton, David. *This Rough Game: Fascism and Anti-Fascism.* Gloucester, U.K.: Sutton, 2001.

Rentschler, Eric. *The Ministry of Illusion: Nazi Cinema and Its Afterlife.* Cambridge, Mass.: Harvard University Press, 1996.

Richards, Jeffrey. "The British Board of Film Censors and Content Control in the 1930s: Foreign Affairs." *Historical Journal of Film, Radio, and Television* 2, no. 1 (1982): 38–48.

Riviere, Joan. "Womanliness as Masquerade," 1929. In *Formations of Fantasy,* edited by Victor Burgin, James Donald, and Cora Kaplan, 35–44. London: Methuen, 1986.

Robertson, Ritchie. "Historicizing Weininger: The Nineteenth-Century German Image of the Feminized Jew." In *Modernity, Culture, and "the Jew,"* edited by Bryan Cheyette and Laura Marcus, 23–39.

Rogen, Michael. *Blackface, White Noise: Jewish Immigrants in the Hollywood Melting Pot.* Berkeley: University of California Press, 1996.

Rosenfeld, Natania. "Monstrous Conjugations: Images of Dictatorship in the Anti-Fascist Writings of Virginia and Leonard Woolf." In *Virginia Woolf and Fascism: Resisting the Dictator's Seduction,* edited by Merry M. Pawalowski, 122–36.

———. *Outsiders Together: Virginia and Leonard Woolf.* Princeton, N.J.: Princeton University Press, 2000.

Schneider, Karen. *Loving Arms: British Women Writing the Second World War.* Lexington: University Press of Kentucky, 1997.

Schuchard, Ronald. "Burbank with a Baedeker, Eliot with a Cigar: American Intellectuals, Anti-Semitism, and the Idea of Culture." *Modernism/Modernity* 10 (2003): 1–26.

Schulte-Sasse, Linda. *Entertaining the Third Reich: Illusions of Wholeness in Nazi Cinema.* Durham, N.C.: Duke University Press, 1996.

Schuman, Frederick. *The Nazi Dictatorship: A Study in the Social Pathology and the Politics of Fascism.* New York: Knopf, 1936.

Schwerdt, Lisa M. *Isherwood's Fiction: The Self and Technique.* London: Macmillan, 1989.

Scott, Bonnie Kime. *Refiguring Modernism.* Vol. 2: *Postmodern Feminist Readings of Woolf, West, and Barnes.* Bloomington: Indiana University Press, 1995.

——. "The Subversive Mechanics of Woolf's Gramophone in *Between the Acts.*" In *Virginia Woolf in the Age of Mechanical Reproduction,* edited by Pamela Caughie, 97–114.

——. "Woolf, Barnes, and the End of Modernism: An Antiphon to *Between the Acts.*" In *Virginia Woolf: Themes and Variations,* edited by Vara Neverow-Turk and Mark Hussey, 25–32.

Sedgwick, Eve Kosofsky. *Between Men: English Literature and Male Homosexual Desire.* New York: Columbia University Press, 1985.

——. *Epistemology of the Closet.* Berkeley: University of California Press, 1990.

——. *Tendencies.* Durham, N.C.: Duke University Press, 1993.

Shapiro, Susan. "*Écriture Judaïque:* Where Are the Jews in Western Discourse?" In *Displacements: Cultural Identities in Question,* edited by Angelika Bammer, 182–201. Bloomington: Indiana University Press, 1994.

Shuttleworth, Antony, ed. *And in Our Time: Vision, Revision, and British Writing of the 1930s.* Lewisburg, Pa.: Bucknell University Press; Associated University Press, 2003.

——. "In a Populous City: Isherwood in the Thirties." In *The Isherwood Century: Essays on the Life and Work of Christopher Isherwood,* edited by James J. Berg and Chris Freeman, 150–61. Madison: University of Wisconsin Press, 2000.

Silver, Brenda, ed. "'Anon' and 'The Reader': Virginia Woolf's Last Essays." *Twentieth-Century Literature* 25, nos. 3–4 (1979), especially Silver's introduction, 356–441.

——. *Virginia Woolf Icon.* Chicago: University of Chicago Press, 1999.

——, ed. *Virginia Woolf's Reading Notebooks.* Princeton, N.J.: Princeton University Press, 1983.

Silverman, Max. "Re-Figuring 'the Jew' in France." In *Modernity, Culture, and "the Jew,"* edited by Bryan Cheyette and Laura Marcus, 197–207.

Singer, Isidore, ed. *The Jewish Encyclopedia.* 12 vols. New York: Funk and Wagnalls, 1901–6.

Smith, Victoria L. "A Story Beside(s) Itself: The Language of Loss in Djuna Barnes's *Nightwood.*" *PMLA* 1, no. 14 (March 1999): 194–206.

Smith-Rosenberg, Carroll. *Disorderly Conduct: Visions of Gender in Victorian America.* New York: Oxford University Press, 1985.

Snaith, Anna. *Virginia Woolf: Public and Private Negotiations.* London: Macmillan, 2000.

Sontag, Susan. "Fascinating Fascism." *The New York Review of Books* 22, no. 1 (February 6, 1975): 23–30; republished in *Under the Sign of Saturn*, 73–105. New York: Farrar, Straus and Giroux, 1980.

———. "Looking at War: Photography's View of Devastation and Death." *The New Yorker* (December 9, 2002): 82–89.

Spender, Stephen. *Poems*. London: Faber and Faber, 1933.

———. *World Within World: The Autobiography of Stephen Spender*. London: Faber and Faber, 1977.

Stetz, Margaret. "Esther Khan: Antisemitism and Philosemitism at the Turns of Two Centuries." In *Antisemitism and Philosemitism in the Twentieth and Twenty-First Centuries: Representing Jews, Jewishness, and Modern Culture*, edited by Phyllis Lassner and Lara Trubowitz, 119–37.

Strachey, John. *The Menace of Fascism*. New York: Covici-Friede, 1933.

Suchoff, David. Introduction to *The Imaginary Jew*, by Alain Finkielkraut, translated by Kevin O'Neill and David Suchoff, vii–xviii.

Suh, Judy. *Fascism and Anti-Fascism in Twentieth-Century British Fiction*. New York: Palgrave Macmillan, 2009.

———. "Woolf and the Gendering of Fascism." In *Virginia Woolf and Communities*, edited by Jeanette McVicker and Laura Davis, 141–46. New York: Pace University Press, 1999.

Surette, Leon. *Pound in Purgatory: From Economic Radicalism to Anti-Semitism*. Chicago: University of Illinois Press, 1999.

Syberberg, Hans-Jürgen. *Hitler: A Film Made in Germany*. Translated by Joachim Neugroschel. New York: Farrar, Straus and Giroux, 1982.

Szobar, Patricia. "Race Defilement in Germany, 1933 to 1945." In *Sexuality and German Fascism*, edited by Dagmar Herzog, 131–63.

Tamagne, Florence. *A History of Homosexuality in Europe: Berlin, London, Paris, 1919–1939*. New York: Algora, 2006.

Theweleit, Klaus. *Male Fantasies*. Translated by Stephen Conway. 2 vols. Minneapolis: University of Minnesota Press, 1987.

Thurlow, Richard C. *Fascism in Britain: From Oswald Mosley's Blackshirts to the National Front*. New York: Palgrave Macmillan, 1998.

Todorov, Tzvetan. *On Human Diversity: Nationalism, Racism, and Exoticism in French Thought*. Cambridge, Mass.: Harvard University Press, 1998.

Tratner, Michael. "Why Isn't *Between the Acts* a Movie?" In *Virginia Woolf in the Age of Mechanical Reproduction*, edited by Pamela Caughie, 115–34.

Trubowitz, Lara. "In Search of 'the Jew' in Djuna Barnes's *Nightwood*: Jewishness, Antisemitism, Structure, and Style." *Modern Fiction Studies* 51, no. 2 (Summer 2005): 311–34.

"Wandering Jew." *Encyclopaedia Britannica Online*. Accessed March 30, 2009. http://www.britannica.com/EBchecked/topic/635269/wandering-Jew.

Warren, Diane. *Djuna Barnes' Consuming Fictions*. Aldershot, U.K.: Ashgate, 2007.

Weil, Lise. "Entering a Lesbian Field of Vision: *To the Lighthouse* and *Between the Acts*." In *Virginia Woolf: Lesbian Readings*. Edited by Ellen Barrett and Patricia Cramer, 241–52.

Weininger, Otto. *Sex and Character*. Translator unknown. London: Heinemann, 1906.

Wells, H. G. *Experiment in Autobiography*. Vol. 1. London: V. Gollancz and Cresset Press, 1934.

——. *The Outline of History: Being a Plain History of Life and Mankind.* Rev. ed. London: Cassell, 1920.

Wenders, Wim. "That's Entertainment: Hitler (1977)." In *West German Filmmakers on Film: Visions and Voices,* edited by Eric Rentschler, 126–31. New York: Holmes and Meier, 1988.

Westman, Karin. "'For her generation the newspaper was a book': Media, Mediation, and Oscillation in Virginia Woolf's *Between the Acts.*" *Journal of Modern Literature* 29, no. 2 (2006): 1–18.

Wilde, Oscar. *The Collected Works of Oscar Wilde.* 5th ed. Edited by Merlin Holland et al. Glasgow: HarperCollins, 2003.

Wiley, Catherine. "Making History Unrepeatable in Virginia Woolf's *Between the Acts.*" *Clio* 25, no. 1 (1995): 3–20.

Williams, Keith. *British Writers and the Media, 1930–1945.* London: Macmillan, 1996.

Williams, Keith, and Steven Mathews, eds. *Rewriting the Thirties: Modernism and After.* London: Longman, 1997.

Winkiel, Laura. "Circuses and Spectacles: Public Culture in *Nightwood.*" *Journal of Modern Literature* 21, no. 1 (1997): 7–28.

Witte, Karsten. "Introduction to Kracauer's 'The Mass Ornament.'" *New German Critique* 5 (1975): 59–66.

Wittig, Monique. *The Straight Mind and Other Essays.* Boston: Beacon Press, 1992.

Woolf, Leonard. *Quack Quack!* London: Hogarth, 1935.

——. *The War for Peace.* London: Routledge, 1940.

Wussow, Helen. "Travesties of Excellence: Julia Margaret Cameron, Lytton Strachey, Virginia Woolf, and the Photographic Image." In *Virginia Woolf and the Arts,* edited by Diane Gillespie and Leslie Hankins, 48–56. New York: Pace University Press, 1997.

——. "Virginia Woolf and the Problematic Nature of the Photographic Image." *Twentieth-Century Literature* 40, no. 1 (1994): 1–14.

Yoshino, Ayako. "*Between the Acts* and Louis Napoleon Parker—the Creator of the Modern English Pageant." *Critical Survey* 15, no. 2 (2003): 49–62.

Žižek, Slavoj. *The Sublime Object of Ideology.* London: Verso, 1989.

Zwerdling, Alex. *Virginia Woolf and the Real World.* Berkeley: University of California Press, 1989.

homosexuals, treatment of
  in Britain, 21, 202, 222, 233, 237, 273n4
  and emancipation movement, 204–5,
    273n5
  in Nazi Germany, 7, 21, 61–62, 200,
    205–6, 232, 273–74nn5–7
  *See also* homophobia; lesbians; sexual politics
Horkheimer, Max, 8–9, 27–28, 33–34, 85,
  207, 227, 260n9
  *Dialectic of Enlightenment*, 27–28, 34, 85,
    227, 260n9
  *See also* Adorno, Theodor; culture industry
House Committee on Un–American Activites
  (HCUA), 253n13
Howard, Leslie, 255n24
Hussey, Andrew, 25, 251n3
Hutcheon, Linda, 46, 255n30
Huxley, Aldous, 35, 50, 54, 256n35
Huyssen, Andreas, 12, 34, 85, 99, 107, 260n8
  *Great Divide*, 12, 34, 85
Hyman, Paula, 153–54
Hynes, Samuel, 60, 257n43

*I Am a Camera* (Van Druten), 66–67
identity, 11, 14, 16–19, 21, 41, 48, 72, 75, 84,
  94, 104–5, 121–24, 134–35, 149, 154,
  159–61, 196, 201, 209, 217, 226–28,
  246–47
  gender, 84, 88–89, 107, 111, 122, 137, 154,
    201, 260n13
  national, 16–18, 19, 94, 134, 144, 146
  racial, 141, 144, 146, 149, 155, 157, 160–
    61, 169–73, 184, 189
  sexual, 18, 88–89, 237, 240–41, 94,
    122–24, 154, 200, 208–9, 212, 216–19,
    221–28, 237–41
Ignatius Loyola, Saint, 99
imperialism, 15, 44, 76, 175
Institute for Sexual Research (Berlin), 204
Institute for Social Research, 27. *See also*
  Adorno, Theodor
Isherwood, Christopher
  biographical information, 3–4, 6, 10, 13,
    16–17, 187–88, 210–12, 243
  *Christopher and His Kind*, 14, 61–62, 66,
    119, 192–93, 210–11, 250n9, 272n61,
    275n18
  *Goodbye to Berlin. See Goodbye to Berlin*
  and life in Berlin, 10, 16, 58, 61–63, 69–
    70, 112–14, 187–88, 194–95, 210–11,
    275n17
  *Mr. Norris Changes Trains*, 211

as narrator in *Goodbye to Berlin*, 16,
  59–63, 69–70, 116–19, 189, 193, 212,
  219, 256
and sexual identity, 17, 21, 201, 211–12,
  219, 275n15, 275n19
writing strategy of, 13, 16, 18, 60–61, 63,
  65, 93–94, 155, 187, 200–1, 208, 210–
  12, 21657n42, 257n43, 275n19
Israel, Wilfrid, 193, 272n61
Italian fascism, 5–6, 168
Italian National Fascist Party, 5–6, 168, 231
Italy, 167–68, 173, 231
Itzkovitz, Daniel, 144, 163

Jardine, Alice, 84, 93, 259n5, 267n8
Jelavich, Peter, 68
Jewish assimilation, 140, 142, 144–47, 154,
  159, 161–63, 174, 180
Jewish badge, 167–68, 270n37. *See also*
  Jewish yellow star, Nazi
Jewish culture, 153–54, 157, 158, 170, 196
*Jewish Encyclopedia, The*, 166–68, 173,
  263n30, 270n35, 270n39
Jewish history, 100, 147–48, 157–58, 161–62,
  165–68, 170, 172–74, 196, 263n30. *See
  also* Christian-Jewish relations; Jews,
  treatment of
Jewish refugees, 49, 143–44, 150–51, 178,
  184, 197, 245, 267nn9–10, 267n13,
  272n61
  Aliens Act (1905), 143, 267n10
Jewish women, portrayal of, 91, 117–18, 123,
  153–54, 176, 186–87, 190–92
Jewish yellow star, Nazi, 167–68, 270n37
*Jew's Body, The* (Gilman), 149–51, 162–63,
  165, 181, 269n31
Jews, representation of, 4, 11, 20, 54, 90–91,
  99–100, 117–20, 139–97, 245, 254n21,
  266–67nn7–8, 269nn26–31
  in *Between the Acts*, 91–100, 149, 174–75,
    179–86
  in *Goodbye to Berlin*, 117–20, 149
  in modern literature, 141–43, 154–55
  in *Nightwood*, 149, 150, 156–74
  and sexuality, 154, 163, 181, 186, 190–94,
    261n19
  and stereotypes, 118–19, 140–42, 145–50,
    159–64, 175, 180–81, 184–89, 196–97,
    266n5, 267n13, 268n20, 269nn31–32
  as Wandering Jew, 150, 156–57, 159, 171,
    174, 270n43
  See also *écriture judaïque*

masses, the (as concept), 6–7, 8–9, 11, 23,
25–28, 32–33, 99, 230, 249m4. *See also*
crowd mentality, spectatorship
Masteroff, Joe, 257n48
*Maurice* (Forster), 211, 275n18
*Mein Kampf*, 7–8, 23, 26, 31, 41, 55–56,
140–41, 144, 150, 164, 169
*Men Without Art* (Wyndham Lewis), 236
Micheler, Stefan, 204
militarism, 56, 96, 104, 232
*Mischling*, 164–65, 167. *See also* Nazi race
doctrine; race mixing
misogyny, 4, 79, 113, 119, 123, 125, 140,
232–33. *See also* sexism
Mizejewski, Linda, 68, 217
modern industrialization, 26, 43
modernist art/works, 3, 12–14, 33–34, 222,
244, 246
modernist experimentation, 3–4, 7, 10–14,
18, 29–30, 33–35, 39–42, 65, 70–71,
85, 142–43, 158, 212, 244–45. *See also*
avant–garde art; resistance: literary
modernist period, 5, 7, 82–83, 112–13, 141–
42, 149, 154, 180, 222, 245–46
Modern Woman, the, 4, 19–20, 79, 82–83,
88–91, 98–99, 105–7, 113, 117–19,121,
137, 141, 259n6. *See also* Flapper;
women, representation of
*Mortal Storm, The* (Bottome), 254n21
Mosley, Oswald, 6, 36, 178, 264n38. *See also*
British Union of Fascists (BUF)
Mosse, George, 84, 125, 182, 203, 237, 259n4
motherhood, 93, 109, 114–16, 126, 161,
171–72, 261n20, 265n43
Motion Picture Production Code ("Hays
code"), 255n23. *See also* Hollywood
movies. *See* cinema
Mulvey, Laura, 87–88
Munich agreement (1938), 36
Mussolini, Benito, 168
myth, role of, 82, 109, 132–33, 150, 216,
217, 227, 229, 233, 241. *See also* history,
role of

nationalism, 5, 19, 43, 44–45, 56, 259n4
National Socialism. *See* Nazi ideology; Nazi
party
Nazi aesthetics, 4, 5–7, 9–10, 13, 29–32,
47, 79, 97, 115, 132–33, 213–16, 220,
227, 249n4, 252n11. *See also* anti-Nazi
aesthetics; fascist aesthetics
Nazi cinema. *See* cinema: Nazi

Nazi government. *See* Germany, Third Reich
Nazi ideology, 4, 7–10, 18, 64, 92–93, 123,
129, 148
and the Aryan race, 47, 64, 79, 90–91, 146,
148, 153, 160, 216, 236
and eugenics, 91–92, 200, 217–18,
262n21, 268n17
and femininity, ideas of 83, 91, 108, 114–
16, 120, 122, 126, 136, 153–54, 158,
191, 261nn17–18, 264n43
and Jews. *See* Nazi race doctrine
and *Kinder, Küche, Kirche* (Children,
Kitchen, Church), 91, 116, 122
and the *Männerbund*, 154, 200, 216
and masculinism, ideas of, 5, 82, 85, 140,
152–54, 163–64, 182, 200, 220, 236–37
and myth, 47, 217, 227, 229
and nostalgia for past, 47, 209, 213–16,
276n21
pseudoscience in, 107, 152–53
and sexuality, 91–93 112, 114, 158, 200,
206–7, 209–11, 218, 225, 232, 259n4,
261–62nn18–25, 274nn10–11
and the *Volksgemeinschaft*, 68, 79, 91, 115,
216
Nazimova, Alla, 125
Nazi Party, 6–7, 9, 18, 24–25, 58, 64, 93, 111,
215, 262n25
Nazi propaganda, 4, 9, 38, 48–50, 66, 72,
75, 79, 91, 99, 116–17, 123, 134, 152,
254n20
Nazi race doctrine, 4, 7, 20, 30, 32, 36, 48,
55, 90–91, 96, 117–19, 140, 144, 148–
49, 160, 165, 167, 185, 187–88, 194–95,
266n3. *See also* antisemitism; Aryan;
Jews, treatment of
Nazi resistance. *See* antifascist writers; anti-
Nazi aesthetic; resistance
Nazi soldiers, 68, 76, 92, 215
Nazi spectacle, 4, 6–11, 23–34, 39–41,
47–51, 58–66, 70–75, 79, 86, 93, 107,
111, 121–23, 131–34, 148, 158, 169,
194–95, 245–46
and illusion of harmony and unity, 4, 7–11,
17–19, 25–26, 29–33, 48–51, 117, 148,
184, 214–15, 245, 252n11
and image, 4, 7, 23–24, 29–31, 41, 122,
131–32, 245
mass rallies/meetings, 7–8, 24, 25–27, 30,
32, 44, 169, 262n25
and female image, 82–83, 86–91, 93, 107,
123–24, 134, 136, 158

and consumption, 84–87, 89, 99, 104, 106, 111, 182

and the female spectacle, 86–91, 121–24, 130–32, 259n6, 260n13

in *Goodbye to Berlin*, 111–21

Jewish, 153–54, 176, 186–87, 190–92

and mass culture, 83–85, 93, 107, 108, 260nn8–9

and the Modern Woman, 82–86, 88–91, 98–99, 105–7, 117–19, 121, 137, 141, 259n6

in *Nightwood*, 121–36

as symbol/icon, 82–94, 112–13, 119, 130–31, 133, 136–37, 259n1, 259nn4–5

*See also* gender construction; Jewish women; patriarchy; Modern Woman; sexism

Wood, Thelma, 17, 221

Woolf, Leonard, 37, 57–58, 100, 177, 233, 256n32

*Quack, Quack!* 256n32

Woolf, Virginia

biographical information on, 3–4, 6, 10, 14, 14–16, 34–35, 37–38, 88, 94–96, 177–78, 232–33, 243, 254n18, 271–72nn51–52, 277n34

and Englishness, 47–48, 177, 241

and Jewishness, 16, 100, 155, 175–78, 251n13, 263n30, 271n46, 271–72nn51–53

and politics, 42–45, 56, 94–96, 100–101, 175–76, 185–86, 231–32, 250nn9–11, 256n38

on propaganda, 15, 24, 42, 44–45, 250n11, 254n18

public vs. private, 16, 34, 42–43, 45–46, 48–51, 57–58, 109, 253n12, 255n31

on the Spanish Civil War, 100–101, 263n31

and writing strategies, 13–16, 18, 24, 37–38, 93–94, 96, 104, 109–10, 155, 200, 208, 246, 254n19

See also *Between the Acts* (Woolf)

Woolf, Virginia, works

"Anon," 45–46

*A Room of One's Own*, 53, 104, 130, 243

*Between the Acts.* See *Between the Acts*

*Carlyle's House*, 272n53

"Cinema, The" 37–38, 253n17

*Diaries*, 48, 98, 100, 251n13, 256n20, 277n34

"Duchess and the Jeweller, The" 175–76, 271n46

"Leaning Tower, The" 57, 250n9, 253n16

*Letters*, 177–78

notebooks, 100, 251n5, 264n34

"Professions for Women" 263n33

"Thoughts of Peace in an Air Raid," 101

*Three Guineas*, 3, 14, 15–16, 18, 42–43, 56, 58, 95–96, 98, 100–101, 175–76, 231, 263n31

*To the Lighthouse*, 110

*Years, The*, 271n46, 272n53

"Work of Art in the Age of Mechanical Reproduction" (Benjamin), 8, 28–29, 59, 252n7, 253n18

World War I, 15, 37, 43, 91, 267n10

World War II, 4, 15, 30, 36–37, 47–48, 56, 92, 96, 174–75, 243, 252n9

Munich agreement (1938), 36

yellow star, 167–68, 270n37. *See also* pink triangle

Yiddish culture, 153–54

Yoshino, Ayako, 43–44

Zuckmayer, Carl, 113, 264n40

Zwerdling, Alex, 96